I0569766

DR. DORA WASHINGTON

UP *from these* ASHES

RESCUED, RESTORED, AND REDEEMED FROM CHILDHOOD TRAUMA

For permission requests, email purposewriter12@gmail.com

www.towerofhopeministries.com

Cover Design: Bayley Holt @bayleyholtdesigns.com

Editing and Page Design: Ashley Hagan @Inkwellwriters.com

Paperback ISBN: 979-8-9912247-0-3

Hardback ISBN: 979-8-9912247-2-7

eBook ISBN: 979-8-9912247-1-0

DEDICATION

To my God, who is my Rock, Fortress, and Deliverer: Your Healing power transformed my life. It is because of Your hand, heart, and help that I am not a statistic. You worked it all out for my good.

To my husband, my teammate and friend on this adventure: Your sacrifices, prayers, and unwavering commitment allowed me to focus on my passion and purpose.

To my beloved deceased and alive siblings, who have been my pillars of strength and unwavering support as best you could: Your faith inspired me to persevere, keep the faith, and to overcome.

To my precious son, who fills my heart with immeasurable joy: After healing I can fully appreciate the gift you truly are. No matter the challenges life brought us, the one thing that will always remain is you are my son, and I am so thankful for you.

To my first husband: Thank you for the 23 years of trying to understand me and for telling me, "You can't make sense out of nonsense." Those words helped to reset my brain. You know the full story. May God reward you double for all the years you suffered with my illnesses.

To my nieces and nephews, who suffered transgenerational trauma: You are a symbol of strength, perseverance, and tenacity. You are continuing to pass on the legacy of faith to your children. We didn't have much, but the one thing we had—FAITH—is bigger than anything we can imagine.

And to the survivors of childhood trauma everywhere, whose courage and resilience defy all odds. Your strength, healing, and determination are a testament to God's power. Give it all to God and watch Him turn it all around for your good. May this book encourage you and give you hope.

ACKNOWLEDGEMENTS

I would like to thank God for His presence throughout the years of writing this book and for picking me up from the ashes of pain.

I would not have been able to complete this project without the continual support and vision of Deborah Antoine, my internal editor. Her unwavering support and dedication to this book helped it to reach its full potential. Your encouragement and determination kept me going.

I would like to thank Ashley, my amazing editor, for allowing the Holy Spirit to guide her throughout the editing process, her attention to detail, and commitment to excellence. Our meeting was an answer to prayer.

I would like to thank my Tower of Hope Ministries family, especially the volunteer staff (Tiffany, Christian, Shaneice, Teri and Angela) for helping me to lead and for trusting that God sent me to help lead you to freedom. Your love and support are unequaled. You are the Esther of our time. You are trees planted by the rivers of waters whose leaves flourish continually. Your compassion, empathy, and resilience inspire me to keep moving forward. All of you are my daughters and sons.

I would like to acknowledge the unending debt I owe to those who prayed for me, supported me, helped me to recall difficult experiences in childhood, and made sure I ate while working long hours on the manuscript: Thank you Brenda, Evelyn, Charlotte, Dorothy, Mitchell, Deborah, Tiffany, Christian, Symone, and my Tower of Hope Ministries Family.

I would like to thank Dr. Felitti, whose groundbreaking Adverse Childhood Experiences study showed me I wasn't crazy, but something crazy happened to me.

I would like to especially thank:

My family of choice parents, Momma June and Dad Al, and Momma Strong, for your unswerving support ever since we first met. You make sure I am always included and welcomed in your hearts and homes.

My spiritual daughters who were born in the beginning, MeLisa, Shirley, Shaquia, and Grace: You were chosen by God to be trailblazers. You were there on the first day to witness the powerful move of God.

My other adopted spiritual daughters Tiffany, Christian, and Symone who witnessed behind the scenes challenges: Your loyalty, commitment and dedication have meant so much to me.

My TOHM Volunteer Staff, Tiffany, Christian, Shaniece, Teri, & Angela who continue to go above and beyond to help others heal: Your sacrifices have not gone unnoticed.

My spiritual son, Willie, who was one of the first men to complete all three phases of the program.

Ms. April my dearest sister, who supported me and was there during the back to back losses.

My cherished friends, Deborah, Sondra, Karen, Benita, Phadra, Steve and Marilyn who have stood by me through thick and thin: Your laughter, late-night conversations, and shared dreams have made life infinitely better.

My financial supporters who continued to support me so I could focus on my purpose and my writing. May God be gracious to you and reward you for the kindness you continue to show to me and Tower of Hope participants.

My counselor, Ailene, who allowed God to use her. My life was forever transformed by God's Anointing that destroyed every yoke.

My Mentors, Katherine and Perry who continue to help me be the best leader, mother, sister, and friend. Your calling and purpose redefined mine.

My God-sent family Alfred, June and Momma Sandy, Momma Dorothy H, who supported the challenging times of ABD, loneliness, and deployment. Your heart of compassion made sure I was always included. Your support and love taught me supportive parents can come at any age. I am equally grateful for the pillars of strength from my living biological sisters (Brenda, JoAnne, and Evelyn). They have been and remain the pillars of Strength, Hope, Perseverance, and Faith in God upon which I stood.

TABLE OF CONTENTS

Introduction

Declaration

Chapter 1: My Earliest Memories   1

Chapter 2: Rules of the House   8

Chapter 3: Another Attempted Murder   11

Chapter 4: The Effects of Childhood Trauma   18

Chapter 5: The Weight of a Name   21

Chapter 6: Heartbreak on Wheels   28

Chapter 7: Time to Leave   37

Chapter 8: Foster Homes   42

Chapter 9: The Stranger I Knew   47

Chapter 10:Lessons Elsie Taught Me   52

Chapter 11: The Bus Driver   56

Chapter 12: A Dark Time   60

Chapter 13: Vagabond   66

Chapter 14: A Place to Call Home   72

Chapter 15: Church   82

Chapter 16: The Fall from Heaven   85

Chapter 17: The Cycle of Abuse   91

Chapter 18: I Am Somebody Special   95

Chapter 19: High School Years   99

Chapter 20: Abuse Changes Things   104

Chapter 21: Role Reversal   107

Chapter 22: Shoplifting Senior 110

Chapter 23: Second Chance 119

Chapter 24: A New Outlook 125

Chapter 25: College Daze 132

Chapter 26: Give Beauty a Chance 140

Chapter 27: When Drake Met Sally 145

Chapter 28: Buy the Cow 153

Chapter 29: Elsie's Legacy 159

Chapter 30: Pregnancy 169

Chapter 31: Bundle of Blessing 175

Chapter 32: Growing Up with Michael 181

Chapter 33: Changing Careers 185

Chapter 34: Prepared but Unprepared 191

Chapter 35: Life 101 195

Chapter 36: My Gift, Michael 200

Chapter 37: Michael Making a Difference 207

Chapter 38: Family Time 211

Chapter 39: Jailhouse Little Rock 213

Chapter 40: Forgotten Purpose 219

Chapter 41: Watch Out for the Big D 225

Chapter 42: The Wake Up Dream 231

Chapter 43: More Layers 236

Chapter 44: The Truth Shall Set You Free 243

Chapter 45: A New House and a New Job 251

Chapter 46: A Volcanic Eruption 259

Chapter 47: Moving to Missouri 266

Chapter 48: Michael and Me   275

Chapter 49: God's Detox   279

Chapter 50: When Church Hurts   285

Chapter 51: The Eyes of God   288

Chapter 52: Joplin   295

Chapter 53: Journal Benefits   303

Chapter 54: Springfield to St. Louis   306

Chapter 55: The God Who Speaks   315

Chapter 56: No Escape   322

Chapter 57: The Long Journey to Freedom   330

Chapter 58: Cracks in the System   338

Chapter 59: Healing Matters   344

Chapter 60: Emerging from the Traumatose Coma   351

Chapter 61: The Stranger   358

Chapter 62: Walmart CSR   370

Chapter 63: Romantic Restoration   382

Chapter 64: The Wedding   394

Chapter 65: A Guardian of Freedom   399

Chapter 66: Beauty for Ashes   403

Chapter 67: God's Global Positioning System   413

Chapter 68: When Pain and Purpose Collide   417

About the Author   424

References   425

INTRODUCTION

For years, I believed the things that happened to my siblings and me were called *life,* so I was never despondent. I was invariably the one to encourage, inspire, and help others. I didn't know that I was destitute most of my life and suffered complex trauma throughout my childhood—multiple traumas that were pervasive and had profound effects. According to the statistics on the outcomes of Childhood Trauma, I now know I could have been disconsolate, laden with chronic illnesses and diseases, or never made it out of my childhood alive. Many survivors of Childhood Trauma continue to relive their abuse in adulthood through irrational behaviors, mental illnesses, debilitating fears, suffocating insecurities, unmentionable secrets, tormenting nightmares, and deep-seated emotional and psychological pain.

Many would rather die with the lie of what happened to them than live with the truth about what God can do about what happened to them.

Hospitals, cancer units, and emergency rooms are filled with people who are sick from medical diseases that have roots in abuse suffered during childhood. No survivor escapes the long-term consequences of Childhood Trauma because it engulfs everything and everyone around them and all aspects of life: emotions, intellect, identity, personality, behavior, and relationships with family, children, co-workers, and employers. It is by the grace of God that I have healed from the effects of Childhood Trauma and can share my story so that others might find hope and healing. I hope that by telling my candid story, I can help other survivors of trauma become overcomers.

Sadly, until I'd lost everything, I didn't know I needed healing. I knew I had issues but didn't think I had aberrant behaviors. Well into adulthood, I thought what I experienced as a child was ordinary. My siblings and I often talked about our pain and abuse, but we never saw it as unusual. We thought all families were like ours, so we talked about the abuse and found laughter, not in what happened to us, but in the insanity of it. It could be easy to judge us for making light of serious situations, but we needed to know what we experienced was real, and we found a non-threatening way to talk about it.

When I was a child, the adults who were supposed to take care of me were my mother—a woman who had nine unwanted and unloved babies before she had me —and her boyfriend, a man biologically related to only three of her children. My mother and her boyfriend called themselves *married* because they had lived together for over twenty-five years. They drank alcohol daily and settled conflicts more often with their fists or other weapons than with words, as their children became scarred, fractured, broken, and damaged in ways that were not always visible.

My parents were consummate torturers. They were supposed to take care of us, but instead they branded us with hot poker irons, burned us on a hot stovetop, broke our spirits, and gave us concussions, all while starving us. They even incompetently hung one of us by the neck from a tree overnight. She survived, but only barely. None of us survived the terror of the constant fear of who would be the next victim of their rage and hatred. None of us survived unscathed or undamaged. They denied us even the necessities of food, clothing, and shelter. Nine of us grew to adulthood with the hallmarks of Childhood Trauma: undereducated, personality disorders, post-traumatic stress disorder, chronic illnesses, debilitating fears, emotional numbness, and inadequate executive function. All of us existed in survival mode, unable to live authentically.

Even the Geneva Convention has standards on how to treat prisoners and civilians when captured during wartime. Any person or government caught violating the standards is charged with torture and cruel, humiliating, and degrading treatment. Yet, despite documentation of the horrific crimes of assault, burning, and hanging of their children, my parents missed being on the list of most dangerous couples. The lack of intervention by the community and state demonstrated to us our lack of value.

As an adult, I understand my parents were not just misunderstood, well-meaning, childhood fairy-tale parents with a few issues. My parents did evil, sadistic things and could have raised serial killers and misguided, evil adults. At least, that is how many stories turn out for children raised by parents like mine. God, in His tender mercy, miraculously protected my siblings and me from such awful outcomes. While we acted out and did things we regret, most remained kind-hearted, loving, and compassionate.

All of my surviving siblings and I have had profound difficulties in adulthood. In my case, multiple breakdowns, chronic illnesses, estranged relationships, impulsive actions, and great despair combined to send me looking for answers. My story, however, is also the story of my brothers and sisters. We lived together and suffered together. When one of us was harmed, the rest of us were present for the terrifying savagery and post-abuse neglect. Most of our injuries never saw an emergency room or received any kind of treatment. As the youngest, there were six of my siblings still living at home as I grew up who shared the same fate of abuse. None of us could climb out of our pit to help the others. If one by chance escaped, they ran for dear life for fear of being killed if someone caught them. Two barely escaped with their skin. Four remained destined and determined to survive the worst. We hungered for mental, emotional, and spiritual freedom, yet we could not attain it. Our stomachs craved food, our tongues longed for water, and our hearts yearned to feel love; though sometimes our lives were in danger, we did not die.

As an adult, I carried the stigma, shame, and betrayal of abuse like a mother carries her child. I was careful to keep my shame-baby in mind, and if I tried to forget her, she hunted me down like prey until she sucked the dreams, hopes, and aspirations out of me. She leeched my heart, mind, and soul with negative thoughts until I was weak and could not feel, think, or love.

At the age of forty-two, after multiple breakdowns and chronic health issues, God made me aware that He had healing in store for me. I read *Self Matters* by Dr. Phil McGraw and felt he described me and my situation. I was desperate as I searched for answers. My sense of self and everything that I thought important was lost: my marriage and relationship with my son, my perceived relationship with God, and my enthusiasm for my job. Most of my friendships and family ties were tenuous. I was alone, going through a divorce, adjusting to a new job in a new state, and had no distractions. It was the ideal setting for healing and for me to meet God. I came to the end of the self I had created from the emotional and mental pain and discovered my true self at the beginning of where I met the One True God.

As I read *Self Matters,* I followed Dr. Phil's suggestion and listed the various abuses I endured during childhood. When I did the exercises recommended in Dr. Phil's book, I acknowledged the giants of emotional pain and mental anguish as I came face to face with the dragons of Childhood Trauma. During the night, pain haunted me through tormenting dreams and nightmares. During the day, mental anguish incapacitated me and left me afraid to drive. During those times, I realized something terrible happened in my childhood that left me unable to think, behave, or function appropriately.

Childhood abuse and suffering left an indelible mark on me, my ex-husband, my son, my dreams, goals, and legacy. I dared to dream things would be different for my child, with hopes that he wouldn't suffer the emotional upheaval, divided heart, sleepless nights, and the trauma of his grandmother's past and his mother's present. I prayed that he would climb out of the pit of abuse, valley of shame, and hills of depression to find sure-footedness on the mountain of hope. I never meant for him to carry transgenerational pains, much less load him down with them. It caused me anguish when I learned I unintentionally passed on my trauma—and its aftermath—to him.

I was in a private prison of pain after separating from my husband, feeling the loss of his support and the loss of my relationship with my only child. I felt I had let down the people who cared for me, and I didn't know who I was, why I was, or how I was. That was when I cried out to God.

God, I don't know if You're real. I believe You are, but I've had such bad experiences with church people called by Your name that I'm afraid to talk to You. I want to tell You I am messed up. I'm in desperate need of help. I can't love like I want to. I can't think like other people, and I'm always sick. I don't know who I am. I don't even care about my feelings. I care about others more than I do myself. I heard You are a healer, and I need healing. I have lost everything, including my sense of self. If You had anything to do with my pain and abuse, I want nothing to do with You. But if You are the God I read about in the Bible, I want You to heal me. If You heal me, I will tell the world what You did for me, and I will never be ashamed of You.

I thought that prayer was the end, but I learned it was only the beginning. The Holy Spirit guided me to write prayers, affirmations, and declarations for my mind, thoughts, body, identity, and purpose. The more I recalled my childhood, the more debilitating nightmares and tormenting dreams I suffered. I had panic and anxiety attacks. Many times, I felt I'd rather die than wait for them to pass. Now, I realize I needed to relive the past briefly to live the present and future permanently.

For nearly a year, I feared I might die in my sleep. It felt like I was in the spiritual operating room, with God performing surgery without anesthesia. Everything was unstable. It seemed death would have been so much easier, but God did not give me an easy out. I had to fight to live my adulthood—like I fought to survive my childhood.

While the healing process was the most difficult thing I ever did, it was also the most rewarding. I have not been required to relive my Childhood Traumas since facing them and processing them. I can talk about them now without pain, not because I suppressed them, but because I processed everything that happened and allowed God to fully heal me from all of it. I was able to put things into perspective and understand why I struggled to stay emotionally connected to people, why recurring negative thoughts and chronic sickness tormented me, and why I was unable to form strong bonds in relationships. Finally, I was able to understand why I distrusted Believers. It wasn't that I was crazy, but something crazy happened to me.

I am grateful to Almighty God, who truly heals the brokenhearted and binds up their wounds. Because of His healing power, I can love more deeply, gain control of my thoughts, and focus them on His promises and goodness. I am healed from sickness, and I can form a community once again with a church family. I am a living testimony of God's healing power and restoration—not because I am perfect, but because He is so loving and compassionate. Each day, I wake up to thank God for His goodness and grace because I know my story could have ended differently. For this reason, I resolved to help others like me who think no one can reach them, who think they are too old, too young, too broken, too sick, too messed up, too whatever. Those individuals are the ones I pray this book reaches and speaks to the depths of their souls, bodies, and spirits to know *if God did it for me, He will do it for them.*

I never thought someone like me, who suffered so much trauma, could be free. Free to love, free to feel, free to think, free to know I am not what I have been through. Thanks be to God, there was hope for me, and if you're reading this, there is hope for you, too. Your life may be full of chronic disappointment, pain, and grief, but if you are a Believer and love God, that is NOT the end of your story. Like me, your story is unfinished until you shout the victory, know peace, and experience freedom.

My horrendous childhood grew into an adulthood scarred by the long-term consequences of Childhood Trauma. Until I healed, I did not live the life of goodness, blessings, and purpose God intended for me. If you are not living a life of abundance, blessings, and purpose, it is not the life God planned for you. I am grateful for the revelation that it was not God's Will but Childhood Trauma that held me in captivity, but I am more grateful for the revelation that God would set me free. I give thanks to the God of my faith who freed me as I cried out to Him to deliver me from my prisons. I am also grateful to God for His resurrection power—the power He gives to all those who believe in Him.

It is God's power that takes the most calloused, obsessed, oppressed, demon-possessed, sinful people and turns them into saints. They are not perfect people, but they grow in perfect love for God's people regardless of their economic status, race, religion, size, or gender. I was like the blind man in the ninth chapter of the book of John who longed for Jesus to pass by and heal him. God told me what to do—and I did it—and I was healed, like the man whose vision was restored. God is passing by you today. I pray you will stop long enough to allow Him to heal you. Then you can join me as I sing that old Negro Spiritual, *"Free at last. Free at last. Thank God Almighty, I am free at last."*

Whatever your situation, you can be free as well. Whether it's a physical prison because of choices you regret, a mental prison where you struggle with confusion and tormenting memories, an emotional prison keeping you from feeling or loving or putting you in one abusive relationship after another, a financial prison from the economic decisions you made and the remainder of choking debt, a sexual prison controlled by your ravenous desire to have your sexual needs met at any expense, or a spiritual prison caused by damage from so-called men and women of God who misused their authority and power—God can deliver you. He has already made provisions for you to heal.

Your first step is to repeat the following prayer:

Lord, I repent of my sins. I make You my Lord and accept You as my Savior. Use my life to bring You glory. I ask You to heal me like You healed the blind man and Dora. Let me do greater works for Your name's sake. In Jesus' name, Amen.

If you prayed the prayer above, email me at purposewriter12@gmail.com and let me know so that I can add you to our prayer list and keep in touch with you.

Your humble sister in Christ,

Dr. Dora Washington

Declaration

I decree and declare today that I will rise up from these ashes of Childhood Trauma

I shake myself from this weight

I shake myself from from the ashes of my past

I shake myself from the flames consuming my present

I shake myself from the dust of oppression, depression, and disease

I shake myself from the soot of addictions, abandonment, and anxiety

I shake myself from the ruins of self-pity, self-doubt, and self-sabotage

I shake myself from the burning habits of procrastination, negative thoughts, and defeat

I shake myself from the smoldering ruins of emotional pain, PTSD, and mental Illness

I shake myself from the hidden embers of physical, mental, emotional, and sexual abuse

I shake myself from the scorching fear of failure, poverty mindset, and negative self-talk

I shake myself from the inferno of low self-esteem, low self-worth, and the inner critic

I shake myself from the bondages of perfection, pride, and the false self

I loose myself from the remains of abuse and triggers of Childhood Trauma

I rise to the abundant life of hope, healing, and purpose Jesus promised me

I rise with a new determination and resilience to triumph gloriously over trauma

My Prayer for You

Lord, I ask you to open the eyes of every person reading this prayer to see in the Spirit that You are lifting them from the ashes of Childhood Trauma. Set them free from the things they remember and the things they suppressed from their childhood. Because You rose from the grave, they, too, can rise from the ashes of abuse to freedom. May they have a God-encounter as You transform them, and let them be a testimony to Your healing power. Let all who know them say as they said about Jesus:

SHE/HE IS NOT HERE!
SHE/HE HAS RISEN!

In Jesus' name, Amen.

Chapter 1
MY EARLIEST MEMORIES

We lived in a red, tar-paper covered house in rural Arkansas until I was four or five years old. We lived in the country, with few neighbors. The house seemed huge, no doubt because I was so small. There was a front room, a wide hallway, a large kitchen, and three bedrooms. There was a bathroom but no running water, so neither the toilet nor the tub was operable. We kept the bathroom clean but told visitors that the toilet didn't work, so the bathroom was unused. The boys' bedroom contained an iron bed with a hole-filled mattress. Although their mattress wasn't as torn as the one in the girls' room, it was full of urine like the mattress the girls shared. Loss of bladder control often happened to us because of our terror-filled days and horror-filled nights. We were anxious, and our bodies stayed on alert. Our mattresses probably held more urine in them than cotton batting. Our rooms reeked with the smell.

My earliest memories as a toddler were the screaming and hollering of my older siblings as our parents beat, burned, tortured, and verbally abused them. I would stand frozen and silent, too afraid to cry and too young to understand what was happening as my parents took turns scorning, cursing, and tormenting my three older sisters and two brothers with hot pokers from the fireplace. It was only by the grace of God that I survived. Even though I wasn't as physically abused, our parents knew that if the younger children watched the suffering of the older ones, we would absorb a warning that outlasted the lashings, kicks, punches, beatings, and burns.

I witnessed my siblings' torture and felt helpless and hopeless as they screamed. My body froze in fear each time my parents attacked one of us. The terror accumulated daily, and I lived in constant dread that I might die. It affected my body in various ways. Often I felt like I couldn't eat for hours after each sadistic episode. What I didn't know then is that HPA hormones (cortisol, epinephrine, and adrenaline) flooded into my brain and organs when I could find no relief from the terror visited upon my siblings and me on a near-daily basis. That's also where my adult disordered relationship with food had its roots.

No one ever wanted to be the first to fall asleep or the last to get up, so we only half-slept. We never knew how or when we would be awakened. It was common to be asleep, then inexplicably on our feet with ears ringing from a broomstick broken across our heads. Other times, we felt a deep pain on the top of our skulls from an iron spoon's thud or the sting of a tree limb whipping across our backs. Fear was constant. It crept through the house like spiders and hid in cracks and crevices. Fear was an unrelenting companion.

Although we tried to be attentive to what our parents demanded—closing doors, picking up socks and cotton fluff, or the crumbs we dropped—we sometimes forgot to do some things, and the wrath of Buck and Elsie would rain down. We wanted to please our parents in hopes they would love us and beat us less. We thought maybe then we could have a normal life. To us, anything that was the opposite of our experience was normal. Normal would be freedom to play, eat when hungry, bathe in acceptable places instead of ditches, and receive a phone call from a classmate without fear of having to spend the night outside the house in the dark as punishment. Normal life could mean freedom from marathon sessions of rubbing my parents' feet, the luxury of uninterrupted sleep, and being allowed to make mistakes without fear of beatings or burnings. Normal would mean we were free to explore and dream of how we would make a difference in the world.

Instead, we blamed ourselves when they punished us. We thought there was something we could have done to prevent it. I overheard my school friends talking about things they did over the weekend, and none of it included witnessing their siblings burned or taken into foster care. Classmates and neighbors seemed to have normal childhoods with working parents who clothed, fed, and provided shelter. That was not my childhood experience. Our abuse included having to watch my parents physically fight each other, periodically not having a mother at home, and lacking the basic necessities of life like clothing, food, and water. Although my stepfather worked at a steel factory, there was never enough money to feed us and my parents' insatiable desire for alcohol.

Although I don't have a clear memory of getting physically beaten before I was five, the dread of a beating by my parents remains a staple in my memory and body going back as early as two years of age. To my sympathetic nervous system, they may as well have done it to me. I experienced my parents' rage and felt the demonic hate radiating from them each time they lashed out at my siblings. I absorbed my siblings' screams of fear and cries of pain. Even when I wasn't the one beaten, I was forced to witness the abuse and feel the demonic rage of my parents. When any one of us was tortured, we all endured the mistreatment and verbal invectives that accompanied it, letting us know that we were nothing and of no value and would never be anything special.

For most of my adult life, I felt sorry for my abused brothers and sisters because, as the youngest, I escaped some of the more injurious torture. I thought I was somehow less damaged. It wasn't until I began to research Childhood Trauma that I realized watching the abuse, witnessing the beatings, smelling their skin burn, seeing blood oozing from them, hearing their screams, and touching the swollen welts on their bodies affected me psychologically in many ways. Watching our parents abuse and torture my siblings was like secondhand smoke; it was doubly damaging because not only did I have to see it, I had to feel their fear. Soon, fear took residence inside my body, mind, and soul.

My brother Mathus had a serious heart condition. The doctors told Buck and Elsie to be very careful with him because he could stop breathing at any minute. Consequently, he got a pass on the abuse the others suffered. They handled him with kid gloves. He ate, slept, and played when he wanted. He received special attention that none of us received. I often wished I was sick, too, to avoid the beatings. The downside to that was that Mathus still witnessed our abuse—much like me when I was too small to abuse physically—and he knew the fear of the terror and torture we experienced.

When I was five, I recall my parents putting me out of the house for something as mundane as not picking loose cotton fluff off the carpet or falling asleep at 3:00 a.m. while rubbing Buck or Elsie's feet. Spending the night outside the house terrorized me. Sundown at the red house meant bedtime was near. We could see the light disappearing as darkness hovered above the trees, encroaching on the house. There were no streetlights, so darkness extended as far as we could see once the sun descended. Rural darkness is a thick blackness through which I could not see my hand in front of my face. I feared a bear or a wolf would eat me because I heard them howling, and I knew they were in the woods near our house. It didn't help that my sister Briana and I once witnessed a huge, colorful snake slithering across the road. It was swollen and looked like it had eaten something almost as big as it was. We stood transfixed as we waited for it to cross. It moved slowly across the dusty road, and we ultimately decided to ease away without drawing its attention to us. The memory of the snake burned into my mind, and I was reminded of it each time I had to sit outside in the darkness. I was apprehensive about the possibility of the big snake's return.

One of my earliest memories is seeing my sister Maureen hanging from a tree in the front yard. Her hanging came at the end of a long, brutally violent episode during which my parents terrorized my ten-year-old sister. It was a day filled with violence and threats of more violence. It began when our stepfather, Buck, beat Maureen nearly unconscious because she hadn't drawn water from the pump. When she tried to run from him, Buck grabbed her and stomped her to the floor. My siblings had gone to school. I was the only one not yet old enough, and I trembled in the corner of the room where I witnessed his cruel savagery. She had thick welts and deep gashes from a sturdy limb broken off a tree and used to beat her, leaving her body marked by wounds.

Buck and Elsie continued their violence when Maureen went outside to wash. They called her inside the house several times to ask her who she thought she was before slapping her to the floor. I followed her everywhere she went, but not when Buck or Elsie called her. Each time they called her into the house, they told her to stand before them. They asked her a question, and before she could answer, they knocked her down. They did this several times before I heard the word *lesson*. My siblings arrived from school just in time to witness Buck and Elsie's vile plan to teach Maureen that lesson.

I remember Elsie saying, "We need to teach her a lesson. She thinks she's grown, doing things the way she wants to instead of how I tell her. She's a liar, and her lies can get us in trouble," she continued. "Let's drag her down the road. That'll teach her." She kept spinning out possibilities. Each of her suggestions grew wilder. "We can starve her. Maybe we can take her somewhere and leave her. No, someone might hear her and call the police on us. Let's hang her from the tree. We don't have to kill her. The hanging will kill her. Then, if anyone asks what happened, we can say the kids were playing around the tree and hung her from the tree. She'll get what she deserves."

Maureen had been born a twin. Her sister, Dot, died around the age of six months, possibly from Sudden Infant Death Syndrome. I only have the word of my older sisters, who said Elsie preferred Dot over Maureen. Elsie—who had the infant twins and one-year-old Marcus at the time, in addition to Jake (2), Ava (3), and Denise (7)—was undoubtedly overwhelmed and may have suffered postpartum depression or psychosis. My oldest sister Denise said in those days she changed and fed Maureen, Jake, Marcus, and Ava because Elsie cared only for Dot. Denise told stories about the ways Elsie neglected all her children except Dot, and when Dot died, Elsie's grief turned into rage at Maureen for surviving. It puzzled me why Elsie loved Dot so much and neglected the other twin. Maureen paid for surviving infancy by becoming the target of Elsie's grief rage over the loss of her other child.

Even though I was too young to understand what hanging meant, I felt my siblings' fear as we shook and trembled. Marcus (11) and Jolene (9) tried to convince seven-year-old Mathus and five-year-old Briana to help them stop the hanging, but they were too afraid to intervene. Marcus was physically disabled from polio but wasn't afraid to fight Buck. Jolene and Marcus knew if they tried to save Maureen, Buck and Elsie's fury would turn toward them, and they would probably be hung, too. They had to choose what they could do: watch Maureen hang or confront their parents. They were still young, but they knew right from wrong. In their eyes, this was so wrong, they were willing to fight. Marcus stepped up and stood in front of Buck and told him to beat him instead, while Jolene screamed for them to hang her instead of Maureen, but it was no use. Buck and Elsie wanted Maureen to suffer, and there was no changing their minds, so everyone positioned themselves to watch.

We watched as Elsie and Buck worked together to secure Maureen's position on the tree. They worked together to hang their child as if they were the best of friends, even though they fought like mortal enemies on other occasions. They hung Maureen with a rope around her neck so that her heels were slightly off the ground, requiring her to exert exhausting energy to stay alive by standing on her tiptoes. She wasn't high in the air, but her feet dangled by inches off the ground. Maureen screamed as she squirmed and kicked, pleading, "Let me down, somebody, please help me. I won't do it again." She begged until her voice grew faint, becoming only a whisper as her hands clawed at the rope, and she became exhausted by her efforts to keep breathing.

My siblings and I watched helplessly from inside the house. We could hear her moans, but our parents would not allow us to go outside, cut her down, or comfort her. I can't recall much more because I believe my brain shut down to protect me from the terror. I was only two and a half years old and Maureen was almost eleven, but I still recall the feelings of abject terror expressed by my siblings as they talked about the possibility of death. We blacked out and slept fitfully while Buck and Elsie slept the way they usually did—without thought to their daughter hanging from a tree in the front yard. We woke early in the morning to see the eerily motionless body of Maureen still hanging from the tree. It was our first experience of what we assumed was death. My oldest siblings, Denise (18), Ava (14), and Jake (13), had already run away from home, so we didn't have the benefit of their experience with the loss of Maureen's twin to inform our exposure to Maureen's hanging.

My parents were up early to go fishing. We could hear their conversation about trying a new location that reportedly contained the biggest catfish of any place around. Elsie and Buck went fishing frequently, and they often got up at 5:00 a.m. to fish as the sun rose.

Before they left, Buck cut the rope holding Maureen, and her body fell to the ground like a stone. At first, we assumed she was dead. Buck left right away without even checking for a pulse while we wept bellowing cries and prayed loud prayers to the only God we knew, fearing Maureen was gone. I can't explain how children of a young age knew such faith, but we did. We hoped she could still be alive. Now I know it was because we wanted so badly for her to live.

After her body fell to the ground, we stood around and continued to pray for what was probably only a few minutes, but it seemed like hours. Someone noticed her eyelids flutter and her fingers twitch. Her head lay in Jolene's lap, and she began to move a little more. We ran to get her some water and dropped it, little by little, into her mouth. She could only take a few sips at a time as she slowly revived. Marcus, Mathus, and Jolene carried her into the house because she was too weak to walk. While Buck and Elsie were away fishing, we celebrated because we knew a miracle had occurred. We thought the revival of Maureen was the end of the hanging episode because she didn't physically die. What we didn't know was the other types of deaths she suffered. The day she hung, Maureen died in ways we would only gradually realize as we struggled to make sense of such a senseless crime against our sister.

Maureen became a zombie, staring silently into space at school and home. Her previous love for school turned to resentment. The school used to be her sanctuary, but she later told me that after the hanging, it was as if she went from one workplace to another because she had to muster up the effort to think and learn when previously schooling required little exertion from her. While no one outside of the family knew about the hanging, many knew something happened to Maureen by the change in her personality and demeanor.

Maureen grew older, but my siblings and I know that the Maureen we knew died the day she was hung. Her hopes and dreams died with her. After that day, she never aspired to do much, and her personality changed entirely. She became compliant and non-confrontational. Whenever we asked her something or gave her a choice, she said, "It don't matter. I like whatever you like."

Maureen was eight years older than me and my sole caretaker until the hanging incident. My older sisters later told me that before the hanging, I was like her surrogate child. She was affectionate and helped feed and tend to me. She carried me around as if I were her baby and treated me with the only tenderness I can recollect. She fed me, put me to bed, and cared for my needs before hers. My sisters told me Maureen was my first *mom*. Although I mostly have to rely on what my siblings told me about our relationship, one thing I will never forget is the pain I felt when Maureen was eventually removed from our house by the child welfare agency. As a child, I didn't understand why I was so happy to see her when I visited her, and then despondent and cried uncontrollably when I left. I now know the deep emotional pain indicated the special bond we once shared.

All of the siblings noticed the change in Maureen after the hanging. We had now lost *two* siblings, Maureen and her twin sister. I lost the only mother figure I knew. My sisters told me I often stood between Maureen's legs or cradled in her arms. After the hanging, Maureen pushed me away and said, "No, Jean, sit down," or, "Get down, you can walk." (My family called me by my middle name to avoid confusion with a Dora who lived nearby.) Years later, in adulthood, Maureen and I talked a little about the hanging. I knew not to pry whenever she talked about it. I learned to wait for what she shared. As best she could, Maureen helped me understand she had lost herself and created a different world in her mind, a place where she convinced herself no one could hurt her—or even see her. She said she worried about me and what might happen if she were injured more severely or even killed. She said she couldn't allow me to be her baby after the hanging because she didn't know if she would be around much longer to take care of me. She thought that if she pushed me away and stopped being so motherly toward me, I would learn independence and not need her so much.

Chapter 2

RULES OF THE HOUSE

We did not return to the life we knew before the hanging because our lives centered around the even greater fear of what our parents might do next or who would be the next target of their torture. Buck and Elsie used the threat of hanging and greater violence to scare us into silence and submission. We knew we had no chance against our parents, so we learned how to protect our hearts, go hungry without complaining, cry in silence, wear dirty clothes, take baths in ditches, lie to outsiders to protect our parents, and never tell anyone anything about what happened in the house.

We were resigned to starvation, burns from hot pokers, and daily lashings with extension cords, thick tree limbs, belts, and ropes. We became used to beatings with broomsticks, iron spoons, skillets, or anything within easy reach if we didn't run away fast enough. There was no one to rescue us. We had no choice but to live through it. Looking busy didn't prevent lashings, but it did postpone them. Buck and Elsie made sure we stayed occupied. We learned to wake up when our parents got up and go to sleep when we saw them doze off. Hunger, chores, abuse, and injuries were constant companions. For us, weekends lasted too long. Time spent at home never went by fast enough, while school days were too short. To ask for food would be asking for a whipping, so we seldom discussed food. I learned early not to feel or acknowledge hunger. I could live without eating, much like a child enduring a famine.

Whenever we did eat—which, at home, was not on any kind of regular schedule—we wondered if it was our last meal. We knew the routine: the rattling of the pots and pans grew louder, and then the boys would eat while the girls stayed busy until they finished. After the boys finished, Elsie called the girls in for the leftovers. Marcus and Mathus were the first to eat. Despite his physical limitations, eating first was the only special consideration Marcus received. We could hear the boys telling Elsie how good the meal tasted while we waited our turn to eat.

Elsie was an exceptional cook. She was the cook everyone wanted to hire because she could make opossums taste like chicken. We children didn't know the difference between possum and chicken because it tasted so good.

She baked a possum and made a gravy for it. It was delicious! We learned not to ask *what it was* if we couldn't identify a meat item. It didn't matter. We had no luxury of choice. It was *eat what is before you or die of starvation*. The smell of onions and bell peppers filled the air, drowning out any tainted scent or gaminess of the animal. Elsie's cooking made the lashings almost tolerable, but she cooked infrequently, sometimes only once a week. Fresh kale picked from the neighbor's yard, candied yams, homemade rolls, and blackberry cobbler from the berries picked by Jolene and Maureen somehow turned our dysfunctional group into what I thought might be a family—if the idea of *family* had something to do with the convening of everyone to eat the huge meal Elsie cooked.

There were a few rules for mealtimes. One was that leftovers from a previous meal must be eaten first. We believe this was because we seldom had food, so Elsie didn't want to waste any by allowing leftovers to spoil. Two, we were to eat *all* the food on our plates. Three, we could not draw any attention to ourselves while eating or by conversing with each other. No burping or gagging was allowed. We ate our meals in silence. There were never any complaints about the food. There wouldn't have been because it was so delicious. My only complaint was that I didn't like eating cold or old food, so instead of growing a tough stomach for food, I developed a weak stomach for certain foods and leftovers. I especially remember the leftover biscuits. They didn't taste right, so I hid several in my pants or jacket until the old ones were gone before asking for fresh ones.

Please let there be enough for us to eat, was our prayer. We prepared a table—of sorts—and hoped goodness and mercy would follow us. The girls were prohibited from sitting at the table because we dropped food on the floor. The sister siblings sat in a silent circle on the floor, but we didn't care where we ate as long as we were allowed to eat. I can see now how much like feral kittens we must have appeared, eating the unfinished remains of the boys and relegated to sitting on the floor.

I learned how to spell Busch, Schlitz, and Budweiser beers and Wiederkher wine before I learned how to read books because they were what I saw most frequently. The big letters on their labels were unmistakable. I saw those labels because Elsie drank daily and left her bottles sitting around the house. Buck had no leisure of drinking during the week because he had to go to work and couldn't afford hangovers, so he mostly drank on the weekends.

Not only were we physically neglected, but we were also educationally neglected. Our teachers often assigned us homework, but no one dared open a book at home for fear of a beating. Avoiding talk about school and books at our house was an unwritten rule, and it illuminates the extent of educational deprivation we endured. It was difficult to develop a love for education in an anti-education home. Reading a book signaled to Buck and Elsie that we thought we were better than they were and would *go somewhere and be somebody*. We never understood what that phrase meant, but we heard it often enough and with such venom that we knew it must not be a good thing. We never wanted to telegraph a negative message to the adults, so we pretended to be busy doing anything except reading a book or studying. We learned to stay busy, whether scrubbing the floor for the fourth time, dusting the records on the stereo console, picking fluff from the carpet because we didn't have a vacuum cleaner, wiping the iron bed frame, or washing the walls. Sometimes, we simply pretended to pick the clover in the yard. As a result of Buck and Elsie's abhorrence of education, we were well into our teenage years before we could tell time. I only recall time being relevant to us in the morning so we didn't miss the bus and during the weekends as we wished the hours away. The less time we had with Buck and Elsie, the better off we were. Ironically, I don't recall my older siblings ever asking about the time or sharing stories from books they read. My home environment was challenging for me because I enjoyed school and reading. I memorized poems and conversations from characters in the stories I read at school and rehearsed them in my mind at night. It is a miracle that I took great interest in what Buck and Elsie tried most to discourage: books.

Chapter 3

ANOTHER ATTEMPTED MURDER

Less than a year after Maureen's hanging, she and Jolene were set on a hot, wood-burning stove and held there while the heat from the fire burned them.

Like many low-income families in our area, our parents routinely swapped and bartered for food. Neighbors regularly shared proteins (chicken or pork) and ingredients such as sugar, flour, and butter. One night, while my parents were at a local juke joint, Jolene gave a frozen chicken to a neighbor who had given us a chicken a few weeks earlier. Jolene thought nothing of returning the favor as we did many times. However, when Buck and Elsie returned home drunk, they accused Jolene of being too grown and stealing their food to give to the neighbor. There was no satisfactory explanation to calm Buck and Elsie. They were furious and blamed Maureen, who they said should have known better than to allow Jolene to give away the frozen chicken. Buck and Elsie were determined to avenge their loss by once again torturing the girls. Even though Jolene tried to protect Maureen by pleading her responsibility and apologizing for the mistaken charity, our parents determined both girls should suffer. Buck demanded that the girls take off their clothes.

Buck and Elsie heated the stove by stoking it with wood until the stovetop was orange with heat. I watched as Buck lifted Maureen's naked body—the only mother I knew—and held her to the heated stove long enough for her skin to begin melting off from her belly button to her lower back, the skin normally covered by underwear. The burns extended down her legs to her knees. I saw her lose consciousness, and then so did I. Horror. Terror. Fear so deep that even at the age of three I could feel it flowing in my veins, vibrating in my cells, and pounding in my pulse until my brain shut down and refused to accept the gruesome barbarity happening in front of me. Maureen lost consciousness from the physical pain of the burns while I passed out as my brain tried to protect my childish understanding of this hideous atrocity.

True to Buck and Elsie's sadistic nature, they burned Jolene the same way they did Maureen, but undoubtedly, God held Buck's hand and refused to allow him to hold Jolene on the stove as long as he'd held Maureen. Jolene's injuries were slightly less severe. She has scars, to be sure, and the psychological shock of the burns contributed to several self-harming tics and obsessive-compulsive disorders throughout her adolescence and adulthood. I only know about Jolene's burning because my brothers and Briana told me. My mind shut down and took my consciousness to protect me from seeing both of my sisters burned and scarred for life.

No one could touch either of the girls. They could not tolerate clothes touching their skin. They stayed home from school until the burns scabbed over. Because Maureen was more injured than Jolene, when the girls were allowed to go back to school, she struggled to sit down because of her pain. When she would get up, she could barely walk. The teachers and school administrators asked questions, but no one interfered with what happened at home. Buck and Elsie had threatened the school officials several times, bullying them into keeping a tight lip about things going on in our family.

Elsie repeatedly warned Maureen about nosey people. "Nosey people will get in our business. They will take you away, and we will never see you again," she'd say. "Those people ask all kinds of questions." Maureen was old enough to know what Elsie meant when she said *those people*. She meant the people at school. "So if they ask you what happened, you have to tell them the truth. That I accidentally hit you in the eye."

Maureen agreed with Elsie that she would tell them the truth and repeated Elsie's lie back to her. "You accidentally hit me in the eye. If I don't tell them the truth, they will take me away, and I will never see you again."

How we children wished someone would be nosey enough to help us! The school district was more willing to risk our lives than their reputation from public scrutiny by other parents. Regardless of our hunger pangs, physical scars, and emotional wounds, the school staff chose to look the other way. Neighbors knew something was wrong, but no one did anything or even asked questions. "What happened to all the nosey people?" we children wondered. Eventually we discovered there was one nosey neighbor.

It was a few months after the burning that my sisters disappeared. I'm sure the news of our abuse spread to the community because of the nosey neighbor who was a notorious gossiper. She was the one who reported Maureen's and Jolene's burning. News spread quickly because of the phone party line. I heard that people sharing the line lingered on the phone and listened to others' conversations.

After the burning of my sisters on the stove, my siblings and I were abruptly removed from our home for the first time by a government agency. I was affected more than I knew. Maureen and Jolene went to a hospital for medical treatment and remained separated from us for the rest of their childhoods. Maureen was hospitalized for months. When she was released, she went to a foster home. Jolene went to a different foster home and was later placed in a girl's reform school for her defiant behavior toward adults. The rest of us were kept together and sent to a foster home where we remained for a few days. To my knowledge, Buck and Elsie were never charged with wrongdoing.

Again, my world turned upside down because not only were we taken from our home, but we were taken from one another through separation. I wouldn't see Jolene again until I was an adult. My memory of her left with her, but I saw Maureen again a few years later. She came by the house with an older man she was living with to say hello. I didn't know either of them, but I felt a familiar closeness to Maureen that I didn't feel for Jolene when my siblings mentioned her. Because I didn't understand any of what happened to keep Maureen out of our home, I stayed fearful and on alert after they left, afraid I would do something that would remove me as well.

After the burning incident, the four remaining siblings—Marcus (12), Mathus (8), Briana (5), and me (3)—were placed in a single foster home. We stayed in this foster placement for only about a week, but it was a week of starvation since the foster family barely fed us. We questioned whether we were better off than we'd been with Buck and Elsie. The adults ridiculed us and our parents, frequently making snarky remarks about our lack of hygiene, ragged clothes, and odd behaviors. I guess they hadn't seen the type of badly abused, wolfish creatures we presented. They weren't ready for our hunger and desperation.

We were only gone long enough to upset our parents. Ultimately, Mathus led our nighttime escape, with me trailing my siblings, a diaper flapping around my legs as I tried to keep up. I was too little to understand what running away meant, but I know we ran away from the foster home together. I recall the fear and nervousness surrounding the situation. My siblings were older and faster, so they ran off and left me in the darkness. The scene of me running down the street in my diaper is still a vivid memory. Little did we know that going into foster care and then bouncing back and forth between Buck and Elsie could be as abusive as what we had already endured. I don't recall how we ended up at my parents' house, but we did. Even as a toddler, I didn't want to return home because I knew it was not a good place.

After Maureen and Jolene were taken out of the home, the other four of us prioritized our survival. We didn't talk about the burnings and beatings. Buck and Elsie ingrained in us that Maureen and Jolene did something wrong and that whatever happened to them was their fault. Abuse always blames someone else. The narrative was, "They did something they weren't supposed to do." We constantly feared that we might do something we weren't supposed to and suffer a similar fate. I knew our parents burned them, but I didn't accept they did it intentionally, nor did I understand the complexities of what happened. My denial of Buck and Elsie's culpability was a coping mechanism—a way of trying to control the soul-destroying thoughts about the brutality my sisters endured.

After removal from our home at age eleven, Maureen visited occasionally but never spent the night. I couldn't understand that. I begged her to stay with us, but she wouldn't stay. Occasionally, Buck and Elsie visited Maureen at the house where she lived with her foster family, and Briana and I would go, too. These visits did not make sense to me either. Buck and Elsie acted as if nothing had happened. Those visits were difficult for me because I always felt a sense of grief and separation anxiety when I was with Maureen. I felt a closeness with her because she had cared for me and mothered me when I was young, and I cried sometimes when Buck and Elsie drove by the house where she stayed. Each time I saw Maureen and then had to leave, I felt like a part of me stayed with her.

No one explained why she left our house. As a young child, I didn't understand that the brutality of the burnings finally got the attention of local child welfare officials, who, until then, ignored reports of our abuse. I was too young to understand the nuances of child abuse and custody and how state child welfare officials monitored them.

My narrative was *Maureen ran away because she wanted to be with a grown man*. The thought that the state took her away because my parents abused her so badly did not occur to me. My oldest siblings—Jake, Ava, and Denise—had left home and moved on with their lives. At the age of three, I had no way of knowing that my teen siblings were still minor children. I thought they were grown adults, but looking back now, I can see why they didn't finish high school or go to college since they were also consumed with survival—away from Buck and Elsie!

In my twenties, I began to understand why each of my siblings eventually left home—some voluntarily, others by state intervention—but I was more disappointed that they didn't rescue me. I felt like they knew our parents were abusing the children still in the house, and the older ones should have intervened. It took years to see their addictions, chronic health issues, and dysfunctional lives through the lens of trauma and find the perspective to see their wounds and inability to help me during their suffering. The paradox is that because I was the youngest and benefited from the state's intervention on behalf of Maureen and Jolene, I was able to get a formal education and had the resources that they lacked to persevere to find healing from trauma. I can now help my siblings understand what happened and help them heal from their adverse childhood experiences.

As an adult I recognized that I blamed myself for Maureen leaving because I felt responsible for her absence. I thought I whined too much, annoyed her, or was too much of a baby for her. I vowed that when she came back home, I would be a big girl and stop wetting the bed. I would do whatever she told me to do. And though I tried, it would be a few years before I could stop wetting the bed. Lack of bladder control is common in abused children. In *Bladder Control and Enuresis*, it reported that "a child who was predisposed to upsetting events (such as divorce, separation from a parent, or accidents) before age five was more likely to be a bedwetter, and children exposed to four or more disturbing events had around double the risk of experiencing bedwetting than those not exposed to such events."[1] But it wasn't the bedwetting that kept my sister away.

By my fourth birthday, I knew Maureen was removed from Buck and Elsie's custody and was never coming back to live with us. I couldn't understand how or why she was a part of another family when she was *my* sister. All six of the younger kids in our family lived together at one time, but her new family was even bigger than ours. Each time we visited, which wasn't often but was frequent enough for me to have a vivid memory, there were about fifteen people present. The driveway had only one car parked there, so I knew they were all family. I tried to figure out how they fed all those people because Elsie and Buck could barely feed their six children.

Maureen's new family, the Smiths, seemed very close and protective of her. When we visited, there were children our age who played outside and did kid things. They ran around chasing each other, playing hopscotch, and jumping ropes. I noticed there wasn't an adult hovering over them or speaking harshly. They seemed to be at peace. I was jealous of Maureen's relationship with them and the freedom those kids seemed to have. I wanted to tell them

---

[1] Douglas, J. W. B. 1973. "Chapter 15: Early Disturbing Events and Later Enuresis" in *Bladder Control and Enuresis*, 109–17. Spastics International Medical Publications. William Heinemann Medical Books.

she was *my* sister, and I loved her and wanted her to return home, but those emotions were not allowed when Buck and Elsie were around.

It wasn't until I was an adult that I understood why the Smith family looked at us like we were strangers and didn't deserve Maureen. They didn't dislike us kids, but it seemed that way to us. They disliked Buck and Elsie and wanted them to know it. They were not kind to them and did not invite them into the house, so whenever we visited Maureen, we would sit in the car while she stood beside the car and talked with Buck and Elsie. I tried to believe that the Smiths were using Maureen and couldn't possibly love her as I did, but in my heart, I knew they loved her, and what was more unbelievable was that she seemed to love them.

A few years later, I heard Maureen was pregnant and living with her baby's father's family across town. That only made me sadder. In my mind, Maureen chose someone over me and rejected me. That equated to *she didn't like me, I was a bad person, no one loved me,* and *I was unimportant.*

I wondered why my parents let their teenage daughter leave home and live with someone they didn't know. I didn't realize that Buck and Elsie had no input. Their custody terminated when Maureen was twelve. Buck and Elsie only had occasional contact with Maureen because her foster family allowed it. I had still not processed or understood the trauma of Maureen's burning and removal from my parents' custody. Even years later, I simply wanted her to be with me again. Later, I didn't understand why Maureen lived with the family of her children's father. She gave birth to a little girl, and Elsie loved to see her, so we occasionally visited the baby. She had another child after a few years and then another one. By the third child, it was clear that Maureen was at home with her new family, and our home would never be hers again.

By the time Maureen was eighteen, she had a family I longed to be a part of. Her in-laws helped raise her children, whereas Buck and Elsie only visited. Maureen's in-laws were the family she never had. I lacked the perspective to see that an eighteen-year-old mother of three was not necessarily someone to envy. True to research, Maureen's inability to think critically caused her to make unwise choices with men. Her children's father couldn't provide for them, nor did he understand the responsibility of fatherhood. He, too, survived multiple childhood adversities. Maureen did not intentionally harm her children. She loved them, and everyone knew it. However, the cycle of abuse continued because their father was not a significant part of their lives. Although we were unaware if Maureen was physically abused by her children's father, the emotional and physical neglect undoubtedly left her with even deeper psychological scars.

Chapter 4

THE EFFECTS OF CHILDHOOD TRAUMA

For years, I struggled with the belief that we were bad children. I thought I had the worst family in the world. I didn't understand why my older sisters didn't call, visit, or show love toward me after they moved out. Occasionally, they'd come by, but only to drop off their kids. After I got older, I understood because I didn't want to call, visit, or show them love, either. It wasn't about them; I escaped that horrible part of my life and never wanted to be reminded of it again, so the less I saw of them, the better. Eventually, I learned they felt the same way.

Research for my dissertation on Childhood Trauma brought clarity about the abuse my siblings and I suffered and the reasons why we did things in adulthood. Learning how trauma changes the structure of the brain helped resolve many questions about my behavior, thoughts, and beliefs. The parts of the brain most impacted by trauma are the amygdala, hippocampus, and prefrontal cortex. The amygdala controls emotions, memory, and the body's fight or flight response. The hippocampus supports memory and learning. The prefrontal cortex works along with the amygdala to regulate emotions by sending cues that all is safe. For CT survivors, the prefrontal cortex does not send the cues that everything is safe, leaving them in a continual panic. Traumatic events cause the amygdala to become hyperactive. Trauma changes the hippocampus' structure and function, contributing to impairments. Lastly, brain regions change after trauma, so the prefrontal cortex, which helps with critical thinking and decision-making, is impacted. In addition, people who have suffered violence or abuse or were in a natural disaster are more likely to develop PTSD, which also changes how the brain functions.

Even with age and experience, survivors of complex childhood trauma are often at a disadvantage in the critical thinking process. During a traumatic experience, a child's brain restructures and the prefrontal cortex shuts down, leaving only the survival brain to function. Functioning primarily with the survival brain is why Childhood Trauma survivors make impulsive decisions to quit jobs, relationships, and important commitments, and even give up lifelong dreams only to discover later they could have done things differently. Decisions are often made on impulse without considering the options and potential consequences. As a life coach, I always suggest trauma survivors get wise counsel before making life-altering decisions. I encourage them to surround themselves with family and friends who have good character and are discerning to help them make wise choices in relationships, finances, education, and other areas they struggle to understand. Survivors need to know their tendency to ignore warnings and follow every shiny object that captures their attention, which can lead to much more heartache than simple disappointment. Survivors need to understand that because their safety was rarely regarded by those who abused them, it makes it difficult for them to know how to safeguard their bodies or their hearts.

I overcame each struggle in childhood but not without losing something. With each struggle, I lost more of my integrity, dignity, mind, heart, emotions, hopes, and dreams—and even my appetite for food. I had no time to focus on my growth, learning, or self-actualization because I fought to survive. Self-actualization is the level of psychological development when a person realizes their full potential, but it can only happen after basic physical needs are met. As a child, I continuously struggled to find food to eat and a safe place to sleep, so I was unable to indulge in self-discovery or experiment with things I enjoyed. My loss of self disrupted the core of my personality. When my personality was disrupted, my identity was at risk, because instead of reacting naturally to a situation, I reacted the way I believed I was supposed to act—or had been told to act—or that I thought pleased others. Disrupting my core personality increased the likelihood that I would develop a personality disorder. Several variables contribute to Personality Disorders (PD), such as type of abuse, age when the abuse occurs, and whether the abuse was acute or chronic. While I am not a licensed therapist and do not diagnose clusters of personality disorders for myself or others, I can identify those specific behaviors I feel I exhibited before God healed me.

Schizophrenia may not be classified as a disorder by the American Psychological Association, but it is a mental condition with which many sexual abuse survivors are familiar. Schizophrenia is manifested by psychotic behaviors and delusions involving the loss of—or breaking from—reality. After an emotional and mental breakdown, I described my thoughts and behavior to a psychologist who told me I exhibited psychotic behavior. I denied it because I thought I knew people who were psychotic, and I was not one of them, but of course, at that time, my thinking was delusional and distorted.

For most of my life, my memories were fragmented. There were things I only remembered as my siblings brought them to my attention. Other times, I remembered things differently than my siblings. Yet, there are things I remember as if they only happened yesterday. I now know that disordered memory is related to PTSD. My brain suppressed my primary memories of many of the traumatic events until I was well past forty years of age and began recovering them. Healing from trauma allowed the suppressed memories to appear with the missing details from my siblings' reports. As a healing adult, it became imperative that I examine the memories from an adult's perspective to find and understand the context of many of them. I suppressed memories because of the terror associated with them due to my childish lack of power and comprehension. My brain registered the terror even more than the brutality because I was too young to understand why my parents hurt us.

Looking at the memories from the vantage point of adulthood, knowing I survived, I can see how damaged Buck and Elsie were. I can see how they perpetuated a cycle of abuse because they had also endured abuse. I was able to discard the terror and see them for the impotent, frustrated, childish adults they were, taking out their anger and resentment on the impotent, helpless, and hopeless children they'd brought into the world.

Chapter 5
THE WEIGHT OF A NAME

Although I didn't know the entirety of my family's story, I knew enough to feel shame when I went around non-relatives or when introduced as *Elsie Mae's or Buck's child*. I was at a friend's house and overheard the adults talking about my parents and how they burned my sisters. "How could parents do that to their children?" they'd ask. "They should be punished, just like they did those kids." Sometimes, I felt intelligent and confident until someone said, "Poor thing, she has seen so much and been through so much already." I didn't know what they meant when they talked about what I went through, but whatever it was, I knew it was not good. I didn't understand what they were discussing until I was an adult because I thought most children went through similar things.

My parents had no friends because the people who knew them didn't like how they treated us. However, no one seemed to live by their scruples at drinking time because they became Buck and Elsie's drinking buddies. During my parents' sober periods, the neighbors didn't visit, call, or chat. It's funny how liquor changes people and who they can be around.

When Buck and Elsie went out on the town, they often came home with black eyes and scratches from fighting one another. Drinking encouraged them to fight. It didn't matter that they were driving. I recall many times when they drank, drove, and fought while we rode in the truck bed and watched them. On one occasion, Elsie snatched the steering wheel from Buck while he drove, and the truck ended up in the ditch. My parents fought like enemies until they got home, but as soon as they walked through the door, Buck and Elsie were a united force against us. In the house, they were friends, and we were their enemies.

It's sad, but true: we were glad when they drank because they'd *forget* to beat us. Hangover days, though, were the worst. They would blame us for anything and everything. We got used to getting kicked in the face for dozing off while we compulsorily rubbed her feet or combed his hair. We became accustomed to freezing water thrown on us at 3:00 a.m. amid their shrieks of laughter. They kept a pitcher of water filled and ready for when they noticed us dozing off. We learned to sleep lightly, anticipating beatings, and on alert to get locked outside in the pitch-black darkness. There is little wonder why we now have sleep disorders. We took naps but rarely, if ever, could sleep on our floor mattress or have an undisturbed night of rest.

Often, I tried to stay awake through the night, on guard for whatever Buck and Elsie discussed or prepared to do. I couldn't afford to fall asleep. I thought it would be easier to endure if I saw it coming rather than be unexpectedly jolted from sleep. We lived simultaneously exhausted and hysterical. The damage of their sadistic practice of torment left my body in a sustained state of fear. My body and mind were wired for danger. My siblings and I have shared as adults how we are seldom able to enter into deep sleep. I believe it's because we were afraid of flashbacks or nightmares if we allowed ourselves to fall asleep. We suffer from chronic illnesses and disorders such as heart disease, diabetes, Grave's disease, PTSD, strokes, and nerve damage.

For years, I feared Elsie and Buck would hang me, like Maureen. At the age of forty, I finally understood how witnessing the hanging and the burning of Maureen and Jolene changed my life because I had to accept that chaos and madness filled our childhood. I had to admit I had no safe place. We didn't have a healthy living environment. When parents don't provide safe environments for their children, the children are on a path to emotional, mental, and physical problems as adults.

I learned more about torture and cruelty from my parents than I ever learned from a textbook. I learned the multiple types of cruelty people are capable of. I learned that adults can break and destroy children and act as if it's an amusing game they're playing. I learned that other people—even the ones paid to take care of children—will stand by and let the abuse happen, especially when the children are poor and powerless. I learned that abused children taken from their parents are often abused by other adults, especially by the foster care system that is supposed to protect them. I learned that abused children absorb the message that they have no value other than prey and that their feelings, voice, and potential don't matter to the world. From that, I learned how to be insincere and untrusting of people, to ignore my feelings, and give them no value. I did not believe I was valued and felt my existence mattered to no one. I was stuck on survival and never matured to self-actualization as a child. According to psychologist Abraham Maslow, if basic needs are unmet, individuals can't grow to meet their love, esteem, and self-actualization needs.[2] Basic needs must be satisfied before one can find love. Living at the survival level explains why I thought the way I thought. As a young child, I was stuck on getting my basic needs met and unable to think past that obstacle.

Even after experiencing the abuse from my parents, I couldn't have predicted the impact it would have on me as an adult. I attributed the thoughts and feelings I had to the temporary resentments children often had of their parents, occasional irrational fears, and wishes that their parents would die. It wasn't until I got older that I began to understand the despicable things my parents did to us, and that most other children did not suffer such abuse. Years later, I wrote a list—of what I could put a name to—of what my parents did to us. I sorted it by calling it Trauma A to Z. Even with an entry for each of the twenty-six alphabet letters, there was more to list. I counted a trauma for all the alphabet letters and then some.

No mother in her right mind would intentionally do the hideous things to her children that my mother did when she tortured us without any remorse. She did not know how to love any of us, even though she occasionally favored one over the others. I do not believe my mother was in her right mind when she abused us. Her actions show me that she was mentally ill, manic-depressive, and most probably suffered from undiagnosed schizophrenia.

Some days, she would lie in bed for long periods and make us rub her feet. As soon as we fell asleep, she gave us a swift kick that sometimes sent us flying into the wall. When she wasn't in bed, she was drunk, delusional, and depressed. She frequently made us search for a mysterious, non-existent letter from President Kennedy. She stayed up nights pacing the floor and making us clean an already spotless house. On many of those sleepless nights, she drank alcohol and accused my sisters of sleeping with Buck. From day to day, we never knew what she would accuse us of doing. It didn't matter if we were innocent of whatever we were accused of because she beat us anyway. She must have had a mental illness to continue having children when she did not want them, only to try killing some of them with life-threatening abuse.

During my early and middle childhood, we moved from the red house and lived in a trailer Elsie and Buck purchased after selling some land. We still had no running water, and we had six people living in an even smaller space. At

2 Kenrick, Douglas T., Vladas Griskevicius, Steven L. Neuberg, and Mark Schaller. 2010. "Renovating the Pyramid of Needs: Contemporary Extensions Built Upon Ancient Foundations." Association for Psychological Science - APS. *Perspectives on Psychological Science* 5, no. 3 (May): 292–314. Doi: 10.1177/1745691610369469.

twelve and sixteen, Mathus and Marcus ran away from home one day, and no one reported them delinquent or missing. Elsie and Buck saw their sons leaving home as giving them fewer mouths to feed. The boys moved in with some friends and extended family members. This left only nine-year-old Briana and seven-year-old me at home.

I am not sure what affected Elsie, but within a few years of the burning, she also ran away more frequently. Something bothered her so much that she couldn't stay with us. It may have been the alcohol that upset her mind and caused her discomfort. Many late evenings, she smoked a cigarette and paced back and forth. She called anyone she thought was still awake and told them her woes. It never failed that someone came to pick her up in a short time. Often, she left in the middle of the night. It became a frequent pattern when I was seven to nine years old to go to bed with her at home, but when we woke up, she was gone.

Perhaps Elsie left because she had increasing mental challenges and needed to get away. After all, she had back-to-back babies for fifteen years and didn't get a break until I was born, since I am the youngest and last of her babies. She was in jail a few times for drinking and driving when the boys were home, but left repeatedly while Briana and I were still in elementary school. She would leave for weeks or months at a time, and eventually, she stopped coming back. We seldom knew where she was. I can remember the stress and shame of not knowing where she was or what might happen to her. Often, I thought about telling people who asked about my mom that she had passed away because it was easier to accept and required less energy and emotional involvement.

We heard Elsie lived with her twin sister, a male friend, a niece, or a stranger. Buck told us she wasn't a fit mother, so he wouldn't let us stay with her. We lived with Buck most of the times she abandoned us, but he often dropped us off at a neighbor's house or the home of one of our older, independent sisters so he could go to work. Neither Denise nor Ava drank alcohol, and neither did their spouses, so we didn't worry as much about being beaten at their homes. Denise's husband occasionally made us strip and whipped us. He was as mentally deranged as our parents, but we still preferred Denise's house over our own. However, the chaos, yelling, and sometimes fighting made us feel we were only exchanging one chaotic household for another. For a long time, neither Briana nor I questioned Buck because we knew Elsie was unstable by her decisions when she returned home from her escapades.

Many nights, Briana and I slept in hospital room chairs or Buck's car because our stepfather thought he was going to die from asthma. These episodes only occurred when Elsie left him and went to live elsewhere. The stress of having to raise two girls on his own may have contributed to his psychosomatic symptoms. He could have also been having panic attacks. In the years we rushed to the emergency room, he had only one asthma attack; none of the other dozens of trips required medical treatment. Buck went to the hospital—just in case.

Elsie's abandonment undoubtedly wounded his ego and damaged his confidence. In his mental delirium, he picked us up from school and went directly to the hospital. Briana and I knew the routine. We pulled up to the Emergency Room entrance and parked. We waited in the car through the night, expecting him to have an asthma attack, but except for the one, he never had an actual attack. During those hot, smothering nights, we thought we would die from the heat or the mosquito bites. When we woke the next morning, our bodies were swollen and covered with bites. He drove us home barely in time to catch the school bus. This was our routine two or three nights a week for a few years.

The nights in the car seemed much longer than at home. Hours crept by as we waited for morning to come so we could return to school and eat breakfast in the cafeteria. Sometimes Buck made us go inside the hospital, and sometimes he made us sleep in the car. Inside the hospital, we sat in waiting room chairs. Buck wouldn't allow us to take blankets or pillows to the hospital because he didn't want the hospital staff to think we were homeless. The only person who seemed to notice us was the security guard who walked around to check the doors. He saw us sitting in the waiting room chairs, but I never saw him question Buck.

The hospital security guard locked the front entrance doors, forcing emergencies to enter through the emergency room. With a sad look on his face, we heard his unspoken words. *I wish there were something I could do to help you.* Still, he didn't offer pillows, blankets, or anything that might ease our hunger. I'm sure he wondered why we were there weekly, often on consecutive nights, but he, too, chose to turn away from our unspoken pleas for help.

When we waited in the car, we lay in the back seat wondering whether it would be the night Buck died. We learned to accept the constant threats of his death and our impending fatherlessness. I'm still not sure why we thought either of those things would be so bad. At the very least, it would've stopped the abuse from him. From my abused child's brain, I can understand why we feared for his life. Traumatized children often want to remain with an abusive parent due to attachment issues, shame, guilt, or because they don't recognize the maltreatment as abuse. We thought we would be homeless if something happened to him because he refused to allow us to live with Elsie.

Nights in the hospital were some of the most difficult times of my life because we had to learn to ignore hunger pangs. We had no meals inside the hospital or outside in the parking lot. The only time Buck was admitted to the hospital, it was only for a night, and he made Briana and me sleep in his room. I slept on the end of his bed while Briana slept in a chair. Buck gave half of his food to Briana and me for our dinner when the staff brought his meal. Every other night, we couldn't tell Buck we were hungry, sleepy, or that we needed to finish our homework because we feared his assaults. We didn't know when it was okay to laugh with him because one day he would laugh and play with us, while the next day he would beat us for looking at him. These episodes taught me to ignore my needs because the person with the drama was a higher priority. This early introduction to self-denial carried into adulthood. If someone had a problem, even when self-inflicted, it was of higher priority to resolve than my responsibilities. I often delayed addressing my needs to help someone with theirs.

Briana developed real survival skills during those hospital stays. I know God was with us because He made it possible for Briana to find a clothes hanger each time we went to the hospital. I was too afraid to enter a patient's room and get a hanger out of the closet, but she found one each time she went looking. We might have died if not for her courage and skills. I didn't think God heard the prayers of thieves, but He heard our prayers because coins came out each time she used the hanger in the vending machine, which we used to purchase items to eat. Some nights, we foraged for food in the patients' rooms while they slept. Briana's job was getting the food, and I was responsible for being on the lookout. I feared someone would catch her, so I watched and prayed while she worked the machine or entered patient rooms. I asked God to *please not let her get caught!* because we were hungry. I never asked Him to stop her from taking the patients' food or money.

We justified our thefts by telling ourselves it was allowable to get money from the machine because we weren't trying to steal; we were hungry and needed food. The food wouldn't come out of the machine unless we put money in, so when the money fell from the machine's coin box, we put it back into the machine to purchase the nutritionally deficient snack foods.

Before long, we held bags of corn chips, cupcakes, peanuts, and chocolate candies. The nut snacks helped fill our stomachs and provided some energy to stay awake as long as we could in case Buck needed us to run and get the medics from the Emergency Room. Buck never searched for us, even though we usually stayed inside the hospital working the machines long enough that he should have been concerned. I am thankful the hospital staff didn't catch us. Our situation was already deplorable; we certainly didn't need the stress of criminal proceedings.

Briana criticized my skills as a lookout because she said I was too scared—and I was. When a coin fell on the floor, I feared someone would catch us after hearing the noise. I often wanted to put the stolen items back. Even while eating the food, I was afraid of being caught. I did not enjoy the food from the vending machine. I ate for hunger, not for pleasure.

To address my fear of being caught, Briana told me that we would starve if we didn't do what we needed so that we could eat. A few times, she almost got caught because I froze when I saw someone coming and forgot to cough to warn Briana. They say *God helps those who help themselves*. We helped ourselves to the chips, cookies, and drinks and never forgot to thank God for them.

We knew the hospital staff by name, and they certainly knew us. Still, no one called the Department of Human Services (DHS) or reported us sleeping in the chairs or in our car in the parking lot, which helped to cement my belief that no one cared about us. The hospital staff acted like they never saw us. I often wondered if we were invisible.

Chapter 6
HEARTBREAK ON WHEELS

I never got used to Elsie being at home because I never knew when she was going to run away. I say *run away* because sometimes she told us she was leaving and warned us against telling our stepfather because he would try to get her to stay. Or, she would leave with no advance notice in the middle of the night or while Buck was at work.

"Your mom left you," our stepfather, Buck, would tell us. "She just walked away. I don't know if she'll ever be back." Then he would add, "I do all I can for you. If you stay with me, you'll be fine. If you go with her, you'll be on the streets or dead because she will drag you into bad places." What he said rang true. I sometimes overheard conversations about Elsie, and they were never complimentary.

I didn't love Elsie, nor did I feel loved by her. She didn't hold me or express affection toward me. When she left, I didn't miss her or want her to return. Our stepfather wasn't as mean to us when she was gone. He seemed more relaxed when she left and didn't beat us as much. Now I know it was because he wanted us to choose to stay with him. After all, he knew our preference for him would make Elsie look bad for leaving us and bring sympathy from the neighbors. Sometimes, Buck tickled our armpits or made funny remarks about something we said or did. We'd make ourselves laugh at things that weren't funny because at least he didn't beat us if we laughed. I didn't like the tickles because I wasn't ticklish, but I ignored how I felt to make him happy. Sometimes, it was a relief to smile—even if my smile was temporary and fake.

I was excited when Buck wanted to teach me to drive. When he first sat me in his lap and put my hands on the steering wheel, I could barely see over the wheel, so he put a pillow under me to make it possible to see through the windshield. Driving lessons were one of the few positive things in my childhood, although they only lasted a few weeks. When I asked him why I couldn't drive anymore, he said it was because I told him I would drive fast. I knew that was only an excuse not to let me drive, and I was hurt. I didn't think of the dangers of an eight-year-old driving. Also, we lived in a rural area where parents allowed their children to drive as soon as their heads were higher than the steering wheel. So the real problem for me was that he took my driving privileges without explaining why. Instead, he began to let Briana drive. I thought he would have us take turns, but he didn't. I resented Briana because Buck favored her. He allowed Briana to sit in his lap and *drive* from when she was six, but not me. Buck's refusal to teach me to drive was the next in a long line of insults—parental abuse, foster parents' neglect, family disintegration, Elsie's abandonments—and I realized I no longer trusted the adults who were supposed to take care of me.

It took a long time to stop feeling guilty and blaming myself when Buck stopped teaching me to drive. I watched and cheered for Briana as she drove us around. He only allowed her to drive when Elsie was away. Elsie was not interested in teaching us to drive, nor did she want Buck to teach us. My older siblings told me Elsie would accuse them of being attracted to Buck or having an affair with Buck. Perhaps this was why Buck wouldn't allow us to drive when Elsie was home; she might have thought the same about Briana and me. When Briana was ten, she sat in the driver's seat and steered the car alone while I rode in the back seat, smiling and wishing I was her. I couldn't believe, as smart as Briana was, that she believed the only reason Buck wouldn't let me drive was because he feared I would drive too fast. Sometimes, she agreed with him about things he said or did to me, probably to stay in his good graces, and this was one of those times. I felt he didn't trust me like he did Briana and manufactured a reason to deny me driving.

Driving was one of the many things I did not get to do that Briana could do. She got money out of the vending machines, built a fire, and cooked food outside for the family when there was no gas for the stove. We had a gas stove, but when Buck and Elsie didn't pay the bill and the gas was turned off, Briana built an outdoor fire with kindling wood and cooked meals for the family. She drove a car, spoke up for herself, and wasn't afraid to fight. Briana loved Elsie, even running away with her and returning without consequences. I admired and wanted to be like her because she could think on her feet and was street-smart. Regardless of what happened, Briana survived.

The achievement that made me the most jealous was something Briana had nothing to do with—she could style her hair into a ponytail. I couldn't get a comb through my hair, let alone style it. I worshiped her. Briana was savvy, beautiful, and frequently complimented. If not for her, I would have died of starvation. She found food for us when I was too weak to walk. I looked to Briana, not my parents, to get us food. I knew I could depend on her. She was my closest friend. I could endure almost anything as long as she was with me because she was everything I wasn't. I admired her tenacity and courage.

One day, Buck promised Briana he would buy us bicycles when she graduated sixth grade. At the time, I didn't know why we got bicycles. I only knew Buck bought us both shiny new bicycles. Years later, Briana told me the story behind the bicycles: Buck approached her about having sex with him and promised her a new bicycle if she did. She was not quite twelve years old at the time. I believe Briana was street-smart from Elsie's womb. She made him think she was fine with his plan to have sex with her because she knew if she didn't go along with him, he wouldn't take her to see Elsie. It was part of her escape plan. She thought beyond her years.

We learned to distrust Buck if he said he was going to do something because his words meant nothing. I learned at a young age the difference between reality and what sounded good. Buck told people what sounded good, and we knew the reality was that he probably would not do what he said. His promises usually degenerated into disappointment. What should have been a happy day was overshadowed by the fear of *what if he's lying again?* When he said he would buy new bicycles, I didn't expect it to happen, nor did I give it a second thought. Buck had raised my hopes too many times when he said he was taking us to our friend's house, Ruth's Dairy Bar, or Denise's house, and when we reminded him, he would say, "I'm not going anywhere. I just said that." His promise of bicycles was as empty as his other promises. We were pleasantly surprised when he came to school for an early dismissal.

Briana ran into my classroom to get me. "Let's go! We're going to get bikes today!" she exclaimed.

My teacher was kind but very firm. I knew not to get up and run out of the room without a nod from her. My sister slapped the note on her desk and told me to come on. I saw the nod from the teacher and ran, giggling, out of the room. Buck was outside, standing beside the car with his hands in his pockets, smoking a Camel cigarette.

"Y'all ready?"

"Yes, sir," we said in unison.

I distrusted Buck. I still thought he could be lying and that he might change his mind and take us home. I heard Buck tell more tall tales than Briana did because when Briana sometimes ran away with Elsie, I stayed with Buck. On several occasions, Buck told me we would visit them, only to get in the car and find out that he had lied to me. I couldn't raise my excitement to the bike level yet.

Unbelievably, Buck took us to a local hardware store and allowed us to choose two bicycles. I momentarily forgot the beatings and burnings and the removal of my sisters from our house. I even forgot for a second that Elsie had left again. Those difficulties couldn't compare to my pink bike with a banana seat and pink and white fringe on the wide handlebars. I forgave Buck for his abuse. For that moment, he was the best stepdad ever, and the dreams of him dying or wishing he was dead made me sad because, for now, he was a good stepdad. I wanted him to live—for now.

Briana must have known Buck was in a good mood and to ask a favor while the asking was good. She asked him if he would take her to see Elsie, and he said he would. Again, I thought he only said *yes* to make Briana feel good. Briana never gave a hint or let on that anything was less than what it appeared. We were close, but she was more perceptive than me, and she recognized things I missed. Also, she knew not to ask me to hold anything other than my breath because I couldn't keep a secret. She knew I would tell Buck. I don't know why, but I'm sure I would. Like Briana, I tried to win his favor and make him think I was loyal to him.

We enjoyed our bikes for a week. We rode every evening after school. It was okay with us that we had no food to eat because Buck didn't have enough money to buy groceries after he bought the bikes. Our new bikes solved our problems.

The following Sunday morning, we woke early and ran outside to ride our bikes. We rode until Buck called us into the house and told us to get dressed because he would take us to our Aunt Bessie's house (Elsie's twin) to see Elsie. When Elsie left, we often knew she went to Bessie's house. Briana jumped up and down like she didn't remember how Elsie abused us. She seemingly forgot the knot on her head from the broom, the welts on her arm from the extension cord, or the burn scars on her feet and legs because she received no medical treatment. Why was she so happy that we were going to see Elsie? Normally, Briana behaved beyond her years, but not in this situation.

Briana hugged me and started singing, *"We're going to see Momma, we're going to see my Momma."* She was happy to be with Elsie, but I wasn't. I was sad that Briana wanted to visit her. We were getting what we wanted because she told Buck what we wanted and he did it. What could be any better than that? We weren't starving anymore. We had no food in between paychecks sometimes, but now he had credit at Littlefield's grocery store, so we could at least get lunch meat, bologna, liver cheese, hog-head souse, and bread. We took trips to see his sister, whom we called Aunt Sim, and Buck let us go to our friend's house and spend the night sometimes. We weren't going to the hospital as many nights as we used to, and we could sleep through the night without freezing water thrown at our faces. However, Buck occasionally bribed Briana and made her put hot sauce and chicken poop on my fingers to keep me from sucking them because he still got a sadistic kick from our expressions of emotional pain and anguish.

I thought Briana was happy. I thought we were fine. I thought the bike was enough. I didn't know why, but going to see Elsie made me nervous. I asked Briana why she wanted to see Elsie, and she said, "I miss her," as tears welled in her eyes. I couldn't relate at all. I didn't miss Elsie and wished she'd stay completely out of our lives. I wished my sister felt about Elsie like I did, but I couldn't change Briana's feelings.

I knew Briana loved Elsie. It made me sad when Elsie ran away with Briana sometimes. It is normal for abused children to want to remain with their abusive parents and even to defend them. Abused children's brains are wired to fear and are alert for abuse. Stockholm syndrome undoubtedly contributed to Briana wanting to live with Elsie and me wanting to live with Buck because a *trauma bond* forms between a victim and their abuser. We both developed a strong sense of loyalty to them despite the damaging bond. Subconsciously, I may have been waiting for the day Elsie might take Briana from me again.

I forced a smile for Briana's sake. "I will be glad to see Mom," I said. I knew she would tell Elsie what I said because they were close, so I spoke few words after that. We arrived at my Aunt Bessie's house in Heth, Arkansas, a few hours later.

Before Buck fully parked the car, Briana jumped out and ran inside to hug Elsie. As soon as she hit the ground at Aunt Bessie's house, Briana knew Buck couldn't touch her because Bessie's place was untouchable. Aunt Bessie had sons who loved her and Elsie; they would fight Buck if he put his hand on Briana while she was there. No one dared touch her or Elsie.

When Buck and I walked in, Briana and Elsie were still in the back part of the house. I stood in the front room like I wasn't welcome to the back with them. When they came out, Briana stood behind Elsie as Elsie made small talk with Buck. His visits never lasted long and usually ended with, "Sugar, the girls need you. Why don't you come home?"

I wanted Buck to shut up. I screamed silently at Elsie *I have a bike. I am quite well. We get things we like when you are not at home. Don't listen to him. He's speaking for himself, not for us. Don't come back! We don't want you!*

She gave him her usual, "I'll come home when I'm good and ready." Even though we'd barely arrived, Buck got up to go and told us to get our things. Briana didn't walk toward the door with us. Instead, she stood behind Elsie, who said, "Briana's not going with you. She said she wants to stay with me."

I thought I would die. I burst out crying while Elsie and Buck went back and forth with words. "She's old enough to decide who she wants to stay with," Elsie said.

"No she's not, and she needs to be in school," Buck retorted.

This went on for what felt like an eternity. Buck begged Elsie, and I pleaded with Briana, but neither one budged from her position. After this deception by Briana and Elsie, my dislike for Elsie intensified because I felt she took my sister from me. I left feeling like I would die because Briana was the sole person at this time who I felt took care of me.

The ride home from Elsie's place was lonely. I cried on the way home but ensured Buck didn't hear me. He tried asking a few questions, but I pretended to be asleep so he would stop talking. The tears kept falling. I couldn't stop them. My best friend, Briana, was gone, and I didn't know if I would see her again. Although we weren't allowed to discuss Maureen and Jolene, I still missed them. To me, Briana was as gone as they were. I closed my eyes, but I couldn't sleep.

Restful sleep evaded me during the period of grief after Briana left. For several nights, I dozed off only to wake up frantically gasping for air and afraid to go back to sleep. I frequently fell asleep in the classroom because I was so tired. I had no energy or desire to go outside and play, and I was glad when recess was over. I now know I was grieving Briana's friendship, leadership, and companionship. The fact that she left me duplicitously and without warning only intensified the feelings of betrayal and loss.

Briana broke my heart, but I couldn't tell Buck how hurt I was. I knew I had no one to talk to or play with except my neighbor's daughter, Tisah. Her mother, Ms. Charlotte, was a kindergarten teacher. She was kind and encouraging and said positive things. She and her husband Weston called me by my nickname. "Jean, you are so smart. You can be whatever you want to be," she'd say. Their words didn't mean much to me then but often replayed in my high school and college memories. Throughout high school and college, I visited Ms. Charlotte and her family because they knew my childhood adversities and continued to tell me I was strong and could overcome my past.

I couldn't control anything except my grades, so I always made school the object of my determination. When I was in third grade, I even stayed up late to learn a poem about the Loch Ness monster. *He sleeps till noon, then makes his feast,* I chanted repeatedly. It was hard to see the words because our electricity was off due to failure to pay the bill. We had a coal oil lamp, but I knew to memorize as much as possible at school so that I could practice at home. I saw the poem as a chance for praise and an opportunity for Ms. Taylor, my third-grade teacher, to tell me how smart I was. I couldn't pass up the opportunity for positive recognition. After I recited it, she praised me, establishing a pattern I followed from grade school to college.

I knew I wanted to be a teacher because Ms. Charlotte was a loving and caring teacher. She inspired me. She was tall and wore glasses. She looked under the frames and gave me a big smile. It made me feel so good when she showed concern and asked if I had eaten. I loved how she cared for her children. She provided green vegetables and healthy snacks and made sure they ate their food. We ate apples and oranges when I played with Tisah. The best thing about being around Ms. Charlotte was when she took me to her classroom during the summer break to prepare for the fall reopening of school. Her classroom allowed me to dream. I don't think she genuinely needed me to clean. In retrospect, I think she established an amicable relationship with Buck to spend time with me and help me. I envisioned teaching children like she did. She had a soft voice that she rarely raised. No matter what mischief I did, she never yelled at me. I wished I could be in her class, if only for one day.

I was in elementary school when I helped her clean the classroom for her kindergarten students. Buck let me help her for a few summers. After we finished, she rewarded me with a good, hot meal. I didn't want to go home but never let her know because I thought she might not let me come with her again. I wanted her to be my mother and teacher. She was my first example of Christ and a great one. I so wanted to be like her! I didn't know that one day I would become a teacher because of the love and kindness she showed. I loved my students the way I felt she loved her students.

I was nine years old when Briana decided to stay with Elsie. After Briana left, it became obvious how boring Buck was. He frequently called people and whined to whoever would listen—mostly older, lonely women—about how Elsie split us up and that she was a bad mom. He griped about how she didn't do anything for us. The neighbors didn't like Buck either, but it seemed they preferred him over Elsie. When she left, he became a man in better esteem. The neighbors said it was a shame that Elsie left me, that Buck did his best to raise two smart children, and they gossiped about how Elsie "stole" Briana. He told so many tales about Briana and Elsie that I began to doubt things happened the way I remembered them.

If he wasn't on the phone talking about Elsie, we were down the road at a neighbor's house or at my oldest sister Denise's house talking about Elsie. Strangely, Denise and Buck had a good relationship. She called him "Daddy" even though he was not her biological father. Whenever we went to Denise's house, she cooked for us, and Buck ate and watched TV. They laughed and talked about Elsie. Sometimes we stayed with Denise for a few days.

Denise was my oldest sibling. She spoke with a loud, strong voice. I was afraid of her because she threatened to beat Briana and me with a broom. I found out as an adult that she was only teasing, but I was terrified of her as a child. Denise had running water, towels, and food. She made sure we ate when we visited her. She threatened me time after time about taking her towels, but I continued to steal them. Somehow, I think she understood. I liked being with Denise, and I liked going to her house because she had electricity and I could watch TV, but I also felt unsafe when her husband, Reese, was there. Everyone knew he inappropriately touched children, but no one did anything. He first began touching and fondling me when I was six. Once again, I met adults who kept silent about the abuse I suffered. When Briana and I visited Denise, Reese made us pull down our pants and lift our shirts. He told us he wanted to see if we were women yet.

On one occasion, Buck told someone Elsie kidnapped Briana while he was at work. That lie got him a lot of sympathy from women. They offered to cook and clean, and he took some of them up on their offers. He was interested in them, but none of them seemed to like him enough to stay. He sang the single man's song of suffering until he wore out the notes.

I was the faithful one who stayed with Buck, but despite Briana's absence, he refused to give me more driving lessons. After she left, we stared at each other. He didn't want me to stay. He wanted her to stay. I knew Elsie didn't want me to stay with her, either. Buck and Elsie both tried to win Briana's favor. I guess they both knew if it didn't involve school, I wouldn't participate. Sadly, this wasn't my first experience with rejection.

Briana's friends asked about her. I picked up one of Buck's habits when I learned to stretch the truth and tell them what sounded good. I said, "Briana went to stay with Elsie for a while, and I'm here. We'll switch places when she comes back." They accepted what I told them. No one followed up to ask any more about Briana, and of course, she and I never switched. I only told the story to make us look like a normal family with parental problems. I had no idea what *normal* was, so my story was demonstrably pathetic, but it required less explaining and defending of my situation.

From time to time, Buck took me to visit Elsie and Briana, but it wasn't the same. I didn't want to stay with Elsie, and Briana didn't want to stay with Buck. My relationship with Briana changed because we kept secrets from each other. I couldn't trust her not to tell Elsie how I felt, and she couldn't trust me not to tell Buck what she thought of him. Briana and I tried to convince each other of the things the other was missing. She reminded me that she could see boys and eat Elsie's delicious cooking without attending school or being in by a certain time at night. I reminded her of Buck's rules, curfew, school, and good cafeteria meals. Neither of our scenarios appealed to the other. Briana didn't want to live with Buck, so eventually, he stopped taking me to visit her.

Chapter 7
TIME TO LEAVE

B riana and I have always been different. I was book smart, and she was street smart, and we both got smarter in those ways. I envied the life she described, but she didn't seem jealous of my life in the least. The most excitement I had after she left Buck's was reading books and watching the Ingalls in Walnut Grove on TV's *Little House on the Prairie* when I visited Denise. I read many kinds of books, but due to the stress of my childhood, I couldn't remember much of them in detail. I remembered more of Elsie's true romance books I read in secret than the age-appropriate Judy Blume stories.

My fourth and fifth grade years are little more than a blur. The saddest times of my life were when I was alone with Buck. He didn't abuse me as much after Briana left, but during those years, I stayed anywhere from two weeks to a month at a time at any one of eight different homes. Buck would drop me off, but he didn't communicate why he left me at different houses, so there was uncertainty and instability each time he uprooted my life. I now believe Buck dropped me off when he couldn't care for me or was mentally unstable, because he left me with them for days, weeks, and even months.

Most of these houses were family homes headed by older women. One of the homes belonged to the Williams family who lived down the road. Two homes were comprised of women who lived with their adult sons. Two widows housed me and provided a home to several older children. One home had children of many ages, and one woman had a nephew five years older than me that she raised. Miraculously, I escaped abuse in these homes. I am thankful as I write this that Buck didn't leave me with Denise for long periods because her husband might have succeeded in his attempts to rape me.

I had plenty of food and was allowed to take long baths, but I felt like a stray dog searching for food from one house to the next because of Buck's instability. Most of the women head-of-households were older people who went to bed as soon as the sun went down. I was often lonely, and many nights I lay in bed crying, wondering where Buck, Elsie, and Briana were. Those long nights seemed to last forever before the next pick-up and drop-off. The homes had televisions, but I also had to turn in when the Big Mamas went to bed. I was glad when Buck picked me up, but he generally only kept me for a few months before he dropped me off without explanation at someone else's house.

Although I continued to make good grades, I had no one to praise or applaud me. The primary consistency in my life was my elementary school friends. However, we had little more than a school relationship because everyone in the community knew what Buck and Elsie did to us. Most adults wanted little to do with them or their children.

Two years after Briana left, I was eleven. Buck had devolved from benign neglect to overt malevolence—much like he was when my older siblings and Elsie still lived with him. He weaponized anything he could pick up to hit me. He hadn't done that for a while, so I was taken aback when he started doing it again. He woke me up after I'd gone to bed to rub his feet, comb his hair, or massage his legs, and if I fell back to sleep, he kicked me in the chest. When he was angry, he slapped me and hit my head with iron spoons. It was a new level of violence following Briana's abandonment, and I wasn't about to endure his abuse again. I was the only one willing to live with him and expected him to be less despicable. I was willing to take care of him and the house, but when he began hitting me, I started thinking about how to run away.

One morning, Buck once again hit me in the head with a steel spoon. Even though I made it to school, my head hurt throughout the day, and I was in a daze for the next few days. Something didn't feel right. After he hit me, my head ached and tingled for months. Undoubtedly, I had an untreated concussion and a possible traumatic brain injury. I repeatedly missed the bus to school. I struggled with time management and had trouble remembering what time I needed to leave the house to get down the road to the bus stop, and Briana was not there to help me.

At that point, I made up my mind to leave Buck. I was motivated to leave for several reasons. I was tired of his useless trips to the hospital and of the hunger and fatigue I suffered. It didn't matter to Buck that he didn't need to go to the Emergency Room for a medical reason; it made him feel better to be there. But now Briana was no longer with me to help find food. Another reason I wanted to leave Buck was because whenever the phone rang, I felt upset and anxious. I knew I couldn't receive phone calls because Buck said I wasn't paying the bills, so I dreaded hearing the phone ring, fearing someone might have gotten our number and called me. He said that party lines charged for each call. Party lines were shared phone lines, which meant neighbors knew the calls—and often the callers and conversations—each phone on the shared line received. I was afraid that if my friends called, Buck would find out and beat me.

One morning, Buck said someone called me and that when I got home he would have something for me. I anticipated a beating, and knew Buck didn't make idle threats. The only time he told the truth was when he said he would beat us. Whether he intended to beat me or not made no difference. The fear registered in my mind, and the terror made a believer out of me. I decided I had endured enough beatings and witnessed enough burnings. I refused to be beaten or terrorized anymore.

A year or so earlier, Buck had allegedly called and reported Elsie as a homeless, unfit mother, so the state removed Briana from Elsie's home and took Briana into custody. Briana was placed in the home of a relative—great-uncle Harold, the local pastor of a large congregation. Briana said the Department of Children and Family Services (DCFS) removed her from Elsie's because Buck repeatedly called DCFS and told them Elsie and she were living on the streets, but Briana eventually admitted she was removed from Elsie's custody because she missed too many days of school.

Shortly after Briana moved, Buck took me to visit her at Harold's house. Briana said she received a monthly check from the state, opened a savings account, and that a church member, who was a well-known seamstress, made new clothes for her. I thought maybe if I ran away, the state would do the same for me as it did for Briana. I was surprised at how healthy and beautiful she looked! She smelled nice and lived in a warm, clean house. I could tell she had baths while I didn't. Her hair was clean and beautiful. She looked like a model. I could imagine her in a shampoo commercial. Briana looked as if her life was a success. Her improved living situation undoubtedly planted the seed of running away in my mind. Of course, the abuse watered the seed until it grew tall enough and gave me the strength to run away.

The day of Buck's threat, I planned my escape. This time, I took a page from Briana's book on keeping people in the dark about what I did. I acted like things were fine at home. I caught a ride like I did occasionally with my sixth-grade teacher, Mr. Kragin. He taught school and drove a bus in my town, but he lived about twenty miles away in the same town as Denise, my oldest sister. I asked him to drive me to Denise's house. Mr. Kragin wasn't suspicious because occasionally Buck paid him to drive me to Denise's house. My family knew Mr. Kragin and trusted him, even though they shouldn't have. He was known to bring students (including me) alone into the science lab. But I knew if I lied and told him that Buck told me to catch a ride with him, he wouldn't think anything of it. After Mr. Kragin dropped me off at Denise's, I walked to the Youth Services Agency about three miles away instead of going into her house.

It wasn't difficult to find the Youth Services Agency, and I hadn't let Denise know I was coming, so she wasn't expecting me. While I walked, I fantasized about the monthly check I would receive and how I wouldn't be abused anymore. I dreamed of staying in a nice house, having as much food as I needed, and wearing decent clothes—because that's what happened to Briana. Of course, that's not how it happened for me, but as a child, I could only think so far ahead.

As soon as I walked through the door of the Youth Services Agency, the secretary told a social worker named Marla that I had run away from home because my stepfather beat me. Marla was a beautiful, young, black woman, immaculately dressed in a beige linen suit with brown pumps. She had a pointed nose, a small mouth, and lovely curly hair. She had photographs of her three daughters in her office, and I instantly liked her and wished she was my mom—a feeling I frequently had when faced with warmth and a perceived functional family.

When I had visited Briana at Harold's, she gave me step-by-step instructions on what to do to be placed in a foster home and get a check, as she did. Unfortunately, I didn't know what to do when Marla asked me questions. Marla didn't ask Briana the same questions she asked me. I later learned the difference between Briana's status and mine was that DCFS removed Briana from Elsie's custody while I voluntarily removed myself from Buck. My big runaway plan ended at the Youth Services Agency. I had no idea what else to do beyond trying to get *rescued* like I thought Briana had.

Marla took me to her house for a few days instead of sending me directly to a foster home. She said it would give her time to do the paperwork and find out what to do with me. I was excited and afraid as Marla drove us to her home. My mind tortured me with *what if* questions: What if they don't like me? Where will the agency send me if the foster family doesn't like me? Will I have a room of my own? How long will I live with them before they send me to my next home? Will the kids at the new foster home beat me up? Will I still go to the same school? The silent questions dominated my thoughts.

Marla spoke to me as if she heard those voices in my head. "My kids are going to love you. I told them you were coming, and they're waiting for you." I didn't understand what that meant, but it sounded good that someone was waiting to see me. She lived in a beautiful, beige brick home with three bedrooms, a bathroom, living room, dining room, den, and a huge kitchen with a stand mixer on the countertop. When I walked into the living room, I thought I was on the set of a TV show. There was a plush, beige sofa, loveseat, and chair, wall-to-wall carpet, and a large stereo. Family pictures stood on the end tables and hung on the wall. Also on the end tables were lamps that matched the sofa and the carpet. When I stepped on the carpet, it was so soft I thought, *I could sleep here if they have no bed*.

I felt like Marla's house was home, and I wanted to stay there until I graduated high school. I imagined Marla's family as my family. I visualized them at my high school graduation, and because Marla talked on the way to her house about the importance of going to college, I began planning my future.

Marla introduced me to her family, and we immediately liked each other. Additional pictures of her daughters were on the table in the entryway. The baby was a beautiful, little, curly-haired girl. In the photo, her two older daughters stood next to her and her husband. They wore various shades of red. I wanted to burst out crying because I wanted a family like that. I shoved my tears in my throat and swallowed because I didn't want to show any signs of emotional instability. I thought that would discourage them from letting me stay.

Chapter 8
FOSTER HOMES

I stayed for about a week at Marla's. After that week, she sent me to Ruth, my next foster home parent. Ruth's home was new. I had never spent a night in a new home. Ruth had no children and lived in a beautiful, brick home with running water, towels, and food in the refrigerator. Her kitchen had a huge, open space where she could simultaneously stand, cook, and watch TV. The dining room had a glistening chandelier above the table. She had a large living room with furniture that looked new and unused. Ruth's house had hardwood floors with carpet only in the bedrooms.

I had never lived in a home with running water—not in the red house, the trailer, or the mini camper I had just left. Denise's house had running water, so Ruth's home wasn't the first I had experienced, but now I had towels and a private bathroom! Ruth's house felt so much safer than Denise's house. I was overwhelmed with the luxury and feelings of unworthiness and became emotionally over-stimulated. I wondered how long I would be with Ruth. *What if I spill something on the floor?* I was ashamed, and wondered what Marla had told her, fearing Ruth might put me out. I didn't have to haul jugs of water or get by with little food, but fear of my stepfather finding and punishing me for leaving him stayed with me, regardless of how far I got from him.

At Ruth's, I was in a better place physically but in a worse place emotionally because these were new feelings and emotions to get used to. I have learned people assume that when they rescue a child from adversity, the child should be happy and forever grateful. In reality, only when the child is in a safe place is she or he free to feel and the body to return to homeostasis. Before then, the child is in survival mode. When she or he can finally settle down, the child is angry, withdrawn, fearful, distrusting, and often defiant. That is what happened to me. I became frightened and anxious the moment I was in a peaceful place. I was afraid that Buck would find me. I questioned whether I ran far enough. I warned the Youth Services Agency that if they sent me back, I would run away forever. I know now the Youth Services Agency staff read my parents' records and reviewed the documented abuse—which was only the tip of the iceberg—as well as the injuries that demanded medical treatment and couldn't be hidden under clothing from mandated reporters like doctors and school personnel. I was in no danger of the Agency sending me back to Buck.

My first night at Ruth's house was too quiet. I was used to the trauma drama from my dysfunctional parents. That first night of safety was stressful because I went from extreme abuse to no threat of abuse. The voices in my head and the fear of abuse did not allow me to enjoy the peace. The solitude was overwhelming. I wanted to run away again, but Ruth was too nice.

Before living with Ruth, I had no time to think about my parents' dreadful treatment of me. At her place, I had plenty of time. I tried reading books, watching TV, taking long baths, and talking to my new school friends on the phone to fill my time. I cleaned the house, folded the clothes Ruth bought, and did homework, but nothing worked to distract me from the consuming anxiety. I had fearful thoughts about Buck kidnapping me from school or coming to Ruth's house and beating me or injuring her. I had nightmares of him chasing me, even though he never came. As far as I knew, Buck only knew that I ran away. I didn't think he knew I'd gone to the Youth Services Agency and was in the Agency's custody, but I still feared he would find me and try to bring me back. Presumably, the Agency did let Buck know I was in their custody, since they had documentation of our abuse, but he never came looking for me.

After only a few months of living at Ruth's house, she told me Marla was coming to get me. I didn't care where I went as long as I didn't go to Buck or Elsie. I wondered whether I had done something wrong. She never told me anything I did, so I was left to guess what happened. Maybe I didn't make the bed correctly or wash the dishes well enough, or perhaps the school staff told her something. Neither Ruth nor Marla mentioned anything about returning to Buck's, so I didn't either. I waited anxiously for my new home.

I learned the upside of being an asset from staying in the various drop-off homes where Buck left me from time to time. I knew that when I showed people I could offer something they wanted, they were happier to let me stay with them. I worked hard to prove I deserved to stay so the host family would give me a room.

I never once considered someone might like me because I was nice or simply worth being liked and accepted. I felt I could only offer my skilled labor—cleaning. I could out-clean most adults. I learned how to clean from Elsie. She made us scrub the floors and pick the carpets and rugs for fluff and debris since we didn't own a vacuum cleaner. After the red house, Buck and Elsie bought a new trailer with green carpet and no running water. The trailer rapidly depreciated, and we lived in it for only about a year until Buck and Elsie bought a small used camper. We had no running water in any of the homes I lived in with Buck and Elsie, so I had years of experience cleaning without water or cleaning products. I was an advanced cleaner.

When I returned to Marla's, I thought *Finally, a real home for me.* I lived with Ruth for a while and disliked the quiet and drama-free environment, but I fell asleep at Marla's house the first night. It may be because there was a lot of noise and questions from Marla's daughters, and I was used to a house full of people. I was only there a few minutes before helping with the youngest child's potty training. I felt like a big sister. Living with Marla's family gave me purpose, and I felt needed. My heart and mind determined that this would be my *forever* home.

Life events were special when celebrated by Marla's family. I celebrated Easter several times at Aunt Sim's house, but no Easter was as wonderful as the first one with Marla and her family. They celebrated Easter at the house of the matriarch, Grandma Lucinda. Grandma was loving, witty, and accepting. Everyone loved her, and I loved her, too. She cooked homemade dinner rolls, ham, macaroni and cheese, greens, chitterlings, pound cakes, and cobblers. Children my age were present, and I enjoyed every minute I was at her house. I was accepted. I wasn't isolated or rejected. Maybe the girls were a little jealous of the newcomer getting the attention, but the jealousy didn't last long. Everyone received beautiful Easter clothes and huge Easter baskets with candy, toys, and coloring books packed inside. We had Easter egg hunts, played games, and ate as much and whatever we wanted.

Before Easter at Grandma Lucinda's house, no one had given me an Easter basket. An Easter basket was a luxury—more than I could imagine! After my first Easter at Marla's, I couldn't wait for the next one. Buck used to allow Briana and me to go to church with the Williams, an older couple who lived down the road, but their Easter service was nothing like the one with Marla's family. At the Williams' church, we had only an Easter egg hunt, and I was grateful for it because I found about eight eggs and ate every one of them. Marla's Easter celebration, however, made me feel special. Whatever Marla did for her biological children, she did for me. Every day I spent with them, I loved them more and more. They were a true family who celebrated their love for each other. I fantasized about living with them for years.

Occasionally, I bribed Marla's girls to help clean their rooms and do some chores. I cleaned up after everyone. Marla didn't ask me or make me do it. I simply did it, and I did it every day. I desperately wanted to impress Marla, so

I volunteered to do it. I seldom relaxed. I thought they wouldn't need me if I didn't keep the house clean. I fell asleep in class because I cleaned early in the morning and late at night so Marla's family could see my value. I felt that if they needed me, I would have a place to stay. I was older than her girls and felt responsible for the cleaning. It was ingrained in me to clean, clean, clean. It was my currency. I liked living with them, and I wanted to earn my keep.

Cleaning up after everyone, doing my homework, and brushing and combing the girls' hair was hard, but I loved it. The problem was I wanted excellent grades, too, so I was busy until I fell asleep at night. I didn't want to leave the delicious homemade French toast, bacon, eggs, and orange juice we enjoyed every morning or the homemade rolls with roast beef, mashed potatoes, and green beans Marla made for dinner.

Marla's family was my dream family, the home where I thought I would live forever—until the night the dream turned into a nightmare. One night after I'd lived with them about six months, I was jolted out of sleep at 3:00 a.m. by a hand between my legs and a light shining underneath the covers of my bed. Marla's husband had left his bed and crept into the room where I slept with their toddler. He invaded my private parts with his searching fingers. I jumped and opened my eyes to see him holding a finger to his lips, saying *Shhh.* I didn't know what was happening, but I knew it made me feel like I did when Denise's husband, Reese, touched me. I knew *this was not good,* and it was yet another assault by a man on my body. Once again, my world fell apart. I knew I had to leave. I knew in that instant that my dream of a family cheering for me as I crossed the graduation stage would not happen. I didn't know where I would go or what I would do, but I knew I could no longer stay at Marla's.

In my mind, revealing her husband's assault would cause Marla's family irreparable damage, and I could not be responsible for that. I did not tell Marla that her husband sexually assaulted me because I loved her and her children. My first instinct was to protect them. I find this to be a common trait when I talk with adults who have experienced child sexual abuse. Survivors routinely protect the families of the people with whom they live, which in turn protects the perpetrators. Eventually I did explain it to Marla, but it was years later as a healing adult.

The next morning, I implemented my escape plan. I lied to Marla and told her that my sister Denise needed me to help with her children—even though I knew I couldn't go live with Denise. I had stayed with her before and knew what would happen if I returned. I tried to think of other places I could go but couldn't think of any good options. The only place I could think of was Elsie's house. I couldn't tell Marla my intention because she knew how abusive my parents were, and I thought she might try to send me to another foster home. My trust in agencies was gone. It was time for this eleven-year-old to trust herself.

Briana had updated me a few weeks before and told me Elsie had a place of her own. She received a disability check because she had thick corns and callouses on her feet and couldn't stand long enough to work. Briana told me Elsie wasn't the same as she'd been when we were younger. She said she was nicer. I told myself that Elsie would not abuse me again because I was older and could leave if she tried to hurt me. I would leave her in the same way I left Buck. I had reached my limit with physical abuse from them. I didn't know if Elsie would allow me to come live with her, but I felt that was my only alternative. I didn't know what to expect at Elsie's or whether she would beat me, but it was a chance I had to take.

I made the wrenching decision to run away from Marla's home. Once again, I assumed the huge responsibility of keeping another family's secret. I felt like a family's future was in my hands, and I knew well how to keep secrets. After all, I didn't tell anyone the things I saw my parents do to my siblings. I didn't want to cause Marla's family to split up. I didn't understand that if they split up, it would be her husband's fault, not mine.

I tried to prepare Marla's heart for my departure. I hinted to her that I needed to go help Denise. I thought she and her daughters needed to know I was leaving, and it was best not to announce the day I intended to go. I thought my approach would be gentler if they didn't know the day. I left Marla's house that day and knew I wouldn't return. I explained to Marla's children that I needed to leave and live with my sister. They cried, and it felt good to see someone cry for me. I was sad to leave them. Seeing them cry meant they loved me and would miss me. The truth is, I never wanted to leave. I didn't tell them the truth: that I left because their father came into my bed.

I cleaned the house one last time. I learned from Elsie that a house wasn't clean until you scrubbed it with bleach, so I left them with a clean house as I walked into the unknown. My eyes teared up as I headed for the bus stop. With my books and my life in my hands, I left everything else behind me.

Chapter 9

THE STRANGER I KNEW

Elsie lived alone in a tiny duplex house on the corner of a busy street. It looked like it could use a paint job from the outside, but the yard was well-kept. I didn't know what to expect when I knocked on the door. It had been almost three years since I last saw her. I was nervous because I had no feelings for her. I was emotionally numb. It felt like I would be living with a stranger, and I only knew what Briana had told me about the stranger. A part of me hoped I would get to know her. I thought I might get to do some of the fun things with Elsie that Briana talked about.

When Elsie opened the door, she didn't greet me. Instead, she asked how I got there. She didn't reach out to hug me, and I didn't reach for her. I told her I left Buck, walked to her place, and wanted to live with her. Beyond answering her questions, I didn't know where, what, or how to continue talking to her. She had me come in, and we both pretended to watch TV. She said nothing, and I didn't know what to say. I expected her to break the silence with her derogatory comments about my hair or how much of a burden I would be, but she surprised me. She didn't talk about my hair or face or turn me away. A few minutes later, she stood up and said, "Let's look at your bedroom." I wished I could have loved her as Briana did, but I felt nothing as I followed her, eyeing her kitchen and sneaking a glance at her bedroom. After passing the living room, the kitchen was the first room on the right. Her bedroom was on the left, next to mine. I spotted the iron bed in her room as I walked by. The iron bars were unforgettable because of how often we bumped our heads on them.

The rooms were larger than I expected. My room was tidy, with a single twin bed neatly made with a pillow and quilt. There was a wide window above the headboard. The room had walls that I could decorate and a door I could lock. It had no bedside table, but I was okay with that. My stomach felt tight and uneasy as Elsie showed me around. I know that feeling was fear because I felt unsafe around her. She showed me the bathroom with a long tub with claw feet and a toilet that flushed. This was a plus. I could not go back to using slop jars and outhouses after living with Ruth and Marla. There was nothing fancy about the place, but it was a definite upgrade from the red house and the campers. No decor or anything personal made it feel like home. There weren't any pictures of us hanging on the walls or sitting on the end tables. The walls needed paint, but that didn't matter to me because there was running water.

Elsie and I stood in the room like strangers. She said nothing but, "This is your room." Those words would have been appreciated at one time, but not as much after what I had been through. The awkwardness was palpable. I felt ashamed for not choosing to live with her earlier like Briana had and then showing up without notice. I didn't want her to feel like I was using her. I knew that was part of the reason for the awkwardness. What do I say to a mother I don't know? If she were a stranger, I could have made small talk, but she wasn't a stranger. We shared a past filled with hateful abuse and terrifying torture. I was more uncomfortable with Elsie than I was with my foster parents, Ruth and Marla. I didn't know if I had made a mistake by coming to live with her, but I decided to make the most of it.

Finally, she said, "I cooked. Are you hungry?"

Even if I was not hungry, I would have said I was if only to eat her cooking. I was so excited to eat her cooking again, and I couldn't wait to tell Briana. *Guess who's eating at Elsie's house now?* I thought no one cooked as well as Elsie. She could make anything taste delicious. She made tasty meals out of raccoons, possums, and anything caught moving. Elsie's cooking was so good that I would tilt the dish toward me to be sure to get the last drop of gravy or soup and then lick it clean. This time, there was soup in a pot on the stove, and it smelled good.

"What'd you cook, Momma?" I asked.

Her cooking evoked intimacy and fond memories of when she told Briana and me to pick blackberries so she could make a blackberry cobbler. There are only a few times from my childhood that make me smile. Hunting for blackberries with Briana is one of them, despite the huge snakes we were exposed to as we reached into the bushes to get the bigger berries. We couldn't return home without enough blackberries to cook the cobbler, so we risked a bite from a poisonous snake to avoid a beating.

"Your aunt shared some deer meat, so I made a stew."

That did not sound like a good meal or something I wanted, but I was hungry. It had been a few years since I had eaten wild animals, so my palate was not excited about eating deer. Also, I heard Elsie talk about how dry deer meat could be, so that didn't help. I found a bowl in the cupboard and served myself. It was so delicious that I thought she misspoke because it tasted like beef stew.

Then she said, "It tastes like beef, but deer meat is a little drier."

I didn't find it dry at all; in fact, it was delicious. Elsie went into the living room and continued watching TV. I brought my stew and sat on the couch across from her. We stared at the TV as if we could not look at each other. I talked about my teachers and how much I liked school. She said, "You've always been good in school, especially math." I was surprised by this, since when she and Buck were together, academic achievement made them angry. Now it seemed to be the only thing she'd praise me for. While I lived with her, I tried to impress her every chance I got. I'd give her random facts about animals, cars, history—anything to prove to her that I was smart.

Our life gradually fell into a pattern. Watching TV occupied most of our nights and weekends. I learned that we both liked westerns. The only programs she liked that I didn't were soap operas. She had watched *All My Children, The Edge of Night, One Life to Live,* and *General Hospital* when I was younger, and she still watched them years later.

One day, I came home early from school, so we watched *All My Children* together. It never took long to know what happened in soap operas. I caught up within a few days, even though it had been at least a year since I watched it. I only watched soap operas so I could have a conversation with Elsie. I liked Jenny's character because of her friendship with Jesse. Jenny had a good heart and liked people for who they were. No one could come between her and Jesse. It was something I never had. I also liked their story because Jesse was poor, and no one expected him to make it. I liked Angie because she loved Jesse to the end. She was black and beautiful. She had *good* hair, something I wanted, and Elsie usually reminded me I didn't have it. I didn't like Erica Kane because she was vile and immoral. I didn't know what morals were, but I knew I didn't like manipulative people.

That day, we stared at the TV like we always did to keep from having a conversation. To break the ice, I asked, "What did you do today, Ma?"

"Mr. Raylor came and took me to the grocery store. I looked for some mustard and turnip greens, but they didn't have none. I went to two grocery stores but couldn't find them anywhere."

"Where'd you finally get them?" I asked because I smelled them simmering on the stove when I walked into the house.

"Ms. Smith told me about the city garden where they have mustards, turnips, and collards for free. You have to pick them yourself, so I picked a mess."

"I can go and pick you some more if you want," I added. I would say or do anything for her to love me. I was desperate.

"Briana came by and brought a mess, too."

How did Briana know Elsie wanted some greens? I lived with Elsie, and I didn't know she wanted greens. I could feel myself getting upset and thought *Briana already spent her time with you. Can she please let me spend time with you without her popping up or saving the day?*

Elsie's remark about Briana turned me off. Whenever she talked about Briana, I couldn't help but be upset. I was mad, jealous, and envious all at the same time. There were so many things about Briana that made me jealous. Briana's skin was much lighter than the rest of us and she had a beautiful face, long, wavy black hair, and a shapely body. She was street smart, much like Elsie. Men and women gawked at her. I think one of the reasons Briana attracted attention was because her race wasn't immediately apparent. She looked biracial and was sometimes mistaken for Hispanic or Italian. I thought she was beautiful and exotic.

Flashbacks of how I intentionally hurt Briana flooded my mind. I used to find ways to get to her. She didn't know what she was ethnically, but I knew what I was. I was Black. To appease my selfishness and jealousy, I partnered with her friends when we were younger and made fun of her. Once we were older, I could see how my treatment of her damaged our relationship and her self-esteem. I missed our closeness. I think one of the reasons Briana turned to men was because we had no strong sisterly bond. Our sibling rivalry interfered with my love for her. She and I went through a lot together as kids, but our bond was tenuous once she decided to leave Buck and me. Fortunately, as we got older, we were able to repair some of the damage and rebuild our relationship.

I yawned and told Elsie I had homework to finish.

She said, "OK, stay up as long as you want. I'll head to bed a little later."

I kissed her, something I saw Briana do when she left the house.

"Night, Ma." Briana called her Ma, not Elsie, so I thought I'd try it. Maybe calling her Ma would make me feel closer to her. It didn't.

Elsie began to talk a little more after a few months. At first, she seemed not to trust me or thought I was coming to spy for Buck. I told her I didn't want to live with him, but she didn't believe me. I got to know her a little better even though I felt like I was living with a stranger. I didn't sleep much while living with Elsie because I was afraid. Now, I know I was suffering from residuals and triggers from the abuse she heaped on me in early childhood.

One evening, I told Elsie about Jesse, an older man who liked me. I told her I saw him a few years ago, and he liked me then, but I hadn't seen Jesse since I ran away from Buck's house. I only saw him at Buck's because sometimes Buck carpooled to work with Jesse and a group of men. Jesse used to stop by at least once a month and pretend to see Buck, but he would wink at me to let me know he liked me. I was excited to think about the possibility of seeing Jesse because I was eleven now and fully-developed, and I wanted to be like thirteen-year-old Briana. She was dating an older man, and I wanted to as well.

Briana and her boyfriend often came over to visit Elsie and me. They seemed very happy together. She was almost fourteen, and he was almost twenty-seven, but who cares about age? What did age have to do with it? No one ever attempted to protect us from men, so we thought it was perfectly normal to be with men who were completely too old and inappropriate for us. We had never heard the term *statutory rape,* so we had no idea that we were used and abused. Briana's boyfriend had a car. He wasn't my type, but she and Elsie both liked him. They took me to the store, and Briana rode in the front seat like a grown woman. One night, I dreamed I was sitting in the front seat of a car driven by an older man. I could barely wait until it was my turn to make Elsie proud. If I got an older man with money, I thought she'd be proud of me.

Chapter 10
LESSONS ELSIE TAUGHT ME

Briana may have had an older man, but he had no job. Her boyfriend was a hustler who begged and swindled people out of their money. To outdo her and earn points with Elsie, I would have to find a man with a job. I wanted to make Elsie proud of me like she was of Briana. *Perhaps then I will be her favorite,* I thought. My thoughts must have taken wings because I was at the store a few weeks later and ran into Jesse. He had frequently hung around Elsie and Buck, so we weren't strangers. Few people came by the house to visit Buck and Elsie, but Jesse's family sometimes did. The few visitors Buck and Elsie had were mainly men. I realize now these men didn't come by to pay a friendly visit to Buck and Elsie—they were pedophiles who set their eyes on Briana and me. I was unaware that they were nice to us because they hoped to be allowed to have sex with us. They pandered to Buck and Elsie to get time alone with us. I was too young and naive to see their intentions.

"Jean, is that you?"

I turned around and saw a tall, light-skinned man. He was thin and had the most beautiful white teeth and thick, wavy hair like Briana. His sisters braided it for him, which made it even curlier.

"Hi, Jesse."

"My, you turned into a beautiful young girl." I smiled at him. "What'cha been up to?" he asked.

"In school." What else can a pre-teen say to a grown man?

"Hey, where ya living now? I heard you left Buck."

"With Elsie," I replied.

"Do you think Miss Elsie would mind if I came by to see you?" he said, smiling big and coming closer. People around there called her Miss Elsie.

"I'll tell Elsie I saw you," I said, walking away. I spotted the lady who brought me to the store. I didn't want her to see me talking to an older man. She might think bad of Elsie and that I was fast. The secrecy and *don't tell* mentality Elsie and Buck put in us when we were little followed me throughout my adolescence and adulthood.

"Tell her I'll come by Wednesday."

I didn't say bye. I just smiled and kept walking.

He really wants to see me, I thought.

I heard he was married and had children, but he liked me. I didn't know much about married men except what I had learned from Elsie, Reese, and Marla's husband. I didn't know I wasn't special and that he was a pedophile and had probably been watching me since I was born. I saw Elsie in action with many men. When she lived with Buck, men would come by the house sometimes. She would flirt with them, smooch with them, and sometimes dance with them. She would invite them in to the house and keep the bedroom door locked. We knew she was up to something because she would ask us to let her know when Buck was coming home. I didn't think she would be upset that an older man liked me. I had already prepped her about Jesse before, but I prepared Elsie some more when I got home.

"I saw Jesse in the store, and he wants to visit me."

She said, "He can come see you. I like him. He's a nice man." She didn't ask any questions about him, and I didn't volunteer any information, mainly because I didn't know much about him except that he had a reputation for liking young girls. We lived in a small town where abuse was ignored by those sworn to protect—and predators were protected—so we were not warned against pedophiles.

Sure enough, Jesse came by on Wednesday. He greeted Elsie. She hugged him, and they talked like old friends. He smiled and winked at me while he talked to her. I felt good about him because Elsie approved of him. She said Jesse came from a good family. I hadn't seen her laugh and talk as much as she did with him. She talked more to him than she did to me. I thought to myself, *I have outdone Briana.* They talked and reminisced seemingly for hours.

Jesse asked Elsie how she was doing, and she asked him about his mother and family. As he stood up to leave, she walked him to the door. I stood near the TV, pretending not to hear them talk.

He turned and said, "Ms. Elsie, can I take yer girl out for a little while?"

I thought he was a decent man to ask Elsie if he could take me out. *Elsie is right. He really is a nice man.* The things my family exposed me to distorted my thinking.

"Yeah, she can go," she replied.

A few nights later, Jesse picked me up like he said. When I got into the car, he asked me to get into the back seat. Even though it was clear he was only interested in using me for sex, I wasn't opposed to it because I thought he was a nice man, and I had Elsie's approval. I talked about school, homework, and living with Elsie. When he finished, he told me to tidy my clothes. Then he took me to Joe's Dairy Bar. I thought this must be how Briana feels when she's with her boyfriend, but I was mostly thinking how proud Elsie would be because my boyfriend had a job. A boyfriend meant having sex like a grown up, and a boyfriend with a job meant he gave me a few dollars, and I could give them to Elsie to help pay bills. She never asked me for money, but I knew she had very little, and even though I was only eleven, I wanted to help her. I thought it was perfectly fine for me to be with a grown man because I used the standards of Reese and Marla's husband who sexually assaulted me. I reasoned that at least I consented to Jesse. My thoughts of right and wrong were skewed. My experience was limited, and I could not discern what was good for me. My evaluation of men was deficient since most of the ones I knew had sexually assaulted me, and sexual assaults were a common experience. Some men who sexually assaulted me made me feel attractive because I heard of other girls they sexually assaulted.

Everyone knew Joe's Dairy Bar. It was known for ice cream, greasy burgers, and hot dogs. Joe, the owner, was an oversized man of medium height and wide build. He had oily hair to go with his greasy burgers, but he made the best burgers in town. He was rude and acted like customers bothered him, but his rudeness didn't stop his customers, and there was usually a line of people waiting to order. Breathing heavily, Joe slid the window open and asked what I wanted. I'm sure people thought I was Jesse's daughter. I could feel them staring at me. I was petite and with an older, extremely tall man. I am sure no matter how grown up I acted, I looked like a child.

"Whatcha want, Dora?" Jesse asked.

"I'll have a double cheeseburger, fries, chili, a chocolate shake, and an ice cream cone.

"Is that all?" he said

"Yep."

"What about Ms. Elsie?" he asked.

It made me like him more that he was concerned about Elsie. I ordered for her, too.

"Give her a Frito pie with mustard," I said.

"What about a drink?" he asked.

"Grape drink." Her favorite was grape Nehi soda.

Jesse pulled his billfold out. I saw a roll of dollar bills, some five dollar bills and a few twenties. I was beyond impressed. He handed me $20 for

Elsie. I was too young to know that the exchange of money meant I was legally a child trafficked for sex by my mother. I was oblivious to the fact that Jesse paid my mother to have sex with me and added a tip in the form of food from Joe's Dairy Bar.

Jesse ordered a burger and fries. We ate our food in the car before he took me home. It was about 9:00 p.m., and Elsie was already in bed. Jesse came into the house to give her the Frito pie and express his gratitude, but she didn't leave her room, so he called out, "See you later, Miss Elsie Mae."

She yelled back, "OK, goodnight."

I was happy to give her the money. I knew she needed money and would be very proud of me. I had seen Briana do it, and Elsie seemed to love her so much that I knew she would love me. She was lying down reading a book, something she did often. "I got this for you, Momma." I folded the twenty dollar bill to see her reaction as she unfolded it and looked at it.

"Thank you, Jean."

Because I gave Elsie money for the first time, I felt I meant something to her and made her proud. I felt valuable when I gave her Jesse's cash. I slept soundly that night. When I stirred in my sleep, I wondered how happy I made Elsie. The visits with Jesse went on for several months. Each visit was similar to the first. I still did not understand the terms *pedophile* or *prostitution*. Now I understand that whether you tell your child to bring you money or not, allowing the child to go out, accept money from, and be in the romantic company of an older man without supervision is prostitution. My mother first conducted this with Briana, then with me. We were allowed to leave the house with adult men who gave us money, which we gave to our mother. Undoubtedly, Elsie did to us what her mother did to her. We were too young to know that the adults who should have protected us violated the law. Our prior physical abuse damaged us too much to have any expectation that adults would protect us. We so *normalized* our abuse that we had no idea we were not living the same lives as other pre-teens.

Chapter 11
THE BUS DRIVER

Living with Elsie finally gave me the opportunity to talk with her about my biological father. Our conversation began when I shared with her the talk from kids in elementary school. I told her the kids on the bus laughed at me because the bus driver, Mr. Lonnie, made me sit in the tiny compartment between him and the driver's side window. She didn't respond, so I continued. I was awkward and afraid as I told her that he trusted me to collect money from the other students who purchased candy from the supply he sold to the bus riders. It seemed he went out of his way to be kind to me. Mr. Lonnie also gave me money and candy.

Elsie responded, "He should have given you more than that."

Her answer confused me. I didn't know how to interpret her meaning because she didn't explain or answer my question. My siblings said Mr. Lonnie was my dad, but Elsie didn't confirm. I used to think Buck was my dad. In this memoir, I call Buck my stepdad, but growing up, I called him Daddy. What did Elsie mean by saying Mr. Lonnie should have given me more than money and candy? I wanted to hear more but was afraid to ask more questions. I knew this conversation was an opportunity, but I hesitated. I wanted to know if it was true that Mr. Lonnie was my daddy. That moment felt appropriate to tell Elsie about him, so I told her everything.

In elementary school, I got on the bus each day knowing exactly where to sit. The bus was quiet in the mornings with sleepy children, and Mr. Lonnie focused on me. On the rowdy, loud, and chaotic afternoon bus, I could sit with someone for a few minutes, but as soon as he missed me, he'd look at the large rearview mirror until he spotted me. I knew that meant I had to move to my tiny box seat beside him. Sometimes I didn't immediately sit next to him because I wanted attention from him when he looked for me and said, "Jean, you need to get in your assigned seat."

He was alert and observant. Somehow, he watched the road and the students, too. He was a no-nonsense kind of man, especially with the Black students. In a fight, it didn't matter who started it if the quarrel was between a Black child and a White child. In mixed-race conflicts, he deemed the White student the victim and evicted the Black child from the bus. If a fight happened between two Black students, he asked what happened, but if it was between a Black and a White student, he didn't ask what happened. He simply suspended the Black student. My youthful sense of justice was offended by his practice, and even at a young age, I thought he was afraid of White people.

Mr. Lonnie routinely had bananas, apples, oranges, assorted brand cookies, gum, taffy candy, and lollipops to sell. I politely refused when he offered money, but he made me take it. I accepted the candy for my siblings and me because we were hungry.

I finally got enough courage to ask Elsie, "All the kids say Mr. Lonnie's my daddy. Is he my real daddy?"

All she said was, "Mr. Lonnie is your daddy. You look exactly like his family. They all got duck lips." I didn't hear the rest of what she said because I could only wonder what duck lips looked like.

In elementary school, my siblings called me *Duck Lips* for years. Finally, I knew why. I hardly slept that night in anticipation of going to the library the next day and checking out a book on duck lips. As soon as I finished my classwork, I went to the library. Unsurprisingly, there was no book on the subject. I read about ducks and tried to understand why my siblings called me duck lips, but I could find no explanation. I could not see any resemblance between my face and a duck, but I spent my teenage years self-conscious of my lips.

As time passed, Elsie and I talked more than when I first showed up, but we still didn't have much of a relationship. I was emotionally numb. No matter how I tried, I couldn't feel close to her. She seemed to make no effort to be close to me, either. Now I know it is because we never addressed the elephant in the room—the horrific abuse she inflicted on me and my siblings. My mind wanted to trust her, but my heart allowed no trust. I was no longer physically afraid of her, but I was still emotionally terrified. I had a room to myself, but I was afraid of everything.

I was skeptical of teachers and anyone nice to me. I felt like no one would believe me if something happened, so even small classroom disagreements went unreported. When I fell asleep at Elsie's house, I often woke up breathing heavily. Now, I realize those were panic attacks. My body and mind stayed in a constant state of fight or flight. The abuse manifested in my physical and mental health and behavior. I didn't feel peace in Elsie's house. Even though I finally had a room, running water, electricity, and a little food, I couldn't settle in. I had to sleep with the light on because I felt unsafe.

My body couldn't return to homeostasis. I had frequent nightmares of her and Buck beating me. I had peace when I lived with Marla—before her husband shattered it—but after a few months of living with Elsie, I was exhausted from lack of restful sleep. Many days after lunch, I fell asleep in history class. History was one of my favorite subjects, and I didn't want to miss it, but Ms. Brown's room was the safest place I could find. My body sought refuge in sleep, knowing that Ms. Brown would protect me. I felt safe in her class because she was a no-nonsense teacher, and I saw her stand up for bullied students. It also helped that she was tall and confident. I overheard her tell other teachers when they overstepped her boundaries. I wanted to be Ms. Brown because I wanted to be strong, courageous, and able to tell people they better not touch me again or else.

Elsie had no car, but she went everywhere she wanted. Her twin sister often picked her up to go fishing or shopping at a thrift store. Her friend, Mr. Raylor, came by at least once a week, gave her a few dollars, and took her to the store. I don't know how Mr. Raylor knew, but he came when she needed, whether to go to the store for cigarettes, groceries, or something else. Even as a child, I knew they liked one another. He was a tall, thin, poorly dressed older White man who seemed to have a crush on Elsie and her twin sister. He looked to be at least forty years older than Elsie. When we were little, we'd see a truck driving 10-15 miles per hour and run into the house to tell Elsie he was on the way. I couldn't believe he was still alive and had come around to visit her. I don't know how Mr. Raylor managed to find Elsie because he was well into his eighties, moved slowly, and had one eye covered with a black patch. I wondered if a man shot his eye out because he had a reputation for messing with married women. Elsie and her twin sister knew him well; he bought things for them when they needed something. I suspect he had some kind of twin fetish which they exploited for financial gain. I thought that it was unusual how both sisters had a relationship with him. Whether they liked or used him, I knew something wasn't right. He came around to visit Elsie until she died. I didn't see him again after her death.

Our next-door neighbors believed in God and were kind to us. Elsie liked them, and they liked her. They asked us to go to church with them several times before Elsie agreed to go. The church van picked us up, and I rode in the back with Elsie. I had never been to a Caucasian church. The congregation welcomed and catered to us. They asked if we needed anything and sat us near the front of the sanctuary. I stayed close to Elsie. The church folk told us that Jesus came into the world to die for us, and through Him, we were free to live a blessed life. They extended the invitation to give our lives to Jesus. They explained why we needed Jesus in our lives. Elsie didn't go down the aisle and accept Jesus, but for her to agree to attend church services was a big deal. I watched her closely as she sat quietly during the invitation. When they asked her about accepting Jesus, Elsie told them she had already accepted and knew Him. I prayed to God, and I was under the impression that knowing God meant a person lived a life that reflected their knowledge of God, so Elsie's statement was a source of confusion. She openly admitted and confessed how good God was and that she believed in Him, yet her behavior, lifestyle, and her treatment of us gave no support for her statement. Nevertheless, I felt special as Elsie and I sat side by side in church that day. It was her and me for this short period of my life.

Chapter 12
A DARK TIME

A few months later, my world changed again. Christmas lights twinkled on every street as people prepared for the annual Christmas parade. The Christmas parade was a big event in our small town, eclipsed only by the fall high school Homecoming parade and football game festivities.

After school on Thursday, December 6, 1979, a month before my fourteenth birthday, I walked into Elsie's house. When I opened the door, I heard a voice moaning, "Um, um, um, um." I saw what looked like a river of blood flowing down the hallway, stopping at the doormat. There was a lot of blood. Down the hall, I could see the blood trailing from Elsie's thin body, which had slumped over on the floor as if she had recently been sitting up. My heartbeat accelerated, and I couldn't think. The fight, flight, or freeze response was activated. I wanted to collapse (freeze). I knew what I saw was not good, and I didn't want to know any more than that.

I thought perhaps someone went into the house and shot Elsie. Frightening possibilities flooded my mind. I ran to her, knelt, and asked what was wrong. I didn't know or understand what shape she was in. I panicked because I didn't know what to do. Trauma had buried my emotions from the beatings and burnings I experienced. I was in shock from seeing blood, but I didn't cry.

In a state of emotional numbness that I undoubtedly inherited from the beatings and burnings, I ran into the middle of the street and jumped up and down, screaming. I screamed and hollered, "Elsie is dying! Elsie is dying!" The people next door heard my screams and ran to call 9-1-1. An ambulance rushed Elsie to the nearest medical center, where she was airlifted to a hospital in a larger city.

The panicked state of running into the middle of the street is a normal reaction for a child who has suffered trauma since birth. Anything out of the ordinary causes excitement. Seeing the blood made it worse. I was not devastated by anything that followed finding Elsie. I responded from my trauma brain created by her abuse and was probably secretly glad to see her suffering after what she did to us. There were many times in childhood when I wished she and Buck would die, but not this time. I wished they'd fallen dead during our beatings. They never did, so I got over it, but I didn't wish for them to die as a daily thought. The abused child wanted freedom from the pain, but she was no longer beating me, so I didn't wish for her death.

I may have thought I was an adult, but the authorities didn't. Police officers came along with the ambulance, and they told me I had to go stay with my older sister, Denise. The initial report was Elsie was doing well and would be home the following week. I didn't know Elsie had been previously diagnosed with cirrhosis of the liver. I don't know how long she knew about the diagnosis. She never told any of the children, so none of us knew. I heard Denise talk about Elsie's care. Elsie and her doctor shared a birthday on December 20th. Her doctor said he would celebrate his birthday with her, and Elsie was looking forward to celebrating her birthday with him. Even if she hadn't returned from the hospital, he promised to celebrate with her.

On Sunday, December 16th, we received two phone calls from the nurses reporting that Elsie was not doing well. Denise and Briana rushed to the hospital an hour away. Because of my youth, and no doubt affected by memories of long hospital nights with Buck, I chose not to go with them to the hospital to see Elsie. I remember thinking that she'd be home in a few days, and I would see her then.

I was oblivious to death knocking at my mother's door. I put some records on the stereo and hopped around, singing gospel songs like "Will the Circle Be Unbroken," "I'm Coming Up the Rough Side of the Mountain," and "When the Doors Swing Open." I had no idea those songs were prophetic even as I sang them. My life to come found me questioning whether I could ever break the cycles of abuse, pain, and suffering. Future me felt like I came up the rough side of everything—not only the mountain.

I cried as I danced around the kitchen. I couldn't stop the tears from flowing even though I had no idea what was happening. My unacknowledged stress was leaking out as I danced. Sometime later, a call came: Elsie passed away. I didn't understand how that could be, especially since an earlier call said she felt poorly and a visit from the family might encourage her. I was with her the week before, and she was fine. Now Denise said she was dead. It was too much and too sudden for a thirteen-year-old to comprehend fully. My first thought was not that I'd miss Elsie but that I don't have a mother. She wasn't the best mother, but we were making it work. Then my thoughts shifted to *What's going to happen now? I have no place to go. I have to find someone to live with. No one will take a thirteen-year-old into their home. Where will I go?* I was sad, not because my mother died, but because I had no place to go.

I could only think about surviving and how that would look. I called Jesse to take me to the hospital. I didn't cry on the way because I didn't know I needed to. Jesse tuned the radio to grown-up music, and I felt like an adult sitting in the front seat. I wasn't feeling sadness because I couldn't comprehend what was happening. I snapped my fingers to the beat and was glad to ride with him. Though I didn't feel sad, I did feel several emotions about Elsie and the moment. I felt guilty, selfish, and regretful for not going to the hospital, but I dismissed my feelings and emotions as I reminded myself how mean she was.

While I felt I shouldn't be with Jesse, I thought it would be okay because he could care for me. He liked me. I didn't know that it was unacceptable for me to live with a man twice my age, nor was it allowable to have a married adult pedophile take me to the hospital. He broke state laws, boundaries, and moral codes. Yet, my family never questioned anything. Childhood Trauma is so pervasive in its affect of critical thinking that it often leaves adult survivors unable to make wise decisions or understand the difference between right and wrong. Such was the case with my adult siblings allowing a grown, married man known to be a pedophile to pick me up and bring me to the hospital.

When I arrived, no one asked how Jesse knew to bring me. Even if I had told them, they would have been fine with it because they knew him. Everyone except Denise's husband Reese acted as if Jesse bringing me to the hospital was fine. Reese didn't like the idea of Jesse driving me, so he refused to speak to him. Reese wasn't trying to protect me from Jesse, though. He simply wanted me for himself. By the time I arrived, the staff had removed Elsie's body from the room. When I walked in, the family was crying. I didn't know what to do. I had no tears. I went to each person and touched their back as if to say *I'm sorry for your loss.*

I felt lost, but not a loss.

Seeing my family members cry finally permitted me to cry. I don't know why I cried other than from the effect of seeing the grief of those I loved. I didn't want them to think I didn't love Elsie. Briana's eyes were fiery red and swollen. I felt sorry for her because she had lost her mother. I hugged her, and she broke down even more. I couldn't help her. Now, my tears were falling, but there was no sadness. I was sorry for my sisters because they experienced a loss. Elsie hadn't told anyone about her diagnosis, so her death was particularly unexpected. My sisters loved Elsie despite what she put them through.

Everyone left the hospital and returned to Denise's house to process the shock. I thought Denise would make me ride with her, but she didn't. I rode with Jesse and had a very distinct feeling of being alone. I looked at the sky through the front windshield and thought, *I'm alone in this big world. Everything is going to change now*. I was sad to leave Elsie's home and have to find another place to live. I was tired of changing houses and cleaning people's houses just to have a warm bed. I cried a little, thinking I wouldn't see Jesse again because wherever I went, the adults in charge might not be as lenient as Elsie. Somehow, I knew it wasn't right for me to see Jesse, but none of the adults around seemed to know it was wrong—or illegal. And I was right: after Elsie's death, he stopped coming to see me.

The family made funeral arrangements for a service held three days before Christmas Day. That was a sad Christmas, not only because Elsie passed away, but because I had to try to figure out where I could go. I was too stressed to focus on the death of Elsie because I had to figure out who could take me in. I thought about living with Elsie's twin sister but heard she was much like Elsie. Men loved her. I didn't want another Elsie. Elsie's sister never left her children like Elsie, but she did some unscrupulous things, so I eliminated that option before they laid Elsie to rest.

I took foster homes off my list of options. I had had enough of the late-night prowls of the men in the homes, of starvation, and of ridicule from the foster parents. I crossed out Briana because she had no place of her own. My heart dropped because I knew I had older siblings, but I also had reasons not to live with any of them. Reese had made it clear to me for as long as I could remember that he had plans to use me for his sexual gratification. I considered the Williams family, Buck's neighbors who lived down the road who had often kept me when Buck went off drinking or checked out, but I reasoned he had probably told them such bad things about me after I ran away from him that they would never allow me to live with them. After all, I was not the same little girl they once knew. My head hurt from thinking, and my heart hurt from the possible rejection. It's hard to describe how alone and abandoned I felt.

At the funeral, Elsie's children filled the front row of the church. Her siblings sat in the second row. As she lay in the casket, I looked at Denise, Ava, Marcus, Mathus, and Briana, who were crying. Maureen and Jolene were present; like me, they didn't cry. I thought tears indicated a love for Elsie. My feelings were numb, and my thoughts were all over the place. My most pressing thought was that she *would never beat, whip, or be mean to me again*. She didn't whip or beat me while I lived with her the second time, but my memories of the early childhood abuse were haunting. I tried to ignore them because this seemed an inappropriate time to think about how the deceased abused me. I wanted to miss Elsie, cry for my loss, and think of why she would be missed like my siblings did, but I couldn't. Nothing came to mind when I glanced at the casket. I continued to look away because, whenever I looked at the casket, I saw her and remembered how she abused me. I thought this was the end of her reign of terror. We were about to bury her, and my memories were already digging her up. I felt remorseful because I had little to memorialize except the pain she caused.

I hadn't seen some of my siblings in a while, so the funeral provided a family reunion. My siblings, except Jake, lived within a 15-20 mile radius, but none of them had visited Elsie while I lived with her except Briana. Briana was supposed to be living with Elsie, but she was never there because she lived with her boyfriend's family, which is why the bedroom was free for me. Most of my siblings were teary-eyed and probably thinking about losing their mother, but I was thinking about how I could spend more time with them. Since I was the youngest, I hoped some long-lost family member would offer me a home, but they didn't. They didn't give me any special attention or concern. I felt like an orphan because my mother was dead, and returning to Buck was not an option, especially after knowing for sure he was not my father. Once I ran away, I refused to accept any kind of beating again. Also, Buck was sick and dying. He didn't attend Elsie's funeral. Shortly before Elsie was hospitalized, someone took me to visit him in the hospital. This time, he actually had a reason to be there. I remember feeling bad that I'd run away from him, even though my reasons for running were because he abused me, and it probably wouldn't have been long before he asked me for sex like he did Briana. He had a new girlfriend who was supposedly taking care of him, but he died shortly after Elsie did.

My real father, Mr. Lonnie, had been nice to me as a child, but that didn't mean I could live with him. He was a preacher, and I'm sure he hadn't made a public statement confessing his sins of adultery. Neither Buck nor Mr. Lonnie were viable options.

The funeral wasn't long. I had nothing to say in the funeral service, so I kept quiet. As I sat staring at Elsie's casket, I kept thinking, *You left me—now what will I do? Who will I live with?* It was uncomfortable, not because she was my mother, but because I felt pressure and stress to perform. I felt like my family wanted me to say she was a good mother and to show grief by crying. They kept passing me tissues. They assumed I was distraught over losing my mother, but I wasn't. I was emotionally numb, and I couldn't fake what I didn't feel. I didn't think anyone would understand my plight and not judge me for being a terrible, selfish child. I thought they expected me to break down at any minute, or maybe I wanted to break down to meet a perceived social expectation. I didn't break down because I wanted it to end. I felt nothing but a creeping numbness moving through my emotions. My thoughts focused on where I could live, not on Elsie's passing. I had a lot of work and little time to do it. While they paid their last respects, I looked for a place to stay.

Denise introduced me to different people. "Jean, this is Elsie's cousin, uncle, friend . . . ." I didn't recognize their names or faces. I looked around for some of my friends and teachers but didn't see any. I wanted to be honored and seen at Elsie's funeral. I wanted some sympathy. For a brief moment, I felt I was somebody special at the funeral when we rode in funeral cars. Since I was the youngest, I sat in the main car following the hearse. I wanted to sit with Briana, but she rode with her boyfriend. I remember the long ride to the burial site as we drove down the dusty roads, around the curves, and over the creeks to a graveyard. I sat next to the window, my eyes filled with unshed tears. I saw townspeople pull over to honor the dead by allowing the funeral procession to pass. I felt recognized when people I knew pulled their vehicles over. Buses, cars, and motorcycles moved to the side of the road and waited as the funeral procession passed. Again, I felt special, as if it were my big day and not as if I had only recently lost my mother.

Ashes to ashes and dust to dust. Tears welled up again when I saw Elsie's casket lowered into the ground, but I didn't feel emotional. I shed a few tears when I saw how hurt Briana was, but I had no tears for Elsie. I didn't understand the finality of it or that burying Elsie was forever. Even so, I felt something each time someone threw a handful of dirt onto her casket. As I watched them, I thought, *That's my mother,* but in my heart, I only felt that they buried *that lady.*

As I grew up, I wished a thousand times I had said goodbye to her. I didn't want her to be angry with me. I believed for years that I was selfish for not visiting her at the hospital. As an adult, I understand that I made a childish decision not knowing all the possibilities that day, and that's all right because children aren't responsible for the consequences of adult decisions. I have now processed it and released it.

Chapter 13
VAGABOND

Before they finished throwing the dirt on Elsie, I resolved to make it in life somehow. I decided my best option was to stay briefly at Denise's house. I was afraid of her husband, but at least I knew I had a temporary place. We said our goodbyes to Elsie and each other. I felt strength momentarily because I heard several people tell my siblings, "Y'all take care of Jean now. She's the youngest. She will need your help."

I heard them reply, "We will take care of her."

I should have known they were acting like Buck. They said what the people wanted to hear. I held on to their words this time because I needed them, but *take care* to them must have meant for them not to let me die in their care. The funeral had scarcely ended and everyone acted like nothing happened.

I was already trying to find another place before I told Denise I would live with her. *I can stay at Denise's until school is out in the summer, but then I must leave. If I stay at Denise's, Reese will do the same sexually abusive things to me as he did to my sisters.* I had heard stories of things he had done to my older sisters and his own children, and I didn't want them to happen to me. I had no peace about the decision because I didn't know where to go once the school year ended.

All I got that Christmas was the box of oranges, apples, and candy that Reese traditionally put together for each person in the house. We received a box filled with goodies with our name on it. That holiday is still a blur to me. I only recall the candy box and wishing Christmas would go away. It was much ado about nothing and caused me too much pain. The Christmas lights, Santa, and songs did nothing for me that year because I was plagued with thoughts of *What will I do when Reese tries to make me have sex with him? Where will I go? Who will help me?* It was more than a thirteen-year-old could handle.

I lived in terror at Denise's house. I was too afraid to sleep alone. Denise was afraid, too. She feared the dark and liked to sleep with the lights on. She called for me to come to bed whether I was ready or not. I was afraid of the dark, too, but I was more afraid of Reese than darkness. When Reese worked the overnight shift, Denise had me sleep with her. At the time, I didn't understand her fears, but now I believe it to be the result of abuse from Elsie and Buck as well as from Reese. I found out later that he physically, emotionally, and verbally abused her. I was glad when Reese worked because I got to sleep in Denise's bed. I was in the habit of staying awake long into the night, waiting for Elsie to return from the dead. Elsie used to tell me about dead people coming back to torture the living. After her death, I looked for her to return in her favorite long, ankle-length housecoat with her hair in a bun, but she never did.

I used to think I was the only one who believed Reese was crazy. I later learned everyone in the family thought he was crazy. I never wanted to be around him, but he forced me to interact with him. He was the very friendly pedophile in the neighborhood who made sure he bought the kids popsicles, popcorn, and candy. He eased his way into the hearts of unsuspecting children with his deviant friendliness. His ingratiating behavior especially appealed to the little girls with no father or who didn't have anyone to explain what was inappropriate. Every kid on the block liked Reese because he spent money trying to impress his neighbors. He bought ice cream cones, freeze pops, and sandwiches when the ice cream truck came around. Whatever he bought his kids, he bought the neighborhood kids, too. I knew from what others had told me that whatever he gave me came with strings of expected sexual favors attached, and I didn't want to feel like I owed him. I couldn't enjoy his treats like the other kids because I knew the hidden expectations. I learned how to talk to him in order to get my school supplies. I had to have pencils, pens, and paper, so I made promises to him I never planned to keep, telling him I would have sex with him and that I wouldn't tell my sister a thing.

I did whatever I needed to do to make good grades, stay in school, and be somebody. I thought I was smart, but what mattered to me more was that others thought I was smart. I didn't think I had anything else going for me. My family's name disgraced me. People who knew us labeled us nobodies, making my siblings and me regret our family name. I believe the *nobody* mentality emerged when I saw how Buck and Elsie disgusted people. My parents were not well-liked. I felt I had to prove to people that I was somebody. Conceived in adultery, I was battered and shunted from house to house and uncared for by people who had no love for me. The only positive thing about my life was my intelligence, academic capability, and trust in God to be with me.

There was little talk about Elsie after her death other than someone stole the furniture from her house. When the moving van went to empty her house, the furniture was already gone. No one knew who helped themselves. The emptiness of Elsie's house stuck in my mind. When the furniture disappeared, Elsie's physical disappearance was complete. Visiting her house and seeing its emptiness affected me. My mother's death was finally front and center; until that time, I might have been in shock. It was another illumination of how cruel and uncaring people could be, but it was also another reminder of how predators take advantage.

I was at Denise's house for only three weeks when I felt a hand under the covers one night. It was Reese. I made a noise, and he quickly left the room, but from that night on, I was distracted at school from lack of sleep and thoughts of what might happen the next time he came in, especially if I refused to engage in his sexual interactions. At night, I stayed awake as long as possible to remain vigilant in case he returned. By day, I struggled to pay attention in class, afraid of what he might do that night.

When Reese worked the second shift, he usually got home around midnight after Denise was asleep. Everyone knew it took a tornado to wake her once she fell asleep. When Reese came home, he woke me up and made me do things like fetch a glass of iced water, pull his socks off, pull the bedcovers over him, or empty the slop jar (the bucket he urinated in overnight when he didn't want to leave his bedroom). While living in his house, I hardly slept when Reese was home.

It was almost summer, and I was tired of making promises to Reese that I had never intended to keep. He was tired of my broken promises to sleep with him if he bought school supplies and ice cream treats. I had no intention of allowing him access to my body. One day, he told me, "This is the last day where I am gonna be fattenin' frogs for snakes. When I come home tonight, you better have something for me, or something bad gonna happen to everybody in the house. I'm tired of being the only one hurting."

Up to that point, I had been able to keep him away from me, but I now knew my time at Denise's had run out. I was barely fourteen but knew exactly what Reese's comment meant. I had heard my stepfather tell Briana he was tired of *fattenin' frogs for snakes*. After he made that statement, Buck stopped buying clothes for Briana for a while. He meant he was tired of financially caring for someone else's child, only for others to get the credit and the benefits.

After Reese's comment, I strategized to execute a plan to leave Denise's house. I decided to leave like I left Buck's and my foster parents' homes. I was an experienced runaway. I didn't trust people enough to believe they would make the best decisions for me, so I had to decide for myself. I heard how some people once tricked my older sister, Jolene, into thinking they were helping her, only to have authorities pick her up. I wouldn't let that happen to me. I didn't want the Department of Human Services (DHS) staff to send me to another home of their choice. The home where they sent my siblings and me when we were younger wasn't safe. They didn't provide the necessities for us, so my siblings and I ran away because they mistreated us and did not feed us. I believed I could do a better job of finding a place. I certainly couldn't be any less competent.

Later that same day, I went outside to think. Sometimes, being in Reese's house was too much for me. I had too much fear and anxiety about both staying and leaving. It was a beautiful afternoon at sunset, and I walked around the neighborhood to do some self-talk to overcome the fears of leaving my sister's house—another place I called home. I thought, *You remember how your sisters and brothers ran away from the foster home when you were a little girl, and they ran off and left you, but when you turned the corner, you saw them? You remember when Elsie nearly backed the car off the wooden bridge when she was drunk, and you prayed that she wouldn't drive into the river? You remember Hosner, the high school junior who bullied you, and how he tried to beat you up on the bus, and you were so afraid to ride the bus that you'd rather miss school than face him? You prayed, and miraculously, he became your protector. You remember how you and your sister had no food to eat, and she put a clothes hanger in the hospital vending machine and food came out? You remember how you went to school and couldn't eat lunch because you were afraid of the beating Buck promised you, but when you got home, he didn't remember? Remember?* Recalling times when God came through for me strengthened my faith and helped me believe that if He did it then, He would do it again. I knew God would be with me, and I had to leave.

Before I knew it, the sky was almost dark. I must have walked for more than an hour before I became aware of where I was and what happened. I knew I could do whatever was required to protect Denise's family, and God would be with me. Reese's words repeated in my mind: *Something bad is gonna happen to somebody tonight.* I couldn't let anything bad happen to my family.

I went back to the house and told Denise about Reese's threat. I felt like I had to protect myself—since no one else did—and do something to help Denise and her kids. I loved my sister and wanted her to know what Reese was up to. I knew the right thing to do was to tell her about her evil husband. She could have made me feel better if she had said, "Girl, he's not crazy. He's only playing," but she didn't say that. She encouraged me to leave because of him. She knew I couldn't keep fighting him off and making up excuses to avoid sex with him. She was afraid of him, too. I can only imagine how trapped she felt in a marriage without anyone to protect her and where she couldn't protect her children or help her youngest sister. I've helped many women through the years who found themselves in Denise's situation: powerless, hopeless, and unable to see a future free of fear. At that moment, however, I had no idea of my future, only that I was determined to get out of Reese's house and dead set on making something of myself.

Tears welled in Denise's eyes. I thought she was a strong woman because she escaped much of Elsie and Buck's abuse by dropping out of school and running away from home. I'm sure they never filed a missing person report. When I met her at age five at the beginning of kindergarten, she was twenty. When I visited her as a child, she pressed and curled my hair when no one else would touch it. She pierced my ears. Denise was gruff and made lots of threats to beat Briana and me with a broom, but she never hit or even spanked us. When I was older, I told her how afraid of her I had been. She was shocked that I thought her threats to beat us with a broom were serious because she said she was playing with us. She reminded me that she never hit us.

Perhaps Denise's closeness to Buck threw me off, especially since she knew how he treated us. She and Buck were friendly. I watched them play cards and share cigarettes. When Buck needed something, he asked Denise to do it for him. She seemed like a daughter to him, so in my childish thoughts, I may have assumed she could carry out her threats.

Sadly, Denise escaped Elsie's and Buck's abuse only to run into Reese's abusive arms. She married Reese while still in her teens and only learned about his mental problems afterward. Reese's flagrant disrespect of her in front of others made me think that's how all men were. Several times, I found her with swollen lips and black eyes. She said she fell in the bathtub, but I knew better. From an early age, I began to calculate what I now know are boundaries—or hard limits. One of my boundaries is no physical abuse. I learned from my older siblings and was able to stay clear of physically abusive men.

When I was younger, I blamed Denise for her fears and felt she should have protected me. I was barely a teen when I lived in her house, but as I matured, I realized Denise did what she could. I'm certain that with Reese, she looked for a home and stability rather than a husband. She was more like his daughter than his wife since he was nearly twenty years older.

I was devastated that I had to leave Denise because I had gotten to know her and trusted her. She told me she would miss me because I was a big help to her. We hugged, and she promised to visit me. We both knew that wouldn't happen unless she sneaked to see me. Reese wasn't the visiting type. Once I left his house, he wanted nothing to do with me because I shouldn't have left. Leaving was final for me, as far as I could see. That's why it was painful. I was correct. I don't recall Denise coming to visit me after I left, but I calculated that into my plan.

Chapter 14
A PLACE TO CALL HOME

Denise looked amazed when I laid out my plan to live with my great-uncle and great-aunt, Harold and Agnes. They had one grown daughter who had already moved away. Briana had lived with them after DCS took her away from Elsie. Briana found them too strict and had run away to live with her boyfriend. My sister Ava lived with them off and on as well. Ava had passed her GED, had left her husband and children, and was attending college with her new, younger boyfriend, but she would stay with Harold and Agnes during the breaks. That gave me hope that they would take me in as well.

Denise said they were a good choice. Her approval made me feel better. I felt a tinge of excitement. I remembered how Elsie spoke of Harold. She said he was a powerful teacher and preacher of the Word of God. Harold was Elsie's mother's brother, so he was Elsie's uncle. The whole family knew that Elsie didn't raise her children. Whenever Elsie's name was mentioned, Harold shook his head and said, "I expect anything to happen to her children." I took that to mean that he had little optimism for us to succeed. I was excited to think I could finally be free from physical, mental, sexual, and emotional abuse. I hoped that since they already knew my plight as a child of Elsie, they might be willing to help me. I didn't know for sure, but I was optimistic for a change.

I wanted to tell my nieces and nephew I was leaving but didn't want to see them cry. I wanted to take them with me because I knew the sad situation they called home. Instead, I grabbed my school bag, homework, and a few pieces of clothing, and jumped into Denise's car. Harold and Agnes lived fewer than five miles away, but it felt like Denise was taking me to another state.

Lost in our thoughts, neither of us spoke during the drive. When we arrived, the big, beautiful house looked empty. With a beige brick exterior, I thought it was a mansion sitting on a 1.5-acre corner lot with an expansive green lawn surrounded by a fence. A pecan tree stood near the driveway, surrounded by an installed fish pond. I guessed it was a fish pond because there was neither fish nor water in it, so it looked more like an empty retaining pool in the well-maintained lawn. I walked slowly toward the door while admiring the lawn, noting the size of the house and the beautiful white swing on the porch. I sat briefly on the porch swing, in my own world, until Denise beeped her car horn to remind me to knock on the door.

I never considered Harold and Agnes might refuse to allow me to stay with them in the same way it didn't occur to me that Elsie could have said no. I was so consumed with leaving my sister's house to protect her and her children that I didn't question if they might turn me away. It didn't cross my mind because I knew I could give something most people needed—domestic help.

I heard feet slide beyond the door and an attractive woman opened it. I knew she wouldn't recognize me as her great-niece, so I introduced myself. I didn't recognize her, either. She indicated that I should follow her. We walked through the living room on our way to the kitchen. The living room was unlike any room I had seen before. It was spacious and tastefully decorated like a room in a home decor magazine. It had expensive end tables and an oval coffee table in front of a fireplace. We walked into the kitchen, where I smelled something delicious simmering on the stove. I didn't wait for Agnes to ask me any questions.

"Hi, I'm Jean. I'm Elsie Mae and Buck's youngest daughter."

She looked like she wanted to say, "Not another one."

I went on, "Elsie passed away, and I don't have anywhere to go. I stayed with my sister Denise, but her husband tried to make me have sex with him. I didn't want to, so I ran away. I know you all don't have children living with you, so I came here. I have no place to go." I blurted it out quickly, hoping she didn't hear everything, but I needed to get it out.

That was a mouthful. She picked up a big spoon and stirred the pot. It looked like dumplings. "Well, I have to talk to my husband about you staying because you are a girl," she said. I didn't know her husband, Harold, my great-uncle, but I believed everything would work out for me. My expectations were high because Elsie talked about what a great man he was and how he helped people. Call it stupidity or child-like faith. It was probably a little bit of both. "Who brought you here?" she asked.

"My sister Denise dropped me off."

She looked at me suspiciously and asked a question I couldn't answer. "Why didn't she come in and speak to me?"

I could anticipate what an adult might want to know, but I hadn't thought that far ahead. I now understand that it looked suspicious for an adult to drop a child off without saying anything. Perhaps Denise knew Agnes would ask questions she couldn't answer, and one of them might have been *Why can't she live with you? You are her oldest sister, after all.*

"I don't know. Denise said she had to get home and cook for her husband." It sounded like a made-up answer. I needed a legitimate excuse for Denise's actions to explain why my twenty-nine-year-old adult sister didn't come into the house and verify my story to Aunt Agnes.

"Okay, I'll talk to Harold tonight when he gets home, and we'll let you know what we decide." That was not what I expected to hear. I expected to hear, *"You poor thing. Of course, you can stay here. I'm sorry about your mother passing."* Not a word of that.

I stood with tears welling in my eyes because I felt rejected, in limbo, waiting for someone to have mercy and give me a place to stay. Harold and Agnes were my last hope before homelessness. Agnes looked like she wanted to say, *Here's another one of Elsie's kittens with nowhere to go,* but she didn't say that. I asked if I could use the bathroom, and I barely made it inside before breaking down. I prayed, "God, I don't have anywhere to go. Please let me stay here. Please don't let them make me leave. I want someplace to call home." After praying, I decided to help God fulfill my request. I came out of the bathroom and began cleaning. I was tired mentally, physically, and emotionally, but I couldn't stop because I needed to prove to Agnes that I would work hard to earn my stay. I cleaned for a few hours, dusting, sweeping, mopping and even cleaning the refrigerator. I went from room to room cleaning—like a maid.

The refrigerator contained lots of food and a variety of beverages. Cooked food was packed and stored. I had never seen such an abundance of food! There were trays of stored food from days, maybe weeks ago. While cleaning, I wasn't thinking about the work I had to do to clean the fridge. I was only thinking about the foods I could eat. I knew I would never go hungry again. If this was anything like heaven, I wanted to go.

Aunt Agnes was sickly and couldn't get around well. She dragged her feet when she walked, and I knew she would appreciate the cleaning. I thought *Even if they don't like me, they will like my cleaning services.*

"You'll have to sleep with Aunt Sally tonight," Aunt Agnes said. I knew there was another bedroom because Briana and my older sister, Ava, slept in it during the periods they lived at Harold's, but I didn't want to act ungrateful. I was thankful to have a place to lay my head where I had no worries about anyone coming in to threaten or assault me. As if she read my mind, Agnes said, "The other room is for guests."

She indicated where I would sleep. "You will sleep here on the left side of the bed near the door. Sally panics if she can't sleep on the right side, so don't try switching sides with her," she instructed. Anywhere except outside was fine with me.

I cleaned the forbidden guest room. It had a beautiful queen-sized bed with a matching dresser and nightstand. I would have loved it to be my room, but Agnes told me it was for guests. I wondered how Briana and Ava qualified as *guests* while I didn't. I tried to wait for Uncle Harold to come home so they could talk and let me know if I could stay, but by 10:00 p.m., he still wasn't home, and I was tired. I asked Agnes if I could lie down until he came. I acted as if it was fine if they made me leave, but I did not have a plan C. I thought, *Surely they wouldn't put a young girl out at this time of night.* I was sure I had a place to stay, if only for the night.

I never slept well at Denise's house because I feared Reese would rape or kill me. In Harold and Agnes' house, I felt free. I understood what Dr. Martin Luther King meant when he said, *Free at last. Free at last. Thank God Almighty, I'm free at last!* I slept through the night for the first time in a long time. Looking back, I am in awe of how God protected my nervous system throughout my childhood. I never slept deeply for fear I would be jolted out of my sleep by a beating or burning. Normally, I woke frequently during the night to make sure no one was in the room or trying to physically or sexually assault me. Not this time. Even Aunt Sally's snoring didn't wake me. That first night at Harold and Agnes' house, I slept undisturbed. It seemed like a good sign.

The next morning, I asked Aunt Agnes how I could help her. She told me to bathe Aunt Sally, her sister-in-law who lived with them. Sally was Uncle Harold's sister, my great-aunt. Family said Aunt Sally lost her mind and couldn't understand or communicate with people. She had long fingernails that looked like claws. Her sudden outbursts of singing songs and incomprehensible conversations revealed her mental challenges, but I wasn't afraid of her. I later learned a few church congregation members didn't want to be around her, but she didn't bother me at all. Her handicap was only mental.

It only took a comb and a brush to bring her mind to the present. When I combed her hair, she talked and yelled at me like someone in her right mind. I can only wonder what abuse she must have suffered that left her mind in multiple pieces. Uncle Harold said her husband beat her for many years until, one day, her mind left her.

"What did I say?" she would yell at me. "I said, 'Don't comb my hair!'"

It didn't matter if I intended to comb my own hair; she always warned me not to comb her hair. I thought if I touched it gently, she would see I wouldn't hurt her. I didn't know that other church folk had been impatient and hurt her head when they tried to comb her hair, causing her to become suspicious and untrusting. She didn't care who I was or how gentle I was. She did not want me to touch her hair. Her hair was silky soft with curls like Shirley Temple as if rollers set it. I sprayed it with a little water. I had never seen black hair this soft and curly. She had thin locks of gray and white curls that had not been permed or straightened. After a few prayers and lots of pleading and patience, she finally allowed me to comb through her hair a few times. Like a toddler, she twisted and turned, pulling her head back and forth.

Aunt Sally was eighty-five years old. Caring for her was a lot of work, but I was glad I could. I was relieved to help Harold and Agnes with Sally because it meant I had value. I learned to find and fill a need from a young age because I perpetually needed something. Aunt Agnes couldn't believe I washed and combed Sally's hair and bathed her because Sally didn't like to bathe either. Sally let everyone know she didn't want a bath. That was another battle. God gave me favor with Sally. That evening, I put Sally to bed. Aunt Agnes thanked me profusely, but I was grateful to do it because I needed a place to stay, and once again I thought that if I was useful, Agnes and Harold might let me stay.

Uncle Harold was seventy-six, but he was energetic and seemed more like a fifty-year-old. He was up early and off to work in his office at the church, where he spent twelve hours a day, Monday through Saturday. He had an excellent work ethic but wasn't the house-cleaning kind. Agnes had a leg and foot infirmity and could not keep up with the housekeeping. She was partially disabled for eight years before I arrived, and I saw an opportunity for me. They had previously hired church members to come and assist her, but none of them worked out. I remember thinking, thank God they didn't because God sent me. If they allowed me to stay, it wouldn't only be because I was a child and had nowhere to go. I could meet their need for household support. They could use my cleaning skills and home health services for Sally.

I knew I needed to prioritize the cleaning order, beginning with the parts people would see when they entered the house. The foyer, informal den, bathroom and kitchen were the first areas. I cleaned the dining room next, which barely needed cleaning since it was rarely used. A picture of Uncle Harold's and Aunt Sally's mother sat on the fireplace mantle: my great-grandmother. She was Native American, and she was beautiful. You could tell by my grandmother's and Aunt Sally's cheekbones they had a lot of Native American genetic heritage in them. Next to that photo was a black and white picture of Harold and Aunt Agnes' daughter. She looked glamorous. Her skin was flawless. I hadn't yet cleaned the room where both doors stayed closed. Aunt Agnes called it the formal living room. It had a light aqua-colored carpet with matching furniture. The details on the couch were hand-carved. The sofa had a big armrest that rolled inward. I had already bounced on it when Agnes was in another room. It was beautiful and comfortable. I didn't need a bed. I would gladly sleep on the formal living room sofa, but Agnes told me this room was off-limits. It looked practically new, even though it was nearly forty years old.

The third morning I woke up at 6:00 a.m. and started my morning cleaning duty, as I had done in the foster homes. Harold and Agnes were up early, but I knew to wake before them if I wanted to impress them. I learned early on that adults didn't care about helping me or providing for my needs. What mattered was that I attended to *their* needs. I learned to observe their needs and help them. Afterward, they often asked if I was hungry and offered me some money or a place to stay. This pattern rarely varied.

Their house was one where the church members could drop by anytime, morning or night. I felt responsible for keeping it spotless because it represented them, but more importantly, it defined me because I was there to help them. It was my job now. So, by 8:00 a.m., the house was spotless. I mopped the kitchen, bedroom, and den, cooked Sally and Uncle Harold's breakfast, and dusted the furniture. I was outside sweeping the front steps and sidewalk when Aunt Sally came out. She sat in the swing, which I later learned was her favorite place. She greeted everyone who passed by as if it was her job. No one passed the house without Sally calling, "Hello sir, Hello, ma'am." Her boundary was the porch, but she often ignored it and went outside the entrance to speak to the passersby.

I finished sweeping the steps and returned to the porch as Sally pulled out a round, clear bottle filled with something brown and put it to her mouth. I didn't know what it was, so I grabbed it. She snatched it away and almost scratched me with her long fingernails. I thought it was too early to fight with her since I hadn't officially received permission to stay with them. Still, I knew I couldn't allow her to drink or eat something dangerous.

Sally yelled, "Gal, give me my snuff back." I inspected the snuff jar to be sure it was snuff. I accidentally inhaled a little of the aroma and began to choke and gasp for air. She thought that was funny and told me, "Gal, if you had minded yo' business, dat wouldn't happen to ya. Hep yossef." Sally would frequently tell me she didn't need my help whenever I tried to do something she didn't like.

She called everyone *baby* because she couldn't recall names. I hoped her mind would return and she would remember me one day, but that never happened. "Baby, can you help me please? Can you put some of this in the bottle for me?" She wanted to pour snuff from the big bottle into a smaller jar she pulled from her pocket.

"Thank you, baby," she said, looking up at me with beautiful gray eyes and high cheekbones. It seemed to be a genuine smile. *How can she be crazy?* I questioned. *Is she truly crazy, or does she act crazy to repel people?* She walked back into the house to put away her large bottle while putting the smaller bottle into her apron pocket.

Uncle Harold came out as Sally went in. It seemed like an opportunity to have a conversation with him. He was a tall, thickly built man of few words who seemed to perpetually rush to his next destination. "Later," he said as he strode swiftly to his truck. He did everything quickly but hadn't yet taken the time to have a meaningful conversation with me. When he finished eating breakfast, he simply said *thank you*. He was a taciturn man. I had heard many wonderful things about him. I was overjoyed to be living with the man my mother adored. She spoke so highly of him as a man of God that I felt my problems would disappear if he prayed for me. When my mother was dying, he stopped his truck and ran into the house to pray for her. After his prayer, I believed she would live. I understand now that I had more faith in Harold than in God.

My family admired him as a wealthy uncle, so he had my attention and respect before I moved in with him. I wasn't sure why his prayer didn't save Elsie's life, but her death didn't erase the seeds of his greatness or the miracles she credited him with. Elsie called him a miracle worker and said he could preach the devil himself right out of hell. Occasionally, Elsie turned on the Sunday morning radio to hear him. They wouldn't take us to church, but sometimes they allowed us to listen to Uncle Harold. "That's my Uncle," she'd say proudly. Living at Harold's house seemed like a dream. All the suffering I went through to get to his house didn't seem to matter anymore. All that mattered was that I was there. I thought I was safe forever. I just knew I would have no more pain. I trusted that God sent Harold and Aunt Agnes to rescue me.

Harold drove off, and I jumped up. *Yessssss! I'm staying at least one more night since he didn't ask me to leave.* I allowed myself to dream like I did when I first went to Marla's house. I imagined being part of a church family, learning and growing up with lots of love and support. I thought I might have a future with Harold and Agnes. They didn't say I could stay, but as long as they hadn't told me I had to leave, there was a possibility they would let me live with them. The worst part was the unknown. It looked like it would be a day-to-day stay for now, but I would do everything I could to let them know I was a good fit for them. We both needed something. They needed help, and I needed a home. I swept every dust bunny in the house, picked up every leaf in the yard, and attended to every need of Aunt Sally and Aunt Agnes to help them decide in my favor. I had no money to pay for my stay, but I wanted them to know I had something to offer.

Although it wasn't official yet, I was enjoying living with Uncle Harold and Aunt Agnes. When I wasn't cleaning, I took baths or ate. I thought I was in heaven. I'd heard that everything we ever want is in heaven. I'd never seen such a large quantity of food. Agnes and Harold's kitchen had several kinds of fruit, vegetables, meats, juices, cereals, cookies, milk, soda, and Neapolitan ice cream. *Food at last. Food at last. Thank God Almighty, I have food at last!*

I often stood at the open refrigerator, deciding what to eat. There was an abundance. Overnight, I had gone from a pauper to a princess. I came from a place of shame and deprivation where I didn't know what it was like to have food or entertainment. Now I could enjoy both. I didn't enjoy TV when I watched it with Elsie because my body was constantly alert, and I felt unsafe. At Harold's house, I felt safe.

Aunt Agnes cooked evening dinner each day before Harold came home. I learned how to cook a few meals by helping her, but I was so busy cleaning that I often missed the cooking sessions. I watched and listened as she explained the meaning behind the thick red gravy made with sliced summer tomatoes smothered with onions and simmered in flour. She called it Hoover gravy and said it was a poor man's meal. I liked the gravy and looked forward to eating it. I cooked it several times for my college friends but did not tell them what she said, that it was a poor man's meal. My friends liked it, too. Agnes cooked vegetables, soups, and pies. Her food was the closest to Elsie's I ever had. Although Agnes was sickly, she usually prepared dinner for Harold so he could eat after work. I unconsciously learned what Agnes thought were the actions of a good wife. Preparing dinner was one of the routines I picked up from her and Marla, my foster care mother. They both regularly cooked dinner for their families, and I understood that was a reflection of their love for their families.

While ironing Harold's clothes or standing over the stove cooking, she remained committed to the duties of a virtuous wife. I didn't understand the commitment and unceasing responsibilities of a wife. Aunt Agnes and Marla revealed they had mothers who taught them to love their husbands and be good wives. I figured that was something I probably couldn't do because my mother didn't teach me. Most of the time, I only missed the parents I lacked when someone shared something they learned from their parents. I knew I didn't know much about caring for a husband or children.

It was summer, so I had time to do whatever I wanted. There was a store next door, and when Aunt Agnes sent me for a two-pound bag of flour, she gave me ten dollars and said I could keep the change. I saw that surplus as earnings for the work I did. Never had I been in a place where I could leisurely shop for snacks!

At Elsie and Buck's house, I had no food for days on end. At Denise's house, we had food of a sort. Sometimes, it was biscuits with syrup and butter. We might get bologna and lunch meat on Reese's paydays. But in Harold's house, I had food every day. I could feast all day. I must have gained ten pounds in the first few days, catching up from the years of starving.

In addition to the food and delicacies in the refrigerator, the parishioners cooked dinner for Harold on Sundays on a rotating schedule. I couldn't believe it. Twice a month, someone brought a huge platter to the house after service that had several dishes on it: fried fish, baked fish, fried chicken, baked chicken, ham, turkey, dressing, green beans, potato salad, stewed greens, coleslaw, and yams. On a separate platter were the desserts: sweet potato pie, lemon meringue, coconut cake, pound cake, lemon cake, and chocolate cake. It was enough food to feed us for several days. *Why would someone do this unless it was a birthday or a holiday?* I thought. It was like God was making up for the years I didn't eat. Now I know it to be reverential treatment that members give to their leaders in some ministries.

Parishioners brought Sunday meals to Aunt Agnes and Uncle Harold's house because he was their pastor. It was a way the parishioners honored them and showed love for his dedicated service. I found it overwhelming. I couldn't fathom people doing such a thing. The food tasted like it came from the angel Gabriel's oven. There was nothing needed or missing. I couldn't stop eating even when I was full. I felt I had to make up for the years I had no food to eat. My stomach bulged when I overate, but I was concerned that I needed to eat as much as I could in case they made me leave. Like a squirrel, I planned for the future, saving my acorns. I hoped I had a bright future. I believed the worst was over and things would only get better.

Chapter 15

CHURCH

The first church service after moving into Harold's house was unusually stressful. I had attended church a few times while living in foster homes, but this church was different. It was the first time the fear of a judgmental God registered in my mind and heart, a God who was standing ready to cast me—and everyone else who sinned—down into hell. Until then, even through my pain, I thought God loved me, cared for me, and protected me. I thought He was loving, kind, and gentle. I knew He wanted all of His creation to choose to serve him, but the message I heard in Uncle Harold's church, and what I came to believe, is that I was a sinner who had fallen into the hand of God and that at any time, God was going to destroy me like he did the cities of Sodom and Gomorrah (Genesis 19).

In the short week or so I had been living with Harold and Agnes, I went to church several evenings. Hearing repeated messages of God destroying people and sending them to a place called Hell where there was violent destruction quickly changed my perception of a loving and peaceful God to a mean and angry God. It wasn't long before I became afraid of God instead of fearing and loving Him. The Bible says we are to fear God—meaning reverential fear—but not to be afraid of Him as if He is a horrible monster who does evil things (Proverbs 9:10). God has goodwill planned toward His creation (Psalm 119:65-72), but in this period of my life, I became obsessed with running from Him. I cried because I didn't understand what I was doing wrong or how to stop doing it to appease the angry God I was hearing about. I tried to reason with God by telling Him I was a child and didn't mean to steal the food from the hospital vending machines. I even repented on Briana's behalf. I was confused about why God would send me to hell because I stole food when He knew I was a rag-wearing, starving child. I thought He put those things in my path for me. I thanked Him for giving us food each time we successfully got it out of the vending machine. We only stole food to eat and money to buy the food from the machine. But with this new information about God, I went from being happy to sad because I believed I was going to hell for stealing food. Instead of feeling the conviction of the Holy Spirit for my sin of stealing, I felt condemnation and overwhelming guilt.

I had only been to their church for two weeks before I decided to go to heaven. I assumed Briana made that big decision while she lived there, too. However, congregation members told me Briana unfortunately chose to go to the other place. When I talked with Briana, she sounded fine, but the church folk insisted Briana's soul was destined for hell. Briana said she told parishioners not to touch her and to stop telling her what to do. She said, "They are not God and can't treat me in any kind of way. I know God, too." I prayed for her soul.

I was the first to walk down the aisle at the following Friday night deliverance service. I would do whatever I had to do for *salvation*. I joined a line of people, which surprised me because I thought I was the only one going to hell. I didn't feel as alone once I saw the others. I would do whatever they told me to evade hell. From their description, hell was not a place I wanted to see.

When it was my turn, I stepped up. I held my arms high at the leader's direction until they began to shake and tremble. I saw people faint on the floor after other people laid their hands on them. I didn't want to hit my head on the floor because I didn't know God like that, and I was afraid of pain and injury. A short, stocky man gestured as if to lay hands on me. His mouth had visible foam at the corners of his lips. I pretended to be weak in the knees and laid down gently. I opened my mouth wide to praise God when the foam from his mouth landed right in my mouth. His last meal must have had onions because I could taste and smell them from his foam. I wanted to gag, but I couldn't because I knew they would circle around me to cast out the evil spirit. The church members saw any aberrant behavior as the devil. Instead, I swallowed his onion-y saliva and lay quietly on the floor for a few minutes until they turned their attention to someone else. I got up slowly so as not to attract attention in case someone felt led to lay hands on me again. They clapped and shouted for me. After the service, several people congratulated me for having the courage to go to the altar. I didn't do it because I was courageous or accepted Jesus. I felt I already knew Jesus. I came determined to prove to Harold and Agnes that I would be a good girl, and they could trust me to live with them. They might be more willing to let me stay with them if they thought I repented of my sins. If I were allowed to stay, I could focus on other things and not worry about eviction.

I had lived with Uncle Harold and Aunt Agnes for over a month when I overheard them in conversation. I was cleaning the den, holding a broom in one hand, a cotton cloth in the other, and a bottle of furniture polish. I wiped the corners of the floor where dust collected. I saw dirt as my enemy because it stood between me and the next home to which someone could send me.

"What are we gonna do?" Aunt Agnes asked softly.

"What do you mean?" Harold asked.

"I mean the girl. What are we gonna do about her?"

"She ain't got no place to go. Her Momma and Daddy are dead."

"I know, but we said we would never keep girls." No girls was Agnes' position.

"You're right, but we didn't ask for this one. She came to us. I don't know what to do with her."

"Me either, but she's a girl."

"She keeps the house clean and is good with Sally. You don't get around like you used to. She could be a big help to you."

"Yeah, but she's a girl, and we said we wouldn't take girls," Agnes persisted.

"I think we need to keep her because I don't know anyone who will take her. We can let her stay here for a while and see how it works out," replied Harold.

There was no response from Agnes. She believed strongly in obeying her husband and standing behind his decisions because she also had a prominent position in the denomination. She knew it called for her to say *yes* to his decisions.

That's how I found a forever home where I'd stay until adulthood. I continued to attend church services on days, nights, and weekends. Uncle Harold ensured I studied the Bible because I had to read the Sunday School and Sunday evening class lessons. I began studying scriptures and memorizing them to impress the church people and eliminate any doubt in their minds that I was a heathen. Little did I know that I would learn the meaning of the phrase *hell on earth* from the pastor himself.

Chapter 16
THE FALL FROM HEAVEN

I settled in with Harold and Agnes, even though I had to share a bed with Great Aunt Sally. My stomach was full, school went well, and the church members accepted me as a family member. I experienced what it was like to be a teenager. Harold and Agnes set boundaries and rules, and I liked them. I spent time on the phone talking to my school friends. I enjoyed my *heavenly* experience. Having a home that felt stable, even though everyone else was much older, had a calming effect on me.

Then the heavenly experience turned into—not quite hell, because I had already passed through hell—but if there was a level lower than hell, I went there. As bad as it sounds now, it wasn't hell to me at the time. It was only another thing I endured. Not until years later would I understand what kind of hell I was in. I spent years wondering how—and why—I fell so far from heaven.

On a Sunday afternoon, several months after moving in with Harold and Agnes, Harold drove me to a sparsely populated area about twenty miles from his house. During the car ride, he repeatedly told me he would care for me regardless of what anyone said. That sounded good because I needed someone loyal in my corner. I needed to know I wouldn't have to go to the streets, back to Denise's house, or another foster home. Uncle Harold assured me I would not have to worry as long as he was alive. His words sounded reassuring, but I felt anxious each time he said he would take care of me. Something didn't feel right. I hoped and prayed I was wrong, but the more he talked, the more uncomfortable I felt. His message was familiar; he sounded like Reese and the other men who had touched my body without my permission. Harold's talk of taking care of me sounded like what every man who ever used me for sex had said.

I had been in the situation of a man verbally preparing me for what they expected from me too many times not to understand. I didn't expect, however, that a minister of high repute would be like those other men for whom I had no respect. Harold was a man with a reputation to protect. He was a man who preached the Word of God! That was the shock that shook me to the core. I could not wrap my mind around the fact that a *man of God* was using me like men who made no pretense of loving God or following His commandments. I wished I was dreaming, but I wasn't.

No! God, please don't let this happen. I must be dreaming. I silently screamed *What is wrong with me to make these men want to use me?*

I knew the mechanics of sex from Jesse. I knew that men who used girls didn't expect anything from them other than accommodation. There was no *relationship*—or even affection—to complicate things emotionally. It was strictly transactional.

Before Harold touched me, I made up my mind that I would do what he wanted because I thought if I refused, he would put me out of his house to live on the street. I didn't want to run anymore. I had no fight left in me. My mother and stepfather were dead. My biological father did not acknowledge I was his child. My sisters struggled to mother their children and survive the physical and emotional abuse inflicted by their husbands. The years of surviving physical abuse and torture from my parents combined with years of sexual abuse from men, both related and unrelated to me (sometimes with the permission of my mother), on top of the upheaval of moving every few months, then losing my mother, was too much. I was exhausted and worn down. I had taken care of myself for the preceding three years and needed a stable home to put down some roots for the first time. I needed to know I could stay at one address and be part of a family, however dysfunctional. I had no physical or emotional reserves to keep moving and starting over every few months.

I lay on the back seat of the car and tried to imagine that I was somewhere else, somewhere safer. Like Maureen following her hanging, I mentally escaped to a safer place as the earth and what I thought I knew about Pastor Harold shifted beneath me and became unstable yet again. When Harold and Agnes gave me a home, I thought it was an answer to prayer, a refuge, that I had gone to heaven. Their food was delicious and the house was comfortable, but the price I had to pay was far more costly than I had imagined. Sadly, I couldn't predict that I would pay for that home for the next four decades.

The rides to the country with Harold continued for weeks, months, and finally, years. I already knew how to keep secrets, and this one was no different. Harold had much to lose, so I felt I had to keep this one. It is easy to feel obligated to hide someone's sin when it isn't the entirety of who they are. Harold was an amazing preacher and his church did a lot of good in the community. The community respected him, and people came to him for support and prayer. I felt responsible for protecting his reputation because he helped me by providing a place to stay. In return, I helped him by keeping his secret. I remained loyal to him because *he said* the church people wanted him to send me away, but he didn't. *He said* he told them I had nowhere to go so he wouldn't put me on the street. I was so thankful he let me stay; I felt I owed him my life. I was loyal to him because he was the one who bought school supplies, fed me, and provided a house with electricity and running water. Harold made me feel like he was the only one who was for me, the only person I had. It never occurred to me that there could be another perspective. I had never heard of an older man getting into trouble for having sex with a young girl, so I had no idea that what he stood to lose was much greater than his reputation. He could have been imprisoned and lost his freedom. My ignorance of the law worked in his favor.

None of my siblings checked up on me. No calls, no visits. I felt alone with only Harold, Agnes, and Sally to care for me. I wasn't close to Agnes. She told me early on that she enjoyed having Briana live with them. I understood her comment as a rejection, so I was closer to Harold. Despite his sexual abuse, I clung to him and his promises to take care of me. I lived in a fantasy world where I pretended I was his lover and confidant, keeping his secrets. It would be years before I understood the depth of his betrayal of my loyalty and childish need for protection.

Our visits to the country consistently left me shocked and confused. Each time Harold used me, my body went limp. Instead of feeling like my usual self, I felt weak, as if I could not resist. I thought *I am not here. It is not happening. It must be all right since he is a man of the cloth. He probably knows something I don't know. I've suffered through worse things. I'll close my eyes, and it will be over soon, and I'll still have a nice home and as much food as I want. I will keep my mouth closed. I can never tell anyone this happened because it will destroy his church and family, and I'll be an outcast forever. I can never tell anyone. I'm still a child, but I know some things can never be repeated. If I leave Harold and Agnes, I'll be back in a foster home, and the same thing will happen to me. I have nowhere to go, so I'll keep my mouth shut.* Mentally, I tried to imagine I was further and further away each time. I pretended it wasn't me Harold violated. The voice in my head got louder and louder, and I got quieter as I waited for him to finish.

Agnes told how she kept herself chaste until she married. As much as I wanted to be a virtuous woman when I grew up, her husband—and a few others—had taken that from me. I told myself that I may as well stop running. This is the way it's going to be, so it will be better if I stop fighting it. At that point, I stopped hoping. I had to release hope because it was too heavy to carry. I knew I would be continually disappointed if I continued to hope. I held on to hope after Elsie and Buck burned my sisters. I hoped someone would punish my parents, but they didn't. I hoped Elsie and Buck would die and stop abusing us, but they didn't. I hoped they would change, but that didn't happen, either. I hoped they would tell us they were sorry, but that was only a pipe dream. I hoped they would feel remorse for our injuries and traumas, but they never did.

Regardless of what happened to me, I kept hoping. I hoped living with Harold and Agnes was heaven, but it wasn't. I believed things could and would get better—until I couldn't. I couldn't keep believing my life would improve and set up my emotions and heart for more pain. Each time Harold used me, I lost more and more hope. Letting go of hope was like letting go of life. I felt I was letting go of my life before I could live it.

Many years later during my healing journey, I wrote a poem called "Surrogate Mother" to describe the pain I survived from Childhood Trauma. In it I share how important it is for other people to help carry the dreams of those who suffered Childhood Trauma because trauma may have made them abort their dreams. Sometimes survivors need surrogate mothers and fathers to carry their hopes and dreams for them until they are strong enough to do it themselves.

As many abused children do, I dissociated myself from chronic emotional, mental, and spiritual pain. I ignored and blocked the thoughts, feelings, emotions, and memories surrounding the country trips with Harold. I sometimes wondered if I imagined that he did those things because I tried to believe he didn't. It was extremely confusing to know one thing in my head but feel something different in my emotions. I had to dissociate to block conflicting thoughts to manage home and school responsibilities.

I was in intense emotional and mental turmoil with no sense of direction. Nothing had worked out for me. I couldn't see myself moving forward from Harold's abuse. Harold's abuse felt like the final straw. I could pray past other abuses, regardless of the pain—but not this one. The pain was deeper this time because it involved my soul and my relationship with God. Harold represented the God whom I trusted and believed. Not only did Harold violate me, but he stole God from me because I couldn't understand why or how God allowed him to do such egregious things to a child. I let go of my last hope of escaping my childhood and achieving success in life. I feared I wouldn't make it out of my circumstances. I felt alone in the world with no one to advocate for me. I felt completely lost, helpless, and hopeless. I had little interest in life. I was never suicidal, nor did I experience thoughts of suicide. I was simply numb and didn't care about living because by the time I was eighteen, there was nothing left of me. I traded food, clothing, and shelter for my authentic self. Who dared to judge me? What child would trade something tangible (Harold's provision) for something she couldn't see (God's provision)? Who wouldn't keep something she had instead of trading it away?

I gradually adjusted to the trips to the countryside. I rationalized that it could be worse. After all, I had everything I physically needed at Harold's house. I had friends and a growing positive reputation in the church. I made up my mind after I lost hope that I would go through whatever I had to in order to survive and live in a stable home. Unknowingly, I was willing to trade my authenticity for a perceived *good life*.

There was no way to reveal what Harold did without losing the best place I'd ever lived. Besides, there was no one to talk to about intimate issues, even if I wanted to. Safety and security are important to trauma survivors. Without safety needs met, survivors live in a constant state of fight or flight. I assessed how bad things were with Harold compared to how bad things were with Buck. Harold didn't physically abuse me, so I convinced myself to endure his sexual abuse. At least in Harold's home I had food, clothing, and shelter. I realize my standard of care was pretty low, but it's what I had.

Surrogate Mother

When trauma of abuse destroys the unborn
it's better for the survivor to abort it than live with it and be torn
Give it up or keep it
You say I had a choice but
The hurt and pain speak louder than a small still voice

You say it didn't happen to you, but it happens to many others
So I stand before you now asking you to be that surrogate mother.

Carry the abused girl's dream
Carry the abused boy, too
Carry those who have lost all hope
Carry those who wait for a rescue
Carry the children who struggle in school
Carry those who join gangs for love
Carry the children who need a positive role model
Carry those who cry out and are ignored

Carry the fatherless pain in your heart
Carry the motherless into tomorrow and give them a new start
Carry the handicapped thoughts of equality in your mouth
Carry the poor in your pocket and give to those in need
Carry the orphans in your prayers and pray they succeed

Carry the hungry child's hope and spread it across the land
Carry the dreams of our ancestors in your hearts and the palms of your hands

You carry it whenever you help others
Man, woman, boy, and girl,
You carry it for all God's children
Wherever they may be in the world

You carry it when you help them achieve
You carry it when they can't conceive
You carry it and help them cleave
You carry it, when you help them believe
You carry it.

We must all help give birth to the dreams of others
No one is exempt
For we are all surrogate mothers
Carry it!

Chapter 17

THE CYCLE OF ABUSE

My older sister, Ava, was staying in Harold and Agnes' guest room when I showed up, but she was in and out. She stayed there during college breaks and came and went during summer vacations, mainly on weekends. She abandoned her children—like Elsie left us—and lived in another city with a young man who attended college. Undoubtedly, the abuse from Elsie and Buck affected her decisions.

Ava was exceptionally beautiful. Elsie used Ava as the standard of beauty. In Elsie's opinion, beauty was Ava's light skin, long hair, head-turning figure, and the dimple in her cheek. When we went out, I noticed men and women reacted to Ava's beauty. I understood their reactions because I stared at her, too. I enjoyed watching her dress for going out, and I brushed her hair when she was in a good mood. When I brushed Ava's hair, I imagined what it was like to be her.

When I was younger and experienced almost daily abuse from Elsie and Buck, I sought love—especially from Ava—because I thought she was somebody I wanted to be. I admired her because she had a job and made good money. She had a handsome husband and a beautiful family. I vacillated between wanting to be like her and not wanting a life like hers. I wanted to be like her because she was beautiful, had long hair, drove a nice car, and had a home. I didn't want to be like her because her life came with a high cost.

I was good at ignoring the facts of abuse and the ugly reality of my life. When I needed to escape Elsie and Buck and go somewhere peaceful, I thought Ava's house was my sanctuary. In reality, there was very little peace around Ava. I imagined everyone loved her until I spent time at her house and learned they didn't. Ava's marriage made me afraid to think of marriage and children for myself. Her husband Tommy often accused her of infidelity. She accused him of being with other women. They did a lot of tit-for-tat arguing and fighting. They were both equally attractive, so women vied for his attention like men competed for hers. Tommy was flirtatious, smiling, and talked to women as if Ava wasn't there. When I was in their home, I listened to their conversations and the contemptuous and abusive ways they spoke to each other. I didn't know what love was, but I quickly learned what it wasn't.

When Tommy asked Ava a question, if she *smarted back* as he called it, he slapped her. She would tear into him like a mama bear protecting her cubs. They fought viciously. I wanted to leave, but I knew I was at Ava's because Buck and Elsie were fighting, too. I hated watching Tommy slap Ava and listening to her yell and scream at him.

Through my childish eyes, Denise's house was even worse. Reese beat and kicked Denise until she had swollen lips, black eyes, and a bruised body. Everyone was afraid of Reese because he didn't seem to care if he killed her, nor did he care who saw him beat her. Tommy didn't beat Ava like that—at least when I was present. Tommy and Ava's fighting style was shoving and slapping each other. Both Denise and Ava inherited domestic abuse as part of Elsie's legacy. Elsie left a legacy of abuse that reverberated through the lives of her children. Buck instilled such fear in me that I didn't feel I could do anything for either of my older sisters. Tommy and Ava's fights reminded me of how Buck and Elsie fought. I not only feared that Buck would kill Elsie, but I also worried that Reese would kill Denise and Tommy would hurt Ava from the violent treatment. Both Ava and Denise married to escape abuse from Buck. The irony for both of them is that they found abusive men who were as violent as Buck. I didn't know what a healthy, loving relationship looked like because abusive, violent adults surrounded me.

Ava treated me the way Tommy treated her. She was mean, and I felt like she didn't like me. Both Ava and Denise reflected the genetic makeup of their father, a Creole man from Louisiana. While I brushed her hair, Ava spoke scornfully about mine. Ava and Elsie did the most to make me think I was ugly and had nothing to offer—all because I lacked long, wavy hair. Ava planted seeds of negative thoughts about me and my hair, and her voice remained one of my inner critics long after I became an adult. I now understand Ava mirrored Elsie's treatment of her. Elsie idealized light skin, long hair, and a shapely figure like Ava's, and Ava was hungry for approval from Elsie.

By the time I moved into Harold's, Ava was twenty-five and still beautiful. I heard Harold and Agnes talk about how Ava mentally broke down and left her husband and children for a younger man. They said she was on drugs. She seemed out of it most of the time she was at their house. She slept most days and went out in the evenings. People, especially the church people, talked about her. I hadn't seen her for years, so I was shocked when I saw her condition. I found out that the guest room was not solely reserved for guests; it was Ava's room whenever she showed up. The *guest room* was also Briana's room when she stayed with Harold and Agnes. That room became another symbol of how I wasn't *good enough*—my sisters were allowed to live in it, but I had to share a bed with Great Aunt Sally until her death when I was in the eleventh grade.

"Ava ran away and I told her to come back. I love her, but she won't come back," Tommy would say each time he showed up at Harold's. Even at fourteen, I knew Tommy attempted to manipulate them—like Buck did our neighbors—to get sympathy. I felt sorry for Ava's children because she did the same thing to them that Elsie did to us. Uncle Harold would look at Tommy and say, "Yeah, yeah." I thought it wasn't very pastoral or even caring, given Tommy's distress. Tommy seemed inconsolable. The only thing that made him feel better was talking about Ava. Tommy stirred my memory of when Buck went to whatever house Elsie ran to when she left us, trying to get a glimpse of her.

Sometimes, Harold told Ava to go outside and talk to Tommy. Ava harshly reminded Uncle Harold how Tommy treated her; then she'd yell at Tommy, "You can't make me go back with you!" There were times she reminded me so much of Elsie through her actions and behaviors.

Tommy's appeals to return to him and her children did not move Ava. Then Tommy would cry uncontrollably. I saw Buck cry a few times when Elsie left us, but not like Tommy. I didn't understand his emotionality. Despite his abusive history, I felt sad for Tommy and the children. Years later, I can still remember his crying and her emotional coldness. Ava was numb to his pain or that of her children.

I witnessed men abuse my sisters and then beg them to come back when they left. Each time, my sisters reunited with their abusers, so I equated love with abuse. My childish thoughts were if a man hit me, he loved me. At fourteen, I liked an older boy. As he and I stood outside his house, some boys in a car drove by and whistled at me. The attention amused me, and I laughed. He didn't like how I responded to the passersby, so he removed his belt and hit me. My first thought was, *Wow! He really likes me.* It didn't take long for me to think it wasn't funny or cute. It was embarrassing, so I had to rethink what I thought was love.

I didn't like the harsh words and violence I saw in the relationships around me, so I decided in my pre-teens what I would permit in my adult relationships. I kept my promise to myself to never allow a relationship with a man who had no respect for me. I am grateful to God for sparing me physical abuse as an adult because research continually reports that abuse is cyclic.

The more I listened to and watched the adults around me, the more it shaped my ideas about men, relationships, marriage, children, and parenting. I didn't realize it, but seeing and hearing about Ava made me think badly of her. I thought she was the most selfish woman in the world. The more I heard and saw, the more I disliked her. I vowed never to leave my children because I didn't want to do what Ava or Elsie did. It wasn't until I researched childhood adversities that I learned there was a lot more to Ava's actions. It made me ask, *What happened in Ava's childhood that caused her to leave home when she was twelve years old?* Obviously, she only knew her role as prey to violence because that's the kind of men she attracted. She was undeniably abused and assaulted until she had four children back to back at a young age. Eventually, her traumas caused a mental and emotional breakdown until she checked out of life. My judgmental, religious, pharisaical thoughts said *She must have done something terrible for God to punish her like that*. I didn't realize something crazy awful happened to her and caused her to have breakdowns so severe that she abandoned her family to save herself.

Chapter 18

I AM SOMEBODY SPECIAL

As a child, I deeply desired to study the Bible and know God, so it wasn't punishment for me when I was required to read the Bible for hours to know the stories and prepare thoroughly for Sunday School. I volunteered to compete in regional and statewide denominational Bible contests and often won. By the second summer of living with Harold and Agnes, countless Bible scriptures were ingrained in me. I wrote poems, essays, short stories, and plays based on Bible stories. The youth department put on plays, and I performed in front of large audiences. Invariably, they chose me to write, act, or speak. I wasn't nervous and shy like the other children when I performed. I felt alive when the microphone was in my hand and I had an audience. No one had to coach me on what to write or say. Performing seemed to come naturally. Audiences clapped loudly. Comments like *Amen, You better tell it!* and *She gonna be somebody one day,* erupted from various sections of the auditorium. I felt I had something to offer the world. Speaking to an audience took me from nobody to somebody, and my hope began to return.

One of my favorite Bible story performances was from the book of Esther. Esther was special to me because God chose her to help deliver her people even though, like me, she was the least likely person to be chosen. Several young people were regularly selected to represent the local church, district, region, and state in these competitions. It was my first year living with Harold and Agnes, and I felt this was my big break to let everyone know I was intelligent and talented, so I wrote a poem entitled, "I Am Somebody Special." This poem meant more to me than it did to the audience I addressed. It was prophetic because I did not feel special at the time. Yet, somehow, those words would penetrate my heart and mind years later and let me know my life had value. Many times throughout my life, I recalled this poem written when I was fourteen years old. It is still remarkable today.

Here is an excerpt:

I am somebody special
I am somebody special
because God has chosen me
I am somebody special
because I have the victory
I am somebody special.

Whenever life was difficult or I felt unworthy, I recalled the poem. These words helped carry me through the most challenging seasons of my life. I believe God gave me this poem to show me how much I meant to Him and to convey that I had value. The audience stood and clapped for several seconds after I read my poem. I enjoyed the praise. It said *You are somebody special.* After the event ended, people told me how much they enjoyed the poem. Many church events ended with food in the fellowship hall, so they caught up with me in the serving line. These were not the same members from Harold's church I saw weekly. These were people from the statewide competitions and conventions who didn't know me. They were encouraging, and their recognition was affirming. I thought this must be what heaven is like. No more worries. I could think about growing up, getting good grades, being a teenager, and doing what I liked to do. I thought about getting a job when I got to high school. I thought about having friends, talking on the phone, and which college I wanted to attend. The smallest praise did wonders for my self-esteem.

Finally, I was doing well in school. I couldn't change some things, but education was one thing I could control. Because I didn't know who I was or what I authentically did well, I did whatever people told me I could do—good and bad. My middle school teachers encouraged me. They told me I wrote well. Once again, I believed I could. I worked when I had supportive and caring teachers because I decided that school was where I would soar, and I did. By the time I got to high school, I was academically competitive and confident. I enjoyed classes and loved my teachers. Things were looking up for me.

I loved my ninth-grade classes, but I was especially fond of English and History. I liked to read about the struggles of the past and how people triumphed. I enjoyed the comments from my advanced English and History teachers. They said things like *You've got the hang of this. You need to write more,* and *You leave the reader wanting to know what happens next.* I wanted and needed someone to notice me; school was the place. Church people noticed me, but I had to work hard for God to get praise. At school, my only job was listening, participating, and doing the work. For me, school was the great equalizer. I believed it was the one place I could succeed.

Some of my classmates had parents at home to check their homework, come to parent-teacher meetings, and reward them for making good grades. Not me. My only incentive to learn was to grow up and be somebody and to have food and a home. At Elsie and Buck's places, we had no working toilet or bathtub. We moved frequently and once lived with six people in a small, one-room trailer. There was barely enough room for anyone to turn around. At Harold and Agnes' home, while I had room to breathe and food to eat, they were senior citizens who didn't like to go to after-school activities or get involved in my life. I wasn't their child or even their grandchild. I saw school as my way out.

I never forgot the only time I ever heard Elsie say something good about me. She indirectly let me know that I was smart—even if she didn't think I was pretty. I overheard her telling Ms. Lucy Mae, a neighbor across the field, that I was smart. Elsie only said it once, but that was enough for me to believe I was smart for a lifetime. I held those positive words in my mind long after she was gone. Regardless of her evil actions, I believed what Elsie said about me was true. I thought she knew me best, so I believed her. I had selective hearing because the negative things and vile names she called me somehow didn't stick. I cried when she verbally abused me because I was a child and my feelings were hurt, but I knew I wasn't the things she said. I don't know how I knew; I just knew. Grasping Elsie's words of praise testifies to the power of parents and the words they speak over their young children. Research doesn't support the selective hearing I had. Research shows that negative talk becomes repetitive, negative thoughts, which become the worst inner critics. I can't help but wonder what greater things I might have done if my mother had said more positive things. I accomplished a lot simply because I **once** accidentally heard her say something nice about me.

If I didn't know anything else, I knew I was smart, so I gave high school and college education my best effort. I didn't need reminders of assignments or projects due, which was good because there was no one to remind me. If I didn't do it, no one would punish me. I believe God gave me the desire for education because He knew I had no one to encourage or support me. In a sense, God was my parent. He reminded me to do my assignments and get good grades to be successful.

I leveled the field with my classmates through hard work. Some students were known for their beauty, some for their humor, and others for their money, but I determined I would be known for my brains. I didn't think I had anything to offer except intelligence. I didn't know that trauma had changed the structure of my brain. I had to work harder in math and science classes because those subjects required critical thinking and logical problem-solving —the skills weakened by trauma. All I knew was I needed something to make me believe I was smart and valuable.

I went through extreme adversities without feeling loved by any of my caregivers—nor had anyone told me I was special. Despite that, I felt I was special. I could tell people sympathized more than empathized with me, but I didn't appreciate either of those sentiments because they weren't helpful. What happened in my childhood was difficult, but instead of focusing on how strong I was after going through such trauma, the adults around me focused on the evil of what happened and how damaged I must be. It was challenging to find hope when so many thought my situation was hopeless. The adults around me didn't expect me to succeed. I had no reason to think I was special. I simply thought so, and that made it true for me. What is more, I believed it. I believe God created me with a natural joy, hope, and encouraging spirit because He knew I wouldn't receive it from others along the way.

Chapter 19
HIGH SCHOOL YEARS

I tried not to let negative thoughts overrun me, but it seemed the state favored Briana by giving her a monthly check for $400. The state bought Briana's school supplies, opened a bank account, and gave her money for personal things like clothing. Briana's money from the state had been sufficient to send cash to Elsie regularly while she was alive. I received nothing from the state, which bothered me for a long time. I didn't understand the nuances of the state welfare system and its rules. The state did not consider me a ward, like Briana, because I ran away from Buck to escape abuse instead of being removed from his custody by state officials. That disqualified me from receiving help from the state.

With no income, I seldom bought anything. I had an abundance of food, however, and I felt satisfied for the first time in my life. A few people from church gave me hand-me-down clothes. Still, I felt devalued and rejected. I had to ask Uncle Harold and Aunt Agnes to buy school supplies every year I lived with them. Asking felt like begging. I was uncomfortable asking for anything without giving something in return. I felt indebted to everyone who provided for me. I always felt like I owed adults something and that my cleaning service was the only thing I contributed to the household. I felt inferior since Briana had offered Harold and Agnes funds to offset their expenses in the short time she lived with them. This technicality contributed to my suffering and made me feel like an orphaned child.

As soon as I finished eighth grade, I got a job at the local technical college. It was my first job with responsibilities, and I earned my own money. I still remember the first paper check. It was a summer job as a secretary, and I delivered messages to the various departments. I felt smart. I quickly learned various machinery, mechanics, construction, and business terminology. I was exhausted most days because I had to take care of Aunt Sally, clean the house, go to church, work, and meet Harold's needs. This job was good because it taught me the importance of endurance. I knew I could endure whatever difficulty I faced in the job because the summer would soon end. I applied the same strategy to difficult college classes and life situations as I got older.

In ninth grade, I landed a job at a hardware store. I didn't make much money, but it made me feel responsible. It was a part-time job, but I was determined not to be on welfare and the kind of person some of the church members thought I would be. I thought getting a job and giving Harold gas money to take me to work would prove to him and Agnes that I wasn't like Elsie. Having a real job alleviated some of the emotional and mental pain of the sexual abuse because I didn't have to ask him for money every time I needed something, and I could buy personal items. Harold drove me to work and picked me up after each shift. The dissociation of removing myself from the present helped to lighten the five-minute car rides with him to and from the hardware store. He didn't ask many questions or talk to me during the rides, so being in the car with him wasn't triggering. I dissociated myself from so much, I don't recall thinking about how he sexually abused me. Occasionally, he asked if the hardware store carried a certain nut, bolt, or PVC pipe. Otherwise, it was a quiet commute.

At the hardware store, I learned to manage unhappy customers, solve problems, handle money, and find things to do when I had no customers. I did not want to be fired from the hardware store because it would mean I was a failure, so I worked hard and took pride in my employment. I wasn't taught not to steal, but thankfully I memorized the Ten Commandments and wasn't tempted to steal money from the register. There were some things I decided I would not do, and going to jail was one of them. I had extended family members who lived rent-free in the state's jails and prisons. I knew what could happen if I took money from the register. I was proud to have a job. I learned how to balance home and work responsibilities, school, and the road trips to the country with Harold.

In ninth grade, I met my wonderful algebra teacher. He was short and funny, and he loved algebra. Everything he did or said revolved around algebra. He made me believe I could do anything I was determined to do. He told me my main issue with learning algebra was that I didn't finish my homework. He said, "Perfect practice makes perfect." If I studied correctly at home, regardless of the types of problems on the test, he said I would do well. I felt my algebra teacher's genuine kindness. He encouraged me, and I wanted to do my best. He wrote on my homework paper, MS. ADORABILITY, to let me know I could do whatever I wanted. I was elated that someone I admired saw me and believed in me.

I once told my algebra teacher I would turn in some extra credit work. A month or so later, I still hadn't turned in the extra credit work. He handed me a sheet of paper with a large circle drawn on it. Inside the circle were the words *Round TUIT*. He told me to keep it in my folder to remind me to do my extra credit work and stop thinking I would *get around to it*. He gave me a *round-tuit,* so I no longer had an excuse to procrastinate.

My biology teacher was more intrigued with my life and body parts than he was with the science of life. His compliments and winks made me uncomfortable, but I saw him behave the same way to several other girls, too, and no one said anything. I was used to sexual harassment, so I never reported it. It makes me wonder if the other girls were used to it, too, since none of us reported it. I concluded it was something I said or did that signaled men permission to touch or grab me when I was around them. I didn't tell anyone about the teacher's ongoing harassment because I knew no one would believe me. Harold and the prior sexual abuse I endured made me feel that my body wasn't mine. I experienced enough of a pattern of sexual attention to know what to do: don't tell. He was a popular teacher admired by his peers and the students. He was known as a *cool* teacher. Somehow, I made it through his class and graduated from high school without any teacher forcing me to have sex.

When I became a teacher, I told myself I didn't want to be recognized as a cool teacher because, for me, being cool meant inappropriately crossing boundaries. I was glad when my students called me *caring* instead. I never crossed boundaries with my students. I realized their childhood was in my hands and vowed to protect it as much as possible. I wanted to give them the education, support, and protection I failed to receive.

Abuse from a teacher was on a different level than abuse from a family member. I rated sexual abuse and molestation from teachers on a scale of 1 to 10, with ten the worst and five as tolerable. My ninth-grade teacher-abuser was more likely a five, which meant if I stayed quiet, I was left alone. He did not mentally, verbally, or emotionally abuse me, so I was able to endure. I experienced worse abuse at my childhood home. I knew teachers had the power of grades to leverage for what they wanted, so I never reported him. I feared the life he would have if I revealed what he did. He was married with children, and I didn't want him to lose his family. I didn't understand that losing his family would be a self-inflicted consequence for sexually assaulting a student. Instead, I believed his downfall would be on my hands. Harold's downfall would, too. I didn't comprehend that they might lose their families because *they abused me.* I thought I was the one who might destroy them and their loved ones. Distorted thinking like this is common for survivors of sexual abuse because they often want to protect their perpetrators.

I thought that *No one would believe me because they are fun teachers*, so I had to suck it up. If I reported what they did, things would not go well for me, and I needed the thing I loved most—education—to go well. I was glad to hear my sixth-grade teacher was eventually indicted on sexual misconduct charges. He used to take his students, including me, alone into a science lab, but he wasn't indicted until almost thirty years later. Thankfully, today's students are more likely than my contemporaries and me to report inappropriate behavior. Increasing research shows how adverse childhood experiences affect the brains of children. The last thing abused students need to worry about in school, where they need to use their brains most of the time, is exposure to preventable trauma. Tornados, earthquakes, and mass shootings may not be preventable, but everyone can work to prevent sexual abuse. Some things don't mix with education. Abuse is one of them.

High school was challenging as I adjusted to working, studying, and Harold's twice-monthly trips to the country. I thought I was smart, but algebraic equations and back-to-back Advanced Placement classes made me question my abilities. I misjudged the amount of time required for AP classes. I took them because they looked good on my transcript, the regular classes were not as challenging, and many smart kids were in the AP classes. Once I decided I was smart, I wanted to do what the smart kids did.

AP English and history were my favorites. I could read and write essays about *The Scarlet Letter, Black Boy,* "The Tell-Tale Heart," the Boston Tea Party and the Emancipation Proclamation any time they were assigned. I had to use mnemonic devices to help remember battles, dates, formulas, and stories. Still, I was dedicated to my education. Harold didn't care much about my studies, but he wanted me at church every time the door opened, so I learned to sneak my notes into the church to study. I had little time for homework between going to church and working, and my algebra teacher gave me daily homework assignments. I initially felt guilty for taking schoolwork to church, but I figured God understood and wanted me to make good grades. I asked Him to help me pass tests. He was faithful every time.

I heard students talk about how they were grounded and made to stay home because of their grades. I couldn't imagine having someone who cared about me, much less about my grades. I was very disappointed when I didn't make the highest grade in AP English and history classes. I knew I was smart, but my confidence increased when teachers praised me. It was false confidence, but it helped me in high school.

When I became a teacher, I remembered how I felt when my teachers believed in me, so I made it a point to encourage my less motivated students to find something they were good at. I had to look with a magnifying glass for some of them, but when I did, I magnified it. I often taught students who, like me, had been abused. I felt a connection with those students even before they shared that they, too, suffered emotionally, physically, or mentally. Thanks to my good teachers, I knew exactly what type of teacher I wanted to be.

I was the unannounced student grader in tenth grade. My geometry teacher assigned me to grade everyone's work and return it to him before class the following day. I felt privileged because he trusted me, and I wouldn't disappoint him. I didn't give any of my friends extra points. Still, I wished he didn't trust me so much. He had to know the temptation I faced grading my own papers. Now and then, I would give myself a few points. I figured it was an exchange for helping. It seems everything came to me with a price, even helping others. After three months of grading papers, my teacher asked me to return the graded papers to his house. I knew this would lead to inappropriate behavior, and I declined. I saw a pattern of men asking me for favors.

I took the ACT exam in eleventh grade and scored high enough to get college letters. I was afraid of anything I couldn't conceptualize, so I had to overcome debilitating fear to take the test. College was an idea too big to contemplate. If a college or university accepted me, I knew my family would have questions. I knew I would have to go alone and without family support. People praise the imagination, but to a child who has seen the worst and can only imagine the worst, positive recognition for achievement creates emotional pandemonium. I heard my classmates discuss their big dreams and ideas, but I had none. I only knew I wanted to be somebody, and I wanted a place I could call home. I didn't think I could be somebody yet, but every chance I got, I tried to think about being someone with something of value to offer society.

Chapter 20
ABUSE CHANGES THINGS

In elementary school, I only had to play tic-tac-toe, connect-the-dots, or be on a team at recess to make friends. Elementary students didn't care about my poverty; they only cared if I was their friend. In high school, however, the students were cliquish, and there was enormous pressure to wear certain clothing styles, drive a car, and hang out on weekends with the popular students. I felt like I was destined to be with students like me who were either in foster homes or living with someone other than their parents. I didn't want to spend my lunch break hearing about the fun wealthy kids had at parties, their vacations, or weekend shopping sprees. I couldn't relate to any of those. I felt pressured to prove I was one of them to my classmates. Of course, now I know I competed with myself and my negative thoughts, but my thoughts were real.

Sexual abuse changed my personality, my identity, my self-esteem, and my values. Even as a little girl, I dreamed of being a teacher. Sexual abuse introduced doubt. After sexual abuse, my dreams fluctuated between working a job that required little to no advanced education or training and going into a profession—something that demanded a college degree and specialization. I went from believing I would be somebody to wondering if I could even graduate from high school. In the eleventh grade, I skipped school, snuck out of the house to see older men, took money from Harold's wallet, and stole his car. I became a defiant, disobedient, destructive, and disrespectful teenager. I believe the attention from colleges for the high ACT score opened my mind to the possibility that I could leave Harold and Agnes and live independently. While the idea of going to college thrilled me, it also terrified me because I had no idea how to manage what was required to make it happen.

I felt bad for being disrespectful to Harold and Agnes. I didn't know that I was behaving exactly as research data predicted. Research reports four to five months after girls are sexually abused, 80% of them develop at least one mental disorder, while 55% of them have two. Mental illness found its way to me. I was confused about everything. It was difficult to make even the simplest decisions, and I began years of what researchers call mental setbacks.

I stopped caring what adults thought of me. I hurt and desperately wanted to hurt someone else—not physically, but emotionally. What does a child do with so much hurt? Before Harold's sexual abuse, I was more respectful and focused. Whether in foster care or my sibling's house, I was respectful and focused on education. I knew I had to graduate. Harold's abuse, however, came at an age where I felt it was wrong, even though I had no idea it was illegal. Although I was in church several times a week, rarely was anything said about sexual morality beyond the commandments banning adultery and fornication. I had not yet understood that what happened to me fell into one or both categories. The child sexual abuse I experienced when I was younger didn't affect me in the same way. I didn't know enough about life then and accepted the assaults and child sex trafficking as *normal* since they were common in my family and among my sisters. I became disrespectful, resentful, and cynical after repeated trips to the country with Harold. The price I paid for my compliance and silence far outweighed the stable home I traded for my authentic self. I felt like I had to show the world it couldn't hurt me. I think it was about this time when I stopped recognizing my feelings.

Emotional pain is one of the reasons children are mean to other children. Abused children want someone to feel their pain—even when they are unable to speak about their abuse. I was afraid of men because of Buck's violence against Elsie and her children. I was uncomfortable saying no to men. A friend of a friend hugged me without asking whenever he saw me, and I didn't like it. Yet, I never told my friend or his friend that I didn't want to be hugged. It was an epiphany the day I realized that I don't have to let him hug me if I don't want to. That was a light-bulb moment! I allowed the person to hug me because I thought he had a right to hug me. It took some thinking to realize that liking my friend—who I knew very well—didn't give the other guy access to me, nor was I obligated to honor any of his unspoken desires.

Buck was extremely abusive, so I assumed all men were abusive like him. The men in my sisters' lives were abusive, which confirmed my assumption. Abuse engulfed and consumed me. Harold's church taught me I was a rebellious girl because I made bad choices. I didn't know my decisions were influenced by abuse that changed the structure of my brain. Sexually abused children are more likely to make poor choices in anger, be expelled from school, become sexually promiscuous, suffer identity confusion, run away from home, and be incarcerated—as a result of the abuse. I envisioned a life of abuse, pain, and rejection because my childhood was filled with chronic abuse. The abuse was what I knew, and it wasn't easy to imagine my future self happy, loved, enjoying life, or achieving my goals.

Chapter 21

ROLE REVERSAL

va and I didn't grow up together because she was eleven years older than me and left home before finishing high school, but when I was in high school, I felt like we grew up together. It was as if we switched roles. She did things Briana and I did in middle school. If I didn't hide them, she would steal my clothes and take them with her when she returned to her college boyfriend. We didn't have a relationship because she wouldn't talk to me. Since she initiated it, I obliged her by repaying the same unkind treatment.

Whenever she came home, she was angry with someone about something. Most days she got up, ate, talked on the phone, and went back to sleep like a teenager. She asked Uncle Harold for money, and he gave it to her. It made me angry because when he gave her money, he said he didn't have any for me until the next time because he had given it to Ava. I didn't realize it until later, but Harold had the same kind of sexual arrangement with Ava that he had with me. When I was older, I discovered Elsie emotionally and verbally abused Ava. I also learned that when she was a little girl, she witnessed a murder and never told anyone out of fear she might be killed. I hadn't done research into trauma then, but I understood enough to know something happened to her. Despite that, I still had no compassion for Ava because I couldn't fathom how she could leave her children.

Continuing her teenage behaviors, Ava stole Harold's car a few times, and I knew it. I begged her not to because he might get irritated and put us both out. She was an adult. If she left, she had the option to live with a friend. I was not an adult. If they put me out, I wouldn't have anywhere to go. She was an adult acting like a child, and I was a child acting like an adult. I told her several reasons why she shouldn't steal Harold's car, warning her there would be no one to bail her out of jail if he pressed charges. Each time she took the car, she was able to return it before he knew it was gone, until one night Harold asked for his keys. I told him Ava had them, so he called the police and reported his car stolen. Early the next morning, Ava returned the car and told me to give the keys to him. Police didn't pick her up, and Harold didn't press charges. He simply reported a stolen vehicle.

I was sixteen years old and impressionable, and despite how she irritated me, Ava's wild behavior and car theft escapades influenced me. Even though I spent a lot of time at church, I had several boyfriends in high school. I could only bring a few boys to the house, so if I quit one, I had to wait before bringing another one over, although the rules were different if the boy said he was *saved* or on his way to heaven. One night, I wanted to visit a boy I enjoyed seeing but hadn't invited over yet. I thought if Ava could steal Harold's car without consequences, I could, too. Also, I wanted to be like her because she seemed unbreakable. Regardless of what people said, they didn't seem to hurt Ava. She didn't care if Uncle Harold and Aunt Agnes pressed charges. She didn't care what anybody thought about anything she did.

I got the keys and left as soon as Harold went to sleep. It seemed like a switch flipped; instead of trying to be the best, I decided to be the worst. I told Ava what I was doing and when and where I intended to go. She didn't tell me when she planned to steal the car, but I wanted to tell someone, just in case. She encouraged me to do it and told me I could stay out as long as I wanted. I didn't know she was jealous of me. What did she have to be jealous of? I was only the baby sister. I didn't see my life as much to envy, but I suppose it was a plus since I had no husband or kids. My life stretched out before me without encumbrance, while hers was already permanently weighed down. I didn't realize it, but I had my life ahead of me, and she may have felt the best part of her life was behind her.

I visited my boyfriend for about an hour and stopped to see an older friend with a police scanner. My friend said there was a police report about a stolen vehicle that sounded like Harold's car. Embarrassed, I played it off and made an excuse to head home. My main concern was that my boyfriend didn't find out I stole the car. When I got to Harold's house, a police officer was waiting. Harold had a sad face like I had disappointed him, while Ava stood beside him, smirking. I saw she enjoyed that I had disappointed Harold—not because she disliked him, but because she was jealous of me. I shouldn't have been surprised. It turns out I had barely pulled out of the driveway when Ava woke Harold to tell him I had stolen his car. She was getting back at me for telling on her when Harold asked for his keys. Her betrayal didn't hurt me. I wasn't close to anyone except Uncle Harold, but by then, I didn't care how he felt. Ava later revealed that she told him because he bragged about my good grades.

The police officer didn't handcuff me because he knew Harold, but he put me in the police vehicle and we headed to the police station. For the one permitted phone call, I called Mr. Kragin, one of the teachers who molested me when I was his student in the sixth grade! I know it's surprising. I called him because I thought he would be sympathetic because he knew my situation with Buck and had heard how Briana and I had to sit at the hospital all night long and then go to school. It didn't occur to me that he might also try to make me have sex with him as a favor for helping. Sadly, I didn't call my sisters because I didn't think they would come and get me. I knew Reese wouldn't let Denise get me, nor did I want to stir that hornet's nest again. I knew Ava was the cause of my situation, so she certainly wouldn't get me, and I had no one else I could call.

Writing this, I see the total desperation I experienced in this situation. I was so desperate, I called an abuser instead of my family. I also see I grew up without anyone I could trust in my family. For a long time, I was angry with my siblings because I was the youngest and felt someone should have rescued me. When I was an adult, I understood that regardless of their age and social status, they weren't mentally or emotionally able to help me. I am thankful the state didn't place me with them, or my story might have ended differently. It is easier to take abuse from strangers than it is from family for several reasons: contact with strangers is less frequent than with family, and the closer the abuser, the greater the damage. We are forewarned about strangers but not about family members. I have an unpopular saying due to the high percentage of child sexual abuse by family members: *Those who are close, watch them the most.*

When I called from the police station, I told my former teacher what happened, and he came and bailed me out. Ironically, he didn't try to touch me that night. I'm glad he didn't because I had no strength to run away from him. Also, he spent money to keep me from going to jail, so I might have felt I owed him. He dropped me off at Harold's house. Even though I'm not clear why he rescued me that night, I can imagine that perhaps he did it out of a guilty conscience and the fear that I might report what he had done to me when I was younger. Maybe he thought this gesture would clean the slate with me.

That was the first and last time I stole a car. I didn't steal Harold's car again because of my embarrassment and shame. It wasn't the end of my defiance, but it was the end of my career as a car thief.

Chapter 22
SHOPLIFTING SENIOR

My senior year in high school got off to a great start. I made good grades, filled out college applications, and had a boyfriend and a job at the local hardware store. I accumulated some self-esteem from the college invitations I received. I loved the excitement of senior year, but there were so many demands for payments: the class ring, field trips, photographs, and the graduation cap and gown. I felt I had to have those things but lacked the money to pay for them. I worked part-time, but even when my hours increased, I didn't have enough money to pay for the senior items and events. There were several field trips; one was to attend Mardi Gras in New Orleans and another was to France. My friends went, but I couldn't attend either because of the cost. The furthest I had been from home was a few hours away for church competitions. I wanted to go on those trips, but I dared not ask Harold and Agnes about sending me because I felt they were doing enough by providing a place to stay.

I felt I was a burden to them because they were not my parents, and the only reason they allowed me to live with them was because my parents were deceased. I didn't like being a charity case, but I had no choice. I loved school and desired to participate in activities, but I knew I couldn't because I didn't have the money.

In twelfth grade, I took more of an interest in my appearance. Boys began to notice and compliment me, so I knew I had something other than education going for me. I pretended to need something from the Dollar Store while surreptitiously buying a pair of blue jeans. I knew pants were forbidden at Harold's church, but I didn't care. I hid them in my school bag and changed from the long skirt or dress I wore when I left the house into jeans and a T-shirt at school. I had an urgency to be seen. This was the exact opposite of what I wanted earlier in life. The older I got, the less self-control and self-discipline I had. I did things I didn't want to do and didn't know why. Of all the times I could choose to be like Elsie and Briana and get attention, I chose my senior year. I ran headlong into the things I never wanted to do before. I disappointed myself but couldn't control the feelings, thoughts, and actions that pursued me. I had no idea of my capability, and wrongdoing became a compulsion.

Since researching Childhood Trauma, I've learned that some studies link impulsivity and Childhood Trauma.[3] This helped to explain much of my just-do-it behavior. I didn't think about the consequences. If I thought about it, I did it.

Harold and Agnes paid for the senior pictures and graduation fees, but I had to pay for the other items, such as the class ring, yearbook, and cap and gown. Harold usually gave me money whenever I asked him. It might have been at the back of his mind that I might tell someone what he did to me if he didn't give me the money I requested. If this were the case, he never expressed it. Now, I understand that I didn't want to take money from him because I resented his abuse and rejected his selfish motives. I refused to ask Harold and Agnes for more, so I worked as many hours as possible, but I still didn't make enough money to cover some senior expenses.

Instead of gratitude, I began to feel animosity toward Harold and Agnes. Perhaps I would have been grateful if their help had come without strings attached. I wanted to finish school. I was bright and knew I was headed to college, but I always needed more money. I was determined to keep my tiny amount of dignity, so I searched for ways to get what I needed without begging or giving more *services*. I was older and no longer felt I owed Uncle Harold anything. I was determined to do what I wanted to do. Some things I couldn't control, but others were within my purview. I learned disobedience was rebellion—and God would punish me—but I decided I'd rather deal with God than continue begging Harold for money. I knew Briana didn't have to deal with begging or servicing Harold when she lived in his guest room. I was angry with the state, but the state wasn't a person, so thinking about the inequality was fruitless.

I told Ava I wanted a pretty outfit for my senior pictures, and she had an idea of how I could get several outfits for free. I told her I didn't want to sell my body or sleep with men for money to buy the clothes I wanted. She convinced me that mall stores practically gave away clothes by allowing people to walk in and take whatever they wanted. I could see from her wardrobe it worked for her.

Ava described a simple process. We would go to the mall, and she would show me how to get whatever I wanted. Then she said, "If you get caught, give

[3]Regier, P. S., L. Sinko, K. Jagannathan, S. Aryal, A. M. Teitelman, and A. R. Childress. 2022. "In Young Women, A Link Between Childhood Abuse and Subliminal Processing of Aversive Cues is Moderated by Impulsivity." BMC Psychiatry 22, no. 1 (March): 159. Doi: 10.1186/s12888-022-03770-0.

them a fake name and Harold's phone number. I'll answer when they call, pick you up, and take you home. They have to release you because you don't live in that town."

I had no idea of the truth of that, but it sounded good, and I was up for the adventure, even though I had no reason to trust Ava after she snitched on me to Harold. I should have remembered the experience of going to the police station and calling a former teacher to bail me out. Ava was twenty-eight, abandoned her children, and bounced between a college boyfriend and Harold's house. None of those things indicated trustworthiness. Nonetheless, she could have said, *Drive the getaway car for a bank robbery,* and I would have said, *OK, maybe no one will see me.* Though she evaded capture, I knew she shoplifted because she had a closet full of new clothes. If anyone could teach me how to do it—and get away with it—Ava could.

One of the saddest things about abuse is that it robs people of the ability to think critically. Abused children often depend on others to think for them. That is a problem when the trusted person lacks critical thinking skills or has Childhood Trauma of their own. Trusting them is like throwing dice; it can end up going either way. Traumatized people often end up trusting someone whose thinking is equally compromised because they may think, as I thought, that anyone's idea is better than theirs. I thought because Ava was older, she had more experience and knew something I didn't. I thought because she was older, she must be smarter, and I trusted her to calculate the mistakes I could make. I thought she'd tell me if an idea was bad, but when she went along with me, I thought it must be a good idea.

Most times, I couldn't see past the getting-away-with-it moment. I never envisioned getting caught. I was relieved to learn, through brain research, that the left hemisphere is damaged during abuse, which is a reason why a person who had complex trauma can only see themselves escaping the crime, or whatever it is they are trying to get away with.[4] They cannot conceptualize the possible outcomes and weigh the risk-versus-reward when deciding to move forward with a bad idea. Ava's idea sounded great to me. I needed clothes, and she had a plan. What could go wrong? I completely ignored how messed up Ava's life was and the risks shoplifting posed to my goal of finishing high school. Abused children have a propensity to hope the next person who shows interest in them is genuine and will help them without taking advantage of

---

[4]Hart, Heledd, and Katya Rubia. 2012. "Neuroimaging of Child Abuse: A Critical Review." *Frontiers in Human Neuroscience* 6, no. 52 (March): 1-24. Doi: 10.3389/fnhum.2012.00052.

them. They are usually too trusting or not trusting enough. Survivors are the most hopeful of people while also the most distrusting. Although they experience the worst from people, they continually look for the best. Survivors have difficulty distinguishing who is trustworthy despite the person's character or behavior.[5] It doesn't excuse the dumb things I did, but it certainly helped to know things were working against me that were out of my control.

Ava's plan was to coach me to steal. She assured me I would not get caught and that she had done it many times. What could go wrong, right? I was ready. I had the script and was jumping to play the part. I told Harold and Agnes I would be on a school field trip and wouldn't return until late that evening. Harold believed me, or at least he didn't ask questions. Although we were going to a city with a large mall ninety minutes away, I was confident I would be back by nightfall. It seems unbelievable now, but I had no idea that things could go wrong. Ava set it up for one of her friends to drive us for my first visit to a mall. Previously, I had only been in stores in the small towns where I lived. The mall was full of things I wanted. Ava coached me on how to steal and what to do if caught. I should have learned my lesson after the stolen car incident, but I was a slow learner in this type of life lesson. It made no sense that I wanted to be like Ava almost as much as she wanted to be like me.

We both thought I would get away with it. Ava had never been caught, and if I followed her directions, I should be just as successful. I justified stealing by saying I needed the clothing for senior events. I was tired of wearing long cotton dresses, leg warmers and penny loafers. I wanted a different look because I was on the cusp of entering the adult world. I rationalized that taking something without paying for it was no different than what Briana and I did when we were hungry. I would look so pretty. I had the grades for success, and now I needed the look to fit in with my graduating classmates. I left out one calculation: they had parents taking care of them. I had guardians who simply provided a place to live—a big difference. I also justified my intention: *"The government took care of Briana, but I have no one to take care of me."* My distorted thinking excused my misbehavior, which is common among Childhood Trauma survivors. Excusing and justifying my behavior made it easier for me to take things that were not mine.

[5]Cikanavicius, Darius. 2019. "Trust Issues That Arise from Childhood Trauma." Psych Central. https://psychcentral.com/blog/psychology-self/2019/09/trust-issues#1.

I did exactly what Ava said to do. I chose three outfits, tucked them tightly under my shirt, and headed for the door, but a security officer stepped into my path and asked me to come to the office. He said *please*, but I knew there was no option to refuse. My body skipped *fight* and *flight* and went directly to *freeze* mode. I stood unmoving when the security officer asked me to follow him, but his nudge woke me up. The guard took my arm and steered me to a back room. I knew I was in trouble. My heart rate increased. I had to use the bathroom. I wanted to cry. I tried to figure out what happened because this was not what we rehearsed.

Questions flowed quickly. *How did anyone see me? Where did they get a back room? There were so many people in the store. How could they have singled me out?* Bible lessons screamed in my mind: *Thou shalt not steal. Thou shalt not covet.* I even created my own commandment, *Thou shalt not get caught,* but I broke mine, too. I knew I would be punished for doing something I shouldn't have done.

My age and experience were against me because I couldn't see past the outfits. When caught, I immediately fought anger, resentment, and hatred for Ava. I believed she knew I might get caught. The security guard asked several questions, and everything Ava told me to do and say meant nothing to him. I began to cry like a little girl. There was no one to help me. My life flashed before me because I didn't know or understand the law. My closest encounter with law enforcement was the stolen car incident, but I was released so quickly that I didn't experience jail or the true consequences of violating the law. Some people learn the first time they misjudge a situation. For others, sadly, it takes pain to adjust their mindset. For this incident, I thought I would go to jail for a long time.

"Who brought you here? What's your name? Who are your parents?" He spat out one question after the other.

I refused to answer his questions. I watched *Perry Mason* on TV. I was prepared to be yelled at and for the guard to try to make me talk. I thought *I can't get my sister in trouble. She won't talk to me again. She tried to help me.* Then my thoughts switched to *She set me up. She is jealous of me. She doesn't want me to graduate. I'm going to jail. Why did I do this when I know it's wrong to steal?*

"I'm sorry. I was wrong. Please forgive me," I said to the security guard. I thought he would feel sorry for me and would release me. I wasn't sorry for taking the clothes, but I was truly sorry I got caught and that our scheme didn't work. That was the extent of my thinking. I knew I couldn't tell the truth because Ava told me not to give anyone my real name. I thought he would let me go if I gave him a fake name. Then maybe everything would go as planned. Ava forgot to tell me one thing. When a minor gets caught, the adult who retains the child must find a legally responsible adult to whom they can return custody of the minor.

After what seemed like hours of grueling questions—but was probably only a few minutes—I broke down. I told the guard everything as I sobbed. "I am a high school senior, and I have to go back to school. I have semester exams. If I fail, my whole life is ruined. Please help me. Ava told me to do it." In my childlike behavior, I thought a simple apology was sufficient. How silly of me to think if I apologized to a security guard, my circumstances would change.

The guard said he would have released me into Ava's custody if I hadn't lied about my name. Once again, Ava led me astray. I found out later that she waited in the car for me for a few minutes; when I didn't come back out, she left, leaving me there alone. Now, I was required to have someone bring proof of my name and show evidence that I was a high school student. The guard would only release me to my legal guardian with that proof. Harold and Agnes seldom heard the phone ringing, so I knew no one would answer the phone calls from the security guard. This time I was convinced I would go to jail.

The mall security guard didn't handcuff me. That made me feel less like the criminal I thought I was. I didn't resist as we walked to an official vehicle with one officer in front and another following me. Tears flowed during the ten-minute ride to the precinct. A police officer called the phone numbers I gave her, but no one answered, just as I expected. There was no choice but to hold me in jail, so she made me put on a jail uniform. I cried inconsolably and thought I wanted to die. By then, I was emotionally numb from the physical and sexual abuse. The world and everyone in it no longer mattered to me. During this ride, my hope vanished. Reality set in.

"Jail," I sobbed, "But the inmates will kill me."

No one responded. All kinds of thoughts ran through my mind. *I am not an adult. I don't want to be raped. I promise I won't do it again. What happens now? I made a few bad choices, and I'll have to drop out of school. There goes my dream of being somebody.* My negative thoughts raced from zero to sixty in three seconds.

I braced for the worst as I walked into the cell with two cots and someone already there. I didn't know this person. How could they leave me with her?

She was a tall, thin, dark-skinned girl about my age with a short haircut. She looked like she lived a hard life.

"You take the bottom. I like the top," she said in a deep, bass voice.

I prayed, *Lord, please help me.* I didn't know what to expect, and I was terrified. Catastrophizing set in. Catastrophizing is when your mind exaggerates the negatives of a situation. It is dangerous because irrational thinking continues to feed on the worst outcomes.

My knees shook. I was going to play like I was bad, but when faced with bad, I froze. I didn't want her to make me her girlfriend, so I started crying. "I will give you whatever you want. You can have my shoes, my dress, and my earrings. Just don't touch me, please." She hadn't even threatened me, but I was so afraid she would, I just blurted all of that out.

She looked at me as the cell door clanged shut with an expression that said, *What you got?* even though it was obvious I had nothing. Neither of us had any personal property. "What did you say you would give me?" she asked.

I trembled. "I will give you my shoes, dress, earrings—and I can get you some money." I thought but didn't say *Girl, you can have anything you want except my body.* I knew some things were sins, while others were an abomination to God. To me, woman-on-woman sex was an abomination to God. The church called abominations *wicked* sins. I wasn't taught about what I would consider to be moral sins, like stealing, fighting, and premarital sex, but I knew what I believed to be wicked ones, and sex with a girl wasn't something I could ever do.

"Ok, but when you leave, if you don't do what you said, I will find you," she said.

She looked as hard as she spoke, and I believed her. She looked like she could gut me like a fish. I didn't want to worry about her showing up at my house. I knew I would give her whatever she wanted.

I voluntarily told her I had fifty dollars. I planned to buy something at the mall as a coverup for what I stole, but I didn't get the chance to check out. I hoped she didn't ask for more money because I had none and didn't know where to get any. My cellmate told me she was there for skipping school, burglary, fighting, and stabbing someone. I didn't interrupt her, mainly because she looked a little unstable, and only the two of us were in the room.

I prayed for God to send someone to rescue me, but He didn't. He allowed me to learn this lesson the hard way. I became a prayer warrior overnight. God was on my emergency call list. I felt every ounce of ambition, courage, and determination take wings as I cried. My cellmate said, "Stop that crying! Jail is not the place to do that. People here see crying as a weakness." I immediately dried my eyes, and the strength returned to my body. The power of words!

Dinner was unappetizing. The pinto beans and cornbread looked like hog slop. I sent my meal back untouched. I knew how to ignore hunger pangs from the practice I had in childhood. When breakfast was brought to the cell, I understood why Elsie cooked for the jail whenever she was taken into custody. I thought jail food must be good because Elsie's food was good, and she was frequently arrested for fighting or drunkeness, but when I looked at the food in front of me, I didn't want it. The oatmeal looked like soup, and the yellow puddle looked like powdered eggs—probably from the same government surplus that supplied school cafeterias. The toast was dry, and I didn't see any jelly. Another meal left untouched.

I was in jail for a day before Harold answered the phone, and I would have to spend three nights in jail before my court date. I decided I had a case for a lawsuit because keeping me in this place was cruel and unusual punishment. I loved law and history, but I didn't like that it applied to me now that I had personal experience of how the law worked.

After I had been in jail for two days and heard my cellmate's story, I felt sorry for her. She encouraged me and was knowledgeable about court procedures. She had been in the criminal justice system since the age of ten. She assured me stealing was not a serious offense and that the judge would probably let me go but assign probation.

She coached me on what to say when I stood before the judge. "I am in school, I make good grades, and I am about to graduate." She said the judge would be lenient when I showed him I was a good kid who made a poor choice.

"Unlike me, who keeps coming before him," she added, looking away.

I saw how sad she was. I felt sorry for her but could only think about my situation. *What if Harold doesn't come and get me?* I wanted to tell her a good story and give her hope as she did for me, but from what she told me, things didn't look good for her. I could only look at her and say, "I hope everything works out for you."

The day of my court hearing came, and I was hopeful but sad. I woke up early and thought about the direction of my life. I felt sad because I was such a burden to Harold and Agnes. I was grateful to them for taking me in. I didn't yet understand Harold wasn't doing a good deed for the sake of helping me. He had ulterior motives. I thought *They are older, and this is how I thanked them. Shoplifting could go on my permanent record. I can't do stuff like this unless I want to be in here like these other criminals. A conviction can keep me from attending college and getting a better job. A criminal is not the me I want to be.* The soul-searching did me good. It made me rethink what I wanted to do with my life.

Chapter 23

SECOND CHANCE

The court appearance was much like my cellmate predicted. The judge asked for my school records, which Harold produced. The court must have notified him to bring them. After I gave thanks for the school records, my thoughts quickly switched to shame and wondering who Harold might have told about my jail experience. I heard many testimonies at church when the speaker didn't understand confidentiality or appropriate discretion. They openly shared their run-ins with the law and other personal family information. I was afraid Harold had shared my story, and I didn't want anyone to know I was arrested. Some of them already thought I was scum, not worth scraping from the bottom of their shoe. Hearing that I shoplifted would validate their opinions. Sadly, I didn't think about this possible consequence before deciding to steal clothes from a store in the mall.

The pomp and formality of court proceedings was impressive. The judge, a tall man in a black robe with gold tassels, entered as the bailiff said, "All rise." It was clear that he was somebody special. At that moment, I clearly understood what it meant to be somebody. I said several times that I wanted to be *somebody* but had no idea what it meant—much less what it took to be somebody. The judge looked like he was somebody, and I am sure everyone under his authority thought he was. In that instant, I realized he controlled my life. He had the power to change the course of my life or to give me another chance.

Several other people waited to be called by the judge. They were arrested and detained over the weekend and were in court to learn if their detention would continue or if they would be released to return later for another hearing or trial. I was the sixth person called to stand before the judge. I felt like a criminal. My knees shook, and my breath was ragged. I feared this incident would label and stereotype me as unsalvageable. I silently prayed for mercy that God would allow the judge to see that I was a good kid.

My cellmate had told me to say only *Yes, sir,* in reply to court questions. "The judge doesn't like excuses," she said.

The court clerk said, "You are to plead Guilty or Not Guilty with an explanation." I wanted to plead guilty with an explanation, but I heard the more anyone talked, the angrier it made the judge, so I needed to speak clearly and briefly in a loud voice.

I wanted to tell the judge about my abusive childhood and how my older sister influenced me to steal. I wanted him to know how I found my mother dying on the floor and how I had to live with Harold and Agnes, who were like great-grandparents to me. I wanted to tell him I wasn't allowed to wear pants, play sports, or do many other things, so he'd feel sorry for me. Instead, I focused my goal on getting out of jail. I wanted to go home and finish high school.

"I plead Guilty." I knew what those words meant but did not comprehend their weight. I only knew I needed mercy. If I lied, I thought the judge would get angry. The truth was, I stole something and got caught, and nothing else needed to be said. For the first time, even if only to myself, I acknowledged that it wasn't Ava's scheming that made me steal. She influenced me, but I chose to go with her to do something I knew was wrong. Trauma had completely skewed my thinking. I blamed Ava until that moment in the courtroom when I took responsibility for my actions. I realized I chose to steal, which led to a loss of freedom, rather than wear the old clothes I owned and be the queen of my destiny.

That lesson would be one of my great life lessons because it taught me that I was responsible for my actions, regardless of who or what influenced me or even what happened to me, and that those actions have consequences for which I am also responsible.

It taught me someone else's actions had nothing to do with mine. No one can make me do anything I don't want to do. Others can only make the fear of not doing what they say greater than the fear of doing it.

Remorse for my actions flowed through my body. I felt momentarily paralyzed and motionless. I was in shock. The weight of what I did finally hit me. I dropped my head and silently sobbed as I reflected and asked *What are you doing, Dora? You're too smart for this. You can be whatever you want to be. Don't settle for this powerless life.*

The judge looked down to flip through my school records before looking at me like he knew me. "You are doing great in school. You've only had a few days of absence. You have not been in my court before. I will let you go home today, assuming you won't return. Is that a correct assumption?" he asked, gazing directly at me.

I wanted to jump over the partition, hug him, and say, *God bless you, judge! I promise you will never see my face again. I won't be back!* Whatever would make him understand that I'd learned a valuable lesson. Instead, I simply replied, "Thank you, Your Honor." He didn't seem to care that I thanked him and was appreciative, but I wasn't put off.

"Who is she being released to?" he questioned.

Harold didn't answer, probably because he hadn't heard the judge. So he asked again. "Who is she being released to? Will you be responsible for her?" he asked, looking at Harold.

I received my first lesson in *mercy.*

Harold stood with his head hanging down, then walked from his seat and stood beside me, and said, "She is being released to me, Your Honor."

"I don't want to see her here again. I expect her to do great things. She's smart and capable of doing anything she wants to. I don't even want this to go on her permanent record. I am giving you a second chance. Do you understand?" he asked, his eyes boring into mine.

It took everything I had to hold it together because I thought *Why is the judge so kind? He doesn't know me. Why is he telling me this?*

Something inside me said he could see it. He somehow knew this mistake would not define me.

The judge gave me a second chance. He could have sent me to a juvenile detention school, where teenage criminals would have surrounded me, but he didn't. This second chance meant everything. God does watch over babies and fools. I felt the judge saved my life. It was the difference between giving up my dream to be somebody and resolving to make it happen. I was willing to keep trying because a stranger believed in me—a stranger who wasn't asking me for anything or taking anything from me.

"Yes, sir. I understand," I replied.

I left the courtroom with Harold and Ava, who came for the opportunity to see me humiliated and in fear for my life. Ava brought me a change of clothes, so I changed from my jail outfit and was on my way to the car when I remembered my cellmate. For half a second, I thought about leaving without honoring my promise to leave some money in her account. However, in the next half second, I remembered that she could find me and do some serious harm. She helped me prepare for court, and I felt she earned my tennis shoes, clothes, and earrings, so I told Harold and Ava to go to the car while I ran back inside to ask the matron to give the bag of clothing to my cellmate. I put the fifty dollars in her account, as promised. I don't know if she ever received it, but I kept my word. I didn't want to be like my stepdad, Buck, who never kept his word. I felt good walking away from the courthouse as if I had done something right, even though I had done something wrong to have to be there in the first place.

I returned to school with a fresh outlook on life. I felt like God gave me a second chance. I missed a few days of high school while in jail and court, but I learned a big life lesson. To avoid making poor choices in the future, I focused on the thought that if I had been sentenced to jail, I might have become a high school dropout. I concluded the only thing I had to offer anyone was my brain, and I couldn't allow anyone or anything to interfere with it.

To this day, I am grateful for the early correction of getting caught and the lesson in responsibility from my *Abba Father*. It undoubtedly kept me from future jail time or even prison time. As I matured, I recognized that I wasn't as smart as I thought I was. I was arrested for trying to get something the easy way. It taught me to work hard for what I want.

I often wished I had parents to teach me the everyday things about life, simple and complex, such as not taking things that are not mine even if I believe I need them. People may let a child's mistakes go unpunished, but adults face adult-sized consequences. Life will get hard, but others have gone before you to show you it can be done. Now I understand that having loving parents does not guarantee lessons are learned. It only means they would have taught and corrected me when I was wrong. Since I had no parents to do that, God was my parent. He disciplined me as a parent disciplined a child—lovingly but firmly.

If I had parents to discipline me when I first stole a coat at school, I would've likely learned my lesson earlier. In third grade, I committed my first theft, except for the candy from the hospital vending machines. We moved to a new place, and I had no coat. I didn't even have a warm sweater because Buck and Elsie didn't buy us clothes. I was cold when I saw a classmate's abandoned coat. It looked warm, so I took it home. I thought if I took the coat, no one would know. I don't know what made me think the girl wouldn't miss her coat or that her friends wouldn't recognize it and know I stole it. If anyone said something, it would be my word against theirs. I had no concept of evidence. Trauma brain makes people look stupid because it interferes with critical thinking and problem-solving.

I wore the coat to school the next day, and the teacher asked me to bring it to her. I began to feel anxious. The teacher said she wanted to see if it was mine because someone was missing a coat exactly like the one I had on. Through the entire ordeal, she allowed me to maintain my dignity. I was upset and frustrated because I had taken someone's coat, and they wanted it back, and I would be back where I started—cold and coat-less. Thankfully, neither the girl I stole the coat from nor the teacher made a big deal about the coat. The teacher returned it. I was visibly angry about returning the coat, but the teacher didn't seem moved by anger. She politely removed the coat and looked at the tag on the back. The girl said it was hers because her mom had written her name on the tag.

Until the shoplifting incident, I had never felt guilty for taking things that weren't mine. I felt I was justified. Today, I understand why I shouldn't have taken the girl's coat, the gum from a girl's gym bag, the cheese puffs from the lady down the road, the packages of taffy from the candy lady, or money from the sick people at the hospital. It's the principle of taking things that aren't mine. My first steal without consequences opened the door to take more things and led me to believe there wouldn't ever be any consequences. According to research, jail time is not unusual for trauma survivors. In fact, 98% of people in prison experienced at least one trauma before age eighteen.[6] From that day I was determined not to be part of the CT jailhouse statistic again.

The judge saw my abilities when he reviewed the school records. The positive seed he planted stayed with me, and I wouldn't allow anyone or anything to dig it up. I continued to have doubts about who I was because of what I lost from the sexual abuse, but the one thing that never changed was the belief that I was special and that God chose me to do great work for Him. *One day, I will be somebody!* I cherished that thought.

That day in court, I was motivated to put foolishness behind me because I was old enough to understand that my actions had consequences. I had a new lease on life. I had gone to jail, and I was determined never to go to jail again. I repeated *I will go to college. I will study hard. I will get a good job. I will have a beautiful family. I will be successful. And I will never look back or come back to this place again.* God taught me to speak affirmations over myself long before I came to understand the importance of them.

---

[6]https://compassionprisonproject.org/childhood-trauma-statistics/

From the day I left court, I knew I had to be my own cheerleader. Although Ava and I continued to live together at Harold's, we didn't talk about the incident. I pretended like nothing happened. Instead, I committed myself to putting my best foot forward. I determined that, against the odds, I would make it. My new goal was to graduate high school, earn a college degree, and get a job to make a difference with my life. This goal guided most of my decisions for the next few years, except for a few mishaps. Although I hadn't yet defined what *being somebody* meant, at that point in time, *to be somebody* meant to finish high school and go to college.

Chapter 24
A NEW OUTLOOK

Until my weekend in the county jail, I didn't realize how much I wanted to graduate from high school. Graduating was my priority, even though I knew I didn't have to. There was no one to demand I graduate. No one I knew cared if I graduated. I could drop out of school, and no one would have said a word since none of my siblings graduated. Ava and Briana finished the Graduate Equivalency Diploma (GED) after dropping out of high school. If I stopped going to school, the only requirement would be to get a job. Despite this, I was determined to graduate.

I felt restless when I stayed at home. Staying at home reminded me of who I was, while life at school showed me who I could be. When I was a child and Elsie made me stay home with her, being out of school felt like a punishment. Accepting another disciplinary action was preferable to missing school.

Following the arrest, I excused my absence from school by telling people I was sick. I never told anyone where I spent that time. I didn't feel persuaded to get up in church and give a testimony of how the Lord delivered me from jail. I hoped neither Uncle Harold nor Ava felt the need to share my testimony as their testimony, as others sometimes did. A few rumors about me spread in the church, but the true story remained untold. I was glad because I was already ashamed of what I had done. In the past, some congregation members warned Harold and Agnes about taking in stray children after two of my older siblings lived with them before me. They left a bad taste in the congregation's mouth and eyes. I heard my brother sold drugs, and the congregation threatened Harold about allowing such criminal activity in his home. I was thankful the rumors about me were squelched.

Three months before graduation, anticipation was heavy in the air. Most of the seniors began to feel it around February. I had a dream booster—jail—so I was motivated and ready to do what I needed to graduate. I wrote applications to colleges and essays for scholarships and grant applications. I was determined to leave Harold and Agnes' house. Alone with no parents, siblings, or other relatives to direct me, I still felt my steps would lead me to a new world—a world I was afraid of. Where would I go? Who would support me?

Although Ava had been in a college setting, she offered no guidance as I prepared to attend college.

I gravely contemplated which college to attend. I didn't know how I would get there or what would happen, but I knew my first step was to get there. At times, the thought of college overwhelmed me. I had no answers—only the determination to go. The same perseverance that pushed me to graduate from high school would get me to college—and through college to a degree.

I had a high school acquaintance from the bus stop. We only exchanged small talk at first, but in my junior year, we talked more. She was a year older than me. She planned to go to a college two hours away. She agreed to stay in touch with me and let me know how she liked it. She called several times during my senior year to encourage me to apply to the college she attended. That was a great idea because I felt uncomfortable going where I knew no one. Her suggestion gave me a possibility to consider. By mid-March, I decided I would go to her college. Out of fear of rejection, I didn't apply to other colleges. I decided to go where I knew someone and could feel safe. I still didn't know that safety was not something others provided.

By myself I applied to go to the same college as my bus stop friend, met the deadline, completed the paperwork, filed the financial aid application (FAFSA) and paid the fees. I had a new outlook on life—in time for a new life. I was ready and set to go.

My mind cycled through worries and fears, and they were my invisible companions. Fears lie dormant in survivors until an experience exposes them, such as fear of rejection, failure, being hurt, or being abused. When I realized I needed transportation to college, I had to overcome my fear of riding buses. They seemed dangerous to me. I hadn't yet flown anywhere, so I couldn't fathom attending a college out of state. I hadn't heard from the college or received a letter of acceptance, so I thought they rejected me. Even after receiving the acceptance letter, I thought something bad might prevent me from going. Then, I imagined that college coursework would be too difficult, and I would fail and be kicked out. I was afraid I wouldn't be able to manage during the breaks, I would have no friends, or not be smart enough. I was afraid of ridicule. Survivors experience so much pain and loss that negative thinking becomes the norm. Pain and loss integrate with their thoughts, emotions, and lives for a lifetime—long after their actual pain and loss ends.

I was prepared for my world to change but not to be transformed. Many times, I cried because I realized success was up to me. I had an insatiable desire to be a world changer, transform lives, and help people. One of the reasons dreaming of success was difficult was because I hadn't seen any family members go to college, graduate, or make a difference in the world. There was no role model or blueprint to follow.

High school graduation went as I expected—no one in my family would be there except Briana. My family members probably didn't know I was graduating, and since none of them had graduated high school except with a GED, it didn't mean much to them. Graduation meant everything to me. I had few positive role models, no successful relatives, and no idea how to make my dream come true.

All I had was a dream to be somebody, faith that it would happen, and a determination to let nothing stop me.

Graduation from high school was the first step. I was the first of at least three generations of my family to graduate from high school. I was on my way.

Briana was the only family member who attended. Harold and Agnes made nothing of the achievement. I didn't expect them to attend the commencement ceremony. They were in their late seventies by that time and consumed with church activities and responsibilities. Neither of them could see or hear well, so it was pointless for them to go.

A brief silence followed the announcement of my name, a pause as if the speaker was reading the name of someone not present. For most students, there were cheers, slaps on the back, and signs held high by their friends and family. I felt the awkwardness of the silence following my name, but I held my head high and walked across the stage to receive my diploma. I was proud and felt like I had won a major award.

After the graduation ceremony, students rejoined their parents and families. I looked for Briana, who had driven from Memphis to attend. She and her three small girls were there; seeing them was like having an entire family present. She hugged me and headed back to Memphis. It didn't bother me that my family didn't come to my graduation even though most of them lived nearby. I didn't expect them to come, and I didn't invite them. We weren't close, and they didn't keep up with me. Unless Briana had told Denise, Maureen, or Marcus, they may not have even been aware. At that point in my life, I didn't know where Jolene, Jake, or Mathus were, and Ava wasn't interested. I had other things to fight for—family support was not one of them.

I was more mature after graduation, but childish behaviors persisted. That summer, I didn't want to be home by midnight, clean the house, go to work, or service Harold. He didn't even approach me about sex my senior year, proof that he knew he was taking advantage of a young girl who didn't know she could say no. Some weeks I barely went to Harold and Agnes' except to change clothes and go back out. I was doing the same things I had seen Ava do when she came home. I knew I couldn't go into Harold and Agnes' house after midnight, so I stayed out all night if I didn't make it home before the curfew.

I changed, but I couldn't explain it. I spoke up for myself. I made quick decisions about transportation to college, choosing a roommate, getting a new job, and how I would travel home on school vacation breaks. I was often overwhelmed by negative thoughts and increasing fears as the summer rushed toward fall. With college starting soon, I feared something bad would happen because transitions were difficult. The change triggered hyper-vigilance. It felt like childhood, when I routinely expected something terrible to happen.

I was well into my forties and studying the effects of trauma on the brain before I understood how Childhood Trauma altered the structure of my brain and influenced my decisions. I had never heard of Childhood Trauma before attending graduate school for a doctorate. I didn't know that my family could be a poster advertisement for CT! Childhood Trauma even damaged my spatial intelligence, causing difficulty with spatial concepts and patterns. It was difficult to conceptualize distance, location, time, and space,[7] and going away to college challenged me in those areas.

I was thankful to learn there is hope for the thing most damaged by CT— my brain. Neuroplasticity allows the brain to reorganize and grow neural networks. Researchers once believed the brain did not grow further after reaching a certain age. However, more recent research reveals the brain continues to change as it learns new information and is affected by environmental and pharmaceutical influences. Unfortunately, I didn't learn this until much later!

Another important part of the summer following graduation was spending time with my boyfriend, Dwight. It was easy to fall for Dwight. He was easygoing, gentle, compassionate, and never raised his voice at me. He was the first boyfriend who seemed to care about me. I enjoyed seeing him, and I

---

[7]Golledge, R. Encyclopedia of Applied Psychology, 2004, Development of Spatial Cognition: A Multidisciplinary Effort.

cared what he thought about me. I never felt judged by Dwight or his family, but it may have been because they hadn't heard the bad reports about my family. If they did, they didn't let me know or treat me as if they knew. Dwight had a huge family with ten siblings and a married mother and father. When I visited, I stayed busy helping with the younger siblings. They loved me, and I loved that they loved me. I reasoned that Dwight wouldn't break up with me if his parents and siblings liked me, so I worked extra hard to prove to them that I was a good fit for him. I would do anything for others because it made me feel like I had value.

That summer, Dwight and I were like a couple in love. We spent day and night together. I never wanted to leave him. I thought I could be with him forever. I am unsure if he felt the same since he never told me. It was more than a summer fling because we spent so much time together, so I was devastated when he cheated on me. I worried Dwight loved the other girl more than me because she was older and had a child. I assumed she was more experienced and thought I couldn't compete. For a brief minute, I actually thought Dwight would like me more if I had a child, so I contemplated motherhood for about half a second.

Dwight's infidelity was sort of my first relationship heartbreak. I say sort of because in twelfth grade I dated Rudolph before Dwight. His mother's church was in the same denomination, so I saw Rudolph at church events. Rudolph was unkind and critical of me and my family. He repeatedly reminded me that I was a nobody after his mother told him about our family abuse. He'd say, "Hey, I heard you were running down the street naked because you had no place to go. I bet your nose was snotty when you were little," and, "Do you know who your daddy is?" Rudolph's ridicule lowered my self-esteem and made me cry, but I didn't quit him because my sisters taught me how to keep an abusive man. I see the manipulation now, and I am thankful I didn't marry him because that could not have gone well. I believed it didn't matter how he treated me as long as I had a man. My sisters taught me an abusive, incompetent, lazy man was better than no man.

Rudolph was constantly teased and called *baby* because he was the youngest of his siblings. He treated me as unkindly as his older siblings treated him. I've discovered staying in toxic relationships is common among CT survivors, even when they know the relationship is unhealthy. I think it may be because they feel they can rescue the woman or man, don't want to abandon them, are codependent and fearful, or don't want to lose the relationship since they've already lost so much. Some CT survivors risk their lives trying to make an abusive relationship better. I remained in a toxic relationship with Rudolph until I met Dwight.

When I told Dwight how much he hurt me by cheating, he told me he loved me, but he loved her, too. I had never heard of anything like that, but he made it clear his feelings for her were not the same as his feelings for me. At any rate, I resolved that was not the type of relationship I wanted. Yet, I continued to see him because I didn't know what else to do. My sisters showed me how to stay in unhappy relationships.

Dwight and I acted like we were grown until his mom rained on our parade. She said he couldn't come in at any time of the night or early in the morning because he had younger siblings who looked up to him. She was correct about them admiring him. They acted like Dwight was their dad, so I understood why his mother was concerned. Even so, I still liked the *no-responsibility freedom* we had. It was refreshing not to have rules and curfews at first, but when Dwight's mom made him come home, I felt sad that I had no one who cared enough about me to insist I get home by curfew. Adult life was overrated. I needed someone to care enough about me to curb my behavior.

The door to negativity opened again. *Why didn't Dwight's mother correct him when he was with other girls? Maybe she liked the other girls better, or someone told her about my parents.* She never treated me differently. I simply felt and thought differently after she stopped our late-night trysts. The insecurity made me nervous when I was around his family. I thought Dwight's other girlfriends were prettier and had parents and rules—things that made them more desirable. I didn't have those things going for me. I didn't have to be home at all, but occasionally I said I had to go so he would think I, too, had someone who cared for me. Girls left to raise themselves are set up for disaster.

Dwight left for military duty about a month before I went to college. My heart broke when he left. I feared we would go our separate ways once we left our small town, so I held on to him as tightly as possible. We said our goodbyes and promised to wait for each other, but I knew we were not soulmates because his soul was tied to other souls. I continued to call Dwight after we officially broke up. He was almost 4,000 miles away in Anchorage, Alaska, and I couldn't handle it. I had separation anxiety disorder (SAD), although I didn't know it at the time. The emotional pain was so great, I was willing to do almost anything for us to reunite. I wanted to hold on to *what was* because I feared change. People told us we would miss each other less as time passed, but I felt a physical aching when he was gone. I wanted to keep our relationship going. I called Dwight daily, and he called me about once a week. I didn't notice I called him more than he called me, nor did I care. I wanted to hold onto him. It was too painful to think he might forget me. I had finally found a handsome, intelligent, caring boyfriend and would not let him go, even though he had shown who he was by cheating on me and telling me that we were not a love match.

Harold's stories of Elsie and her mother didn't help. "Yo' momma and her momma ran up behind men their whole lives, and you know they thought a man was more important than their children." Harold's stories of Elsie and her mother chasing after men did not deter me from the fantasy man I loved. I created an imaginary version of Dwight and clung to him.

I was so desperate that my monthly phone bill ballooned to $400—a huge debt. This was before cell phones and unlimited long-distance calls. It took every penny I made that summer to pay the bill because Harold refused to pay it. He tried to shame me out of love with Dwight, but it didn't work. I had worn pain, hunger, shame, loneliness, rejection, and dysfunction since birth. The shame of a ridiculously high phone bill didn't bother me. I chose this shame, whereas my parent's shame chose me. I thought I loved Dwight, so this wasn't a real shame. Rather, it was an inability to control my emotions and urges to call him, and there was no shame in that. Hadn't they read Elizabeth Browning's poem "How do I love thee?*" How do I love thee? Let me count the ways*. While she counted the ways, I counted the dollars.

Chapter 25
COLLEGE DAZE

I couldn't conceptualize college life, so I was ill-prepared. I didn't know how to get to the college town or what was expected of me once I got there. I only knew I had to go. When it was time for me to move into the dorm, Harold had a church member drive the two of us because the college town was a long, boring drive more than two hours away. Neither Harold nor the church member was in the mood for conversation, a pep talk, or encouraging words. They weren't even curious about what I would study. Harold often shared his testimony of being a third-grade dropout who rose to a prominent position. He said he was an example of how God could use someone without education. I thought he would be excited that I was going to college, but he showed no interest. I knew it was up to me whether I succeeded or failed.

I was afraid of being alone and friendless at college. The only person I knew was the girl from the bus stop who was a year ahead of me. I wondered how she would treat me once I arrived. I didn't trust others, but I didn't know anyone else, so I hung out with her.

College was nothing like I expected. Changing locations didn't change my negative thinking. I expected it to be a negative experience but assumed I would have autonomy because I would be free to make my own decisions. While it was true that I could do what I wanted, the consequences of those choices were costly because, legally, I was an adult. Like most students, I learned to create a schedule, create rules, and set personal boundaries. I had a lot of *If I didn'ts*. For example, *If I didn't sleep*, I couldn't study. *If I didn't study*, I would fail. I wouldn't have money for expenses and personal items *if I didn't work*. I would get an ugly label *if I didn't monitor my behavior on campus*. *If I got kicked out of college*, I would have to return to Harold and Agnes' house. I soon found freedom, adulthood, and autonomy overrated. I was free, but only to choose for my good because any other choice could take away my freedom.

Orientation leaders told us to watch out for the older students who majored in what they called *fresh meat*. It meant that older students sought out new and younger students for sexual conquests. My naiveté, insecurities, loss of Dwight, and desire for love—combined with emotional immaturity—set me up to be *fresh meat*.

I quickly met a man who was over forty years old. He said he pledged a fraternity, so I was honored he chose me. I didn't know enough to be skeptical of someone his age claiming to be in a fraternity. He chose me because he saw I was young and naive. Women with Childhood Trauma rarely question when a forty-year-old recruits a nineteen-year-old. Undamaged women know it's not healthy or balanced to have such an age difference. One of the saddest things about CT is the impact it has on self-worth. I thought the forty-year-old chose me because there was something special about me. Several times when we were together, he called other women in my presence. It hurt me when he did, but I said nothing. In my distorted thinking, I felt special because an upperclassman chose me. I later discovered he was a senior and knew I was a freshman. He preyed on incoming first-year students. There were times I questioned his activities but dismissed them. I suspected something when I rarely saw him on campus, but he showed up at fraternity events and Greek shows where he took advantage of naive girls. I'm so thankful God watched over me during my wilderness experiences of learning and adjusting to college life. This man was in and out of my life for several years. Several upper-level students had boyfriends, and I wanted one, too, even if it was a facade. It wasn't a big breakup. I matured, and he moved on.

Survivors of Childhood Trauma are at a grave disadvantage because they go through life underestimating the consequences of their decisions.[8] To trauma survivors, few situations are ever as serious as they seem to others. For instance, survivors know intellectually that if they have unprotected sex, they may get pregnant, but it requires critical thinking skills to realize the true ramifications of one poor decision. I didn't think I might get pregnant—I only *hoped* I wouldn't get pregnant. With the examples from my older sisters, it is laughable that I didn't take a proactive approach to family planning to avoid an unwanted pregnancy. This lack of critical thinking skills may be one of the reasons many CT survivors become single mothers. They may have suffered complex trauma and have impaired decision-making skills.

Survivors of trauma are known for *wishing* and making life-changing decisions based on what they *wish* for. While decisions about my personal life stemmed from wishful thinking, I rejected wishful thinking when it came to

---

[8]Kirk, Mimi. 2017. "How Childhood Trauma Adversely Affects Decision-Making." *Pacific Standard*. https://psmag.com/social-justice/childhood-trauma-adversely-affects-decision-making.

my studies. I knew I had to work hard to get good grades. I knew *wishing the professor would give me good grades* wouldn't work because I was the only person expecting anything great. Although I made excellent grades the first year, I still had nagging, persistent, negative thoughts that I might be kicked out. There was no end to the agonizing cycle, but I learned how to keep going despite the negative thoughts.[9]

I learned how to elicit praise from professors. I found they loved themselves and their intellectual abilities, so I encouraged—some might say manipulated—them by quoting them; they, in turn, encouraged me with recognition and praise. I scheduled office appointments to build rapport, which worked for most of them. Sometimes, I quoted my professors verbatim as I expounded on the subject in class discussions. I studied the subject well, so I was confident when I spoke. I took careful notes because I was desperate for praise and to feel clever. Some students argued their point, but I didn't like confrontation or conflict. I still had my opinion, but I didn't feel like I had to convince anyone to agree with me. I needed my evaluators to think I was on their side. I had been around enough arguing while growing up, so I kept quiet and gave them what they wanted to know: that I heard them, that I was learning, and that I could memorize. That's how school became my escape and my security while validating my existence.

I did well academically as long as I could memorize or learn steps, but I couldn't memorize facts or dates in every class. Remembering and understanding were achievable, but applying new learning was sometimes the breaking point for me. Accounting and political science classes were challenging because I was required to solve problems. I hadn't developed the higher-order thinking skills demanded in most university courses, such as analyzing, synthesizing, evaluating, or creating. My critical thinking skills were almost non-existent due to the brain damage caused by trauma. I did not yet know the research about how Childhood Trauma impacts the ability to think critically, so I simply thought others were quicker. I was amazed at how some classmates could look at and solve a problem, whether it required deep thinking or critical analysis. Whenever we were assigned writing or speaking assignments, I did well and often scored the highest in the class. I strategically partnered with someone with excellent critical-thinking skills. I could do the

[9]Kimble, Matthew, Abhishek Sripad, Rachel Fowler, Sara Sobolewski, and Kevin Flemming. 2018. "Negative World Views After Trauma: Neurophysiological Evidence for Negative Expectancies." *Psychological Trauma: Theory, Research, Practice and Policy* 10, no. 5: 576–584. Doi: 10.1037/tra0000324.

creative part in projects, and my teammate would do the critical thinking and analysis. I adapted to my weaknesses and built on my strengths.

During my first year, I decided to be an attorney, which meant I had to take pre-law classes in political science and history. I didn't realize law required skills I didn't have until the political science professor told me, "You don't grasp the concepts of government well enough to major in political science." It was true. I had difficulty thinking critically and understanding abstract concepts. I did well in classes where I could study and memorize things, but classes where I had to analyze ideas and data were challenging.

I left the professor's office defeated. Political science was my major, and in the first semester, he said I lacked the foundation and skills required for the field. I knew I struggled to understand political science theory because it involved humanistic perspectives and scientific skills, but I knew I was intelligent and believed I could do anything I wanted. Now all I heard was that the professor said I couldn't be an attorney. That day was a reckoning because I discovered I wasn't as capable as I thought. I tried to reject my professor's words. His comments, while truthful, left me without direction and temporarily shattered my dream. I went from assurance that I could do the work to doubting myself.

As a child, I said I wanted to be a teacher, but when I went to college, I changed my career aspirations and decided to become a lawyer. I think it was mainly for the the prestige, although I also wanted to advocate for others because no one had fought for me. I had aspired to be a teacher because Ms. Charlotte, my neighbor, was a teacher, and I wanted to be like her. Undoubtedly, I chose to be an attorney because I thought I would fight injustice and make more money than a teacher.

Obviously, my steps were not ordered for me to be an attorney. If the professor had suggested I could do pre-law studies in history or social sciences, it might have made a difference. Still, his flat assessment of my chances in political science effectively ended my attempt to become a lawyer.

To say I was disheartened was an understatement. I tried to repair my damaged self-esteem and injured confidence, but I couldn't. For a long time afterward, I questioned my abilities, and it took years to get it back; even when I got it back, I doubted I could ever be much of anything. It was not the professor's fault, but he could have delivered his assessment of my abilities with more sensitivity. He couldn't know how damaged I was and what a victory it was to just to make it into a college program. Without pointing out my strengths and potential options, his proclamation of what I lacked crippled me. I already operated on the fragile edge of sanity. It seemed that I had to go to college to find out what I couldn't do—and pay to find out!

I survived Childhood Trauma and somehow maintained a modicum of self-esteem despite repeated reminders from my parents and the community that I would never amount to anything. I ignored and shook off their opinions, but the professor's comment sank in this time. It hit me hard. My negative thoughts cycled, *"You're not as smart as you think. You have been lying to yourself. You are a failure."* His comment gave those negative thoughts wings. This time, they meant something. My grades dropped in every class. I'm thankful I had good grades, so even when they dropped, I wasn't in danger of failing, but I no longer believed I could do anything I wanted to do or be anything I wanted to be, and there was no one to change my mind. I prayed for strength to finish the semester.

Thanks to Dr. Watts, world history teacher, I survived the semester. Dr. Watts was a tall, dark-haired man with a deep voice and roots in the Middle East. He had a body twitch that caused his head and body to twist simultaneously, and then he would shake the twitch off by dropping his arm. By the end of class, my neck hurt from watching him move back and forth. He took an interest in helping me and salvaged my diminished self-esteem from the shame I felt about the political science professor's assessment of my abilities. Dr. Watts took me under his wing and emotionally supported me for four years. He even asked me to let him know if I needed anything. Before Dr. Watts, no one had done anything for me without expecting anything, yet he expected nothing! Dr. Watts reminded me that I was intelligent and could succeed in being anything I wanted. I believed I was capable because he told me how smart I was. I earned good grades in his class, and that helped my self-esteem.

Childhood Trauma survivors do better in classrooms where teachers show they care for them, encourage, support, and are patient. Dr. Watts' words gave me the courage to focus, regain my self-esteem, and believe that I could be what I wanted. My self-esteem was so low and my self-confidence so flimsy that one person was able to destroy my determination to believe in myself while the next was able to fuel it. CT survivors are vulnerable to those around them, which is why they must surround themselves with people who can speak life into them and help them develop their skills and talents. CT survivors must identify their strengths and weaknesses and not just take another person's word for who they are and what they can do. One teacher was able to knock me down while another propped me back up. They had the power to make or break me.

At first, I was afraid to get close to Dr. Watts for fear I would be disappointed if he asked for service or a ride to the country, but he never said or did anything inappropriate. It was refreshing to have such a caring, honorable, and helpful professor. I concluded God placed him there for me. Although the FAFSA grant paid for my room and board, I often lacked money for personal items. Dr. Watts had no particular schedule for giving me money, but he seemed to know when I needed it, and he suggested, "Why don't you take this and give it back to me later if you feel like you need to." However, I noticed he gave me more when the campus had big social activities like homecoming. I had a work-study job, but sometimes I didn't get as many hours as I needed and came up short on funds. I liked that Dr. Watts' money was given with no strings attached, and he also made it clear that he was not depriving me of the opportunity to repay him. He didn't expect reimbursement, but his donation was not purely charity. CT survivors need to know that it is not *quid pro quo* when someone is kind to them. I paid him back a few times, which made me feel like I maintained control of the situation and acted honorably.

Dr. Watts was witty and often professionally asked thought-provoking questions. I enjoyed conversations with him and looked forward to seeing him. I even developed a crush on him. I fantasized that he would be romantically interested in me because I mistakenly thought I was his equal. My age didn't matter to the other men in my past, so I thought it didn't matter to any men now that I was no longer a child—another example of how fragile and vulnerable I was. It's good that university teachers get some training in managing students' expectations because having multiple students with similar fragilities each semester must be challenging. A teacher without a solid sense of self and perspective could easily wreak much damage by misunderstanding a student's interest.

I wore short shorts and sat at the front of Dr. Watts' class, smiling, listening intently, and watching his every move. One day, he said, "Ms. Dora, will you stay after class? I need to speak with you." I didn't hear him ask anyone else to stay after class, so I felt special. He got straight to the point. "Ms. Dora, don't you think your shorts are too short to wear to class? I think wearing those shorts is inappropriate for a young lady. You might attract the wrong kind of men because a caring man with character does not want a young lady who dresses like that." He smiled the whole time.

Dr. Watts caught me off guard, so I stared at him, unable to respond. I knew that he said what he did out of caring concern and not because he was interested in fashion or class-appropriate attire. He provided insight from a male's perspective that I had never experienced. What he said was something I should have heard from my family during adolescence. I simply heard a paternal reproof suitable to the situation.

I never wore short shorts to Dr. Watts' class again. Although I was taught by women in the church how young ladies should dress and look, I didn't change my look and attitude because the rules of religious people convicted me or because a man of the cloth said it was wrong. I changed them because a caring man showed concern for me. Dr. Watts taught me more that day than I ever learned in Sunday school or church. I learned I was lovable, that there were men in the world who had discipline, and that someone could care about me without expecting anything in return. His approach helped squash my crush on him and allowed me to appreciate his paternal interest.

Whenever I needed a pep talk, I went to Dr. Watts. He motivated and encouraged me, whether I complained about an unfair professor, whined about not wanting to go home, fretted about getting a job, agonized over summer school, or updated him on my love life. Dr. Watts consistently had wise words for me. He earned my respect, so I listened to him. On one occasion, he asked me who I was dating, and when I told him, I could tell he disapproved. He knew the campus, the students, and the faculty. When I told him about the older man I dated, he said, "He's been here a while, hasn't he?" When I said seven years, he retorted, "Do you think he is planning to graduate?"

I sometimes resented the way Dr. Watts asked questions to make me reflect. *Why couldn't he simply tell me what to do?* He never did. Whenever he gave advice, he framed it as a question. I knew I should think about what he said, but I didn't want to think. I wanted to be told what to do and why to do it because I had lost trust in myself and my ability to make decisions. For those like me with complex Childhood Trauma—multiple traumas that were pervasive and had profound effects—making simple decisions is almost impossible. I often found myself in *freeze* status when I needed to make decisions, and I wanted someone to help me make them. At that time, I didn't know the documented research data of *1 in 3 girls and 1 in 5 boys is sexually abused,* which meant those I asked to help make decisions were probably abused and as damaged as I was. I knew some of them were not any more cognitively competent. Still, I trusted their decisions because of my low self-esteem. There is little wonder why CT survivors either stay stuck in ruts of indecisiveness or get the wrong counsel.

I respected Dr. Watts enough to accept his authority, but he wanted me to think about choices. He said I needed to be sure I understood what I was doing, its impact on me and others, and the consequences of my choices. I did what he said, but the explanation he gave was beyond my ability to comprehend. Following our conversations, I often felt like I had been disciplined. I found out later he mentored several young men and women with no family or friends and provided meaningful guidance. He called us his sons and daughters. That made me feel special. His acceptance of me changed everything. It meant he drew a line that we couldn't cross. Although Harold confused the daddy/daughter relationship by crossing the line when he demanded sexual service, I didn't feel Dr. Watts would betray my trust in him. Dr. Watts demonstrated *I see you as a daughter and nothing else.* After the shorts incident, I thought of him differently. He became someone I trusted, deeply respected, and went to for wise counsel. My relationship with Dr. Watts was the first of its kind for me. He truly behaved like a loving father. He taught me women with self-respect know their value and think, speak, and behave in ways that demonstrate their regard for themselves. His mentorship helped shape my decisions, behavior, and choices.

Chapter 26
GIVE BEAUTY A CHANCE

In my sophomore year, I decided to see if I had more to offer the world. I applied for the Miss Essence beauty pageant. I wanted desperately to gain confidence in my abilities, and I thought winning a beauty pageant would do it. I wasn't popular or in a sorority, but I wanted to try. Entering a beauty pageant could've been described as delusional thinking since I'd never felt attractive or had anyone tell me I was pretty. Still, I was motivated by the scholarship prize. Thankfully, the other contestants didn't look threatening. They probably asked themselves the same question—why did Dora enter a beauty pageant?

I believed there was only one serious contender for the Miss Essence title; she was a senior in a sorority. I didn't think she was prettier, but she was popular, and the pageant prize was for popularity and talent. I knew I wasn't popular, but I was certain I had talent. Sure enough, my competition danced her way into the hearts of the audience and judges while I expressed myself through spoken word.

I panicked when the woman doing our makeup saw the scar on my leg and said I needed to cover it. She didn't ask how it got there. Perhaps she knew from the look on my face that there wasn't a positive story behind it. Tears welled up as I remembered Buck's beating that had left the scar. I had to compose myself. I had to squash my stage fright and quickly regain excitement, knowing the power of expression was my only chance to win the pageant. There was no need for sadness. Makeup covered the scar, and no one saw it—or my deep emotional scars. I reminded myself the abusers were dead and could never hurt me again. I stopped the tears, threw my head back, and confidently walked onto the stage.

My years of church speeches had taught me to write and speak. While living in Harold's house, I often had to write and perform on command. I knew there were many things I couldn't do, but of the few I could, writing and speaking were things I did well. Years of writing for church competitions increased my confidence. My roommate helped prepare me, and I ensured everyone in the college community who knew me was there—especially Dr. Watts. He told me, "You can be anyone you want to be." As I took the stage, I saw him sitting in the front row. I was confident the exterior scars were as well-covered as the interior scars.

There was a microphone and an empty chair on the stage, which made it seem larger and made me feel smaller. I stared intently at the judges, and the words poured out of me. *It Takes A Determination*. I didn't know the words were prophetic at the time, but later I needed to hear and say them repeatedly as I moved through my life.

As I stepped to the microphone, I imagined I was Debbie Allen giving the famous monologue from the movie *Fame*.

It takes a determination to do what you believe is right
To believe in yourself when others despite.
It takes a determination for you to make it
I mean a real inner strength . . . Just to be able to take it.
It takes a determination to say no
When everyone around you is saying yes
To be proud of yourself when you've done your very best.
It takes a determination to achieve your goals
For you to keep looking up
Until the thing you want most in life unfolds.
It takes a determination
To prove others wrong
To believe in yourself
If you have this determination
Keep holding on, it won't be long.

Then came the finale, where I looked at the left side of the audience, to the right side, and back to the center as I stepped to the center of the stage and stood silently for a few seconds, building suspense before I continued:

I hope everyone here tonight has this determination
Determined to give life all you've got,
Instead of dwelling on things in the past
And what you have not.
God didn't put you on this earth
To just sit around and complain
Hold your heads up
You have no reason to be ashamed.
Just remember . . .
If you have this determination

And you have done the very best that you can,
That's when you should just sit back
And give yourself a hand.

I then sat in the onstage chair and slowly clapped for dramatic effect.

The audience jumped to its feet, yelling and applauding. I remained seated as they clapped. They clapped for what felt like an eternity, and I felt like I had done something huge. I thought I was somebody because I was recognized.

I left the stage, but the next contestant couldn't begin her presentation because the applause for me continued. I heard the audience clapping, stamping their feet, and whistling. I loved it because it said they loved me. *They loved me-e-e-e! They wanted more me-e-e-e!* I felt a tiny bit sorry for the next contestant because of the uproar, but only a tiny bit.

When it was time for the announcement of the winners, I heard, "The Talent Award winner is Ms. Dora J McMurray!"

And . . . "The winner of the Miss Essence pageant is Ms. Teresa Posner.

Not me.

It didn't matter that Teresa won the pageant because I won in the category I valued most—Talent. I needed that award to prove to my political science teacher—and everyone from my past who undervalued me—that I was somebody. Of course, neither he nor they were there, but it didn't matter because I believed I truly had a talent, and it was writing. I was convinced I had a talent for creating words that moved people's hearts. It encouraged me to know I was good at something. People who don't know their talent don't lack talent—they simply haven't yet discovered it.

The evening of the pageant, I had the time of my life. People stood in line to shake my hand. I smiled and felt something like when I was recognized for the church plays and competitions. I felt some of the people were genuinely happy for me. They wanted me to win. They saw something in me, too. I didn't know what happiness was, but that night, I had a glimpse of a better life. I didn't understand why people I barely knew could care about me or want me to win because that was a new feeling. I knew I wanted to win because of the scholarship prize, but there was no benefit for audience members. Confused but grateful, I waited until the last person drifted away. Still basking in the glow of the Talent Award, I heard supporters brag about me for the next few weeks. Frequently, I ran into someone who said, "I wasn't at the pageant, but I heard about you." That type of comment made me believe I was somebody special.

When I was younger, a friend a few years older directed the church choir. Jolie attended one of the churches in the same jurisdiction I attended with the Williams family. Everyone praised Jolie. She was good at what she did, even better than some adults. It would have been fine if she only directed the choir, but she was also a singer, dancer, and writer of poems, essays, and short stories. She had remarkable control of rhyme scheme, figurative language, and literary devices. She also loved to pray.

It seemed God had given Jolie everything and left nothing for me. When I asked her how she became so talented, she said she asked God for it. I didn't know it was that simple, so I asked God to give me a talent, too. Jolie's family was as dysfunctional as mine. Her mother had eight children in fifteen years and abandoned every one of them. Even at thirteen, Jolie was strong in her faith and active in the church. She was a respectful, God-fearing middle school student and earned excellent grades. I wanted to be like Jolie, so I asked God to let me write poems. That's the only thing I asked Him to do. I didn't want to be greedy because I had learned He didn't like greed. I thought asking for one talent was reasonable. After all, a man in the Bible had one talent and didn't use it, so he lost it to the man who already had ten talents (Matthew 25). I vowed to use my talent like Jolie used hers. Shortly after that prayer, I became passionate about literature, writing, and poems. Although I wrote poems at Jolie's church when I was twelve, I didn't begin reciting them until I moved into Harold's house. I was fourteen when I first recited my poem for an audience. After that, church leaders often nominated me to write and speak throughout the jurisdiction. I was treated like a *poet laureate* for my church denomination in small-town Arkansas. Talk about being a big fish in a small pond!

At a young age, Jolie taught me God answers prayer. I also learned from Jolie how to love God. She surrounded herself with friends who liked to go to church, liked to pray, and encouraged her. I wanted to be like her. Little did I know that writing and giving church speeches helped to build my confidence in writing and speaking. By the time I was sixteen, I was fully convinced I would be the next Maya Angelou. I continued to write during college, and was even paid to write for special occasions such as weddings, anniversary parties, and high school graduations.

The campus pageant was more than a beauty pageant for me. It was my first secular success. It showed me who I was, and it affirmed my abilities. It helped me by showing me I was more than the abuse I suffered and made me think I was beautiful, loved, and that I had something to offer. I know it wasn't real love, but it was what I needed then. It is obvious I still suffered from distorted and misguided thinking. I believed whatever I set my hands to do, my heart to desire, and my mind to believe was truly possible. I now decided intelligence was not my sole asset. I added *attractive* to my list of attributes. I discovered I wasn't as ugly as Elsie said I was. America was the land of opportunity—or, at least, this pageant was. This pageant meant more to me than I knew at the time. I realized it wasn't as much about my beauty as my efforts to dispel the lies Elsie told me of my ugliness. I entered the pageant because winning it would prove I wasn't ugly. Although I didn't win the pageant, the experience increased my self-confidence and self-esteem because, for the first time, I learned about the power of positive thinking.

The emotional high from the pageant lasted for the rest of the semester. I went from invisible and unknown to recognizable and popular. Boys sought me out who hadn't looked at me before. But that created problems. Before the pageant, I thought I was ugly. I didn't think guys wanted to talk to me. Maybe it was the unfashionable long dresses, no-makeup conservative look, or the poor self-image, low self-esteem, and lack of confidence I wore during those years. I didn't think well of myself, and what I thought came through, not only in conversation but also in my actions.

I briefly hung out with a few party girls but quickly found I didn't want to do what they did at the after-parties. Also, the good girl image became more attractive after conversations with Dr. Watts. He talked with me about the parties and the type of girl who went to them. The conversation was brief and went something like this: "What type of girls do you think are attracted to those types of parties? And why do you think men are attracted to them?" What he said is what I needed to hear. I decided that day I was not that type of girl.

Chapter 27
WHEN DRAKE MET SALLY

I met my first husband, Drake, while studying in the library. We were frequently in the library at the same time. One day, he spoke to me, and I felt a spark of interest, knowing I had caught someone's eye. I thought his speaking to me meant he liked me, but he quickly told me that was not true. My skills at reading people's interest in me were so limited that I thought a spark of curiosity meant he wanted to be with me. I said something irrational and unappealing to him. "Sally 'bout already engaged." I sometimes called myself Sally. Sally helped me say things Dora wasn't courageous enough to say. Adopting or taking on other personas is common for CT survivors of sexual abuse. Once I studied personality disorders, I understood Sally was one of the multiple personalities I developed in response to Childhood Trauma. Before that, I didn't think much about it other than pretending to be Sally made me feel more confident.

Drake caught me off guard and knocked me down a few pegs, stopping me mid-sentence by saying, "Drake 'bout don't give a d---."

My mouth dropped. I thought *He had some nerve*! I did not appreciate it. Obviously, he didn't appreciate my words to him, either. Sally quickly realized she was out of her league and swiftly left the library. Drake was older and more mature. His quick response and dismissal of me made him more interesting to me. It may have been more of a desire to control the situation because I wanted him to know I didn't mean any harm by my actions. I definitely felt an attraction to him, even though his approach irritated me.

After that unpleasant first encounter, Drake quietly passed by without speaking when he was in the library. Sometime later, I ran into him on campus exiting a building I was entering. I took the opportunity to apologize to him. I told Drake I would like to make it up to him for being rude and cook him a nice dinner. He accepted, but once I made the invitation, I had to figure out how to afford the food I wanted to cook for him. I had $7.00 in my checking account. Earlier, my application for food stamps was denied. Some of my friends received them, and getting denied reminded me of Briana receiving a monthly check from the government when I didn't. I had no faith that any state agency could do the right thing.

I promised Drake a *nice* dinner but had to revise that description to *affordable*. I served a one-pan meal of cheeseburger macaroni and green beans with blended strawberry and cherry drink, which cost $6.00. It wasn't as great as Jesus making the five loaves and two fish feed five thousand people, but it was a need met! Our simple dinner initiated a friendship. After that meal, Drake and I frequently hung out together. He taught me how to take a little time from studying and relax. He also encouraged me to stay focused on my grades, to choose the best teachers, and to let go of friends who didn't support my growth.

Drake and I dated for two years. I enjoyed being with him. We were both nerds and frequently studied together in the library. When Drake and I weren't studying, I worked in the library. I spent so much time in the library, my friends knew they could usually find me there. Drake prioritized studying before dating or leisure. I had finally found a guy who was a little street-smart and a lot book-smart. He had started college before me but had to leave briefly because he wasn't ready for college life. When I met him, he was a junior and I was a sophomore. I don't know his college life before, but I know he made up for it the second time. He was focused, determined, and disciplined, and he gave good advice so I wouldn't make the mistakes he had made. I was thankful to have him in my life.

Drake took me to his home on weekends to get to know his parents. He didn't realize it, but he taught me about life, decision-making, and pitfalls contributing to failure. At every opportunity, he would tell me, "Dora, this is why you can't do this," or, "If you do this, this is what will happen." Drake explained the importance of commitment when I considered joining the Army Reserves. He warned about the pitfalls of college—especially time and money management. He warned me to resist non-supportive friends and bad advice and to be aware of the consequences of losing focus. Drake pointed out biased professors and provided strategies to overcome their prejudice. He had a way of explaining things so even the simplest could understand—and I was one of the simplest.

I admired Drake. I respected him and dreamed of having a husband like him. He had a huge family, and they were close, even though there were fifteen. They had family reunions, which was something I had never experienced. His mother, Josetta, had a kind spirit and was the most genuine, caring person I knew. From the start, I loved her. I didn't have to wonder if she liked me because she treated me like she did. I didn't feel the uneasiness with her that I felt with other boyfriends' mothers. I didn't feel like I had to try to win her favor. I could be genuine with her. I believed she was a good mother, so I watched her and wanted to emulate her.

My insecurities stayed under control until Drake introduced me to his brothers and sisters. His family was spread across several states, so for almost a year, I met someone new each time we visited. Most of them only came to Arkansas for holidays and family reunions, but it seemed I met a new family member each time I went home with Drake. I had an idea that I had to look a certain way, play the role of Drake's girlfriend—and potential wife—and fit into his family to be welcomed by them. I had no clue how to do those things, so I did whatever I thought would make them like me. I was the first to offer to sweep, wash dishes, mop, or run an errand. I never refused a request because I wanted their approval and would do whatever it took.

I liked Drake because he didn't care about things most people cared about. He valued me despite my economic status, lack of a car, or sorority affiliation. Initially, I didn't feel I had to prove anything to him, but after a year of dating, I felt the self-imposed pressure of being a nobody creep in. I would often try to impress Drake by buying him a shirt or other small gifts. My bank account went into the red, and then I borrowed money from him to return it to the black. The stress was uncomfortable because it was the type of trauma drama I experienced in childhood. Constantly proving to him and his family that I was somebody was exhausting and took enormous energy, but I concluded that stressful drama was my life. It was exactly the way it had to be. I felt like I was *somebody* following the beauty pageant success, but as soon as I tried to put that *somebody* to the test, the insecurities rushed in. I didn't believe Drake was ready to meet the real Dora.

Drake met the pageant-renewed Dora. She came with false self-esteem, unsubstantiated confidence, and imitation strength. The closer we grew to one another, the more I feared someone would reveal my childhood's details. I didn't want Drake to know that my parents abused us, that I was raised in foster homes, and that I was sexually trafficked and habitually sexually abused. I didn't want him to know that my mother was dead, my biological father didn't acknowledge me as his child, and that I wasn't close to my siblings. I knew I wasn't open and honest with him, but I justified the deceit by telling myself none of that mattered. What was I thinking? Or rather, not thinking? I felt Drake deserved more than I could offer, but I knew I was bright and convinced myself that what happened to my family was normal. I didn't know that I didn't know how to love because I never had a healthy relationship.

I had yet to experience any of the types of love: neither p*hilia* (friendship) nor a*gape* (universal, also called altruistic), and especially not *storge* (familial). Because I hadn't understood those types of love, I was at a disadvantage when it came to experiencing e*ros* (sexual) love. I didn't know what love looked or felt like. I was twenty years old, but emotionally I was only about twelve. Harold predicted I wouldn't be able to find a man to love me, and if I ever snagged a man by chance, he said I needed to marry him ASAP because I wouldn't find anyone else. Sadly, I believed Harold because of his reputation as a church leader and wise man. I felt I had no choice but to rely on him because he gave me a home. When Drake expressed delight in me, I wanted to do what Harold said and marry Drake. I told Dr. Watts about Drake, and he said Drake was smart and a good guy. Drake didn't take any of his classes, but I assume Dr. Watts asked his colleagues about him.

I was certain my past diminished my field of options—there were no other fish in the sea for me. I thought Drake was a nice fish who could teach me things I didn't know or understand about life. I trusted him, and I thought he was wise. Drake told me things he did before we met and the mistakes he made. He had gone into the military to get his life together. When we met, Drake was a transformed man who was six years older than me. He became my mentor, friend, and most importantly, a father figure. What I looked for in a man was someone who could fill the father-sized void in my heart. Drake didn't know it, but he fit the bill. Of course, I didn't recognize any of this distorted thinking at the time.

When I told friends I dated Drake, they were incredulous. They knew Drake because they had classes with him. Drake had a reputation as a loner. My friends talked about his intelligence and told me he was a great catch. Not only did I have the pressure of dating a smart guy, but I also had the pressure of dating a smart guy with money. I had no car, money, nice clothes, or even a firm set of values. I knew why I liked him, but I wasn't sure why he liked me. I desperately wanted someone like him to help me navigate the road called life, and I believed he knew the way. I lacked the confidence to think I was a catch for him—or anyone else. I thought whoever married me would have to settle. It made me sad that I couldn't give him more, but I didn't have any more to give.

After a couple of years of dating and never discussing marriage, we decided to move in together to save money. We talked about how much time we spent with each other and agreed it would be cheaper to move in together. Neither one of us was comfortable with it, but we agreed to do it. We were open to doing things we thought we wouldn't do because we didn't have clear boundaries or values. Roy Disney said, "When your values are clear to you, making decisions becomes easier." We sacrificed personal boundaries and values to save money. CT survivors often find themselves sacrificing their boundaries because others, through abuse and unhealthy relationships, have not respected those boundaries and values. I knew Harold and Agnes would be upset if they learned I lived with Drake. Drake himself told me he wasn't raised that way. For that reason, we agreed to keep our living arrangements secret. While it seemed like a good idea, keeping a secret caused childhood memories to resurface because our secret triggered memories of other secrets I'd had to keep, and the rejection, shame, guilt, and insecurities that went along with them.

My self-esteem took a hit from moving in with Drake—as if it could be lower—because I began believing the things I imagined everyone said about me. I lived with a man without the benefit of marriage! Church people believed it was immoral, but no one knew, so it was okay for now. I repented every night we lived together and asked God to forgive me because I had been taught I would go to hell if I died while participating in sin. Each morning, I was glad to wake up alive. Although Drake told me he liked me and we grew closer, I lived with the fear he would discover the truth about me and leave. One of the worst things about Childhood Trauma is the feelings and thoughts of unworthiness. Regardless of how faithful Drake was to me and how much he did to express his love for me, he could not fix my problem of low self-esteem.

One day, Drake came home and said he'd met someone from my hometown. Until then, I specifically told him only what I wanted him to know about my past. I emphasized that people in my hometown didn't know me and didn't know anything about me, and if he ever heard anything about me, he should ignore it. I feared he might leave me if someone told him about the real Dora. The woman Drake met told him she knew me. I became unhinged, combative, and fearful, anticipating what Drake had learned. I thought the only thing she could have told him was something about my miserable childhood and how I was unwanted, unloved, and undesirable—all of which would have been news to him. I wanted to quit Drake before he quit me. In a flash, I went from *I love you* to *I never want to see you again*. This type of extreme behavior and catastrophizing is typical of CT survivors. Everything is perceived as the worst because of the constant state of fight, flight, or freeze.

Everything is life-altering, and everything is an emergency because of the survivor's inability to analyze and assess.

I was sure the woman from my hometown couldn't have told Drake anything good about me because I didn't believe there was anything good about my past or me. I told him how serious I was about not listening to anyone speak of my past. We had a heated argument that left him saying, "What is wrong with you, Dora? You don't even know what she said."

Drake didn't understand. It wasn't what she said—it was what she could reveal. My secrets were deep, and I didn't want anyone to expose them. I couldn't handle Drake learning the truth because I thought we would immediately break up. I thought Drake would break it off with me after he spoke to her, but he didn't. He never told me what she said. I guess he saw how upset I was and decided to drop it. Dropping it didn't change what happened. Once I felt exposed, I feared anyone could tell him things I didn't want him to know. I felt it was my responsibility to protect my present from my past, and the only way I knew to do that was to discourage Drake from talking about me with others. My behavior was controlling, another feature of an unhealthy self-image. From that point, Drake never let me know if anyone told him anything about me.

Although I was nervous about acquainting Drake with Harold and Agnes, I knew I couldn't keep him a secret forever, so I planned a trip to introduce them. Drake knew I lived in their home, but I didn't tell him much more of my family history except that my parents were deceased and Harold and Agnes took me in. Negative thoughts cycled through my mind and stirred up anxiety: *What if he doesn't like them? What if he doesn't like the church stuff? What if Harold talks too much? What if the church people talk too much? What if Drake found out I was in foster homes? What if my past is too much for him?* I reminded myself that Drake was a good man and would know how to soothe those negative fears. I was not comforted by telling myself that Drake loved me regardless of what anyone said about me, because I didn't know what love was. I felt he cared for me, but I avoided using the word love.

I became more nervous the closer we drew to Harold's for the weekend visit. I believed Harold and Agnes would also see what a good guy Drake was and that he was a good match for me, but the uneasiness didn't come from what they thought about him. It came from what I feared they might tell him about me.

I wanted to appear normal. I wanted to impress Drake, and I wanted him to think I had a family who cared for me. I wanted him to think I had it together. I wanted him to see what didn't exist because I believed he wouldn't want me if he knew the truth. Harold had already told me no one would want me because of my past and warned me to commit to any man interested in me. Drake was my chance, and I didn't want to mess it up. I didn't realize the amount of manipulation, control, and deception I put into getting Drake until after the divorce more than twenty years later. While dating, I led with secrets and deception. Now that I'm healed, I lead with exposure and truths. Misleading someone to think you are someone else denies them the chance to meet the real person. If they meet the real person, they may or may not want to be with them. When I healed, I found I'd rather be with someone who knows my weaknesses, challenges, and disappointments and still wants to be with me than with someone who doesn't know me and chooses the false me. Understanding the importance of that distinction requires character, something I didn't have in my young adulthood. Many CT survivors struggle to develop character. They often think good intentions are enough, so they may lack follow-through, discipline, honesty, and the ability to make good choices. I didn't see it displayed in those around me, and I didn't have those qualities until God healed me and showed me how critical they are.

While visiting, Harold told Drake a story about different kinds of horses. Drake listened intently to him. I was in and out of the room and only halfway heard their conversation, but I walked into the room as Harold told Drake that I was a thoroughbred. That was news to me! Later, Drake said he didn't appreciate the analogy. Harold and Drake were men of few words, and everything they said meant something. I later learned Drake and Harold were engaged in a male power play. Drake was secure in himself and didn't back down to another man; neither did Harold. I felt tension as if they both knew something about each other that I didn't know about them. I felt like an outsider, unable to understand their verbal sparring. Drake told me ten years later that he accepted Harold but felt uneasy around him.

I had suppressed memories of Harold's sexual abuse and wouldn't accept anything negative Drake had to say about Harold. This outlook was part of my protection of Harold. CT survivors typically protect their perpetrators. They either suppress the abuse, want to keep it secret, or act to preserve their fragile sense of self, which often leads to life-long damage to their self-concept.

Before bed Saturday evening, I went into Harold and Agnes' room to say goodnight. Harold and I sat on the side of the bed. He told a story based on the saying, "Why buy the cow when the milk is free?" That idiom referred to unwed couples who lived together. Harold said men don't want to get married when they can get the benefits of marriage (companionship, affection, and sex) without committing to fidelity. I didn't understand the earlier conversation between Harold and Drake, but I had clarity about the cow. In Harold's story, I was the cow who gave free milk, and Harold implied that if Drake got everything he wanted from me without marrying, he would never commit to marrying. I left the bedroom feeling that I had to pressure Drake to marry me to prove to Uncle Harold I was a valuable cow. What a sad commentary on my state of mind!

Drake went with us to church on Sunday. I warned him about the long service. We arrived at 9:30 a.m. and dismissed after 2:00 p.m. I gave Harold an excuse to leave early and return to our college town before dark. I tried to shake the analogy of the cow, but I was bothered for a long time. I feared Drake was using me, which shook my trust. I trusted Harold's words about Drake getting the milk for free and thought Harold had my best interest in mind, even though I had no proof. Twenty-first-century research reveals CT survivors cannot accurately assess risks. When I learned this, it helped me to understand that my inability to make advantageous choices was because my brain's structure changed from abuse. It also helped me let go of the shame of that. Additionally, CT survivors often make the opposite choice of what would benefit them—despite known proof or evidence that it is a poor choice.[10] True to research, it was clear Harold did not protect my interests, yet I chose to believe him rather than Drake.

[10]Kirk, Mimi. 2017. "How Childhood Trauma Adversely Affects Decision-Making." *Pacific Standard*. https://psmag.com/social-justice/childhood-trauma-adversely-affects-decision-making.

Chapter 28

BUY THE COW

I no longer wanted to be the cow who gave free milk. I began hinting that the *free milk* was quickly drying up. I secretly looked at engagement rings and thought about how to nudge Drake to purchase his cow. After a while, I decided he was too shy to purchase a cow, so I decided to help him—in my established pattern of *helping* God when impatient. I thought I would be fine if Drake said no to my proposal. Nothing and no one could shame me anymore. I believed I accepted rejection and shame better when I felt in control. If I asked Drake to marry me, and he said no, I wouldn't be devastated. I knew I couldn't wait for Drake to ask me to marry him, so this was a chance I had to take. Drake had access to his cow for almost three years, but he still made no steps to put a ring on it.

The words came out of my mouth before I rehearsed them. "Will you marry me?" I blurted out over a dinner date.

I didn't prepare. I didn't even know what a proper proposal was. I only knew it was time to change to a more permanent arrangement. I loved Drake as much as I understood love, even though I had no idea—or model—of a healthy, functioning marriage or a lifetime commitment. Wise people might say ignorance is a valid reason to avoid a hasty rush into marriage. I solely knew marriage as a vehicle for producing children and filling their lives with violence and abuse before abandoning them. It didn't occur to me that the only married men I knew were men who cheated on their partners, sexually preyed on children, or were incarcerated. Who did I think I was pushing a nice man like Drake to marry a mess like me? I proposed to Drake out of fear, to avoid Harold's prophecy that I would never find anyone. In fact, I did find someone, and he said yes! I couldn't wait to tell Harold I was getting married —if only to prove that someone wanted me.

How can a marriage go well when built on a foundation of manipulation, control, and deception? Drake didn't do anything to prepare for the engagement. I shopped for the ring, asked him to marry me, and prepared to do whatever needed to make it happen. I had to show Harold somebody wanted me, but I also needed validation. I needed to know that I could attract an intelligent man. Drake met the criteria for a *husband*. He was handsome, kind, caring, intelligent, family-oriented, and had a car. He was even more than I dreamed. I only looked for a man who wanted me. Talk about hitting the jackpot! I hit it big.

We were already living together, so engagement didn't change our day-to-day lives. I neglected pre-marital consideration of important life events like parenthood and the responsibilities that children bring. I failed to consider that I needed a job. I had no job because I had to take more classes to graduate after I changed my major from political science to journalism and then to English with minors in Spanish and social work.

I couldn't wait for Drake to buy an engagement ring. I needed a ring to look the part of a desired woman. I needed the ring to make me feel good when people admired it. I searched for a week in several stores for a ring that made me feel valued. I wouldn't have a ring with a small diamond. It never occurred to me that Drake should shop for the ring or that the groom purchased the ring by tradition. I didn't know how much it meant to Drake, but I knew the ring meant everything to me. I couldn't trust him to get the ring that would make me believe I was somebody, because the ring represented more than an engagement. It symbolized the end of who I was and the beginning of who I would be. It represented no more shame for my family name. The ring meant I was worthy because an intelligent man would marry me. It showed the world I overcame my horrendous childhood and that I was somebody with value and desired by another. I had a lot of expectations for that ring!

I walked around the mall stores until I found a jewelry store that would sell the ring on credit, but I still couldn't find one in my price range. I was desperate. I had to make this happen, or it might never happen—all-or-nothing thinking typical of a survivor of Childhood Trauma. I couldn't find anything affordable. I had a student loan and a financial aid check for the semester, which was about $1,000, and I decided I could charge the rest. I prayed I didn't have to use the school money for the ring, but I had it if needed. Finally, I went to a small jewelry store in the college town and found a ring for $860.00. It was the ring I wanted. It was a round diamond set in 14-karat gold, with a cluster of small diamonds in the center. I purchased the ring on credit, but it was okay because a tiny, affordable ring couldn't make me feel secure and loved.

I decided God answered my prayer when I found the ring I wanted. Drake told me to set the date. Now I'd captured a man, purchased a ring, and set a wedding date. I use the word *captured* because I didn't fully reveal myself to

Drake. I was happy that things moved briskly and in my direction. We planned to marry the following summer. I couldn't wait for a big wedding, nor did I dream it was possible. I was thankful to have a man who wanted me. After all, neither Harold nor I thought it was possible. It didn't seem relevant that Drake knew almost nothing about my background. The depths of deception based on my fear were immeasurable. I hid the physical and emotional childhood abuse, the child sex trafficking, and the teenage years of sexually accommodating Harold. How could I be oblivious to what shaped and influenced me and fail to think that Drake deserved to hear it from me and make an informed decision about his future?

I learned the scripture, "What you have said in the dark will be heard in the daylight" (Luke 12:3). I decided Drake would never know the truth about my past because I didn't have to tell him, and it didn't matter. However, God's word is truth. What I said to myself and others in the dark eventually came to light. The sad thing is these things didn't come to light before we married and had our son, Michael. I twisted the truth into lies and justified my deception of Drake.

I functioned in deception and called it God. I thought God had done the impossible by providing a man who wanted me. I was deluded, to say the least. My reality was nothing but a facade covering a lifetime of abuse. Still, I wouldn't risk Drake finding out. I believed marrying would change my past and how I felt about it. Marla, the foster mother I loved and still saw regularly, let me borrow her wedding dress. I only saw that I had a ring, a dress, and a future, and felt I was in a good place. I would leave my shamefully abusive last name behind. That name reminded me daily that I was a nobody, and it felt like everyone in my world knew it. Getting rid of that name would give me a fresh start. Even today, I find it hard to believe that I thought I could wipe away my previous life with a marriage certificate. I was so deluded, I must have thought changing my last name would erase people's ability to recognize me.

Drake's family was supportive; his mother and sisters attended the ceremony in Harold and Agnes' church. It was a simple ceremony without music, food, or friends. Briana was the only person from my family who attended. She supported me as much as she could. There were eight people in the huge sanctuary. It didn't matter to me if no one came. Harold—the same man who shattered my childhood—officiated to legally marry us in what had to be the saddest element of the ceremony. Harold performed the wedding as an ordained minister. Of course, I didn't see the irony of the older man who sexually abused me for years proclaiming a holy seal on my union to a younger man. All I could think about was changing my name and walking away from the abusive family associated with it.

I was convinced changing my name would change my life. I thought it would erase the pain and stop reminding others of my dreadful past. If only I had simply legally changed my name instead of ruining the life of a man who agreed to marry me without the opportunity to make an informed choice. Drake had no idea he had linked his life to a woman who would struggle for years before losing her mind to find her soul. Now I know I allowed Harold to perform the ceremony because I wanted to please him, make him proud, and show him that someone wanted me. I had to let Harold do the ceremony. Also, I wanted to honor Harold for giving me away since I called him Dad. That the marriage ceremony was performed by the man who sexually abused me haunted me until the marriage was dissolved twenty-three years later. After he married us, whenever I saw Harold, he told me, "Whatever you do, stay together." These words rang in my ears for twenty-three years, but now I know what he meant. He somehow prepared me for a future full of the damage he caused. He may not have known the exact impact of his sexual abuse, but he knew there would be a reckoning. Ironically, it was his words that drove me to get a divorce. I couldn't continue to live in the false world I fabricated and presented to others. I couldn't stay together with Drake in a marriage built on deception. I needed help to figure things out, and there was no one to guide me.

I was disappointed after saying *I do* because it seemed like nothing changed. Drake was kind and wonderful, but that wasn't what I was going for. I knew getting married, living as a wife, possibly a mother, and experiencing romantic times with my husband was a dream some women had, but not me. I dreamed that my new life—and name—would erase the emotional pain and damage from my childhood. I guess my expectations were too high. I expected everyone to treat me differently because I found a man and changed my name. I was no longer one of *them*—meaning my siblings. I felt as though I had escaped. I thought marrying would erase people's negative perception of me, the horrible name I was born with, and the shame that came with my name. When I think about it now, I see how ignorant and naive I was.

Drake's mother, Josetta, was a lovely mother-in-law. Tall with a big, beautiful smile, she treated me as if I were her child. Even now, I can visualize her bright, beautiful smile. I felt she loved me for who I was, not for what I could do. She didn't take sides. When Drake and I had a problem, she smiled and said, "You two will work it out."

Shortly after the wedding, Josetta and I shopped in a local, family-owned store with nice, if pricey, clothing. There were stores with more affordable clothing, but Drake's mother liked nice things. I was surprised when she took me to the coat section and explained that jackets weren't warm enough for winter weather. I didn't know that. I wore a light jacket because it was what I had, and I thought it was enough. She said I needed a coat. I was embarrassed that I had no coat, but her smile and love told me it was okay.

Then she said, "All my daughters have coats." Josetta bought a full-length, red wool coat with a black and red scarf. It was beautiful. The most beautiful thing wasn't the coat—it was the love I felt when she gave it to me. Josetta's kind of love was new to me. Later, I cried with overflowing emotions from her loving gesture. During my healing journey, I couldn't bear to look at the coat because it reminded me of the losses of marriage and family, so I donated it to someone who needed a coat. I wish I had kept it now that I can appreciate the love it represented.

Every year, when the family gathered for Christmas, Drake's mother ensured I had gifts under the tree. Josetta didn't like surprise gifts, so throughout the year when we shopped she had me select the things I wanted. Those items appeared beautifully gift-wrapped under the tree. Her generosity and assurance that the gifts were things I truly wanted touched me. Drake's family was the family I wished I'd had. They ate together, went to church together, and planned activities together. I stopped visiting my family because it was too painful, and I thought marrying into Drake's family would somehow erase the pain and emotional hurt of not having a loving family. Only Briana kept in touch; the older I got, the sadder our family situation became. I see now the pain of wishing my family had reunions or laughed and did things together was too great. It became easier to avoid them because they provoked residual symptoms of post-traumatic stress disorder (PTSD) and triggered sad memories. Years later, my siblings shared how they avoided me for the same reasons.

I vowed to make the best of the wonderful family I married into and not look back at the dysfunctional family I came from. I didn't know that when I buried my family and tried to bury the memories associated with them, I buried parts of me, too.

I thought my fantasy of an erased past had come true until, after we married, I ran into an older lady who knew Elsie and Buck well. She said, "I'm so proud of you. Nobody thought you would amount to anything. If anybody had an excuse to be nothing, y'all did." Drake walked up to us as she spoke. I'm certain he heard her say, *If anybody had an excuse to be nothing, y'all did.* I knew Drake to be the kind of man who didn't allow anything to ruffle his feathers, but I wasn't sure how he would react. I was on the verge of trembling, and I couldn't find a casual way to end the conversation. Drake still did not know the details of my family's abuse. I had only told him that I had a rough childhood. I hurried away to end the conversation, but it was too late. She had already said too much. Drake never acted like he cared what others thought of me, but I cared about the effect of others' words on him. I wanted to tell him that he had married down, but I couldn't. I married him, but the marriage didn't erase the fear that he would realize he had married someone he didn't know because she didn't know herself. When would he realize what a huge mistake it was to marry someone who had no idea how to be authentically herself?

Chapter 29
ELSIE'S LEGACY

Sadly, funerals became the de-facto family reunions for my siblings and me. Funerals offered a brief encounter with minimal conversation focused on the deceased. When I went to a funeral, I saw sisters, brothers, nieces, and nephews whom I hadn't seen in a while. Funerals were red-carpet events because we wanted everyone to know we were doing fine. Pitifully, we dressed as if fashion conveyed health and success. We tried to project financial success and noted the family member who was the most successful. Whether by fashion, finances, or cooking expertise, we competed to outdo each other. We thought if we were successful, it meant that we were smarter and better and had *made it.*

Two of the records I held for the longest time were *first to finish high school and graduate college* and y*oungest to marry, have a child in wedlock, and stay married.* Those were significant accomplishments among my siblings, and those achievements were my identity. However, my quest to hold the title of *youngest and first* meant I fought an invisible competition since none of my siblings were aware of it.

I felt pressured to be the matriarch, even though matriarchs aren't usually the youngest in the family. Still, we were a shattered family whose dreams and hopes were destroyed, and we couldn't afford to stand on tradition. Nothing about my family was normal, so the baby-as-matriarch wasn't unusual. Neither Denise nor Ava could take the position of matriarch because their lives were full of abuse and chaos. Maureen and Joleen were too damaged, and Jolene wasn't around to make any efforts to unite us. Briana's life was the epitome of *trauma drama.* She was unable to manage anything beyond her full house of children. Since my life looked the most stable and successful, I took on the mantle of matriarch. I vowed to make every effort to reunite us away from funerals. It would be many years before I achieved that goal, but for the last few years, we have made an effort to get together at Thanksgiving or Christmas, and we always have an amazing time together!

Looking at my life and the lives of my siblings, it is obvious that Elsie's life is indelibly imprinted on her children. Denise, Ava, and Jake were the product of her first coupling with a man in Louisiana we called the Creole Man. When

Denise was nine, Elsie and the children moved in with Buck. Denise left home at age fourteen to live with a series of older men. She never told us why she left home so early. I suspect it had something to do with Elsie falsely accusing her of sleeping with Buck as she did us. Eventually, Denise married Reese, a man with mental illness who physically and sexually abused his immediate and extended family. Denise stayed with him until his death. Denise's children have personality disorders, addictions, and mental illnesses.

Blessed are those who mourn, for they will be comforted.
Matthew 5:4

Ava left Elsie and Buck's house by age twelve. Ava was often with abusive men, including one who killed his wife. She then married an abusive man and had four children by the time she was twenty. Ava repeated Elsie's pattern of abandoning her children, leaving and returning over the years. By socioeconomic status, Ava's children are the most financially successful of Elsie's grandchildren. Their trauma didn't impede them cognitively as much as it did the others. None of Ava's children were incarcerated. Though they are self-supporting, their emotional damage cannot be measured or calculated. Still, they did not have close mother-child relationships with Ava due to the years of abandonment and rejection.

Blessed are the poor in spirit, for theirs is the Kingdom of Heaven.
Matthew 5:3

Jake was about five years old when Elsie met Buck. Buck treated Jake like lions treat cubs that don't belong to them; Buck wanted Jake out of the picture and often beat him. An acquaintance warned Uncle Harold that Buck was going to kill Jake if he didn't leave the household. What Elsie didn't realize is that Jake also wanted to kill Buck. One day Buck beat the little boy so badly he was almost unrecognizable. Elsie asked her Uncle to take Jake into his family, so Jake left to be raised by Harold and Agnes. By the end of elementary school, however, Jake was selling drugs, though he never used drugs himself. Perhaps he felt his only way to make money was the drug trade. Jake dropped out of school at twelve and ran away from Harold and Agnes' house. He learned about life from the streets.

I didn't meet Jake until I was living with Harold and Agnes. He was twenty-three and I was thirteen. I don't think he had ever seen me before then. I didn't know what to think or say. He was soft-spoken but obviously tough from his years on the streets. He definitely seemed like someone who could take care of himself and others, too. We were awkward with each other. I only knew a little about him, mostly from stories my sisters shared, but I was happy to meet him. He asked a few questions about my life and told me he knew I was a good student. He told me to stay out of trouble, and his concern for me made me feel like I finally had someone who could protect me if I ever needed it. Jake soon married and had children. He and his wife were abusive to one another, yet they were inseparable. It was a toxic relationship. A few years into the marriage, he left the state. I only saw Jake once after that, when he returned to visit his wife and children. His wife and children stayed in the city where I lived, and she claimed not to know where Jake lived. I was not close to his children at that time, though I've developed a relationship with most of them in our adulthood. A year after leaving Arkansas, Jake was found dead in California under mysterious circumstances. Jake's children suffered from their extremely complex traumas of domestic abuse, incarceration of parents, violent death of a parent, and alcoholism—all of which have repeated through the lives of his surviving children. One word to describe Jake would be wild because he acted and reacted like a wild animal without the proper training and care he needed.

Blessed are the merciful, for they will be shown mercy.
Matthew 5:7

Marcus was the first child of Elsie and Buck's relationship. He was born a normal, healthy boy but woke up with polio at the age of four, having contracted it before he could be vaccinated. Polio withered most of his right arm and left leg, causing a pronounced limp. His fingers shrank, and he developed a stutter. The saddest consequence of Marcus' polio was Elsie and Buck's decision to treat him like he was mentally deficient. One day, he was a normal kid; the next, his parents told him he couldn't read or write and treated him as if he couldn't learn. It wasn't long until he began to have difficulty learning. Marcus was nine years older than me. I never thought he was slow. He could count money faster than me, he understood how to fix complicated things like a car, he could drive almost any vehicle, tell time, and comprehend and enjoy the pleasures of life. He was approved for Social Security Disability around age six, so after that, my parents did not try to get educational or vocational assistance for him. He received a monthly check, which was enough for Elsie and Buck.

Marcus was the best big brother any sister could have. He was the one who stood up to Buck and Elsie and told them not to hit us. Even at a young age, Marcus told Buck if he hit Maureen or Jolene again, he would kill him. That memory is etched in my mind because I thought Buck and Elsie were going to kill Marcus. They didn't kill him, but they made his life miserable by making him haul several jugs of water with his handicapped arm, beating him until he bled, and threatening to kick him out of the house. They knew he had no other place to go.

Marcus understood what it meant to have character, a challenge for many who experienced the kind of complex trauma we did. He was known to keep his word. If he knew someone had a need, he tried to help them. He was honest and would not take anything from anyone without working for it. Although he was only a farmhand, his employers talked about his dependability, responsibility, and kindness. Marcus was kind and easily deceived by women who meant him no good. He lived with a few, and they often took advantage of him, wanting what they could buy with his disability check without wanting him. He finally met a beautiful soul who loved him. They were together for over twenty years until he passed away in 2021.

I never thought Marcus was different from anyone else, except for his physical appearance. Nothing kept him from working. He was a great employee and found work to do right up to the end of his life. He worked on several farms caring for animals. In 2018, a bull kicked him in the head while he fed the cattle. Marcus passed out, but miraculously woke up several hours later. He had lain in the field for hours in the torrid summer heat. Marcus didn't tell anyone until months later. When I discovered the injury, I took him to a doctor, who said he was fine. However, his limp gradually became more pronounced over the next couple of years until he could barely walk, and he lost the use of his unaffected arm. A few months before Marcus passed away in 2021, he was diagnosed by a different doctor who said he suffered a heat stroke while lying in the pasture after the bull kicked his head. The heatstroke damaged his motor skills, which explained why he couldn't walk or work much during the final year of his life.

Marcus was a helper because he helped those who needed him and never met a stranger he didn't befriend.

Blessed are the pure in heart, for they shall see God.
Matthew 5:8

Maureen and her twin sister, Dot, were born a year after Marcus' birth, so Maureen was eight years older than me. Unfortunately, Dot died at around six months, probably from SIDS. I don't remember much about growing up with Maureen because I was still a toddler when she was removed from our home by a child welfare agency following the incident when Buck and Elsie burned her and Jolene on the stove. Most of my memories of Maureen were of her infrequent visits. When she visited, she usually brought a boyfriend with her. Maureen had five children and miscarried one. She produced Buck and Elsie's first grandchild, and Elsie was excited whenever Maureen brought her to visit. One of Maureen's daughters preceded her in death. The family believes she never overcame the pain of losing her daughter. She conquered many obstacles and disappointments, but the loss of her daughter was her deepest pain.

Maureen's abuse—beatings, burning, and even being locked in a trunk—spurred our first removal from the family home. Our family's chronic complex abuse left Maureen with visible—and invisible—physical, mental, and emotional scars that never seemed to heal. Maureen was not lazy. She worked in construction and other manual labor usually done by men. She mainly held seasonal employment, and the jobs usually ended after a few months. Maureen's children were unaware of their mother's trauma until her oldest daughter's boyfriend's mother asked where her people were from, and Maureen's daughter told her Maureen's name and family name. The boyfriend's mother gasped and told her Maureen was the one who was burned. Maureen's daughter then asked me what happened, and I told her.

Maureen legally married for the first time in her early fifties and then moved to upstate New York. We hoped this was real love and she would be happy, but the marriage lasted only three years. All of Maureen's relationships were abusive. Maureen passed generational trauma to her children. All of them deal with the trauma differently—whether it's emotional, mental, or physical problems—and they reveal signs of generational trauma. The good news is that several of Maureen's children are learning the effects of trauma, and that's a start.

One word I would use to describe Maureen is strength because she endured vile persecution. True to research about the effects of CT on the heart, she passed away in 2020 from heart disease.

Blessed are those who have been persecuted for the sake of righteousness,
for theirs is the kingdom of heaven.
Matthew 5:10

During the final ten years of Elsie and Buck's *marriage*, Elsie had four children by other men: Jolene, Mathus, Briana, and me. Buck often bitterly complained that he took care of other men's children. Unquestionably, his resentment of Elsie's infidelity added to the malicious ways he abused these children in particular.

Jolene is seven years older than me. Because she was removed from the home at the same time as Maureen, I don't have many childhood memories of her because Jolene was permanently removed. Growing up, I often missed her and longed to see her.

Jolene has a big smile and love radiates from her heart. She was burned at the same time as Maureen, but her injuries did not require extensive care in the hospital burn unit. As adults, we intentionally avoided one another for several years. I know it was because we couldn't bear our shared pain. I was in college when I reunited with Jolene. She was living with her boyfriend when Briana took me to meet her. We visited for about an hour. I was overwhelmed and didn't want to leave. I had many questions that would go unasked until years later.

Jolene told me her life story on one of our many road trips to see Marcus in 2019. I cried so much I couldn't see the highway. The thought of her having to go through her trials alone made the tears come so fast that I couldn't see to drive. I had to pull to the side of the road and cry with her. I felt so much pain when she told me about her experiences. I am so thankful to know Jolene and love her. By 2019, I had learned more about Childhood Trauma and worked with trauma survivors. It hurt so much to think about how Jolene survived burning on a stove, only to suffer more trauma from the people who were supposed to protect her.

After leaving Buck and Elsie's, Jolene lived in several foster homes, but she ran away from most of them only for the state to place her in another one. The cycle continued until, at age ten, she went into a residential girls' school, where she remained for almost two years before running away. Jolene was labeled a juvenile delinquent because she kept running away. She manifested many of the behaviors of traumatized children. In her final foster home, the father raped her, and she became pregnant. Jolene's rapist forced her to have an abortion, but she did not reveal his identity as the father of her child for fear of destroying his family. After that, her foster mother made her leave, and at twelve, she went to Harold and Agnes' house to live, where she stayed for almost a year before she ran away. That was the last time she ran away. At thirteen, much like our older siblings, she decided to live as an adult.

Jolene never dated much, so she was naive when choosing men. She met Buddy in her pre-teens while she lived with her last set of foster parents. He was her foster sister's boyfriend. He gave her his number and told her to call if she needed him. When Jolene ran away from Harold and Agnes' house, she ran to the town where Buddy lived. Buddy was physically, emotionally, and mentally abusive to Jolene, but she stayed with him for nearly twenty years. He had angry outbursts and expressed his rage by beating her. After multiple near-death injuries, she escaped.

Buddy never allowed Jolene to get a job, so she had few marketable employment skills when she left him. She asked God to bless her with a job because she knew she wasn't employable. Happily, she got a job at a fast-food restaurant. She was determined and reliable. She couldn't drive, so she got up early to catch the 5:00 a.m. bus. Then, she walked to work from the bus stop.

Years after escaping Buddy, Jolene dated another man, but that didn't go well because he wanted her to take care of him, and by that time, she had learned enough about abuse to recognize and reject it. She stayed with him for a few years and then made a declaration to God and us: I will be alone before I allow another man to beat or misuse me. She was single for almost seven years before meeting Alfred, the love of her life.

Jolene has been happily married for nearly twenty years. In her mid-fifties, she and her husband adopted three children. She is overcoming trichotillomania and other nerve issues and is a true testimony to the goodness of God. When I think of Jolene, I think of laughter because regardless of what she went through, she maintained her contagious laugh.

For you, O Lord, are good and forgiving, abounding in steadfast
love to all who call upon you.
Psalm 86:5

Mathus, five years older than me, was born with a bad heart. He spent several weeks-long stints in the hospital. Doctors told Elsie and Buck they had to take special care of Mathus. We always believed they treated him with kid gloves because they were afraid he would die and people would think they killed him. This would not have gone well with the other abuse reports that had already circulated through the community and Child Welfare Services. Mathus didn't get beatings like the rest of us. In fact, I can't remember him ever getting hit by Elsie or Buck. Mathus knew they couldn't whip him, so he took advantage of it. He fought Elsie and pushed her down a few times. I remember being afraid that he would hurt her. She would get up and act as if nothing happened.

Although I lacked a close relationship with Elsie, I didn't want Mathus to hurt her. She was still my mother, if only through a biological connection.

We feared Mathus and what he might do. As a teenager, he didn't want to work and couldn't stand for anyone to tell him anything, so he often broke into homes to steal whatever he believed he needed. He avoided detection, and he never went to jail. Mathus told us he has children, but we've never seen them because he never brought them to meet us. He was diagnosed with type 2 diabetes. Mathus was married for five years and seemed to live a normal life until his wife said he was impossible to live with and divorced him. Shortly after, he married again. His diabetes worsened, and he had to have both legs amputated, which deepened his bitterness. He had two stepchildren to whom he was neglectful and verbally and physically abusive as he passed on another cycle of generational abuse. He died from complications of diabetes when he was in his forties.

Mathus was a risk-taker. He loved experimenting and trying things most people feared, like riding motorcycles, driving sports cars, and swimming in deep lakes and rivers.

The Lord is good to all; He has compassion on all He has made.
Psalm 145:9

Briana is next to the youngest of the siblings, two years older than me. She was the other beautiful one—the one who caused people to do a double-take when she passed by. Elsie loved Briana's hair and the way Briana wanted to be around her. I can't say Elsie truly loved Briana, as much as Elsie liked that Briana seemed to love her. While with Elsie, Briana saw things she should not have seen and went places she should not have gone. Elsie took Briana to adult clubs, where Briana saw women and men in sexual activities with Elsie. Briana reported that at least one of Elsie's boyfriends attempted to assault her sexually and that after Elsie left him, Buck attempted to rape Briana when she was eleven years old. Whenever Buck took me to visit Elsie, Briana had wild stories of money and men.

Briana was physically beautiful with long, wavy hair. Her biological father was rumored to be a man of mixed race who looked more Hispanic than Black. Briana told me she never fit in well with the Black kids at school—perhaps because of her lighter skin. Growing up, Briana was hard. She was gruff on the outside, but that rough exterior was her protection. I was soft and would cry quickly. Briana did not cry. She was the one who thought things through, saved her money, and escaped from Buck to live with Elsie. Her sense of self-preservation led to periods of homelessness as well as staying in multiple homes of relatives and the homes of Elsie's boyfriends. That period of instability and negative exposure undoubtedly planted the seed of instability and chaos that bloomed full flower as Briana grew older. Whenever her adult life settled down, she found a way to upset the calm and create new drama, repeating the pattern that began with her time with Elsie. She wanted frequent change, which contributed to multiple unstable, short-term relationships and the births of five children—until she married the man who would be her husband for ten years.

Briana is a hard worker. She worked to support herself and provide for her children from age sixteen. At one point, she had five small children while managing a burger restaurant. She was determined to memorize the entire menu. She studied late at night but found it difficult to remember the many options for each of the menu's burgers. She asked me to help create a strategy to memorize the menu offerings, so I created a mnemonic device that kept everything straight. I was so proud when she achieved her goal.

Like my other sisters, Briana lacked nurturing skills and was emotionally numb, but she did her best to raise her children. Despite her efforts, her children are undoubtedly traumatized from the men she had in her life and the extreme physical, verbal, and emotional abuse they brought. Briana's marriage was extremely abusive. She was injured multiple times, and police were routinely called to intervene in their domestic violence. She refused to press charges or even to report the abuse—a mirror of our lives as children when we protected our abusers by not telling people what our parents did to us. One night, while she was away from their home, Briana's husband was murdered. The case remains open and bubbles up in the media occasionally. Briana deals with the effects of the abuse she suffered as a child and from her husband. Although she struggles with addiction, Briana helps other survivors escape and overcome domestic abuse while she is also trying to overcome the dragons that continue to shadow her.

A phrase to describe Briana is faith-filled because she has a lot of faith in God. She is the one who taught me to have strong faith. From childhood, Briana always believed God would provide and care for her.

***Blessed are those who hunger and thirst for righteousness,
for they will be satisfied.***
Matthew 5:6

Chapter 30
PREGNANCY

I was pregnant less than six weeks after the wedding. Before I had time to adjust to marriage, I was surprised to face an impending birth and the responsibilities that lay ahead. Drake was supportive and happy but worried because he had recently graduated. Neither of us had full-time employment, so we had no health insurance. Regrettably, I didn't know medical insurance was available through the college. I was still six months from graduating, married, and pregnant.

After his graduation, Drake and I moved to my hometown to be closer to Harold. Drake was offered a job in the city where we went to college, but accepted a position where I grew up with a non-profit organization that weatherized houses for needy residents. I was glad because I wanted to give back to Uncle Harold. Agnes had died during our engagement year, and I was concerned about Uncle Harold because a church member said he needed someone to help him adjust to life without Agnes. I was concerned that he would get depressed and die shortly after his wife, a pattern fairly common with long-married couples. Once again, I thought the worst would happen.

I needed two more classes to graduate. One class was in my university's first term of summer school, and the other was in the second summer term at a university near the town where we moved. After the move, I drove daily to a university seventy-five miles away. Driving one hundred fifty miles roundtrip each day while pregnant and living close to Harold and the scene of much of my abuse was a level of stress I do not recommend.

Graduation in August 1988 was a quiet celebration of my greatest achievement. Drake and I drove back to our college town for the weekend to observe the culmination of my life's efforts to be somebody. After years of struggle to find stable ground, to complete the required coursework, and to run from my past, I had a diploma certifying that Dora Wallace (married name) had a college degree and was officially *somebody*. I was too overwhelmed by the stress of the summer classes, first-trimester pregnancy, and taking care of Harold to enjoy the moment. I only remember feeling relief that I had reached the goal I had held dear for most of my life. None of my family members attended, but some of Drake's family came. I was too exhausted to care.

I thought once I crossed the stage, I would feel the cloud of impending danger disappear. It didn't. Achievements don't fill the void of low self-worth or automatically increase confidence. I soon learned I had a sincere desire to save other children from abuse because I could not save myself. That is what would give me confidence.

My first post-college, professional-level job was as an administrative assistant at the Department of Human Services in the town where Harold lived. It enabled me to work and care for him after his wife died. The church had drilled into me about taking care of family even when family didn't take care of me. I was happy to be employed and to contribute to the family income, but taking a clerical job in the city where I grew up was not a smart choice. CT survivors who suffer complex traumas can't make smart choices until they get therapy or healing in their prefrontal cortex.

The clerical job was stressful because part of my job was to retrieve folders for the case managers. The folders were in alphabetical order in a huge file cabinet, and each time I opened the "M" drawer, I saw Elsie and Buck's names. It brought back memories of physical abuse, Elsie's long periods of abandonment, interminable hospital nights, and bathing in the rice ditches from the pump used to irrigate the fields. The unexpected challenges, triggers, and residuals from the abuse flooded my mind. Most came from daily reminders of my childhood when I went to the "M" drawer. Some came from the nature of the work. Other triggers came from working in a place that I believed let me down when I most needed their assistance. I couldn't forget that this office of the Department of Human Services (DHS) and the people who worked there missed our incredible need for rescue when they overlooked our obvious violent abuse and did not permanently remove us from our parents.

I wondered if our abuse was ever officially reported. *Why did the DHS authorities choose to stay silent? Why were we sent back to our parents? Were our parents ever warned to stop the abuse?* These questions lingered in the recesses of my mind, but they came to the forefront when I began working in the same office that ignored our distress. Childhood Trauma had already left my body in a state of fight, flight, or freeze, so knowing what was reported wouldn't be the worst thing that could happen to me.

Some of my family members still received public assistance so I could look at the family file. I felt an oppressive heaviness whenever I walked near the file cabinet with my family records. Like an ominous cloud, it followed me to the break room, lunch, and conferences. It seemed to be everywhere. There was shame when I passed the file cabinet. I felt shame when I heard a family member's name spoken. I was ashamed when one of them missed an appointment, and I had to reschedule it for them. There was shame when I overheard the managers talk about them. I felt ashamed for taking public assistance, even if only briefly. I felt I had failed in every way. I tried so hard to be different from my siblings, but I was exactly like them at this point in my life. It was devastating. I saw them as welfare recipients—assistance that I believed only the poor and destitute should receive. I couldn't distinguish myself from them anymore, even though I had a college education and was legally married. I was back in my hometown because of a choice to help Harold—another case of a victim assisting their abuser—and not because I was stuck with multiple children by multiple mothers/fathers, which was the profile of some of my siblings. Moving back was not a good choice, but I knew Harold had no other family to care for him. Ava no longer visited Harold. He had his church family but no family members.

On top of everything, I was three months pregnant. Although he was unborn, I was sure my baby felt my emotional pain. Most days, my stomach was in knots. The stress eased only when I left the office to go home, but it returned each morning when I walked back into the government building.

On a day when only a few people were at work, I stood at the file cabinet with unshed tears and silently asked *Why? Why so much shame? Why was I born? Why do I want to crawl into a hole and disappear? Why did I get married, much less pregnant, after such a shameful past?* I paused and answered those questions as though I spoke to someone else. I knew I got married because I thought I could leave shame behind with the shameful family name. How could I know shame would attach itself to me and, like a leech, drain the tiny amount of security and confidence I believed having a husband and marriage brought me? My shame played in my mind like a song stuck on repeat. *You think you're something now that you have a college degree, but you'll never be anything. Your family is nothing.* I couldn't pause or delete it. I stood in front of the file cabinet, trying to visualize how I would react if the files reported something different than I expected. Officially, no action was taken to protect my siblings and me. I wanted to know what happened to Maureen and Jolene and whether my parents were arrested or charged. I wanted to know if there was a report of abuse of the older siblings Denise, Ava and Jake—were they abused like the children I grew up with? The biggest question I had was if there was a report of the death of Maureen's twin sister, Dot. I was immobilized by fear of finding out.

I thought *What if I read something I'm not ready to handle?* I was concerned I might be unable to control my feelings and emotions. My heart raced, and my palms sweated. I trembled as I opened the file drawer and needed to use the restroom simultaneously, but I found the file. I thought I would pass out. Before I could remove the file from the drawer, a voice interrupted my thoughts, "They're calling you over the intercom." One of my colleagues stood in the doorway.

I realized I had come to pull case files for the manager and was so distracted by the proximity to my family file that I had forgotten my task. I pulled the requested cases quickly and hurried down the hall to deliver them to the case manager. I never did read that file; I was always interrupted or was afraid of what I would find.

As I walked down the hall, I heard someone say, "Jean, is that you?"

If I were from an honorable family, I would have gladly turned around, but because of my family's past, I knew whoever said my name only knew me through the abuse we suffered. My first name was Dora and my middle name was Jean, and only people who knew me from my childhood called me by my middle name. I moved away for college and hoped I had changed enough that people wouldn't recognize me. I was married and pregnant and hoped I was less recognizable. I didn't turn around until I was sure I had my face and mind in a neutral expression. I had to look my best, think ahead of whoever this was, and anticipate a response to what they might say. I was on guard every day I worked in the DHS office, always alert for what the townspeople might say. Being in fight or flight mode daily was severely stressful.

Slowly, I turned around. It was Carol, someone I knew from my old neighborhood and elementary school. She knew me before I knew her because she knew Elsie and Buck. Her grandparents loathed my parents and wouldn't allow them to mistreat us in their club/adult hangout. Her grandparents told her as much about me as they knew. Whenever I saw Carol, she told me she knew everything about me. The fear of people from my childhood kept me focused on hiding the past. It wasn't until I was healed years later that I realized I didn't need anyone's approval. Once God freed me from me, and I processed what happened and released it, I didn't care who held on to it. I was free.

"Jean! How long has it been since I've seen you?"

"About ten years," I responded.

"Where have you been?"

"College." I knew to answer only the questions asked.

"You work here?"

"Yes."

"How long have you worked here?"

"A month."

"That's so good, Jean."

I got nervous. I feared what she might say next. "You're pregnant?" she asked.

"And I'm married," I replied before she could ask. I inserted that as if it somehow made a difference. My siblings were unwed mothers and fathers, and one of the things I wanted to do differently was to marry before having children. I thought people would see I was different from my sisters. I worked hard to gain distance from my family's shameful reputation, only to find out that because I was damaged internally, shame stayed with me.

"That's good, Jean." Carol said it matter-of-factly as if it were no big deal. I wondered how she could so quickly gloss over the fact that I was married before having a child. It was one of those look-at-me-versus-them moments, and I wanted the recognition of being more virtuous.

"I was recently thinking about your sisters and brothers," Carol continued. "I think about you frequently and wonder what happened to you and your siblings. How's Maureen? It's a shame what your mom and dad did to y'all," she said as she grabbed my hand.

I knew this was coming. Whenever I saw someone from my childhood, they reminded me of what my parents did to us. I stood frozen. I thought I was more mature and able to handle these comments now. I was only a toddler when the most horrible abuse happened to my siblings. *What made people feel like they had to remind me of it?*

I wanted to snatch my hand from Carol and say *I don't want or need your sympathy. I could have used it then, but not now. I made it out of that hellhole. Now, let bygones be bygones,* but I didn't say it. I stood there while she went on about how proud she was of me, but I was more annoyed at how I allowed her earlier comments to affect me. I felt anxious. I wanted to run and hide, but there was nowhere to go. I was where everything began, confronted yet again by someone who knew and didn't help. I guess those folks thought they could alleviate their guilt by saying something pitying to me now. As an adult, I didn't need their pity; I needed their compassion and action when I was a child.

I thought marriage and a baby would change the community's perception of me. I learned people wanted to remind me of their memories, making it impossible to forget what happened. What little of the trauma I managed to forget or repress, the pseudo-well-wishing people rekindled. I felt the trauma in my quivering hands and my watery eyes as they discussed it. I heard the cries of Maureen and Jolene and smelled the stench of their burned skin each time anyone mentioned it. Childhood Trauma was stored in my amygdala—using my five senses to arouse emotions and recall the feelings surrounding the incident.

"She's doing well." What did Carol expect to hear? *Maureen experienced such grisly trauma to her body and mind at a young age that it still impacts her mentally, physically and emotionally.* I didn't think Carol asked out of concern. I think she asked for the same reason everyone asked—they were nosey and wanted to remind me of my lowly station as one of the poorest children who grew up in that town with mentally ill parents. My past was now my present, and it seemed like it would go into my future.

I think Carol felt momentary regret because she shifted the conversation. I could see she noticed my disposition and that I was not pleased. I wanted to break down, runaway, find a place to hide, and never return to that office where people kept reminding me of my past.

"So what made you come back this way?" she asked. What I heard her say was *Girl, if I were you, I would have run and kept on running and never looked back.*

"I moved back to help with Uncle Harold," I replied. It was a noble thing to do, but when people want to think the worst, they are not inclined to hear the best. I felt nauseated, and the room seemed to spin. I mustered up enough strength to walk away. It felt like my feet left the floor, and I floated away from Carol. I prayed as I left, *Lord, please don't let her ask me anything else.* I needed fresh air and headed to the break room.

When I reached the break room, I could feel the eyes on me, as if my co-workers heard the conversation and knew how it affected me. Instead of entering, I walked down the corridor to the exit doors. I didn't have my purse or keys, so they knew I wasn't leaving or taking a break, and they knew I didn't smoke, but I couldn't worry about them or what they might think. I needed protection. I had to get away from everyone in that building. I walked past the smokers and kept going. I had to regroup, or I knew I would break down in front of everyone.

I am not my past. I recalled the speech I used to give as a young girl. *I am somebody special. I am not my parents. I am a good person. I have a degree. I am trying to change.*

The more I encouraged myself, the more I realized I had changed, but people's perception of me hadn't. They lived in my past, and I was living in my present.

I allowed their memories of the past to impact my present. I took a few deep breaths, pulled my shoulders back and decided I couldn't let these people upset me, make me lose my baby, or take me back to my childhood. I was determined to rise above their perceptions.

Chapter 31
BUNDLE OF BLESSING

I hardly went a week without seeing someone who knew our story, and even if they didn't know it, I thought they did. I thought everyone knew it. Each time I saw them, whether in a grocery store, gas station, or a dinner event, my stomach clenched. I forgot how small the world was. I worked at DHS when I was twenty-two, barely ten years after my mother's death. Theoretically, I knew the little town where I grew up was only a few miles away, but I didn't anticipate the townspeople's recognition. I should have known better because what happened to us spread like wildfire. I spent four years in college trying to live down my family's past, only to move down the road to be reminded of it at every turn. Most of our community knew Elsie, Buck, my biological father, and my siblings. The community's perception of us had not changed, and I was left to struggle with shame, guilt, low self-esteem, and no sense of identity.

I had little appetite during pregnancy, and I couldn't unlearn the disordered eating habits I developed as a child. Eating was important because I had gone without food for days or existed on a single apple. While pregnant, I intentionally focused on healthy nutrition. Drake and Briana ensured that I would not skip meals. Briana made sure I ate a home-cooked meal daily. She moved in with Denise during my pregnancy and cooked dinner every evening. Drake and I went to Denise's house after work, ate dinner, and then went home. When I arrived each evening after work, dinner was ready. I enjoyed it because I could sit down and eat. I was a size one when I married, but I wore size twenty-two pants by the eighth month of pregnancy. People often commented that I might have twins because my belly was so huge.

We needed financial assistance, but Drake had a job, so we didn't qualify for Medicaid, and his medical insurance did not cover my pregnancy since it was designated a pre-existing condition. We were approved for the Women, Infants, and Children supplemental assistance (WIC). I was grateful but once again felt ashamed to accept government financial support. We certainly needed whatever help we could get. Stressful flashbacks of my family receiving government assistance reminded me of my sisters' pattern. Being on assistance didn't fit my narrative of escaping the family curse or being somebody.

My emotions were all over the place, no doubt exacerbated by pregnancy hormones. I internalized the stigma of being a pregnant welfare recipient. I felt unattractive, emotionally unstable, and stressed out from being in the town I tried to escape. Although we moved into our own place, I was still stressed because I never knew when or what someone would tell Drake about me. I worried about Drake discovering the truth of my heritage. Back then, all I needed was a television script because I was using the same manipulation, control, and deception I despised in soap operas.

Through it all, I was determined to have a healthy baby. I thought positively, ate nutritious foods, and did what I could to boost my chances for a physically and mentally healthy baby. Drake and I played music, read, and talked to my stomach to let our little one know how much we anticipated his arrival.

One thing that provided peace during my pregnancy was a dream about my unborn son. I dreamed he was speaking in front of thousands of people. Then, I awakened with the revelation of the dream. I knew Michael would be a gifted little boy. True to the dream, he was a gifted little boy who would one day shake audiences with his orations.

Drake did as much as he could to keep my life calm and peaceful. He tried to ensure I avoided Briana's drama with her children, her partying, and the repeated physical abuse she suffered from the men she dated. He knew her actions greatly affected me, and what affected me affected my unborn baby. I treated Briana's kids as if they were mine. I didn't want them to miss out on anything, and I frequently lectured Briana about how her actions affected her children. Research shows childhood exposure to traumatic experiences of abuse, violence, and neglect increases the likelihood of perpetuating maltreatment. Children who experience trauma—without intervention, treatment, or healing—continue the cycle of intergenerational abuse, violence, and neglect.

Our abusive childhoods clearly affected my siblings and me, but I wasn't yet able to connect their adult dysfunctions to our abusive childhood. When one of them did something destructive, I thought it was intentional because I hadn't studied how early adversities restructure the brain and impair decision-making, especially in personal safety. Briana and I were so close that I had to mentally release her several times before I could fully emotionally release her. I always felt an obligation to rescue her and her children from bad situations, but it was dangerous, either because of the type of men Briana dated, or it was too emotionally draining for me. Her unhealthy lifestyle did not align with ours, but releasing her meant letting her go, and I could not let her go. As an adult, I felt responsible for her, much like she felt responsible for me when we were children. It is not uncommon for survivors to feel responsible for family members who make bad choices. Along with false responsibility, survivors take on false guilt and shame. Sometimes I felt guilty for going to college when she didn't. I felt guilty for *making it,* so to speak, while my sister didn't make it.

The co-dependency Briana and I shared was undoubtedly from our mother's many disappointments, emptiness, and neglect. I held on to Briana more than I should have because she was the only sibling who remained in my life. We both needed the stability of knowing that no matter what, we had each other, because that's how we survived childhood. Survival skills don't disappear with adulthood. In fact, by the time we were adults, fears, co-dependencies, and distrust were so deeply ingrained in our habits and psyches that we responded to situations and people from our survival brains.

Pregnancy heightened the effects of my exposure to trauma during childhood. I had bouts of crying with persistent thoughts of having to beat my child, abandon my child, or be unable to love my child. These fears escalated as I awaited his birth. I was fearful day and night. Eventually, the fear of losing the baby became greater than the fear of living with the consequences of giving him life. Above all, I didn't want to harm him. I never had a thought of harming him, but the fear consumed me with thoughts of leaving him with his dad and running away so he wouldn't suffer like we did. I wouldn't do to my child what our parents did to us. I saw the cycle of child abuse and neglect repeated by my brothers and sisters, and I feared it would happen to me and my child. My parental models were Buck and Elsie, Denise and Reese, and Ava and Tommy, so I had a dark view of parenting. The abuse I witnessed and endured was so horrific I would do almost anything to keep from damaging my child. At that point in life, I didn't yet know any of the science in the field of trauma. I thought violent child abuse might be transmitted genetically, and I couldn't risk that.

Thoughts of harming my child spiraled to worrying about how to perform the basic tasks of caring for him. I was convinced I wouldn't know how to change his diapers or feed and bathe him. Although Briana's behavior was inconsistent, I decided she could be my resource. She already had three children and hadn't lost any of them. She showed some mothering instincts when we were younger and taught me how to handle female issues properly. When I didn't know or understand something about my body, I asked Briana. I often turned to her for guidance and direction in caring for my son. Although we both suffered severe trauma, we developed different coping mechanisms. I ran when emotionally overwhelmed, but Briana shut down emotionally or turned to men and substances—all to numb her pain. She often sought out someone in need to be their motherly figure and feel valued. The children in Briana's neighborhood called her mother because she regularly fed them, gave them a place to stay, and bought clothes for some of them.

Two weeks before my due date, I drove through the post office parking lot to put mail in the outdoor letterbox. While sitting in the car, someone hit me from behind. I was rushed to the hospital, where I was kept on bed rest, lying flat on my back until the contractions began—exactly on my due date. I was terrified that it would affect the baby. Although my injuries were minor, concerns for my baby's health and safety were paramount. As I spent the period of bed rest with few distractions, my thoughts threatened to sabotage the positive preparations I made. *What if* questions flooded my mind: *What if the baby is born sick? What if I don't feed him enough? What if he has physical or developmental problems?* I was in no shape to take care of myself, much less an infant. Childhood Trauma affected my ability to think positively, and I worried unceasingly. Self-doubts preoccupied me: *Who do I think I am getting married, having a baby and living in a house? I'm an imposter. I don't deserve to have a family.* The negative thoughts and voices were louder than the ones that said *I deserve this. I survived my childhood. I can do this.*

I was physically twenty-three years old—but emotionally only twelve. I panicked when thinking about what to do with a real baby. Pregnancy affected every part of me. Carrying a baby inside me and feeling him grow was a miracle. I was thankful for the dream about my son speaking to crowds because it gave me hope that he would be a productive citizen, but when I thought about motherhood, fight or flight kicked in. There were days I functioned in a fog, wondering who would teach this baby and what I would do with him. I convinced myself I was incapable of mothering based on my experience with Elsie. The *flight* mode manifested in wanting to run—like Elsie—rather than learn how to mother. I chose to *fight,* which was stressful because it was an interior battle. Others couldn't see or help me with the struggle. I loved my son and wanted him to have a better life than I did.

I understand now that my fear of not knowing how to care for him was unsubstantiated because some innate instincts came with the hormones of pregnancy, childbirth, and lactation to help guide my thoughts in the early days following his birth. I also watched Josetta and thought often of how Marla mothered her children. I avoided comparing my mothering style to my sisters' because I knew they were not the examples I wanted to follow. I acted on the information from the renowned American pediatrician Dr. Spock's book, *Baby and Childcare*.

We researched names but didn't find one we felt was right for our baby until the final month of pregnancy. Someone gave me a book with the names of children. I studied the Bible and knew the importance of names, so Drake and I chose a name representing God. In my emotionally twelve-year-old mind, I thought that if I delayed naming him, it would give me more time to prepare.

Sooner than I expected, it was time to have the baby. I talked with a few mothers about giving birth and took the hospital birthing class, but nothing eased my fear of childbirth. I read a few books, but the books didn't prepare me for what happened. I'd heard childbirth could be a near-death experience, so I thought I had to prepare to die for my baby to live. When the time came to deliver, I had to be strong. I trembled from head to toe. We wanted to have a natural delivery, if possible. I pushed several times. After several pushes without a baby emerging, the doctor said the baby was in fetal distress and would give me one more opportunity to push him out. If the baby did not come, then I would be rushed to surgery—exactly what I did not want. The nurses sterilized my stomach to prepare for surgery.

I said, "Wait, I have one more push." I was determined to avoid surgery. I said a quick prayer and asked God to let him come. I took a deep breath and said aloud, "In the name of the Father, Son, and the Holy Spirit," and gave a powerful push. My son, Michael, came out into the doctor's waiting hands.

For a second, the room was silent. I didn't yet know the power of prayer and the name of Jesus as I do now. Of course, I had read about it and heard it was powerful, but in that moment of desperation, I experienced God's power on a new level in an unusual and unplanned way. I was silent, but I never forgot the power of that moment and how it made me feel when I called on Him in desperation, and He answered my prayer. It would be another twenty years before I would fully understand how powerful it was to call on the name of God for help. Even when I didn't yet know God, He knew me, heard my cry, and helped me.

I was exhausted and anxious when the doctor placed Michael on my chest. Out of the many conversations I had about labor and delivery, none of them mentioned the panic and anxiety I experienced when his skin touched mine. I felt as if I could stop breathing at any moment as he lay on my breast. The obstetrical staff and Michael's father were excited and clapped for the delivery because they knew how close we were to a surgical intervention. I, on the other hand, was terrified as I pleaded silently for someone to help me. They noticed my distress as Michael lay on my chest and rushed to get him. For years, I wondered why I couldn't let him lay bare on my chest or hold him when he was first delivered. Now I know the intimacy of the moment was too much because of the sexual abuse.

Chapter 32
GROWING UP WITH MICHAEL

By the time Michael was a toddler, I realized that I was not fit for parenthood. Childhood Trauma affects every aspect of one's life and distorts one's thought processes. I didn't know what to do or say with a toddler. I fumbled through the baby stage because it mostly required simply feeding and clothing him and making sure he was clean and safe. I couldn't fumble through the toddler stage because it required more parenting, foresight, and wisdom. My exposure to good parental models was severely limited. There was so much I didn't know and feared about parenting that it crippled me from doing what I did know. I had moments where I felt compelled to act on something Michael said or did. One of them was when Michael did something naughty, and I said *no* or *stop* several times, but he continued to insist on getting his way. In one of those incidents, I got my belt and was about to whip Michael when Drake stopped me.

"What are you doing?" he questioned.

"I'm about to whip Michael," I proclaimed angrily.

"No. You're not whipping my baby with that. You don't whip a baby with a belt. He's only a baby," he said, looking at me in disbelief.

I walked away, embarrassed and ashamed, thinking *I didn't even know how to discipline my child.* Fear and negative thoughts rushed in again like life-long friends and began bombarding me: *You didn't know how to be a mother. You are going to hurt your child. You should run away. You are going to be exactly like Elsie.*

For a few days after that incident, I was afraid to touch Michael for fear I might hurt him. I didn't trust my instincts or judgment regarding him after that because I realized I didn't know right from wrong. How could I teach Michael right from wrong when I didn't know the difference between punishment and discipline? This was years before I learned about the long-term impact of physical abuse on a child. I only knew that I could not be trusted to discipline my child when my sole idea of discipline was to punish physically. For years after that, I felt inadequate as a parent. My feelings of inadequacy became so great that I told Drake, "If we ever get a divorce or something happens, I want you to take Michael because I want him to have the best training and love, and you can give him that. I wouldn't know what to do with him, and I couldn't give him what you can." Drake may have thought the same thing because he didn't argue or try to talk me out of my position.

However, from then on, I understood the difference between abuse and punishment. Because I did not have an example of healthy discipline, I would have resorted to what was done to me. Thankfully, Drake taught me how to discipline my son correctly. Unfortunately, many abused mothers don't get training to stop the cycle. Abuse is then recycled from generation to generation.

I was afraid to discipline Michael because I had no idea how to do it. I had no skills or a toolbox of approaches. I was afraid to be with him and worried about raising him alone. I had abandonment issues from the repeated absences of my mother. I thought my inadequacies, insecurities, and low self-esteem would go away once I had a child, but I also thought they would go away when I graduated from college and when I got married, and of course, they didn't. Neither having a child, a great job, nor buying a house helped me develop self-assurance and self-worth. I felt neither Michael nor Drake needed me. I had brokenness and loneliness that neither a child nor a man could fix. How silly of me to think marriage would obliterate my emotional pain and the desire to be loved. I thought motherhood would do it, but it didn't. I tried to find an external cure for an internal malady: multiple abuses and neglect. The internal pain stemmed from my childhood, and unfortunately, nothing obtained externally could cure it. It could only be cured when I addressed it, acknowledged its damage, and applied God's word to heal it.

I continued to fear I might leave Michael, much like Elsie abandoned her children. That thought was perpetually in the back of my mind. I tried to prepare Michael and Drake in case I had to leave. I often told Michael, "You have the best father ever. You are so blessed." I was insecurely attached to Michael because of Elsie's frequent abandonment. I wanted Michael to be fine. I wanted him to know his father loved him dearly. I had no idea of my value as my son's mother and the importance of my connection with him. At that point in my life, I did not understand that a child's mental health, balanced emotions, and a well-adjusted sense of self are developed by input from both parents; the lack of either parent leaves a child with deep emotional wounds.[11] My son grew to adulthood before I understood the true nature of the mother-child bond.

---

[11]McLanahan, Sara, and Gary Dandefur. 1994. *Growing Up With a Single Parent: What Hurts, What Helps*. Harvard University Press. Doi: 10.2307/j.ctv22tnmnn.

The more I felt I didn't fit in with my family, the more I turned to Drake's family, even though I didn't feel I fit in with them, either. I felt accepted by Drake's nieces and nephews more than his siblings. In retrospect, I can see the children were less threatening because I was emotionally immature. I thought the adults saw my weaknesses and lack of confidence. At reunions and gatherings, I felt I had nothing to offer, so I usually reverted to my default contribution of cleaning. I thought cleaning was a universal need. Everyone appreciated the maid. Drake's family never asked me to clean. I felt it was something I could do that was appreciated. Cleaning was something everyone needed and valued, and people rarely questioned anyone's motive to do it. I did it to fit in. It was my way to contribute while staying out of the spotlight. I worked so hard to convince everyone I wasn't the person I thought I was that I couldn't become the person I wanted to be. I didn't hide my authentic self; I had not seen her. I laughed at things that weren't funny, bought things that weren't necessary, said things I thought people wanted to hear, and did a lot of things I never wanted to do—all because I believed they helped me fit in.

My life was a continual search for an unknown *it*—the one momentous, life event that would erase the agonizing memories of my childhood and ease the psychic pain of constantly denying and hiding what happened. As a child, I dreamed of going to college to escape by proving I was academically and intellectually capable. In college, I dreamed of getting a job as far as possible from my hometown to put distance between the trauma and me, hoping the memories would fade when I moved away from the place where the pain began. When I married, I dreamed that changing my name would magically obliterate the painful memories by erasing my family name. When I had a baby, I fantasized that motherhood would excise my wounds and give me a do-over with a child I would not abuse. My child's life could be the childhood I should have had. I thought I could replace the torturous memories with the experiences I would have with my son. I waited for my son to grow up and work some big, prestigious job, making me somebody important.

Somehow, it escaped my notice that none of those milestones brought the relief I ached to find because I would not find it from the outside.

I lived most of my life believing deliverance was around the corner, hoping for a rescue, and repeatedly finding only disappointment and more pain until I learned *it* was inside me and followed me everywhere I went. I discovered *it* was learning how my childhood adversities affected me.

Chapter 33

CHANGING CAREERS

Shortly after Michael's birth, I was promoted from secretary to case manager to Daycare Family Home Registration Licensing Specialist at DHS, and we moved to Little Rock so that I could work at the state office. It was one hundred miles away from where I grew up.

Harold was reportedly dating a woman from one of his churches, and he and I had a big disagreement about what was appropriate and inappropriate. She came to his house at inappropriate times, so I told him the church people were talking and that he must not do such things. For years, there were rumors that he had an ongoing affair with her, so I reminded him of the rumor and the seriousness of the allegations. He told me to mind my business and said he didn't need me to tell him who he could or couldn't date. I decided that if he was well enough to reject my advice and tell me he would do whatever he wanted, he no longer needed me around. Released from caring for Harold, we made the move to Little Rock. I thought I was free and no longer feared running into anyone from my past. I thought moving away from them released me, but it only loosened the grip and provided momentary freedom. I still carried the shame, guilt, and abuse with me like an ulcer in my belly. My secrets were deeply buried, but like an old wound that oozes when disturbed, I was often reminded of my past. Living one hundred miles away only meant I had no daily reminders.

As the Registration Specialist, I had to ensure that registered daycare facilities in family homes maintained compliance with the state rules and regulations for childcare. It was more than a job; it was my mission to save the children under my watch from abuse. I was determined that no children in my territory would suffer abuse. I worked long days, evenings, weekends, and whatever it took to make a difference. I reported even the merest hint of abuse or neglect. I decided if I erred, it would be on the side of caution. The job was stressful because I learned early on I couldn't protect every child. I didn't have enough time, couldn't visit enough homes, or drive to enough locations to be everywhere. The job repeatedly reminded me of my childhood, especially when someone was hotlined. Depending on who they knew, the report might be ignored or dismissed. I had frequent flashbacks of my abuse. I was glad times changed and people were more likely to report the abuse. Even young children know how to call and report abuse. Reports of child abuse were less frequent when I was a child. On this job, the reality was that the agency often ignored or denied the reports it received.

Some of the tragic moments on the job were when I reported abuse and no action was taken. Even when abuse cases were substantiated, the state overlooked them for fear of lawsuits. I felt a wrenching emotional pain, followed by a series of questions: *How can this be? How can people get away with this? How do they abuse children and sleep at night? How do people cover for them?* When this happened, I went to my car and cried because I saw the system didn't work for those it was created to protect. It worked for the parents who had positions and titles and whose careers would be ruined if the abuse of their children became public. Working in that environment kept me triggered and emotionally fragile.

Frequently, my supervisor spoke with me about the abuse cases I reported. When she said, "I'm sorry, there's nothing we can do," I felt a lump in my throat, stomach, and heart. I lost my appetite and felt nauseated. I realized that the position was more than a job. It was a personal aspiration to rescue children so they wouldn't end up like me. I didn't want abused and neglected children to wonder why the system failed them or why no one rescued them. It hurt to think their parents, community, and the child welfare system failed them. I did not want to fail them, too. I truly thought I could make a difference in children's lives. Later, I learned that my job wasn't to save every child. My job was to save those I could and make a difference where possible. Accepting that it was unrealistic to rescue all abused children released me from the burden of my expectations.

I felt guilty when I fell short of my goal, but I couldn't go home in a bad mood every day, nor could I adopt every child in foster care. I had to find a better way to deal with my childhood because I realized that I couldn't prevent children's adversities. Acknowledging that limitation was painful. I was trained to ignore children's pain like others ignored mine. I worked for an agency that was supposed to protect children but did not—just as it failed to protect me. I was overworked, stressed, depressed, and an emotional wreck.

In 1993, I was twenty-seven and burned out by the politics and lack of concern for children at the Department of Human Services. I decided I needed a job where I could help children without the limitations of bureaucracy and politics. Quietly, I heard a faint voice say, *I want to make a difference.* Then another thought followed: *I'd make a great teacher.* I should have questioned that thought—especially since I had no teaching experience—but I didn't. Then I remembered I didn't have a teaching license. Despite those impediments, multiple thoughts about teaching continued to flow. I decided to contact a school district to inquire about licensing. I didn't know the second step, but my persistent thoughts led me to the first step.

Within a few minutes, I decided to change my career. I was somehow totally convinced I would, and could, change lives and be a good teacher. I felt it deep in my heart. I know it sounds unbelievable that I would so boldly consider changing careers when I had no prior experience. It sounded ridiculous to me then, and even as I write, it still sounds wild. I had nothing to lose by changing careers. Even more interesting is that I knew I had to have a teacher's certificate—which I didn't—and teachers needed to love children—which I didn't. My only teaching experience was in Sunday School class at Harold's church. Incredibly, I knew my steps were ordered to go into the field of education.

I had a teacher friend who wasn't certified, and I called to ask how she was able to teach. She told me about a program to help those who desire to teach but lack certification. Immediately, her guidance gave me a feeling of peace. I called the local school district to inquire about the certification program. I wanted to see where this still, small voice would lead me. I thought I had little to offer except a college degree in English. I was unaware of the transferable skills I had from working in child and family services, but they would undoubtedly serve me in the classroom. I had nothing to lose and much to gain. I thought any job would be better than the one I was leaving because child abuse hotlines couldn't trigger me.

The school district's receptionist was vague and didn't seem to know anything about a program where people without a teacher's certificate were allowed to teach. I was not deterred, because I believed I was led to this step. I was still working, so I wasn't in a hurry for the teacher's job. I took my time searching for answers because I needed to ask questions, get feedback, and learn what was required to change careers.

A few weeks later, I heard a radio announcement that the Little Rock school district had teacher openings, and I dialed the number. While on hold, I did some positive self-talk. *It can't hurt. I don't have a teacher's license, but God will open the door if it's meant to be.*

Click. I heard a deep voice, "Ms. Wallace, I hear you are interested in teaching. Are you able to come for an interview?"

Interview? I silently screamed. *No, I can't come for an interview. I am only following my random thoughts. How can you ask me for an interview?*

"Yes, sir," I replied. "But I don't have—"

He cut me off mid-sentence. "Great. Can you come for the interview two weeks from today?"

Mr. Richards wanted to interview me even though I had no teaching certificate. I wanted to tell him that was a waste of his time. The interview wouldn't be for a couple of weeks. That was too long to resist the negative thoughts. This type of time delay causes too much panic and anxiety for Childhood Trauma survivors. The *knowing* inside me fluctuated from knowing to unknowing to thinking a*ll of this is stupid.* For two weeks, I vacillated: I had faith, I had no faith. I was on a terrible roller coaster of faith, doubts, and beliefs, but the closer the interview came, the more I felt at peace. If it were to be, it would be up to God to make the district personnel see something that would make me a teacher.

I needed God to give me love for His children. I had none. I could deal with church children in Sunday School for an hour once a week, but by the end of the hour, I was glad when the bell rang, and the students returned to their families. I knew nothing about school teaching or public school students, but I felt compelled to follow through with the interview. Despite my doubts, the closer the day came for the interview, the more relaxed I was.

On the interview day, I arrived early and sat in the waiting area. I heard my inside voice again. It said, *This district needs you. You have a lot to offer these students. You will make a positive difference.* I had no certification, no teaching experience except church, no psychology in understanding children, little previous desire or love for teaching—or I would have gotten an education degree—and no idea what I was doing or why I was doing it. I only knew that I heard a voice that told me I could teach. I knew deep in my heart I could make a difference in the lives of children.

I knew the school district had enough unstable teachers, and I didn't want Mr. Richards to think I would be another one. I waited for the still, small voice to help me, but . . . nothing. Total silence. I tried to remember why I wanted to teach. Teaching was not one of the many jobs I considered over the years. I loved a few of my teachers and wanted to be warm and caring like them, but I didn't want to teach a classroom full of children. I totally forgot that when I was a child, I wanted to be a teacher or an attorney. Childhood Trauma restructured my brain, suppressed memories, and altered my personality. As an adult, I didn't envision myself as a teacher, but I couldn't shake the newfound desire to teach, nor the mental images of being in a classroom with students. I visualized caring for students who had been through negative experiences similar to mine. I went from no desire to intense anticipation. These strong feelings surfaced during the interview.

I flipped through the office magazines, hoping to find a quote, encouragement from a teacher, or direction from the still, small voice—something I might be able to use in the interview—but nothing jumped out. Where was the voice now? I thought *Following the voice got me to the interview, and now it's stopped talking.* Who could I blame?

The positive, self-assuring thoughts came, then waned while the negative thoughts lingered. *What are you doing? You don't know enough about children to teach. What if you treat them like your parents treated you? You aren't educated enough. Everyone will know where you came from. What if there is someone from your town who knows your story? Is Little Rock far enough away to keep others from finding out?*

I tried to dismiss the negative thoughts, but there were too many. I realized that I had to tell Mr. Richards the truth. Well, not the real truth, I thought, or he won't hire me. I knew I couldn't tell him that a still, small voice told me I should be a teacher. I decided to tell him the other half of the truth: I wanted to make a difference. I had a teacher who changed my life, and I believed I could change students' lives. I didn't know it then, but that was the beginning of developing my teaching philosophy. I felt it deep in my heart and soul, and I knew I was ready. Nothing would stop me.

I was jolted from my private interview when a tall man with a mellifluous voice called me to his office. "I understand you are interested in teaching. I see here you don't have a teacher's certification," Mr. Richards said.

"No, I don't, but I want to teach."

"You have your B.A. degree."

"Yes."

"We are definitely hiring teachers, but we want them to be certified. What makes you think we should hire you instead of a certified teacher?"

I felt courage rise inside me, "Certification doesn't make a person care for students. Certification means they have passed the exams that indicate they have content-area knowledge and understand pedagogy. I have compassion for the students, and I can get the training. I want to make a positive difference in their lives."

He looked down at the sheet of interview questions and wrote something. "Uh-huh. Have you ever been in a classroom full of children?" he asked.

"Yes," I hedged. I didn't volunteer that a teacher was present with the students and me in the classroom. I was six years old, but he didn't ask how old I was. I was around my neighbor Charlotte, the kindergarten teacher with her students and saw how she interacted with them. I saw how they hugged her and how she loved them. It was genuine. I wanted to be that kind of teacher where students wished they were my child.

"I think you will be one of our best teachers," Mr. Richards stated. I didn't believe this man felt this about me because of anything I said or did. I believed God answered my prayer and gave me favor with him. He didn't ask any more questions. I already knew I would be one of their best teachers, not because I stretched the truth of what I knew about teaching but because I felt called to teach.

"I'll sign you up for the Alternate Route teacher certification program. You can start teaching in Arkansas in the fall. You will attend certification class one Saturday each month until you are fully certified. The certification program staff will help you get everything you need. We want you certified to teach on the secondary level, which is middle and high school," he stated. "Is there any grade you prefer not to teach?" he asked.

"Wherever I am needed, Mr. Richards," I replied. "I want to make a positive difference." I am sure I sounded like a politician, but I walked away knowing I would teach in a classroom in the fall. I was so excited! I thought Mr. Richard's interview was the easiest I ever had. I was so thankful to God and that still, small voice.

I gave DHS my two-week notice and prepared to attend the first Saturday certification class. After four years of witnessing the cries of children ignored, I left the agency. Between the limits, bureaucracy, and politics, I just couldn't do the job. I wish I could say I didn't look back, but that would be inaccurate. The truth is, I never had to look back because although I changed my job, I didn't change my life, so the cries of abused children still haunted me. My desire to rescue children continued, and I needed to figure out what helping them looked like for me.

Chapter 34

PREPARED BUT UNPREPARED

Alternative Certification programs help provisional teachers obtain state credentials while working in a school. The certification classes prepared me for pedagogy but not for the social and emotional needs of the students. They didn't prepare me for anti-social student behaviors, student deaths, or social upheaval in the community at my first placement in a school in the center of gang-banging Little Rock. The training before the start of school provided teaching scenarios, support, and every kind of resource and the latest information for anyone interested in teaching. It seemed easy enough. What could be better? I didn't know that it took more than knowledge of subject content and pedagogy to be a great teacher.

We met monthly on Saturdays. I created my teaching philosophy: treat students as I wanted them to treat me. During the training, the instructors spent so much time discussing negative theoretical situations instead of real-life scenarios that some candidates quit the program. Others were fearful but stayed. I told myself, *That won't be me. I will love my students. My students will be the best. I will respect them and show them how much I care for them, and in turn, they will respect me and want to learn from me.* In the workshops before school began, I decided to be authentic, caring, and orderly. I wanted to build strong bonds with my students.

I was in a certification workshop in the middle of July when my phone vibrated. As soon as I could, I played the voicemail. *"Hello, this is Principal Lee. I am calling to see if you're still interested in teaching. You come highly recommended, so I want to offer you a job at Northeast Middle School."* How could I be *highly recommended* without any teaching experience? I heard the district was desperate, but this seemed critically desperate. Maybe the same still, small voice that spoke to me also told the principal to call. The certification staff urged us to snag a job when a principal called. I forgot to ask about the pay, the hours, the first day—anything. I called Principal Lee and said yes! I believed if God orchestrated this, He would continue to work out the details. Where I went was part of His plan. The only thing missing was the students.

I rehearsed the first day of school for a month, practicing the students' potential questions and my answers. I visualized them raising their hands and me respectfully answering every question. I mentally dotted the i's and crossed the t's. I was ready. I was sure I'd thought of everything. I prepared a clean, well-organized room, posted positive phrases and quotes on the wall, and prepared my textbooks for distribution. I created learning objectives and lesson plans for the first month and scheduled every second of class to maximize the learning opportunities. I could see the students sitting at their desks, excited to learn like I had seen on TV and like the certification class taught us. I researched the best practices and was ready to implement them to increase my students' achievement. I believed that students were human, and if I treated them well and with respect, they would do the same to me.

The certification staff said they prepared us for everything we needed. They said we were ready to teach. They even gave us a checklist called the *First Day Checklist.* I was determined to be the best teacher. I had the checklist, and I was ready. I enjoyed the certification workshops and professional training for my new career. I decided I would not do the wrong things my teachers did. I would not make any of my students feel like my uncaring teachers made me feel. I chose to be like the teachers who left a positive imprint on me and made me feel like I could do anything. If I didn't know what to do for the students, I was fairly certain I knew what not to do. I would be one of the best, most caring teachers a student could have. I decided teaching would be the best job in the world.

At one time, I thought everyone else was smarter than me, which created a fear of big exams. I know now it's because I had low self-esteem. I studied for the National Teachers' Exam and failed twice. Before I took it the third time, I prayed and told God I knew He led me to teach. I told Him since He called me to do it, I believed He would help me to pass. I passed the NTE on my third attempt. Passing the NTE allowed me to get my Arkansas Certification. The lesson it taught me would last a lifetime for every project I undertook. One of the lessons I learned was that when God tells me to do something, I needed to do it because everything will eventually have to move out of my way.

I hardly slept the night before the first day of school because of too much excitement and nervous energy. I did a mental check and some role-playing and visualized various scenarios of *if they do this, then I will do that.* I had a fresh manicure and pedicure. Finally, I laid my outfit on the bed next to the outfit four-year-old Michael would wear to daycare. We were both excited. I explained to him *that Mommy would teach the big boys and girls*. I was ready on the outside and the inside—or so I thought.

On the first day of school, I stood at the classroom door and welcomed the students as they filed in. Most of them seemed excited. A few came in and put their heads down, even though it was the first day of the school year. I took note of those students and observed them throughout the class period. I was grateful most of the kids were well-behaved and excited to be in class, but I was drawn to the few who seemed disinterested. Most of the students took seats near their friends, and I could hear them chatting about their summer activities and vacations with a few outbursts of laughter. My attention, however, remained drawn to the students who were extremely quiet, isolated, and unsmiling. I contemplated how to get them involved and interested. In our summer training, we learned much about distracted students but not as much about disengaged ones. I called the roll, made eye contact with each student, and gave them a five-second *I see you* visual connection.

By the time class began, I knew the students who were potential disruptors and needed attention, so I fed their needs with participation and inclusion. By the end of the first month, those students participated and behaved appropriately. I created a safe and respectful environment where everyone was valued. Students saw my responses when anyone bullied others. I let the class know scoffing at each other was unacceptable and that my classroom culture prioritized learning. Of course, I didn't know it then, but I was teaching traumatized students the way I would have wanted to learn in the environment I would have preferred. I made my greatest need the students' greatest need. I couldn't teach in an unsafe environment, and I figured they couldn't learn in one. Research confirms one of the greatest needs for traumatized students is safety. The longer I taught, the more compassion I had for traumatized students. Of course, I didn't know that they were traumatized. I only knew they were like me. I liked teaching students and was confident with them because my insecurities were minimized, and I didn't worry about what they thought of me or fitting in. They accepted me and loved me, and I knew it. I accepted and loved them, and they knew it.

I went into teaching before the big push for teacher collaboration, co-planning, co-teaching, content-area coordinators, and common lesson plans influenced by the No Child Left Behind Act. Teaching changed me because I was in a classroom spending my day with children rather than in an office of adults. I had autonomy, which minimized my insecurities and lack of confidence. I didn't worry about what others thought or their knowledge of my childhood. In the classroom, I could be me. I am thankful for that environment because it built confidence, developed my character, and matured me emotionally while teaching my students to do the same. I now know God led me to teach because it would guide me further in His plans and purpose for me in teaching and training. I would eventually go from pedagogy (teaching children) to andragogy (teaching adults).

Chapter 35
LIFE 101

My first school trauma occurred in my third year of teaching at a middle school. It was the end of the day, the Thursday before Good Friday. We had a long weekend break for the Easter weekend holiday, and I called out to Reggie as he left the classroom, "Reggie, be good and stay out of trouble."

He gave me a big smile, flashed a dimple on his right cheek, and softly replied, "Yes, ma'am. I try, but you know them dudes just try to start stuff."

I thought it was simple enough to avoid trouble, so I said it again. "Be good and stay out of trouble." Looking back, I realize I was out of touch with reality. The city where Reggie lived was number one in the U.S. for gang warfare.

I gave students my phone number but instructed them to call only in times of emergency. Much to my delight, they respected my rule. I taught the students to care for each other. While I couldn't control what they did outside of class, I could control what went on inside the class. They knew we were family, and family supported each other. I realize now I was desperately trying to create the family I knew many of them lacked. I learned love can be taught the same as hate can be, and whichever one was taught the most was the one the students learned.

I'll never forget the call on Good Friday from one of my students. I heard sniffling on the other end when I answered the phone. "He's gone, Ms. Wallace, he's gone. They killed him."

I couldn't ask a question because the caller was sobbing. I assumed she was talking about someone in her family. "Who's gone?" I asked.

"Reggie. They shot and killed him." I almost dropped the phone when I heard that. I had talked to Reggie only the day before. Trauma survivors' response systems remain highly sensitized. I fought back the surge of emotions flooding my body as I tried to calm the student on the phone.

I regained composure and tried not to imagine what happened, although I immediately saw images in my head and became emotionally disturbed. I felt choking fear and painful knots in my stomach. My first reaction was to cry, but

I couldn't fall apart with a student on the phone needing me, so I controlled my emotions.

"Slow down and tell me what happened," I said.

"He was standing on a corner, and they drove by and shot him. They meant to kill his brother but shot him instead," she choked out the words between sobs.

In shock and disbelief, I said, "I'm sure you've got the wrong student. It probably wasn't Reggie." I was in denial. "I will call the police station to clear this up. Don't spread this around until I call you back."

I pushed away the fears, the *what-ifs,* and the nervousness to call the police department. I needed to set this straight before a rumor spread to my students. This could not have happened to my student! Initially, the police refused to give me information. I couldn't handle not knowing, so I continued to ask the officer for information. Finally, I told the officer I was Reggie's teacher and needed to know how to help his classmates. He placed me on hold for what seemed like ages before returning and saying, "Yes, there was a shooting, and yes, a fourteen-year-old boy was killed, but I can't give you any more information. We have to contact the family to identify him."

Somehow, the officer's statement convinced me it was Reggie. I couldn't hold back any longer. "Not my Reggie," I screamed. "God, no!" and I fell to the floor. After that, time passed in a blur. I was shocked, but I had to recover quickly because my students needed me. I had created a nurturing and caring classroom so they were bonded together, and one after the other called. I spent half the night trying to console my students and the other half trying to console myself. I kept trying to figure out how I missed Reggie's gang involvement. I wanted him to be the respectful, quiet boy outside of class that he was in class. I tried to convince myself there was nothing I could have done. I tried to be strong for everyone else while getting little support from anyone else. I learned when students are in emotional distress, they want to be near the teachers they trust to feel their pain and share their distress. I was still an inexperienced teacher, deeply broken emotionally, knowing nothing about triggers and residuals, but I reached my goal of ensuring students knew how much I cared.

The following Monday, one student after another came to my classroom. Some broke down in tears as they came through the door. Others didn't express their pain verbally, but I knew they were hurting. I hugged them and said I understood. Others needed to write something for Reggie, to him or about him, and that's what we did. The first few days following his death, I didn't even try to teach English. I taught Life 101. For some, this was the first time they'd seen a teacher cry or experienced a teacher changing lesson plans based on student needs. Despite any disaster, teachers were to ensure curriculum goals were met by the end of the nine-week term. The curriculum was great, but it had a deficiency. It didn't allow room for humans or life lessons. If I missed teaching the kids about life, I wouldn't be able to teach them the English curriculum, so I learned to authentically integrate life with English studies. I decided to love the students, be compassionate, and help those I knew were struggling because many of them had no one to guide them. I was a teacher, but I became a surrogate mother to many of them in the aftermath of Reggie's death, defending them, checking their grades, encouraging them, and teaching them responsibility. I knew the die-hard, curriculum-driven teachers might have disapproved of the Life 101 class I implemented because it meant a temporary pause of the state's curriculum to address students' needs. Yet, I taught some of the most important lessons students would ever learn—self-care and love. I knew if I gave them what they needed, they would later give me what I wanted: to teach them. I also knew they couldn't learn in an emotionally-charged environment.

My students knew their teacher was right there with them in their pain, and as the funeral approached, their grief intensified. Understandably, Reggie's class seemed more affected by his death. At the beginning of the year, we set classroom norms, and one of the values was caring. I taught them to understand when someone is hurt because people react differently to pain. To my surprise, they learned to do that. Students who did not know Reggie well were sensitive and patient with those who did.

Reggie's family asked me to speak at the funeral, which was held exactly a week after Reggie's killing. I didn't know how I would be able to do it, but I knew I had to assure my students we were in this together, and we would be okay. Speaking at Reggie's funeral was part of being there for the survivors.

The room was packed, as is often the case when a young life is lost. I looked around at the tear-stained faces. I wanted to hide, but I couldn't. My deep emotional wails were not only for Reggie. The emotional losses I had in childhood affected my reaction. I cried many days and nights after Reggie's death, although I didn't understand why I was in such turmoil. I know now it was because I had pent up emotions from unexpressed rage at the injustices of my childhood. I wanted a place to cry until I could cry no more, but I knew I had to hold back my tears to get through the presentation. I prayed under my breath, surrounded by students, waiting for my turn on the program. *Lord, please help me. I can't do this, but I know you can help me. I have to do this for the students.*

Somehow, I found the strength to say the words I thought I could not speak. "Reggie was the kindest, sweetest young man. I am honored to be his teacher. Not a day passed without his hug as he left the classroom." I wanted to give the mourners what Reggie gave me—his big smile. I concluded with these words: "You can carry a part of Reggie with you every day when you wear a smile. Regardless of what he went through, he gave us something that we will never forget: his smile. Take it with you, as I will. We will never forget him." I barely reached my seat before a flood of tears poured down my cheeks.

Reggie's death illuminated several things: relationships with my students helped me as much as it did them, and students looked for someone to lean on during a crisis and to provide reassurance of their safety. I learned students are resilient and can be more understanding than adult co-workers. Reggie's death stirred something that affected me deeply, and I eventually identified unresolved emotional pain. It benefited me more than I can say that my students were a chosen family instead of mere acquaintances. We helped each other rally after a great loss.

As an inexperienced teacher, losing a student deeply affected me. I hadn't been trained in what to do, nor did I anticipate such an event. In fact, there was no mention of losing students in the preparatory program. After my student was killed, I couldn't help but wonder who would be next, so my fight or flight mode strengthened. Stress was constant, and I contemplated leaving the education profession because I questioned whether I could live with the threat of losing another student.

Reggie's death happened too early in my teaching experience for me to be strong enough to handle it. I was unprepared for such a tragedy, but it was unbearable in my first few years of teaching. My co-workers didn't make it any easier. They said things that were not true and accused me of lacking rigor and giving students grades they didn't earn. I took their insults personally. They didn't know I added life and being human to my curriculum. Once the students saw I cared about them more than a curriculum and that I put them first, they helped make up any lost time I spent during emergencies or life events.

It would have helped if my school district had mental health support for teachers who lose a student—especially when that death was caused by violence. There was little support for students and even less for teachers. I didn't realize it, but each time something traumatic happened to one of my students, I was triggered and relived my Childhood Trauma. It was a PTSD response. I was anxious and panicky without knowing why. After Reggie's death, fear tripled in force and came with nightmares.

For months after Reggie's death, I came to school each day wondering if anything bad happened overnight. Living in the top gang-banging city in the state was not good for me. Reggie's senseless death disrupted my sense of safety, and the frequent violence and neighborhood uproars kept me in constant fight or flight mode. I was afraid to drive down certain streets and afraid to let Michael play outside. I was afraid to lose another student to the streets. There was a period when we experienced near-daily losses from our school family. Each time a student was shot or killed, I was triggered by flashbacks of the violence I experienced in childhood that made me question whether my siblings or I were going to die at the hands of our parents. Despite these flashbacks, I was still years from identifying those violent events as Adverse Childhood Experiences and understanding that I experienced such an overwhelming number of them that I was a candidate for post-traumatic stress disorder, personality disorders, and chronic health issues.

I prayed for my students and prayed over their desks every day. I know the power of prayer because I never lost another student to violence. I gave them the love I could give each time I saw them because I never knew when it would be the last. In retrospect, I didn't process or grieve Reggie's death because I was too busy helping students grieve and process it. Years later, I thought of Reggie and unexpectedly burst out crying. I realized then that I still had not fully grieved his death. I thought about him and what I remembered about him, his beautiful smile, and the community's great loss. Then I grieved for how he died a needless death. It would have been painful if he had died from an illness, but I couldn't wrap my head around the senselessness of his killing.

Chapter 36
MY GIFT, MICHAEL

It wasn't as challenging for me to juggle motherhood, child care, and teaching as it seemed for others. Perhaps because I experienced abusive stress as a child, I didn't consider my adult life stressful. I loved teaching and taking care of Michael. Either his father or I read to him every night before bedtime. I thrived with a routine of getting up, getting him dressed, taking him to daycare, teaching, picking him up, going home, and doing it over the next day. On weekends, I graded papers and wrote lesson plans for a few hours. Since I enjoyed grading papers and encouraging students, reading and assessing their work was not a chore.

We had a family tradition called Blockbuster night, a time we set aside to watch rented movies. Having a small child allowed me to relive my childhood and make up for some of the things I missed, especially pop culture, like Disney movies. I often acted childlike with Michael and enjoyed his delight in discovery—something I'm sure I would have had if, as a child, I wasn't forced to remain silent and scrub non-existent debris from rugs.

One of my favorite Disney fairytales was *Beauty and the Beast*. I liked the story because the ugly beast turned into a handsome prince. It gave me hope because it made me feel transformation is possible. I knew it was a fairytale, but any story with a good ending assured me. My childhood reality was horrendous, so I enjoyed hearing and watching stories of courageous people, even fictitious ones. Michael and I enjoyed *Beauty and the Beast* the first time we watched it, so we watched it again the following night. Drake and I noticed that Michael sang and repeated lines from the film verbatim as if he had heard it several times, even though we knew he had only seen it once. We looked at each other in astonishment. In unison, we said, "We have to do something with him. He is gifted." Our son was only two years old at the time.

He learned and mastered many skills well before school age. While he was still a toddler, we taught him phonics and the basic skills of reading. He learned to sound out words and amused us with inventive spellings, such as B-A-K-O-N. He picked up on language quickly. I remembered my dream of a gifted little boy speaking to auditoriums full of people, and I knew it was prophetic.

When he was three, Michael performed speaking parts in church plays. To please Harold, we had joined a church in his denomination and were very involved. Michael performed in our church's Christmas and Easter plays and other local church programs. He quickly learned the lines and was a comfortable performer. He seemed to love it. He went to kindergarten on a high school campus, and his first non-church speaking engagement was on the school's Black History Program, where he addressed more than 700 high school students. They applauded him loudly. I thought they would be critical of him, but instead they encouraged him.

Drake and I were committed to Michael's education and wanted a well-prepared child. I tutored him in English and history in the summer, and Drake taught him math and science. Michael learned vocabulary, read newspapers, wrote essays, created science projects, and solved complex math problems. He studied trumpet and piano, sang, acted, and wrote poetry and fiction. He learned to read music and played by ear for the small church we attended. We rewarded him when he finished his assignments with trips to an arcade pizza restaurant, ice cream treats, or a sleepover at a friend's house.

Michael was the child everyone wanted but didn't know what to do with because he was so intelligent. He was my son, but I was ceaselessly amazed at his intellect and ability to express himself. I often thought *It was a good thing he had a father like Drake or he might not be so smart*. I lacked confidence in my parenting skills and looked to Drake to teach him. Drake didn't know it, but he taught me, too. In the back of my mind, I still questioned if I were like Buck and Elsie because that was what I knew. I wouldn't intentionally hurt Michael, but I still feared the possibility. While I didn't understand love, I understood pain, and I did not want Michael to have the kind of childhood I experienced. I was still unaware of the impact abuse and trauma had on my brain, my self-esteem, my self-worth, or my identity. Only after Michael was an adult and I was in graduate school studying the effects of trauma could I connect the links between my Childhood Trauma and my intellectual and emotional deficits.

Michael's speaking schedule grew until he was the keynote speaker for community programs and organizations. We thought he might be good at other things because he was gifted, so we signed him up for acting jobs with a local talent agency. I wrote monologues and parts for him to recite and coached him to act. A year of practicing, reciting, and acting came and went faster than expected. His acting abilities were recognized, and soon the talent agency staff said he was ready to compete in the International Modeling and

Talent Association competition in New York. We were proudly taken aback. Drake and I coached Michael until we hired a local storyteller known for acting and speaking. A gifted performer, the storyteller taught Michael the techniques of personalizing storytelling and acting. Michael was talented, so we only had to prepare him for the mental and emotional challenges of the competition. Churches, neighbors, and those throughout the state who heard Michael speak were inspired and asked how they could support him. Some of them contributed to the travel fund for the New York competition. If there is such a thing as natural talent, Michael had it. We never had to beg, plead, or prod him to practice. We'd say *practice,* and he would stand and go over his lines. After several months of preparation, it was time to go to New York City.

The school district allowed me to leave whenever Michael had an engagement. They were supportive, and it was a good thing they were because the stress of losing students and missing my son's events could have made me choose another profession. My principals valued me and honored my work at the school, so I never had any problems leaving to support Michael, and I was thankful to make this important trip with him. I had only seen New York City on television and was excited to go there. We were determined not to pressure Michael to compete, but we supported him as long as he wanted to do it and saw it as fun. Michael heard that the biggest toy store in the world was in New York, so I'm sure that played a part in his excitement. Michael and I traveled without Drake because of Drake's work commitments.

The plane landed in New York, and the smell of success seemed like it was in the atmosphere. I had no doubt Michael would win because of the dream I'd had, even though he was competing against kids from all over the United States. The agency enrolled Michael in open auditions for commercials, soap operas, and television shows, as well as the monologue category of the competition. Talent scouts representing national talent agencies and production companies like Nickelodeon were there. My head spun, but I had to keep it straight for Michael. Drake and I wanted Michael to have fun; whatever good happened due to having fun would be great.

Unlike most of his competitors, Michael and I had fun sightseeing after auditions and business meetings on the first day. In New York City, the traffic and noise of honking cars overwhelmed me. The street-level activity made me nervous. I was terrified and excited at the same time as casting directors asked us about Michael auditioning for lead roles in projects. The possibility of us having to uproot our family was too much for me to think about and was an emotional overload. I had to compose myself for Michael because he competed in the monologue category on the second day. He was a natural competitor. The night before the competition, we lay in bed watching TV. I wanted him to be relaxed. We didn't focus on winning, and I didn't bring it up. Drake and I taught Michael to do his best, and we knew he would. All I had to do was make sure he ate nutritious food, slept well, enjoyed himself, and was at the right place at the right time for each competition and audition.

The first two days consisted of acting in various categories, such as toy and food commercials, soap operas, and monologues. I knew the agencies might call him to return for another round of auditions, but my job was to protect him from the stress. Taking Michael away from the waiting area filled with other kids and their stressed-out parents kept him from absorbing their tension. We waited between rounds for callbacks, which provided a great opportunity to take Michael to his favorite store—FAO Schwarz. Michael and I were equally awed by the displays. It was our first time seeing such an assortment of stuffed animals, games, and toys. Michael roamed through the aisles, playing with games, picking up toys, and trying to decide which ones were worthy of attention. We bought a few toys and returned to the venue, where we learned he had several callbacks from Nickelodeon and other agencies. I was confident he would do well. I called Drake and told him, "They want our son! Several talent scouts have called for him. Everyone here likes him. I know he will win the big award." Then reality hit the pit of my stomach, "What do I tell them when they ask when he can start to work or how soon he can fly to Los Angeles?" Drake usually had an answer for everything because he was a thinker, but there was no answer from his end of the phone connection.

"What do I do?" I asked him again in case he missed the question.

"Michael's not ready for that yet, and neither are we. Tell them you have to talk it over with your husband, and you will let them know," he responded. In an instant, the Hollywood dream balloon popped. Even if Michael won, I knew we weren't willing to sacrifice to have a professional child performer in the family.

In my excitement to support Michael's speech and performance talents, I neglected to think through the long-term possibilities. I'm sure most mothers of gifted children, whether in the arts or sports, realize that the end goal of lessons, rehearsals, concerts, and coaching involves performances and competitions. Still, I had not foreseen anything beyond a winner's trophy. There was information in the competition materials about careers for child performers, but it went unseen and unregistered by my trauma brain. It was good that Drake and I steered clear of pressuring Michael and telling him that the New York event was a stepping stone to a Hollywood career. Michael had no idea. He thought the whole experience was an opportunity to improve his speaking and acting skills.

I knew Drake was right, so I tried to console myself. *Why did we come here if we weren't ready?* I knew the answer to that. We agreed on our response. We believed in Michael and knew he was gifted, but we didn't fully understand the sacrifices it took to get into the entertainment world. Neither his dad nor I were prepared for our little boy to be in a role in front of the world.

Several agencies, including Shirley Grant who recruited Christina Ricci, Keisha Knight-Pulliam, and the Jonas Brothers, left messages for call-backs. Ms. Grant only called back those she believed had *it,* and she said to bring Michael in. I would have rather told her no over the phone, but she didn't seem like the kind to take no for an answer, so we went to her booth at the venue. She smiled broadly at Michael, and he smiled back.

"I know raw talent when I see it. Michael has it," she said. "We would like him to come to L.A. to audition for some upcoming movie roles."

Drake and I practiced for this moment, but it was still hard to say it to her. "I have to talk it over with my husband, and I will let you know." She responded with an *Are-you-kidding-me-woman?* expression on her face.

"You came here to tell me you must discuss it with your husband?"

I was embarrassed to tell her our position when I knew many parents would jump at the opportunity. We left her booth. Michael was fine, but I needed a break. Saying no to high-pressure recruiters was stressful. After that, I didn't respond to any other callbacks.

I learned talent agencies don't expect to be put off or turned down. They assume desperate parents are willing to sacrifice their child for a paycheck. When someone comes to them, it's because that person wants to be in show business, not because they only want feedback about their performance skills. Fortunately, Michael thought the auditions were games and felt no disappointment about not going to California for further auditions. He was happy to return home and resume his periodic speaking career.

The IMTA (International Modeling and Talent Association) grand award was presented on day three of the event. For the award night Finale, everyone dressed in formal attire. Michael was excited. He loved to win, even though he didn't know what the win meant, and he loved applause. There was a red carpet for the child actors with flashing cameras from every direction. Michael was gracious, but I was ready to go home. Once I realized that we had no immediate future in entertainment, I wanted to leave. It was a great experience for Michael and me; however, the thought of stardom was too much. I feared what could happen to our family. Even then, I knew something was not right.

I couldn't recognize it then, but my trepidation could be traced back to my childhood adversities. There was a certain predatory nature to the aggressive treatment of procuring child performers for production companies. Scattered across America, primarily in small, rural areas, talent and modeling agencies function to funnel the children of often poor, desperate parents to the entertainment capitals. Child actors are frequently used, abused, and tossed on the trash heap of history, never to be heard from again unless their story is told in a reveal-all documentary. Since the year of our experience, multiple stories of abuse have come from former child actors, whether the abuse was from an industry insider or from their parents desperation for the child's income to assuage their adult dysfunctions. I have no regrets that we took a different path. We knew we did what was best for us and Michael. I know now that we dodged a bullet with our naiveté and unwillingness to allow Michael to get caught up in show business.

At the Finale, the hotel ballroom was packed. The judges completed tallying the scores of the winners in each of the categories. The emcee announced the second runner-up, and I saw Michael look anxious for the first time. "I hope I win," he whispered. The second runner-up left the stage while Michael beamed. Then, the announcer called the name of the first runner-up. Michael jumped up and down because he saw his competitor step away. I wanted to tell him to wait until they called his name so she could have her ten seconds of celebration, but the emcee announced that *the winner was Michael!* We cheered and applauded because Michael worked hard, rehearsed his lines, and did his best. For us, his winning didn't mean we had to do the next step. It meant we were one step closer to discovering what Michael enjoyed doing. We were happy for his success and recognition.

The large, shiny trophy was taller than Michael, and an adult had to help him carry it. As he walked off stage, the IMTA president, Helen Rogers, announced, "There is a young man with a bright future. Keep an eye on him." We didn't know our world was about to change in a major way or that Michael's success opened doors we weren't prepared to walk through.

My trauma triggers and residuals grew worse in New York as I experienced increasing doubt, fear, and a growing distrust of the talent agency that brought

Michael to New York. In addition to fighting the fears and distrust, I had to continually say no to agencies while there and a few times upon returning home. They wanted Michael to try out for a role in upcoming movies or television shows. They thought they could persuade me to move to New York or Los Angeles. The very thought of it made me nervous. I disliked telling people no, but for Michael's sake, I did. All I could think about was how strangers in New York said things like, "I could kidnap your little boy. I want to take him back home with me," and "That is a special little boy you have. You better keep him close." I was afraid to walk too far from the hotel, and I didn't make eye contact with people on the street because I feared they would try to snatch Michael or me.

Co-dependencies also emerged while attending the event, but I didn't recognize them. Without Drake, I felt inadequate. The effects of Childhood Trauma kept my body in fight or flight mode, so I only fractionally enjoyed our once-in-a-lifetime experience. Childhood trauma survivors are often afraid of public success because it comes with fears and what-ifs, such as *What if I fail? What if someone recognizes me? What if someone exposes my secret? What if the perpetrator reads or hears about my success? What if something bad happens to someone I love?* The toxic negative thoughts plagued me. I wished they would go away, but they only intensified. Toxic negative thoughts are difficult to shake without a strategy. My strategy at that point in my life was to pray the words of Psalm 23. *Surely goodness and mercy shall follow me all the days of my life.* I repeated the verses until I believed goodness and mercy were following us, and nothing bad could happen to Michael or me.

Chapter 37

MICHAEL MAKING A DIFFERENCE

y the time we returned to Arkansas, news that Michael had won the IMTA Grand Prize in New York had reached the regional and city newspapers. Shortly after, Michael received a call to speak for the 1997 Presidents' Summit for America's Future. The Summit was held in Philadelphia at the oldest A.M.E. church in the U.S.—Mother Bethel African Methodist Episcopal—and attended by Gerald Ford, Jimmy Carter, Nancy Reagan representing Ronald Reagan, President Bill Clinton, and Vice-President Al Gore. The event organizer said that because Michael was an established motivational speaker, he should speak on a topic of his choice. I couldn't help but think about her words, *"Michael's an established speaker."* He was eight years old, and we were elated by the invitation. For a moment, I thought I could have done great things like Michael if I had supportive parents. I couldn't dwell on that thought because we had to prepare Michael for a summit where he would speak to the living presidents. Drake and I wrote his speech for the event. It was entitled, *"Make a Difference."*

The Summit committee selected children of diverse religious backgrounds from across the United States to speak. Michael was one of four Youth Witnesses on the program. It was an honor for Michael to speak at the Bethel AME Church because of its history. Bethel provided refuge to runaway slaves in 1795, supported the Underground Railroad, and hosted a meeting for African descendants to protest the organization of the American Colonization Society which was formed to relocate free Blacks. Suffragist and Quaker abolitionist Lucretia Mott and author, abolitionist, and formerly enslaved person Fredrick Douglas were among the long list of distinguished freedom speakers who had appeared before the congregation. I could feel the building's history as I took in the beauty of its sanctuary.

The church sanctuary had high ceilings and beautifully stained wood floors, railings, and pews, which gleamed as if they were freshly polished. Michael and the other young speakers sat on the dais, front and center, facing the hundreds of distinguished guests seated in the sanctuary. Drake and I ensured we sat where Michael could see us for support. I felt my motherhood validated because Michael was in the presence of the dignitaries attending the Presidents' Summit. I knew it wasn't about me, but I knew that God used me to bring someone into the world to make a difference. Although the pomp and circumstance of the Summit was emotionally overwhelming, I enjoyed the event. I took a moment to inhale the church's history and history in the making: my eight-year-old son spoke with authority and power as he challenged the audience to make a difference with their lives.

Michael's opening sentence began, *"When I grow up."* Right away, he commanded attention because his voice was strong, and he spoke with courage like a professional. At eight years old, he had three years of paid public speaking under his belt and was not intimidated by a microphone.

I may grow up to be a great painter, like Georgia O'Keefe, and paint a new picture. I may grow up to be a great Boy Scout, like former president Jimmy Carter, and lead the way. At that point, he had to pause for a roar of applause. Michael trained to wait for the applause because it often came during his speeches. Many times, the clapping was accompanied by the stomping of feet. Moments like that sent shivers up my spine.

I may grow up to be a great actor, like former president Ronald Reagan. I may grow up to be a great skydiver and soar from the sky, like former president George Bush.

The crowd erupted after the line about George Bush. Michael couldn't continue for a few seconds because they laughed so hard. Former President George Bush's red face glowed brightly behind his wide smile.

Michael ended with the idea that *I may grow up to be a president and give hope to a new generation, like William Jefferson Clinton.*

Whoever I will be when I grow up, I will be somebody. I will make a difference. What will you be when you grow up? Will you be somebody? Will you make a difference?

Michael didn't forget a line because he was well prepared, but we also prepared for the *what-ifs*. An extended standing ovation kept him on the stage for a minute after he finished, and he enjoyed every second of it. He smiled and looked from left to right and back again as we taught him. When he finished speaking, my beaming smile showed Michael how proud I was. I was on the edge of my seat, hoping he wouldn't be distracted by the crowd or the interruptions for applause. When Michael performed, it was as if I performed. Could I have been someone without doubts and self-consciousness if I had supportive parents?

Cameras, media personnel, high-profile people, and Secret Service agents surrounded the former presidents. Michael performed his speech like a professional, but when he finished acknowledging the ovation, he jumped down from the stage like an eight-year-old boy. Former President George Bush was one of the first to give him a high five. Michael jumped as high as he could and slapped the former president's hand. We received an audio recording and a letter from one of the organizers of the presidential summit thanking Michael for a job well done.

Summit organizers strictly insisted there could be no pictures during or following the event. Apparently, the invited media corps were the only ones with permission to photograph. I'm sure the media was controlled and cleared by security, which meant a smaller media presence than I expected for such a momentous event. Unfortunately for us, this event is documented only in our memories. I would especially like a picture of President George Bush giving Michael a high five when he jumped down from the stage, but that picture may not exist.

Upon returning home, we received a request from then-Governor of Arkansas Mike Huckabee for Michael to be the keynote speaker at his Promise Keeper's event. Governor Huckabee said he heard about a young boy making waves in the speaking industry. Michael captured the audience again at the governor's event and went on to speak at other state and national events.

Each time Michael spoke, I felt as if I spoke. Because of my complex trauma, I couldn't fathom doing what Michael did at his age. I knew I couldn't change my past, but I knew I could change his future by providing opportunities, access, and support. We never pushed Michael to do engagements, and we occasionally declined requests because we thought it was too much for him. Michael continued giving speeches until he was eleven years old. By then, he was an established speaker and helped write some of his speeches, but his enthusiasm waned, and we didn't force him to continue. He began to express interest in music and writing.

It wasn't until I looked at family photographs years later that I realized I lived my life vicariously through Michael. The abuse I suffered in childhood made its way into my entire being and mind. It controlled me and told me who I was and what I could do. The abuse limited every area of my life. The more opportunities came to Michael, the more my limited beliefs were exposed. Limited beliefs are thoughts in the mind that restrict individuals from welcoming new opportunities. They originate from a place of fear and negativity. One of my limited beliefs was that I missed my time to speak, but I was going to make sure Michael didn't miss his opportunity.

I was an abused and neglected child who survived years of physical and sexual abuse, went to college, got married, had a child, and got a job. It looked like I had everything, and I did have a beautiful family. I just didn't know what to do with the beautiful family because I had no model of one during the most crucial developmental years. When children are loved, heard, and provided for, they have the foundation to get through life's challenges. I did not have what was needed to overcome life's challenges or know how to meet those needs.

I wanted to be a motivational speaker, but I gave up my dream of writing or speaking because I believed the trauma was too invasive. I didn't know anyone who overcame the kind of abuse I suffered to achieve their dreams, nor did I have the confidence Michael did. Childhood Trauma is a buzzword now and a diagnosis, but it was a word seldom heard in the 1990s. There was a stigma attached to child abuse, so when I gave birth to Michael, I thought I missed the opportunity to have a career as a motivational speaker. I decided the satisfaction I felt when Michael spoke the words I wrote for him would be the closest I would get to my dream.

Chapter 38
FAMILY TIME

My self-worth was so low, I often wondered what God was thinking when he gave Michael to me. Me! I thought a child prodigy should have a smarter mother. I gave Michael what I had, but I couldn't give him what I didn't know or I didn't have. I was thankful for Drake because he provided the stability and security I needed to raise Michael. Though I was sometimes ashamed to be Michael's mother, many occasions made me proud.

I often thought that if it hadn't been for Drake, I wouldn't know how to raise Michael. When I was pregnant, I couldn't conceptualize how a child would impact my life. I did not foresee the kind of lifestyle changes a child requires, nor did I picture parenting as requiring sacrifice or adaptation. I didn't understand the unspoken rules that children absorb from their parents. I didn't know what *quality time* was or its importance. I had undoubtedly heard of quality time, but I couldn't predict the consequences if a child didn't receive it. As God would have it, quality time was Drake's love language, so we had lots of family time, from bike riding in the country to movie nights and team bowling. I am sure I appreciated our family more than Michael did because I had never had a family focused on its members. For Michael, our caring unit was the only family he knew, and he could take his parents' love for granted.

Although I desired to be a good wife and mother, I realized I wasn't equipped and didn't know anything about either. Thankfully, Drake knew about family and instituted Friday night as family night. We bowled on Saturdays and rode bikes on Sunday afternoons. He arranged the activities. I had no idea what the words *family time* meant because I had no idea what a family was in the true sense of the word. I had seen it modeled by Marla, my foster mom, during my short time with her. My childhood memories of my own *family time* were the few times Elsie cooked and we were allowed to eat her delicious food. In my home, I cooked because we needed to eat, not because I thought it was part of my role as a wife and mother. I didn't know anything about adult roles and decisions. I didn't do what Drake said because I understood his role as husband or considered him the head of our household; I simply did things as he directed. It might have looked like I knew and understood, but I didn't. The saddest and most frightening thing is I didn't know what I didn't know.

Mothering was a foreign language to me. Building relationships and prioritizing my family was an unknown territory. If someone called with a need, I dropped everything and went to them without consideration for how my impulsive decision affected my son or husband. I felt compelled to help others while ignoring Drake or Michael's needs. This was especially true when the church asked me to do something. I acted like God asked me, and church folk took advantage of my lack of critical thinking. I didn't understand that my first obligation was to care for my family. Of course, Drake tried to tell me that, but trauma survivors are known to reject those who love and try to help them only to love those who use and hinder them instead. I justified my rejection of Drake's wisdom by thinking that he was selfish and not generous like me. I felt like Drake didn't understand that God needed me to help the church family. Again, this type of thinking exposed my lack of understanding of God and my inability to think for myself.

While statistics document that one out of every three girls and one out of every five boys is sexually abused, we know a lot of people struggle with critical thinking. I knew little about how to manage a home, how to coordinate the schedules, or how to balance the checkbook. I knew nothing about financial planning, budgeting, or creating personal wealth. With child abuse statistics so high, it's not unimaginable that other married couples go through some of the same struggles as Drake and I did for the same reasons.

My marriage was probably similar to many others. Our focus shifted from one another to Michael, and as he grew older, we didn't know how to bring the focus back to us. Our efforts and schedules centered on Michael. We discussed his offers, prepared his appearances, and worked out the logistics. We celebrated Michael's success and strove to provide enrichment at every turn. There wasn't much time left for our concerns. Because I had no preparation for a healthy, intimate relationship, I accepted the lack of intensity without question. I avoided conflict, so our marriage's superficiality was satisfactory. Neither of us questioned the quality of our marriage.

Chapter 39
JAILHOUSE LITTLE ROCK

A few years after my start in the Little Rock School District, I received a letter from the coordinator describing a specific restructuring plan for eighth graders. I was transferred to a middle school labeled the worst in the district. The building was a former jailhouse, and everything about it resembled a jailhouse—especially the atmosphere. I decided regardless of what the school looked like, it had students who needed me. I was there for the students. Every day, as I walked into the *jailhouse school,* I recalled why I became a teacher—to make a positive difference in the lives of those children. I meant it in the interview, and I cherished every day I was allowed to teach.

I know buildings aren't supposed to be important, but converting a former jailhouse into a school was too much. I reminded myself that students in the other schools must not have needed me, or I would have been sent to one of the other schools. I felt I was exactly where I needed to be. I wasn't angry or bitter about having the most challenging students because I knew they were the ones I was sent to help. I sang to myself, *Don't stop thinking about tomorrow,* as I prepared to teach in a dark classroom without windows.

The eighth grade jailhouse school was my introduction to abused students asking for help. Even though I knew child abuse didn't begin or end with me, I didn't understand how widespread it was, nor was I prepared for it to show up in my classroom. In fact, my personal experience made me a trauma-informed teacher and taught me how to talk to students before the trauma-informed era of the twenty-first century. I knew the following to be true about students:

- students want to be treated fairly
- relationships are the most important things to students
- students need someone to listen
- students have a story, and they need to share it
- students are loyal, caring, and understanding humans and should be treated as such
- students need to be able to trust teachers
- students will learn *for* teachers if not for themselves

- students know when teachers are for them or against them based on actions, not words
- students want to succeed and need someone to believe in them
- students need praise, praise, praise.

I taught my students the way I needed to be taught as a traumatized child. I did what would have made me feel good, said the things I wanted my teachers to say, and cheered them on like I wanted my teachers to cheer me on.

As opportunities arose, I shared my survivor's story with students. I reasoned that telling my story would cause them to open up about their story —and many of them did. I think working with traumatized students was the beginning of seeing how my suffering helped others. My students were the first to hear about my childhood abuse, and it made me feel good to share it. My story of suffering let them know they were not the only ones who were abused. My story let them know that if I made it without a mother or father and grew up in and out of foster homes, they could as well. I noticed how even the students with the most challenging situations worked to succeed because they knew I wouldn't give them a pass. No one gave me a pass because of my situation, and I wouldn't give them one, either. I helped them, but I didn't feel sorry for them, accept lame excuses, or give up on them. I believed they could do it, and many of them did. I loved them, taught them, pushed them, encouraged, and supported them, but they had to do the hard work of never giving up.

In the classroom, Claire sat quietly until a boy jokingly touched her, and then it was as if a volcano erupted. She slapped a boy, cursed at another, and screamed at someone else. I knew something deeper than we could see was bothering her. Each day after school she shared a little more. Then one day she sobbed, "Promise me, you won't tell."

Anxious to help Claire in any way I could, I agreed; however, I should not have made that promise. I momentarily forgot I was a mandated reporter. Mandated reporters are required by law to report suspected or known instances of abuse. Teachers, most school personnel, medical personnel, and social workers are mandated reporters.

"She knows what he's doing. She leaves me at home with him. He does what he wants to me, and then she comes home."

I felt knots in the pit of my stomach, an all-too-familiar pain. "Who knows?" I asked.

"She knows. She does it every time, and I'm tired. I just can't keep doing it."

I wanted to say *OK, that's enough, because if you tell me any more, your secret will have to be told,* but I couldn't. I had to let her finish. I saw she was in emotional turmoil. "My grandmother's boyfriend has sex with me and my grandmother knows about it."

I sat in stark silence. I was face-to-face with the horror I ran from. My student was in an emotional prison, but by the time she finished her story, I was also reminded of my prison sentence. My past haunted me because of what happened to my siblings and me. As a child, I had wanted the school and our community to report their suspicions or knowledge of our abuse. More importantly, I wanted DHS to do something about it. I was now placed in the same position as many of those I criticized for their lack of action and advocacy.

The fear of betraying Claire's trust was stronger than the fear of going to jail for failure to report. I understood her pain. Despite her continued sobbing, I could only half listen. I was nervous, but I wouldn't tell her how upset I felt. I calmed down and closed my emotional prison doors so that I could release her. I fought the triggers and residuals from the similarities in our sexual abuse histories. I withstood flashbacks of faceless men using my body for their gratification. I had to push aside the memory of Elsie accepting money for me and Briana to go with men who were twenty or more years older than we were.

"I don't know what to do," Claire said. "I don't have anywhere safe to go. My mom is in jail, and I don't know who I can trust."

Claire's story sounded like mine. I wanted to cry with her. It was too late to unknow what I knew. I relived my childhood in flashing mental images. I knew sexual abuse existed, but I denied it happened to my students. Perhaps this was part of the dissociation of trauma survivors when things become too stressful. I didn't know how to process my students' confessions that they were sexually abused, so I used avoidance, another technique trauma survivors use to circumvent stress. It is a form of denial to escape or distract from thoughts, feelings, and situations that are triggered by memories of trauma. Sometimes avoidance looks like inventing excuses to reject invitations to events that might be stressful, or abusing alcohol or other substances to numb the feelings.

My abuse and neglect took place more than twenty years before Claire's, but once again, what happened to me was front and center in my mind. I listened to Claire in disbelief while feeling overcome with the thought that children are still abused and neglected. I knew I was strategically placed in that school for my student and others like her. Previously, I thought abuse was limited to rural areas or to poor families, but Claire grew up in an urban center. I was speechless. I didn't want her to tell me everything, because the more she told me, the more I had to report. My thoughts raced. *She has brothers and sisters. They will be separated. I don't want her to be separated from them. She may be abused in a foster home like I was. Lord, I am not prepared for this emotional stuff. It's too much!* I screamed inside.

I knew I had to help Claire and screaming, crying, or running away wouldn't help. Even if I lost my job, I had to help her. "Claire, I know I promised I wouldn't tell anyone, but I can't let this abuse go on," I said as I wiped her tears away, and then mine. "I have to do something. If I don't, this will go on, and I don't want you to continue being sexually abused."

"Please don't tell!" she begged. "They'll take me away from my family."

I knew they would, but I had to help her. I had to do for her what I wished someone had done for me. I reported Claire's situation to the school social worker who contacted Child Services. They did as I anticipated. Claire was removed from her grandmother's home, placed in a foster home, and enrolled in a new school in a new district. About a month later, she called me from her foster home. She said her life was better and she liked her foster parents. I expected her to be angry with me for telling others about her situation, but I found as a trauma survivor that abused children fear transition, so they tell listeners not to report something while they secretly hope the report will result in their rescue. It's an *I didn't do it* sort of situation where they are relieved of the responsibility of the report. Though I never heard from her again, I was glad to hear that foster care worked out for Claire.

Claire's secret and mine were out. Sexual abuse was not something I thought I would hear from my students. Although I grew up thinking everyone's life was filled with abuse, I didn't think my students' lives were as awful. While I thought abuse was common, the reality of it happening to my students surprised me. The confusion vs. denial continuum is wide for abuse survivors, and we frequently swing back and forth, like the variety of emotions that emerged. Despite reminding myself that I did the right thing, I had many nights of sleepless turmoil because I felt I betrayed Claire's trust. I felt I had failed her. How did this happen? For the rest of the semester, I fought the nagging thoughts: *I couldn't help her* and *how did I not notice she was abused?* I thought I had done right by reporting, but I felt guilty for uprooting her from school, friends, teachers, and her one safe environment. The state designated teachers as mandated reporters, so I told myself my job made me do it. Based on childhood experience, I wasn't convinced a foster home was an improvement, but I hoped it was the lesser of two evils—which could still be evil. Concern for Claire's well-being, regardless of how painful, gave me the courage to face the uncertainty of what might happen. I staked my confidence in the idea that one day she would remember a teacher who did right by her.

Although Claire didn't die a physical death, I still felt I'd lost a student. Childhood Trauma sneaked in and destroyed her. The emotional pain of watching her die while I attempted to teach her was unbearable. I wondered how I could have missed this important lesson from students. I found nothing in the teacher's manual on how to talk to a sexually abused student. It said to report the alleged abuse, but there was nothing about providing emotional support for the student—or the teacher—during the process and aftermath of reporting. I searched the manual for dealing with the loss of a student by death, and again, I found nothing. There was a little information about sending surviving students to guidance counselors for grief counseling. Sadly, there was nothing at that time to help me with either of these crises, and I struggled through them alone. At one time, I even questioned whether I missed training in the alternative program that perhaps educators in traditional training programs received. After talking with other educators, I learned I hadn't missed this type of professional development because it was not taught in Arkansas preparatory programs during those years.

I couldn't ask another teacher about it because most of the teachers I knew didn't get as involved with students as I felt I was. In fact, most of them warned me to stay out of students' home lives. I couldn't because I knew students' lives outside of school influenced their school lives. In Claire's case, her grades had dropped steeply and she withdrew from activities she'd previously enjoyed because she contemplated suicide. Until she spoke with me, she thought suicide was the only way to escape her abuser. Students need someone they can trust to guide them when they are lost. It is invaluable to have a caring teacher when they need someone because it might save their life.

For years, I felt I was hoodwinked by the education profession. My lesson plans were prepared. I studied the best practices. I knew how to capture students' attention and set learning objectives. I knew my subject area well, but no amount of reading and studying for an exam prepared me for the adversities students faced or what I needed to do to help them. Education failed to prepare for the most important thing I needed to help the students: time to care. Every second of the instructional hour was filled with things for me to teach them from the textbook, but no time left for me to help them navigate and process *LIFE*. I found it odd, since I believed everything they did involved *LIFE*. Classes were designed to teach them about educational subjects, but nothing about civilization or how to thrive in it. Consequently, I integrated life lessons into my English curriculum. It was as much a part of my teaching philosophy as teaching students to write a five-point persuasive essay. They loved the life lessons, like the one about Romeo and Juliet. We talked about the dangers of rushing into relationships and the tragedies that may follow. One of the life lessons from *Of Mice and Men* was we dream and work on our dream, but there are times we have to reevaluate our dreams to see if they line up with reality.

While teaching in the jailhouse school, I often felt disillusioned. I was certified to teach, but the preparation didn't include the fact that many students weren't ready to learn. Teacher trainers convinced would-be teachers that students came to school to learn. While it is true that some of them did, many of them didn't, and it's not because they didn't *want* to learn. Many students had issues preventing their learning. In the 1990s, teachers were not trained to teach students with trauma. I am gratified that I found ways to help students with trauma, especially since I didn't yet know about the brain damage caused by Childhood Trauma. Even though I was not prepared for my students, I see now that I taught them the ways I learned best, using the strategies and techniques that I developed in college. I taught them to use mnemonic devices for memorization of facts and to leverage their creative thinking by partnering with students who had stronger critical-thinking abilities.

Chapter 40
FORGOTTEN PURPOSE

One day, I received a notice from the administrative office that the school district was restructuring yet again. By then, despite earlier doubts, I was 100% convinced that teaching was my assignment from God. I told whomever would listen that I didn't care where I was assigned because God and students I needed to reach were there. Since I had tenure, the district gave me the choice of where I wanted to go. I could choose from the best schools in the district. I still wanted to help students, but I wanted to help the ones who didn't need quite as much. I had worked with at-risk students for almost ten years, and I thought I could use a break, so I convinced myself that God wanted to give me a break. I was emotionally drained from immersion in my students' lives. When a best friend betrayed a student, I was the first to know. When a parent died or was hospitalized, I was the first to know. When a student was abused, I was the first to know. Restructuring was my opportunity to take a break and make a change.

I was assigned to my school of choice—Little Rock Central High (LRCH), one of the most famous schools in the United States since it was where the Little Rock Nine desegregated Little Rock schools. I would move out of the former jailhouse middle school to teach high school. There was a stipulation that I had to be present at the appointed day of confirmation of the school assignment, but I didn't foresee a problem. I needed to show up and sign my contract for the transfer to be secured. Nothing would prevent me from being there. My future depended on it. Only death could have kept me from showing up to sign that paper. Or so I thought.

When the day came for the appointment to sign my contract, I was at home with a terrible infection. I was so sick, I could hardly walk. I called the central office and was reminded that only the staff who attended the appointment to sign their contract would receive an assignment at the school of choice. "I'm sorry, but if you're not here, we will assign you to a school where we have a need."

That statement hit me like a brick to the side of the head. I saw my future at Little Rock Central High go down the drain. I would stay a nobody. Transferring to LRCH was my ticket to a new life, a higher district professional profile, and an upgrade in reputation and respect. Of course, it was an unreasonable expectation, much like when I thought marrying and changing my last name meant leaving my past behind. Trauma survivors frequently believe that changing their environment, whether with a new job or a new location, will change their reality. They don't understand that their past is part of them and wherever they go, it goes with them.

I was convinced life would be better at LRCH. The students at Central had parents who cared, attended PTA meetings, called to check on their attendance, supported teachers, and above all, understood the importance of education. Central's parents had hope. I thought if I worked there I would be a *real* teacher. Going to one of the at-risk schools meant more caregiving and counseling. I wanted to teach unencumbered by students' painful abuse. I was convinced that could happen only at Little Rock Central High School, which is ironic since the history of the school was built on the suffering of the Little Rock Nine. I was undoubtedly delusional.

Much later in my career, I came to understand that caring, involved parents didn't make me a better teacher. Nearly anyone can teach students who are focused, curious, and ready to learn. What made me a good teacher was understanding and reaching the abused, broken, rejected, and violent students. The fact that I was able to teach, love, support, and encourage those students, many of whom were at risk of dropping out, made me a better teacher. At the time, I wanted validation of my talent and self-worth, and I sought confirmation that I was intelligent. I wanted to be recognized by the District Curriculum Supervisor and the Superintendent of Schools as an outstanding teacher. That validation had not yet come my way, and I was envious of the teachers who were recognized and acknowledged, especially those who received awards. At district meetings, I waited for someone to say *"Great job, Dora! I know you have a difficult bunch."* I gradually learned how important it was to love my work and not be dependent on other people's praise. Teaching was so difficult that I had to love my job fundamentally or I'd have no reason to keep doing it. I learned my motivation had to come from a deep love for students and that I had to know I was doing it for the right reason. I had to know teaching students was my purpose. The desire for validation from others was because of my insecurities, identity issues, and desire to be accepted, all of which came from a poor self-image due to the way I was treated in childhood.

A week after missing the appointment to sign my contract, I was assigned to a school no one wanted to go to. I cried because I heard many of the teachers sent there did not want to teach, and many of the students did not come to school to learn—a bad combination of circumstances. I cried for the incoming students and teachers like me who wanted to make a difference.

I prayed and cried in the days before the start of the school year, hoping God would change His mind. I wanted to be rescued—again. Sometimes we need to be rescued, and sometimes we just need to do the things to rescue ourselves. In this situation, I needed to recall my purpose. From childhood, I wanted and waited to be rescued. Each life decision to *change something* was me crying out to be rescued. I now understand it to be learned helplessness that developed from my childhood feelings of being powerless and unable to change circumstances. I continued to expect a rescue like a typical victim until years later when I did what others did to heal: I faced my horrific past and with the help of God, education, and therapy, began a life-changing healing journey. I allowed God to rescue me.

I told God how unfair it was for Him to send me to that undesirable school. I felt I had done my share of being the trauma teacher for students. I told God I wanted to be transferred to another school, that I needed to be at a school where I could teach. I must have sounded like an ungrateful three-year-old throwing a tantrum. Then I reminded God of what happened to Reggie. What I was saying was *I don't want to risk loving the broken students again.* Can I have some students this time who are not like me? It was selfish, but it was where my mind was.

By the first day of school, God refreshed my memory of my forgotten purpose and promise to help broken and abused students. He also reminded me of why I chose to be a teacher: to make a positive difference and support those He sent me to help. I had forgotten my purpose and that there is often pain in purpose. In fact, in many instances, pain leads us to our purpose. Once I rediscovered my purpose, no matter how hard the job was, I didn't try to transfer to another school. I stayed where He sent me. I learned how to lean into my pain and accept that I was there for the students, not for the school's prestige or popularity among my colleagues. That redirection by God changed my life. From that time forward, I accepted the most challenging students because I knew God gave me everything I needed to help them. The schedulers must have been in communication with God because they assigned the most challenging students to my classes.

I had no doubt that these students would be the best ever because I was convinced I could change their lives. Once again, I declared there would be no student I couldn't handle. Regardless of what the demographics, teachers, or their records predicted, I knew the determining factor was what I would say. I would say they could do it. I knew students who came from extreme adversities rarely came with self-awareness or were prepared for the challenges of life. Many of them came with uncertainty, distrust, and unwillingness to try yet again. That's when great teachers make a difference. I learned to accept the challenge of teaching the unteachable and unreachable students, and I worked every day to change their futures and their lives. I knew the traumatized students didn't come to school to learn. Many of them came to escape an unsafe home or street life. I vowed to create an imaginative place where they would find themselves so immersed in it that they forgot their home life, and that is what they did. Most of the abused children who came to my classroom often didn't want to leave when the bell rang.

On the first day of school I was excited. I sanitized every desk, rehearsed an introduction for the students, made sure the lesson plans were relevant, and wrote an encouraging quote on the board. In previous years I prepared to teach. This year, I was ready to be a teacher. I believed I had the power to change the world. I stopped looking at students as groups and saw them as individuals. I considered each of them would one day touch someone's life and that whatever I instilled in them would also touch that person's life. This is the way teachers make a difference in their communities. I seldom hung out in the teacher's lounge to hear about students' behaviors because I learned early on that students tend to meet expectations. If they are expected to excel, they will, but if they sense expectations of failure, they will do that, as well. I seldom heard anyone share strategies on how to reach a particularly challenging student, but I heard plenty of advice on how to get rid of them. Because I rejected negativity, I was not a teachers' lounge favorite.

I believe my positive outlook contributed to my longevity. Even on my last day in the classroom, I cried because I wondered who would love the children when I left. That's the way I wanted to leave the teaching profession. I wanted to go when I was still excited about teaching, not after losing interest—but that's reason enough to leave, as well. There is a need for teachers with a passion for sparking learning. Students need teachers who go above and beyond to reach them; they need teachers who trust God to help them and their students. Students need teachers who pray for them, teachers who know children's lives are in their hands, and understand they have the power to build students up or tear them down.

Schools need teachers who know there is no student who is unreachable.

My motto was: *There is no student I cannot reach.* I was determined to show everyone that all students can be taught if their teachers care enough. Teachers had to work harder to teach challenging students because it demanded a commitment to overcome the students' defenses and conquer their resistance. My first goal was to reach the students. I wanted them to learn the subject, but I knew I had to reach them with my heart first. The goal of most teachers is to teach their subject first.

Along with hours spent on lesson plans, I spent hours on strategies to help the failing and difficult students. I wanted to show them how much I cared. If a student refused to work, I did not put them out of the classroom or engage in a power play to demand they engage with the material. I said, "I understand if you have a headache. Why don't you put your head down for a few minutes and then try to do a little work?"

I thought students might take advantage of me, but they didn't. They put their heads down for a few minutes, and shortly afterward, I would notice them looking around. I would ask, "Are you ready to start this assignment?" Most of the time they got to work. Others asked if they could return at another time, and they did. Surprisingly, even the students from youth detention facilities asked for—and completed—their homework. I discovered something many tenured teachers didn't know, and it changed how I taught and how students learned. I believe the adage, *Students don't care how much you know until they know how much you care.* I shared my approach with co-workers who had problems, but they often said it wouldn't work for them.

I was determined to do whatever it took to connect with my students because I knew the importance of teacher-student relationships. I was the teacher students talked with to get wise counsel, which was ironic because I had no clue about my own life. The only reason I could help them was because I believed I was in my purpose and that I was sent to help these students. Whenever students had a problem, I thought I could help them. I showed students how much I cared, and I gained their trust. Some were more difficult than others, but I understood why they were defensive. Emotions don't differentiate. It didn't matter that I wasn't the one who hurt them, lied to them, abused them, or failed them. All they knew was adults hurt them, abused them, lied to them, and failed them, so they tried to protect themselves from adults. I understood their defensiveness because I was one of them.

Chapter 41
WATCH OUT FOR THE BIG D

The chronic desire to feel secure in God's love for me—and keep out of hell—eventually took a toll on my mind, body, and spirit. I almost died before I was delivered from religious behaviors. The propensity for the big D (Deception) is common among Childhood Trauma survivors. Unfortunately, I thought the church and its people were sent by God to protect me. Equally sad was my inability to see how easily I was deceived by them. I had little ability to discern what was from God and what was man's weakness and/or evil. I was guilty of doing what many CT survivors do—I trusted the wrong people and rejected the right people.

Many CT survivors have their own stories of deception, and some have two or three. It took years for me to tell my story of deception without shame. My mind and thoughts were so distorted at the time, I was susceptible to believe almost anything. A damaged mind and emotions are a disaster waiting to happen. In my honest belief that God could do anything, and my sincere desire to be used by Him, I thought the opportunity came when I chose to support a sister friend who believed God told her to marry Deion Sanders, a Dallas Cowboys NFL football player.

I'll pause there because you probably need to catch your breath and hold your belly. It's ok, you can laugh now because I can't see you.

Yes, you read that correctly. I believed what my friend told me—that God told her to marry Deion Sanders. In our misguided *obedience to God,* we drove to Texas to attempt to meet him during one of the worst snow and ice storms in the history of that region. The state's transportation authority warned everyone but emergency vehicles to stay off the roads. However, both of us were thoroughly convinced that God spoke to us, and we thought we were obeying Him. We were strong even if no one believed or understood us because we were sure we had the faith of Abraham. One of the worst things about deception is not recognizing it. After all, it wouldn't be deception if it was recognizable.

I ignored every motherly and wifely wisdom in order to go to Texas with my delusional friend. It is embarrassing to admit, but I genuinely believed God told me to go. I see now this plan was flawed on so many levels, beginning with our misunderstanding of the character and Word of God, ignoring my husband's counsel, and ignoring state warnings to avoid travel because of the dangerous roads. This plan was void of wisdom and so many other things. I willfully disregarded my husband and the weather conditions and attributed that to God. I knew the scripture about wives submitting to their husbands, but I decided to use my prideful translation. God couldn't have meant *everything*. I interpreted it as *submitting to my husband as long as I believed he was right*. I thought if God told me to do something, I had to do it. My friend and I had to complete our misguided folly to see the full extent of our deception.

Deceived people are unaware that a loving God doesn't split up families, tell adults to have sex with children, instruct His people to do things contrary to the laws of man (unless the law is in direct violation of God's Word), command people to hurt others, or tell them to remain in a relationship where they are harmed. I left my young son and husband in a blizzard during the week before Christmas to go to Deion Sanders' house. Clearly, my decision was not a direction from God.

Because I functioned in deception, I didn't think anyone understood unless they agreed with me. I needed a Believer who believed in the Resurrection power of Jesus to command the prideful, lying spirits of ego, deception, error, and mental illness to leave me. Instead, those who knew laughed at me and talked about me. Oh, there were many Believers around me, but none told me I was deceived or cast the spirit out of me like Jesus said to do (Mark 16:17).

Childhood Trauma sets up survivors as prime candidates for deception. I see it in many who participate in my ministry today. God is the one who opens their eyes. Students in the program have been deceived about several self-sabotaging behaviors: delusional thinking, life-altering decisions, immoral behaviors, non-faith-based solutions, and leaving their families. Meanwhile they erroneously attribute their decisions to God's leadership. Satan uses deception because he knows the brain damage he caused and how it affects critical thinking. He knows they are not equipped to ask the necessary questions to make informed decisions.

God never tells anyone to go against His Word. His Word says, *"Wives, submit yourselves to your husbands"* (Ephesians 5:22). Because I didn't see Drake pray, I justified my unsubmissive behavior by questioning whether Drake understood the scriptures. Another thing about deception is that it is the twin of pride. I thought that in order for Drake to lead me, he needed to read the Bible, quote scriptures, and fast from eating/drinking. My position was extremely prideful, but it justified my actions. I decided that Drake didn't hear from God like I did, and that's why he didn't understand. In reality, he didn't understand because I wasn't hearing from God and was completely deceived. I had a fantasy of the miracle marriage of my friend to Deion Sanders. The problem was that it was only in my head.

I have learned where there is pride, like in the Garden of Eden, deception lurks. Satan deceived me like he did Eve. I felt justified in thinking *If God tells you to do something, you have to do it. It doesn't have to make sense to you. You should obey God rather than man.* Satan used my desire to please God to twist God's Word and deceive me into thinking I pleased God. It is so important to listen and let humility and wisdom take the lead, because it's harder to be deceived in humility.

When we arrived at Deion's house, a woman I believe was his housekeeper answered the door. She seemed surprised to see me, and probably even more alarmed once she realized that she had opened the door to a stranger—during a blizzard on a day when only emergency vehicles were to be on the roads! I asked for Deion, but she said he wasn't home. I said, "OK, tell him the Lord sent me. Deion will know what it's regarding."

Talk about psychosis! I'm pretty sure after that conversation she either got a weapon or a phone to call the police—or both. As I write this, I can't help but think how many people have killed someone because they thought God told them to do it. How many got married, got a divorce, quit a job, relocated, went to a certain church, or founded a ministry—all in the name of God while He had nothing to do with it?

God may ask me to do something others don't understand, but never will He ask me to do something that goes against His Word. Never.

I knew the Bible but couldn't apply it to my mental disorder. Misguided and delusional believers know and can quote scriptures but don't know how to apply them to their lives. That's how people are able to follow extreme religious doctrine and join cults. I know. All it takes is a person with head knowledge of God without heart knowledge of Him and His character. People lacking heart knowledge of God are dangerous because they are vulnerable to deception. One way to guard against deception is to get the counsel of someone who is honest.

God is Truth and will only move and work in truth. He will not fight a battle that He does not authorize. Our attempt to meet Deion Sanders failed; he wasn't at home, and he never contacted us. Years later, I see how He protected me in my deception, but did not allow me to be delivered from it. I had to go through it so I could recognize it. I used to blame the Texas episode on lack of sleep, exhaustion, and physical illness, but while those things exacerbated the situation, they were not causal. The root of the problem was the structural damage done to my prefrontal cortex due to the Childhood Trauma. Once the structural damage was done, it impacted my critical thinking so my decisions were made based upon my feelings instead of critically examining facts. Apart from the work demanded by my job, my brain was unreliable, but I didn't know it.

Drake was solemn when I returned from Texas. Christmas had passed. I think he experienced unexpressed anger. Still, he didn't suggest I get mental help. I still believe he thought I intentionally did crazy things. Michael didn't ask any questions. When he was over thirty, I asked him how it made him feel when I missed Christmas to go to Deion Sanders' house. He told me he didn't understand at the time until he overheard the family talking and laughing about it. No one asked anything about what happened on the trip, but I could hear their snickering and laughter behind my back. It hurt when they laughed at me, but there was nothing I could do because I was deceived. After Michael shared his memory with me, I was sad that I put him through the embarrassment. I forgave myself when I recognized that I made the decision to go with limited mental and emotional resources.

Although Drake never said *I told you so,* his comments and behaviors spoke for him. When I returned from Texas, Michael was glad to see me, but I could tell he missed me at Christmas. It took several years after my eyes were opened to forgive myself for missing Michael's Christmas. There were no words I could offer him other than *I'm sorry Mommy wasn't here.* Drake didn't pity me. He lit right into me, not in a belligerent way, but in a discrediting way. He said with a smirk, "So, did your friend and Deion get married?"

I wanted to lash out at him, but I refrained. I asked him who he told and he said, "I didn't tell anyone, but Michael told everyone that you and his aunt went to Texas to marry Deion Sanders."

My mouth dropped. At that point, I should have realized this was not of God because if it were, I wouldn't have cared who knew. I was both embarrassed and reassured at the same time. I kept thinking *God wouldn't let her down. They will see when it happens.* Well, it never happened. God didn't let her down because He wasn't in it at all.

I was delusional because I believed Deion would call my friend and they would end up together. It wasn't until a year later when I had my first mental breakdown that God opened my eyes to the lies and deception of the Texas trip. My big discovery? I learned I didn't know God the way I thought I did and that what I knew about God was what I learned from abusive, manipulative, controlling, religious people in my childhood and Harold's church.

I knew something was wrong when I began to feel fearful and experienced panic attacks. My thoughts were scattered. I finally began to question whether God told me to go to Texas. It was too much for me to believe that a loving God would be so cruel as to ask me to go out in a dangerous storm and cause such hurt and embarrassment to my husband and son. Even so, each time I tried to accept that God was not in the Texas deception, I broke down. I began to wonder if I'd misheard God. There was no way I could avoid an emotional and mental breakdown. I suffered significant emotional turmoil recalling the embarrassing trip and returned to suffer humiliation from my husband and his family who heard about the fiasco. Finally, I had to accept the truth: God allowed me to go to Texas to learn about deception. It took such an outrageous experience to jolt me into seeing my behavior as selfish and unacceptable since God was not in it.

That was the beginning of what I thought of as my downfall. Although the Texas deception incident was an emotionally and mentally painful experience, I learned several valuable ways to recognize deception. First, God will never do anything to contradict his Word. Second, anyone with Childhood Trauma should get wise counsel from several people other than those in their circle. Third, regardless of what happens, God will deliver when we trust in Him. Fourth, I learned when life seemed as if it was over because I messed up so badly, lost everything and everyone, and my situation was hopeless, God in His infinite mercy opened my eyes, healed my brokenness, and turned my messes into messages that will help others. While I will always remember the deception, I will remember more that God's mighty hand delivered me from the Childhood Trauma that made me easy prey to deception. I couldn't spend the rest of my life in regret and sorrow, so I chose to teach others who suffered CT how to avoid my painful mistakes. The last thing I learned was God does His greatest works when He redeems us from messes. They are never bigger than our God.

I didn't realize it, but that breakdown was undoubtedly the beginning of my healing journey and learning the truth about the One True God. It took a breakdown for God to break up the fallow ground of lies and deception planted since childhood. Only after I studied the impact of Childhood Trauma did I stop judging myself and feeling guilty for the self-sabotaging decisions I made over the years. The brain damage caused by the trauma is not an excuse for the many poor choices CT survivors make, but rather, it is a scientific explanation that proves when the brain is damaged, it cannot make peak decisions.

Chapter 42
THE WAKE UP DREAM

Recognizing I was deceived in one thing opened my eyes to deception in other areas of my life. Shortly after the Texas incident, I dreamed about Harold chasing his daughter around a yard. I understood in the dream that Harold was chasing her to have sex with her. This was the dream that would change my life because when I woke up, I knew Harold had sexually abused me. I was no longer in denial. After the dream, I was no longer free from doubt about the nature of our sexual transactions. Before the dream, I ignored my discomfort and justified what he and I did because I was spiritually confused and a minor child in desperate need of a home. I didn't understand God's character, and because of Harold's elevated denominational position, I didn't clearly understand right and wrong. The Bible says not everyone should become a teacher of the Word because it is a huge responsibility to teach the Word of God without twisting it. Twisting the Word by saying one thing and doing another causes spiritual wounds (James 3:1-2).

Once a truth is known, it can't be unknown. During the years I lived with Harold and Agnes, I thought the sexual abuse was acceptable because I believed Harold was sent from God, pastor of a church, and in a leadership position in the denomination. Who dared question his authority? Although I was unjustifiably abused by Harold, I had rationalized his behavior, dissociated from the events, and suppressed my memories of the rides to the country.

After the dream, I clearly understood Harold violated me. I already noticed Harold's daughter didn't talk with him much. She lived on the West Coast, had limited phone communication with him, and only visited once while I lived with him. I judged his daughter, thinking she must have been a rebellious teenager and didn't like his rules when she was younger. Still, after living with him and discovering his pattern of sexually abusing young girls, I had other reasons to understand why she kept her distance from him. Years later, I thought about the men in his circle who were predators like him. Several fondled me and attempted to seduce me. I managed to escape and avoid most of them. I can only imagine that Harold's daughter might have had similar experiences.

I suppressed Harold's sexual abuse until the dream jolted it into my memory. I know God used the dream to reveal Harold's abuse. Before the dream, I didn't recognize the abuse. I had suppressed the memory for nearly twenty years, a common behavior among child sexual abuse survivors. The dream stimulated memories of the traumatic events. Because of the low amounts of norepinephrine released during the REM (rapid eye movement) sleep stage, I could manage what would have been overpowering emotions if I recalled the memories while awake. REM sleep is where dreaming and memory work simultaneously. During REM, the brain is extremely active and begins its natural therapeutic work of helping the body process the emotionally-charged events of the day. The brain knows stressful hormones are reduced or shut off during REM, freeing it to process without activating the body's alarm system.

I tried to pray away the dream of Harold and his daughter. I wanted to ignore it, but it remained stuck in my head and repeatedly popped up to interfere with other thoughts. Harold's sexual abuse dominated my thoughts. In a split second, Harold went from foster father to spiritual leader to sexual abuser. As a result of God and the REM sleep phase, I knew what Harold did, but I still couldn't accept that he intentionally did such an evil thing to me. What Harold did was worse than anything other men did to me because he did it in the name of God. My mind began floating between yesterday and today. In an attempt to squelch the memories of the car rides, I wasn't able to accommodate thoughts further away than the day before. Last year, last month, and even last week were too much. I began to question my relationship with God. I loved God, but I didn't think He could love me. I determined a *man of God* couldn't have been evil, so our incestuous relationship must have been my fault. I was the evil one. In my confusion, I could not turn to God. My mind repeatedly fought the truth. I believed I couldn't tell anyone because Harold was a *man of God*—another example of a survivor protecting an abuser. I didn't know it then, but I needed the help of a counselor skilled in treating survivors of child sexual abuse.

Following a month of limited sleep, I became convinced that an evil spirit overcame Harold and forced him to abuse me sexually. I had a breakdown from the unrelenting mental, emotional, and spiritual turmoil. It seemed that everything I learned in Sunday School was no longer true because God didn't protect me from abuse. He didn't punish anyone in any way that I could see for the evil inflicted on me. He didn't prevent me from having a breakdown.

My world shattered with the new understanding that neither God nor Harold nor those who claimed to represent God were who I thought they were. Up to this point, I believed what happened to me was acceptable and that God had somehow sanctioned it, but to understand that I was abused by *men of God* was an indescribable torment. As mentally deranged as it sounds, survivors of abuse have what I call an *uninformed peace*, which means they have a false sense of peace because they have not yet been informed—or understand—that what happened to them was horrific and life-altering. In an instant, Harold was not the loving father I knew and accepted, and God was not the Holy Father I thought I knew. At this point, I didn't know Him as a loving God. We weren't taught in Harold's church that God was loving, but I had always felt He was because He helped me find places to stay, graduate from high school, go to college, and find a good husband. Now, everything I thought about Him seemed false.

I didn't feel I could tell anyone, so for several months I kept the revelation of the dream secret before sharing it with Drake. I was full of shame and guilt, but I was unable to predict Drake's reaction, so I remained silent. I questioned Drake's ability to control his anger. He knew Harold, and I didn't know what he would do to him if he knew the truth. Another reason I didn't share the dream was because I wanted to protect Drake and Michael and was concerned about how my secret would affect them. It must seem ironic that I was the one suffering, but I was more concerned about the potential hurt to others, which is common for CT survivors

After the revelation of Harold's abuse and the return of my memories of the drives to the countryside, as well as the others who knew him and used their relationship to get access to me, I experienced anxiety, depression, and mental exhaustion. I stopped calling and visiting him. It was impossible to converse with Harold as if nothing had happened because of the negative emotional effects I suffered following any contact with him. My love for Harold soured into shunning him since I couldn't talk to him because of the overwhelming negative emotions. I couldn't eat or sleep normally because I was nervous and anxious about the damage to Harold's reputation if others heard that he sexually abused me. I acted like many sexual abuse survivors: I put the perpetrator/abuser's feelings first. I didn't want to hurt Harold or his congregation. I couldn't ask myself what Jesus would do because I couldn't pray. My trusting relationship with God was destroyed, so I remained silent. At the age of thirty-four, I experienced a crushing emotional and mental breakdown from which it took years to recover.

In hindsight, I know I experienced PTSD. Everything frightened me. I was aware I was not myself—as much as I knew who I was then—but I couldn't explain what happened or why. I no longer wanted to be around people because I knew I wasn't mentally stable. I couldn't pray because I thought God allowed Harold to abuse me. I didn't hate God, but I didn't know what to think about Him and couldn't trust Him. I could only quote Psalm 91, which I learned at fourteen. In the madness and confusion, Psalm 91 carried me through the turmoil. God knew exactly what I needed. He knew I didn't trust anyone, so He couldn't have sent a person to me. He also knew I heard from Him but no longer trusted His voice to speak to me because I was too confused by Harold and the spiritual abuse. When the nightmares and panic attacks came, I quoted Psalm 91 repeatedly until I was calm enough to sleep. I quoted Psalm 91 day and night. I'm not sure I believed much in it then, but it was the only thing I could say when I was afraid, panicky, and anxious. I am so thankful I learned the Word before I needed it because as my lifeline, it came to me at times when I least expected it.

I tried to sort out my confusing bewilderment, but I couldn't. My inability to accept Harold's sexual abuse sustained the turmoil. I also find that to be true of many of the people I serve. Their struggle to keep or ignore their secret rather than acknowledge they might have been abused causes them more psychological damage than the pain they experience when they accept the truth and process it.

I thought I was dragging the past into the present of my marriage when I recalled what Harold did. I didn't understand that unprocessed trauma never has to be dredged up because it is always in the subconscious and remembered by the body. Researchers report undeclared memories are stored in the brain and body. Van der Kolk, in his book, *The Body Keeps the Score,* sheds light on how trauma reshapes the brain and body. It further jeopardizes the survivors' ability to trust, engage in meaningful activities, experience pleasure, and exert self-control. The trauma experienced in the past isn't over simply because it happened in the past. My trauma wasn't over until the traumatic emotions were processed, resolved, and stored as a part of my life story. Only then could I move forward.

I felt like a zombie, numb and disinterested in life. I felt hopeless and helpless, unable to sleep or eat. I felt worthless and couldn't focus my thoughts on anything productive. I felt as if my life was meaningless and that the world would be a better place without me. I had no joy and spent a lot of time lying down, exhausted but unable to rest. I often sat dazed and unable to communicate or even talk with people. I lived in complete fear that I would die and leave my son motherless as my mother left me. I was ashamed of what I experienced because no one knew how to explain my erratic behaviors and antics, what caused them, or how long they would last.

The first breakdown I experienced involved increasing emotional numbness and mental confusion until I was unable to function. I had to take a leave of absence from work. After subsequent breakdowns, I could function but experienced more depression and isolation. I wrote poems to help me process my pain. I use the word breakdown because the experiences left me in a constant state of mental confusion, total despair, and thinking I might be admitted into a mental institution. In fact, I believe the only reason I wasn't admitted was because no one forced the issue. I wasn't sane enough to think about my needs so I couldn't suggest anything. Drake saw something was wrong but never suggested medical or in-patient mental health treatment. During these times I experienced inexplicable, utter helplessness.

My thoughts spun in illogical spirals as I vacillated between blaming myself for what I saw was my part in Harold's abuse, to anger and wishing he would die. I wanted the extreme emotional and mental rollercoaster to end. Sometimes I thought because I did not resist him, I invited his abuse of me. Most times I thought I was the scum of the earth and a disgrace to Drake and Michael. I thought Michael deserved a better mother and Drake deserved a better wife. These toxic thoughts eroded my self-worth.

Chapter 43
MORE LAYERS

Almost a year after the dream and the breakdown, I went to speak to Harold. I hadn't told Drake yet about the dream or Harold's abuse because I fantasized Harold would apologize, and we would continue our surrogate father-daughter relationship. He was the only father I knew, so I would have done anything to keep our relationship in place. The only thing I knew to do was pray, so I asked God to fix the situation. I also told God how to fix it, that I forgave Harold, and that I didn't want Harold to lose his church.

I couldn't figure out how to tell a man of the cloth that he did something that left me emotionally and mentally damaged. I wanted to believe he didn't know the extent of the pain he caused. I had dreadful mental images of Harold and Drake fighting to the death, leaving me a widow and Michael fatherless or leaving the church without a leader. My mind was overloaded as I childishly ignored the reality that Drake was a younger, healthier man who could have easily destroyed Harold, but I wanted to protect them.

In my naiveté, I wanted to see Harold because I believed he did not understand what he had done to me. I believed he loved me as his daughter and would be hurt when I told him his abuse contributed to an emotional and mental breakdown. I only envisioned him saying, *I'm sorry. I shouldn't have done that. May the Lord heal you of your wounds.* There was no thought about Harold's intentional deception and selfish abuse. I was about to embark on a period of awakening to the true nature of humans. My eyes were opened to the reality of the capacity for evil, self-preservation, pride, and deception from so-called God-sent people.

On a weekend visit to Harold, I took the opportunity of speaking alone with Harold. Our conversation took place in my car as I drove. I had no particular destination, but I thought it would be less confrontational if I talked to him while I drove. I wanted Harold to understand the depth of the damage he inflicted. He listened quietly as I explained that I knew what he did. I didn't want to tell him that I knew what he did was wrong legally, morally, and spiritually. I wanted to explain the damage that he did to me. Somehow, I thought talking to him would restore our relationship. I wanted to warn him to stop abusing others and to apologize to those already abused. Although I had several successes in my life, I continued to feel I didn't have value and continued to need validation. I felt I needed Harold's approval. This is true for many survivors who try to bury themselves in degrees, positions, and wealth. Those things oftentimes make unhealed CT survivors feel worse because they bring more responsibility, leading to a greater void and loneliness. For this reason, I felt as if I had nothing and no one except Harold and the church.

At this point, my siblings and I hardly saw one another except at family funerals. Harold was the only family I felt I had, and I was ready to forgive him for everything he did. I wanted to forgive him, hoping things would resolve quickly and we could continue as if nothing happened. I tried to convey how the abuse damaged and negatively affected my life. I tried to make him understand that I had an emotional breakdown because of the anxiety and fear brought on by the memories of the rapes he forced me to endure. Still, Harold did not acknowledge his guilt or ask for forgiveness. I had a mental script planned: we talked, he repented to God and asked me for forgiveness so we could continue our relationship. Instead, the only thing that happened as I anticipated was I talked to him. He neither acknowledged nor denied that he sexually abused me. He sat in the front seat and stared through the front windshield as I drove and talked. After nearly two hours of driving around Harold's community, I knew he wouldn't admit he sexually abused me, so I began the fifteen-minute drive back to his house, which seemed interminable. He left my car without a word, and I barely made it the eighty-six miles back to my home before the tears began to flow. I didn't want to break down in front of Drake and Michael in the car.

Though I still didn't know the full impact of Harold's sexual abuse, I knew something was not right. I knew the thing I wanted to resolve was still unresolved. In fact, after the drive, I was more confused. Harold's lack of responsiveness caused more problems; the panic attacks increased in intensity and frequency, along with night sweats and insomnia. It didn't help that the very next Sunday, in an act of self-preservation, Harold told people in his church that I had lost my mind.

I had triggers, such as crossing bridges or when someone revealed their sexual abuse. Immediately, my amygdala registered an alarm that I was again in danger. While driving, I hyperventilated and trembled. When I couldn't cross a bridge, I stopped and waited for the panic to subside, which sometimes took several minutes. I had nightmares and rushed to the hospital several times a month. I called a friend or co-worker to drop me off at the hospital because I remembered how Buck forced me to sleep there, and I didn't want to do that to Michael or Drake. All of the diagnoses were negative. Doctors prescribed several kinds of addictive medications which I usually stopped taking after a short period because they made me feel more anxious, panicky, and groggy. Ultimately, I desperately took Prozac, Paxil, and Zoloft, but none of them were effective. Paxil and Prozac left me physically drained with no appetite, while Zoloft made me feel worse because I would be nervous, irritated, and mentally unstable. My energy and appetite faded. I didn't like the out-of-body experiences the medicines caused. Now I know that I suffered from somatic symptom disorders as well as from a psychological disease called hypochondria that caused me to make multiple emergency room visits.

Drake did not express interest in any of my hospital/emergency visits. He knew something wasn't right but never said anything or suggested I get help except for the one time when I thought I was pregnant and the doctor said I wasn't. I had been hoping for another child and believed I was showing the signs of pregnancy, but the doctor's tests showed otherwise. Some members of the church prophesied that I was pregnant, which increased my belief that I was and later added to my mental breakdown. I learned the hard way that CT survivors need to have several spirit-filled mentors to share their "God told me" instructions before acting on them. If I had done that, I would not have made such terrible mistakes.

When I continued to believe I was pregnant, Drake suggested I see someone. My doctor prescribed Ativan. It caused insomnia and dizziness, but I could live with that because I wasn't driving at that time. I had to choose between my sanity and sleep and dizziness. I chose sanity.

I was awake most of the night. During the day I feared night. I slept very little for years. Lack of sleep added to my deteriorated mental state. I couldn't watch TV. I would read for a few minutes, put the book down and write a few stanzas of a poem due to lack of mental stability. I could only read motivational books by Norman Vincent Peale and Dale Carnegie and listen to motivational speakers like Earl Nightingale and Zig Ziglar. I couldn't listen to anyone who aroused my emotions.

I relived my traumas night and day in disturbing flashbacks. I didn't understand what caused the flashbacks, nor did I make the connection to Childhood Trauma. Even in consultations with doctors, no one asked about my childhood. They simply prescribed medication, which was the worst thing they could do for a CT survivor since survivors are more likely to suffer from drug addictions. The American Society for the Positive Care of Children disclosed that two-thirds of people in treatment centers suffered abuse as children. I see the miracle of how God safeguarded me from drug addictions for a long while because I was prescribed various antidepressants and anti-anxiety medications, stimulants, antipsychotics, and mood stabilizers.

Entangled with the hurt caused by Harold's sexual abuse was the emotional abuse I endured by church members in what I thought was my safe sanctuary. I couldn't attend church for more than a decade after the breakdown, and I spent a lot of time in confusion trying to understand why the church people were so cruel, abusive, and deceptive. I heard my voice say, *It's my fault. I was too trusting.* Then I'd hear another voice say, *It's not my fault. I was a child.* I had unrelenting mental anguish and confusion because I constantly thought about how I could have done things differently so they wouldn't have abused me.

Harold was at the top of the list, but I experienced other sexual and spiritual abusers in the church. When I remembered Harold's sexual abuse, I also remembered other abusers from my childhood. Some of my abusers were Harold's friends. One was a relative who frequently visited. Another was a local preacher who sometimes attended the church. There was a well-known national evangelist. I was afraid to go to the house of another church member because he touched and fondled me while standing at the door with his wife only a few feet away in the back room. I was terrified of what she might do and what might happen to their marriage if she saw him. I am certain he did the same to other young girls. As far as I knew, no one said anything, so I followed suit.

I began to realize that I had allowed myself to be taken advantage of by people in Harold's denomination in ways that were not just sexual, both in his church and in other churches. It was the church community I had been enthusiastically a part of since I lived with him, but now I began to doubt people's sincerity and motivation. I was mentally, physically, emotionally, and spiritually drained because I spent years consumed by earning church people's approval. I needed other people to tell me who I was. In college, I feared I would die and go to hell because I didn't attend church regularly. The religion and the deceptive words from Harold's congregation kept me in fear that I was on my way to hell on roller skates, as they said it. After marrying, having Michael, and living in Little Rock for several years, I felt a pull to get into a church in Harold's denomination. I was afraid I would die and go to hell if I didn't. My family and I joined a church with Harold's approval. I tried to please and impress the people in the church. People pleasing, a common trait for Childhood Trauma survivors, is called *fawning*. Fawning is gratifying others who pose a threat in order to avoid conflict, rejection or pain.[12]

The church dogma convinced me that because of my sinful life, I was headed to hell. God didn't convict me, but I felt condemned by some in the congregation. I slept only three or four hours a night because church members told me I needed to pray more. Upon awakening, I prayed instead of going back to sleep. The interrupted sleep contributed to mental and emotional dysfunction. Research now recognizes sleep problems contribute to depression, anxiety, and suicidal ideations. What I thought to be a good thing by awakening and praying every few hours, instead increased my psychotic disorders. In hindsight, I can see how my childhood adversities robbed me of things many take for granted, such as making wise choices. Thank God, I eventually learned I wasn't required to earn my way to salvation or deliverance. During the times God requires sacrifice, He gives supernatural mental, emotional, and physical strength, as He did with Moses and Elijah when they fasted for forty days. I realized I turned from looking to God and looked to church people for approval. I prayed long prayers and fasted from eating thinking I was honoring God when in reality it was from the desire to please people.

I wanted to be like the religious people in Harold's denomination who talked about how they prayed. I wanted to show them I wasn't spiritually lazy. I thought maybe if I worked hard enough, prayed long enough, and had faith strong enough, they would recognize me as one of them and give me a position of importance. Now I see how pharisaical that was because I didn't feel better after praying long hours. It was prideful—wanting to be heard and seen. I wasn't any stronger spiritually because the emphasis on religiosity drained me. I was exhausted from the pressure of performing religious duties that I hoped would make me feel God's love and acceptance. I went through the motions of attending church, serving, and saying yes to everything the church asked. I tried to please the church leaders and prove to them I had a relationship with God while neglecting my family's and my needs to ensure others' needs were met. This was exactly the type of pharisaical behavior that Jesus spoke against.

---

[12] Walker, Pete. 2013. *Complex PTSD: From Surviving to Thriving: A Guide and Map for Recovering from Childhood Trauma.* Azure Coyote Publishing.

The lack of sleep, extreme fasting from foods, and spiritual deception contributed to my first massive breakdown with its observable effects on my mind, body, and soul. Fasting, praying, and seeking God is great for someone who has learned self-control and knows the character of God. Otherwise, these types of self-denials, along with sleep deprivation, are a set-up for mental disaster. At the same time, my thinking was clouded and my brain could not analyze what had happened or discern what my next steps should be. I couldn't examine the demands from others or my expectations of myself to determine whether they were of God or simply religious. I lacked the fortitude to walk away. I couldn't find the grit to separate from church people so that I could gain perspective on religiosity vs. Christianity.

The spiritual chores were a burden, but I felt compelled to do them or face the belief that I had disappointed God. I wanted to please God, but church work exhausted me! I didn't do it because I loved it—I did it so people would think I was a good Christian. I resorted to what I knew—DOING! Harold never missed a church service in the 50+ years he pastored, and he stressed the importance of showing up. Like a child, I reverted to what I learned from him. I didn't want to miss church services, even when I was ill, because I didn't want anyone to think I was slothful.

After my breakdown, I couldn't listen to television evangelists, or gospel songs, or hold conversations with people about God because it made me anxious and fearful. I didn't know which people were deceptive, so I avoided most of them. I could only go to occasional church services with Drake's family. They belonged to a non-charismatic, small country church. Their quiet service was what my brain could handle since there was no whooping, hollering, or laying on of hands. I couldn't handle any kind of worship that reminded me of Harold's church. Charismatic and spirit-filled outbursts such as running around the church, sudden movements, or howling from people in the congregation or pulpit activated my fear and anxiety. I could only tolerate the bare minimum of listening. I was unable to take notes or understand deep scriptural explanations. Thankfully, the preachers in the country church didn't conduct exegesis or any deep analysis of the scriptures. The country church was the only church I could go to because they didn't pressure me or make me feel like I had to do something for God's love. They didn't make me feel like I wasn't doing enough.

During this time, Drake counseled me because he was the only one I trusted.

He told me, "You will go crazy trying to make sense out of nonsense, so you have to let it go."

His words stung as they sank into my heart and soul. These words remain with me to this day, and I use them when I mentor others trying to make sense of what happened to them. I repeat his exact words. There was no use in wasting time and energy trying to figure out if the abusers understood what they did. For weeks and months, I repeated Drake's words until I was able to release the toxic emotions surrounding the church abuse.

I see deception today in the people I help. Some find their worth and value in serving as I once did. Others find their self worth in giving to others, pleasing others, and receiving praise from others. I understand their need to serve and please others. They believe if they serve others, they are valuable, and it brings them recognition and praise. While serving is extremely important to advancing God's kingdom, it should not be a burden nor should one feel pressured to serve. Coerced service promotes fear and religiosity instead of relationships. God wants us to serve Him and others because we want to, not because we fear feeling less valued. Today I see serving as an opportunity to serve God and His children, not as a job or a requirement. This attitude makes me glad to serve.

Chapter 44
THE TRUTH SHALL SET YOU FREE

I knew I had to tell Drake about my history with Harold. One day while walking at the high school track, I knew it was the day. We walked because Drake knew exercise helped my mind and he often tried to do helpful things for me. As we walked, I unburdened myself and told him that Harold sexually abused me during the nearly five years I lived with him and Agnes. Drake listened without interrupting. When I finished, he didn't look shocked. That didn't mean much because most things didn't upset Drake. I noticed that he withdrew from the conversation as he looked away. He kept his head down and didn't make eye contact.

My heart pounded. I stood before my husband and silently screamed *HELP! HELP! HELP! I need you to tell me this is not my fault. I was a child. PLEASE HELP ME!* Even without a verbal response, I immediately regretted telling Drake about Harold's abuse. When someone shares a painful, intimate, confidential matter, the listener must respond appropriately with the proper emotional support. Drake couldn't give me what he did not have. He was one of the youngest of fifteen children, and his father worked on the railroad and only came home on the weekends. He had trouble expressing his emotions, just like his father before him. Eventually, Drake said he didn't know what to say.

Since then, I have processed how my revelation impacted him. It would have helped me if he had held me in his arms and said, "I'm so sorry, Dora." That alone would have been enough support for me to release the emotional pain I hid from him. Instead, I shut down my emotions because I no longer felt it was safe to share them with him.

I don't blame Drake for his response because I'm sure the horror was unimaginable to him. Drake looked at me, but I wanted to hide my face from him. I felt the fight, flight, or freeze mode activate. Everything in me wanted to fall to the ground in the middle of the track and die. I shivered, even though it was a warm day. My world was shattered, and I needed his support, but he couldn't give it. I wanted to die physically since I was already emotionally dead. I was unaware of any empirical evidence supporting the belief that men aren't as comfortable with emotional matters as women.[13] If I had known, I might have been more prepared for his response. I added an emotional bomb to Drake's discomfort with emotional topics. I understand it was an emotional overload for Drake, but I needed his reassurance.

Long seconds went by before Drake responded. After some time, he said, "I knew something was wrong with your relationship with Harold because of some of the things you said."

"What do you mean?" I asked.

"Once, you said you didn't think you could live without him." When Drake repeated those words, they sounded terribly wrong.

"What else did I say?" I asked. I wanted to hear how crazy I was.

"You said several things and did many things that let me know something wasn't right," he added.

I wanted to know more, but I'm sure he could tell I couldn't handle much more. I almost broke down in shame, thinking about what I had said and done that may have revealed more than I thought. I wondered how much Drake kept from me. I let my questions go unanswered, especially since I could barely contain my emotions from the gravity of the disclosures. We continued to walk, and I wanted to keep talking, but I felt I had shared enough. Drake was not talkative, and talking to him about emotional subjects was not easy. I had not learned how to have courageous conversations because any time one was required, I squelched the instinct to talk to protect what little stability I managed to establish.

I wanted to give Drake a perspective on the life I lived. I needed him to know the emotional pain I felt, but I said nothing. I was too wounded and damaged to fight on my behalf. The years of abuse flowed through my veins, reminding me that I was undeserving of love and respect. Harold had done the worst damage, but every other man who used me was equally guilty. I felt I was good for nothing, not even good enough to be a mother to Michael. Despite the shame of my upbringing, I had made the decision as a parent not to put that shame on Michael. I made sure he knew how loved and valued he was. I was ashamed of myself, for my son's sake. I hated that I put him through my dysfunction. He deserved a better mother, and Drake deserved a better wife. They were normal, but I was damaged and mentally ill. Something

---

[13]Bradley, M. M., M. Codispoti, D. Sabatinelli, and P. J. Lang. 2001. "Emotion and Motivation II: Sex Differences in Picture Processing." *Emotion* 1, no. 3 (September): 300–19. Doi: 10.1037//1528-3542.1.3.300.

happened to me that I couldn't undo. I knew things I couldn't unknow. I carried secrets that weighed me down.

Finally, I could no longer hold back the tears. My tears were a channel to emotional pain. They flowed from my head to my heart and from my heart to my spirit. I thought, "How could God allow this to happen?" but dared not ask that of Him because I thought He would surely kill me. I heard a few times that God loved me and sent His Son to die for the world, but I had not heard He died for *me*. I was concerned about *me*—and what happened *to me*—not the world. My mind tossed to and fro. I cried every time I thought of Drake's lack of response, what God allowed to happen to me, and my fear that I couldn't be a good mother to Michael because of the abuse. Drake didn't have to say anything else because I was now saying it to myself. *I am an unfit mother. How can he ever respect me again? Does he regret marrying me? Because he knows now about Harold, is he wondering about my childhood before I lived with Harold? Will he try to find out more? Will he leave me? Will he take Michael away from me?*

After sharing my deeply private secret with Drake, I beat myself up for the next few weeks. My thoughts fluctuated from thinking it was too much to share with anyone to wondering how Drake could ever understand how painful it was to endure the abuse if we didn't talk about it? More thoughts like *Now, I have to live the rest of my life feeling inadequate, thinking I am a nobody, and worth nothing. I have to accept that I am an unfit mother. I wish I hadn't told him. I can't undo Drake knowing what happened to me. I brought this on myself.*

The walls crashed in on me. I didn't anticipate the impact my secret had on Drake and Michael. I intentionally kept my abusive childhood from Drake because I wanted him to see me as a loving and kind person with a normal childhood. I thought if he knew the truth of the sexual abuse, he wouldn't want me. I withheld life-altering information from him. That was wrong because it prevented me from establishing a solid foundation for a relationship. Marriage can't be built on deception and fear. The truth eventually comes out, and innocent people are hurt when it does. When I minister to other CT survivors, I encourage them to process their truth as it is revealed. Too often, survivors suppress the truth in the same way they suppress the memories of their abuse.

Drake didn't change his behavior toward me, but everything in me changed toward him. When Drake didn't respond like I thought he should have, I shut down and retreated emotionally from our relationship. From that day on, I found it difficult to share with him or to be emotionally expressive. His lack of action resonated in my mind for years. I expected too much from Drake. I expected him to know how to respond to sexual abuse when I didn't know how to respond to it. I'm sure Drake didn't know what his lack of support—or lack of understanding of what I needed during the volatile time following the revelation of Harold's abuse—did to me. Drake didn't know the shame I carried because I did not share it with him. I believed he had the answer to everything because he seemed to always know what to say and what to do in most situations, so I was emotionally unprepared when he didn't know what to do or say. I needed him to say, *Listen, none of the abuse was your fault. You were a child. Whatever happened in your life doesn't, and will never, change how I feel about you. Life gave you atrocious obstacles, but you survived and overcame them. You were dealt a terrible hand, but you played your cards well. We are in this to the end.* Words like that could have helped me to feel I was still worthy, despite the theft of my innocence and childhood.

My life from 2000-2003 is difficult to describe because those were the years I lived in fear and extreme anxiety as a result of the trauma I had endured. I call it my *traumacose* period, but it was no joke. I felt hopeless and unproductive. My only desire was to survive the day and night. Many times I recalled the prayers I made during pregnancy when I asked God to allow me to live to see my son turn eighteen because I didn't want to leave him motherless. During these years, Michael was in high school, and I hoped God would answer me favorably, although I had little optimism.

I was absent from school for most of 2000. My students loved me, and I loved them. I felt guilty for taking off a semester, but the doctor told me I couldn't work and needed some time off. Drake supported my decision to take off work. I couldn't be around people because it made me more fearful and anxious. I spent my days on the couch in a mental state of confusion. I was completely mentally distraught. I could not eat. My primary doctor excused me from work during this time but did not recommend I see a psychiatrist. Drake took care of me because I couldn't cook a meal. I could barely get out of bed due to mental and emotional exhaustion. He took me to doctor's appointments, cooked, cleaned the house, and cared for Michael. Michael didn't usually need help with homework, but when he did, he went to Drake for help.

I returned to the classroom in 2001 the semester following the breakdown. My mental capacity didn't allow me to hold much. When I went back into the classroom, of the 150 students assigned to me, only twenty or so were passing the course. Nearly everyone had F grades. I was overloaded with guilt. It was too much. The students said the substitute was mean and disorganized. They said they did the work but she misplaced it. I knew if that many students failed, it was not a student problem; it was a teacher problem. The principal agreed if the students proved they knew the material and passed the semester exams, I could change their grades. The majority of them studied and passed the semester exam, and I changed their grades.

The principal, students, and the district leaders expressed happiness when I returned, but it was difficult because my mind was unstable. I was terribly emotional. I talked softly and slowly so I could comprehend what I was saying. I couldn't think quickly. The students must have known I was barely hanging on mentally because they were extremely kind. I had fewer discipline problems that year. The students did the work and passed the class.

When I returned to teaching, I was still fearful and didn't talk much to my co-workers. God gave me the grace to teach school, but afterward, I came straight home. I dropped extra duties and focused on getting mentally stronger. To desensitize my social anxiety, our family went to high school sports events which I enjoyed because I didn't have to think. I could enjoy the excitement of the competition. I recall feeling uneasy during the last five minutes of a game because I knew I would face tormenting thoughts once the game ended and my usual life resumed.

I got my first glimpse of hope in 2003 when Drake and I went to the bank and opened a checking account for me. We had a joint account, but I agreed not to use our joint account until I learned how to manage money after repeatedly spending money on unnecessary clothes and shoes instead of paying bills. I know this sounds like a small thing, but to someone who thinks they will die because of their emotional and mental turmoil, a personal bank account was huge. Looking back, I understand this simple act shifted my thoughts from death to life because Drake's action gave me hope that one day my mind would heal and I would manage a bank account. Except for his response to Harold's sexual abuse, Drake seemed to know what to do and say to help me through most situations. I cleaved to his every word. I am thankful he was positive and helped me through the difficult time. Without him, I am certain I would not have made it. I talked with Michael twenty years later to find out how much he remembered about those years. He said, "Mom, you lay on the couch every day. Before that, you went to work every day, so I knew something was wrong. I just didn't know what." Tears welled in my eyes, thinking about how it must have worried him to see his mom in such a poor mental state.

Each day I grew mentally stronger. By 2004, my mind healed enough for me to go to graduate school. I was far from being out of the woods, but I was better than I had been. Drake thought learning would help my mind heal more quickly. I did whatever he told me to do because I couldn't think for myself, and I trusted him.

I registered and started classes, but there was a catch: my classes were a thirty-minute drive, and I had to cross a bridge both ways to get to the campus. God connected me to a neighbor who lived a few houses down the street, and most weeks, I rode to class with her. Occasionally, she had severe headaches, and I had to drive us. I never told her, but I was extremely afraid. I prayed every mile of the commute that I wouldn't have a panic attack. While she was having migraines, I was having panic attacks and anxiety. Neither of us let the other know how bad we were. That is a good thing because we probably never would have driven weekly for two years that way. Miraculously, I never had a full-blown panic attack. The only driving I did during those two years was to class when she had a migraine. By the time we graduated with our Master's degrees, I could drive again, but I still couldn't cross bridges due to panic and anxiety, so my niece often drove me places. No one asked why I didn't drive anymore, and I'm glad they didn't. Being unable to drive and not understanding why was embarrassing enough. I received my Master's Degree from the same university in Conway, Arkansas, where I earned my undergraduate degree.

Though Drake didn't suggest counseling, I sought it while I worked on my Master's Degree. The neighbor I commuted with told me she had panic and anxiety issues and was on medication. I could see she had real problems, but even in my grim state of mind, I felt I was in a better place. Often, we are too close to a situation to have a fresh perspective, because the truth was I was in the same predicament. Listening to her share how her counselor helped her think was new to me. However, I was open to anything at that point because I needed help. My neighbor was a Black woman who admitted she too had mental problems and sought counseling. Admitting and telling others about mental struggles was rare in the Black community. I saw others like me who needed help, but none of us were courageous enough to actually get help. I prayed and asked God to help me find a counselor, and He did. That's when I met Margaret Schell.

I didn't believe I could find a Little Rock counselor who could help me, but I went to see a woman who was listed in my employer's insurance brochure. Margaret was tall and extremely thin, brunette, and Caucasian. She was impeccably dressed and invariably sipped a cup of tea during our sessions.

There was a foul stench in Margaret's office, much like a cesspool, but I felt such love and kindness from her that I ignored the odor. She never hugged me, shook hands with me, or physically touched me—but she touched my heart more than anyone up to that point in my life. She was the first counselor I saw, and I only went to her for a few months. With her gentle voice, she would ask, "How did that make you feel?" I would tell her, and she would listen patiently for an hour. She didn't offer a remedy. She merely listened. I am thankful she didn't try to help solve any problems because I didn't even know I had a problem yet. Most of the time I was in her office, I wept and thought I would explode. I was an emotional bomb. I told her about the abuse I endured. She did not tell me that I experienced Childhood Trauma or that the emotional dysfunction I suffered was a long-term consequence. She didn't use the term *trauma* at all. Margaret's greatest contribution was her listening, non-judgmental ear. I needed someone to hear my story since I could not tell anyone else.

Margaret had a box of tissues conveniently set next to my chair. All I could do was try to keep from drowning in my sea of emotions. She sat about twelve feet away across the large office. At the time, I wondered if she was afraid of me or if she had some sort of illness. I believe now that she was ill because she passed away a few years after I last saw her. By then, I was living in Southwest Missouri. I was one of her final patients. I went to Margaret for several months but only paid her once. She never asked for payment, and I was usually too distraught to remind her. I didn't give her my employment or insurance information, so I don't believe she billed them. It was only after I began to heal that I realized she didn't charge me.

After I moved to Missouri in 2008 and more symptoms of PTSD regularly appeared, along with panic and anxiety, I reached out to Margaret with the intent to let her know I owed her and to ask about continuing our sessions because I hadn't found a counselor in Missouri. I called her several times over a month, but no one answered. When I found her obituary online, I shed tears for her passing. I felt she cared about me and was the first mental health professional I saw after the first emotional breakdown.

My experience with Margaret reminded me that I wasn't the only bird who lost its wings and couldn't fly. I knew others like me needed a new set of wings, and it was my job as a teacher to help them. I created a platform of encouragement and support for students to develop a voice to talk objectively about abuse and to strengthen them to keep going. I believed writing would give them wings and free them from some of the pain associated with abuse. Only the student knew who they referenced in their writing.

Research continues to state the benefits of writing. Writing helps release pent-up emotional pain, so I created a poetry program for students, known as *Poets with Passion (PWP)*. PWP began as a school-wide competition, but word spread and students from other schools wanted to participate, so I expanded the program to include the other high schools in the Little Rock district. *Poets with Passion* gave students a platform and recognized them for using their voices. Each month, PWP had a theme, such as the Harlem Renaissance, betrayal, childhood memories, a significant event, or life's challenges. Students wrote poetry addressing the monthly themes. In 2007, I was recognized for creating *Poets with Passion* and received the Little Rock School District Superintendent's Citation Award.

Chapter 45
A New House and a New Job

Not long after I graduated with my Master's Degree, Drake shared with me a dream he had of buying us a new house. My panic attacks had decreased, but I still wasn't able to "feel" and understand things as others. When he said a new house, I couldn't feel or fathom what it looked or felt like to be in a new house. I didn't bring up the subject of the new house with Drake unless he brought it up. I talked about it and answered his questions regarding a new home, but I couldn't comprehend many of the things he was saying. We went looking for a plot of land not far from where we lived. I liked the plot because it was next door to the school where I taught. In other words, I was thinking I wouldn't have to drive as much while he was thinking about whether it was a good plot of land. I couldn't think beyond the fear.

I recall him asking me about the paint and what color I wanted in the house. When we went to the store to pick it out, I had to keep going to the bathroom because I thought I might have an anxiety attack. I didn't have one, but the threat of it was overwhelming because I didn't want Michael to see me have one. I was relieved when he ended up saying "Ok, let's go with the light beige." Each time I thought I was safe from making a decision, he would ask me about a design or if I liked this light fixture better than another one or this brick over that one. Sometimes we went riding to look at homes. He wanted to know which house I preferred: ranch style, bungalow, or farmhouse. He and Michael were super excited, so I pretended to be as well. I was excited at the thought of being excited but did not have any feelings of excitement.

Oftentimes, I was more overwhelmed. There were too many decisions. Now I believe Drake desired to try to fix my situation. He did everything within his power to get my mind off of how I was feeling and what I was going through. I don't remember moving into our new home. I remember Drake and me going on weekends to look for new furniture. I liked to look for furniture because it was easier for me to make decisions. I remember shopping for the dining room suit. We found a beautiful, brown Natuzzi leather couch, but it wasn't just leather. It was the softest leather I had ever sat on. We didn't know of anyone who owned one like it, and we both wanted it. We had to save for it because it was so expensive. Although Drake asked my opinion on everything, I gave him a simple yes or no. If he liked it, I liked it because if I said no, that would mean more discussion about it. I didn't put up any decorations in our new home. My mind was so distraught, I only put one or two things on the walls.

While I have memories of watching TV on weekends in our new home, I have no memories of building it. I realize now I was unable to participate in one of the most important events in my life next to giving birth. From the outside, it looked like I had it all—husband, son, great job, wonderful friends, degrees, and now a new home. The problem is, I didn't know I had it all.

When we divorced, I didn't understand why I was so hurt that we lost that home since I put little into it to make it beautiful. It took years for me to process losing it. During my near homelessness in St. Louis, it was almost more than I could bear. It wasn't until I finally accepted my role in the loss of it all that I was able to move forward. God restored the most important things —my mind and body. However, I know from studying God's character that He is a God of restoration and will also restore my physical losses.

In 2007, I underwent a grueling application and documentation process to become a National Board Certified Teacher (NBCT). I was interested because the process itself was a deep dive into professional development for improving instruction. Educators across the nation submitted written and video documentation of their practice to the National Board for Professional Teaching Standards in the areas of Content Knowledge, Differentiation in Instruction, Teaching Practice, and Learning Environment, as well as a teacher's ability as an Effective and Reflective Practitioner. National Board certification opened doors to professional advancement and provided a bonus of $5,000 to the school district's salary for ten years.

It is a rigorous process, but it would have been easy for me if I hadn't had a mental breakdown a few years before. By 2007, my mind was rebooting, as Drake called it. It was indeed offline for a few years, but now it was back on enough for me to apply for National Board Certification from a rigorous teacher's program. Drake once described what happened to my mind in a way that was easy to comprehend and accept. He said "Like a computer, you had a hard shutdown. Your brain couldn't take it, so it shut down. It will come back up, but you have to give it a minute to reboot." His explanation helped me not be intimidated by the breakdown.

NBCT was challenging because, as I learned in college, I had difficulty with details and the logical thinking done by the left hemisphere of the brain. With help from Drake and other friends who were critical thinkers, I was able to accomplish everything I needed for National Board Certification.

I was immensely satisfied when I earned the highest possible score in the Teaching Practice and Learning Environment component—the area that measures teacher effectiveness. I wanted the scorers to feel the love I had for my students and recognize my students' comfort level in their responses. I videotaped a lesson with the students' unrehearsed responses. The video revealed everything the scorers needed to know, including my interactions with the students and their learning environment. Before recording, I heard stories about how students wouldn't participate with teachers when they knew they were filming, but the video turned out to be the easiest part of the process. I didn't ask students to be on their best behavior because I believed if they thought I was a great teacher, it would be simply another day in the classroom and they would do their best. The National Board Certification validated my belief that I was made to be a teacher. I was a good teacher, and I made a positive difference in the lives of my students. I am especially thankful God chose me for the profession.

My self-confidence significantly increased as I moved through the certification process. It was painstakingly detailed and significantly beyond my comfort zone. I recognized failure as a possibility since a teacher had only three attempts to pass the culminating exam. I knew teachers who had failed all three attempts, but I still wanted to try it. I was afraid, but I did not allow fear to stop me. God knew my heart. I believed if I received the NBCT certification, I could do anything. It was an actual acknowledgment of success. I was already successful with students, but National Board Certification was peer validation.

The certificate was presented in front of my school district colleagues in an all-employees convocation. I received the award in the same school where I had fought so desperately not to teach. It was a momentous occasion, but as soon as I received the plaque, I heard a nagging internal voice say, *You're still that poor little girl and everybody knows it.* At that moment, I realized that no degree or external validation could outshout the internal voice. Turning it off was something only I could do. I didn't know how to do it, but I recognized it was a personal problem. I realized no amount of money, awards, or degrees, and whatever praise accompanied those achievements, could silence the critical voice of Childhood Trauma.

The same year I was honored with the Superintendent's Citation Award for the *Poets With Passion* project, my mentor encouraged me to apply for a program with the National Education Association (NEA). My mentor said only sixteen educators from across the U.S. would be accepted. I didn't think I could be selected, but because of my increased confidence following the National Board Certification, I cautiously applied. Six months later I received a rejection letter. To me, it wasn't that they were saying, "Not now. Go do some more things with the union and try again next year." I heard them say, "We don't want you."

The next year, my mentor urged me to reapply for the NEA program. He said most people don't get accepted the first time, and he wouldn't accept no for an answer. He continued to call, and I continued to say no. Finally, I told him I would reapply if I could resubmit the prior year's application with only a change of date. He agreed, and I half-heartedly applied to the NEA Internship Program.

A few months later, the National Education Association called to notify me that I was one of the sixteen applicants accepted into the NEA Internship Program. I thought they might call back and say they changed their minds, but they didn't. What an honor! The Internship Program was to prepare the participants to become UniServ Directors. UniServ Directors were placed regionally throughout the US to provide NEA union representation to education employees. Successful graduates of the Internship would secure high-paying positions with the National Education Association. We would leave our classrooms and schools to advocate for the staff who work with students.

Hand in hand with excitement was the anticipation of change ahead. I didn't think much about the work I completed to earn the National Board Certification. Following the process, I thought my mind was stronger. I didn't experience panic attacks during the National Board process, so I thought the panic attacks were a *season* I went through and that they would never return. In consideration of the internship program, I focused solely on the opportunity to help educators, which meant my mind shifted from students to teachers. I began to see myself as an advocate for teachers as my mentor helped me prepare. He told me what to study, what to expect, and what to do. He described it as pledging an exclusive organization. I had survived an emotional and mental breakdown and decided I was no longer afraid to step out of my comfort zone. I was aware that not everyone who loses their mind gets a second chance, so I promised myself to live without fear this time. My mentor said I would succeed if I didn't quit, so regardless of the challenge, I knew I had to make it.

Drake and Michael were excited for me, and I had a lot of local support, but I still did what many CT survivors do: I underestimated the emotional, mental, and physical impact of the Intern program. In my optimism, I minimized the potential challenges and was unprepared for the obstacles I encountered.

I spent the next several weeks assembling outfits and laying out clothes to be sure I could look the part. I thought if I looked like I had it together, people would believe I did. Those accepted into the Internship program were required to live in the Washington, DC, area for two months, and upon completing the program, work under the supervision of an assigned mentor to learn how to be a Uniserv Director. The program paid the expenses, including the mentorship period following the eight-week training in DC. It was an amazing opportunity, and I was determined to avoid revealing any insecurities that could ruin it. We heard NEA paid approximately $60,000 for each intern in the eight-week training program, and I was determined to look the part. Shortsightedly, I didn't prepare academically for the rigorous program or anticipate the emotional effects of being away from home for eight weeks. Naively, I wasn't concerned about the new role. Because I had a deep peace, I knew God ordered my steps to this program. I accepted the possibility that I would leave my students following the training program, and I believed that the *season* for teaching young people would end. My mentor who encouraged me to apply again continued to meet with me to prepare me to leave the classroom, so by the time I left, I wasn't as emotionally attached. Also, I couldn't fully comprehend the possibilities ahead of me because, at this point, there had been no actual revelation of my Childhood Trauma beyond Drake and Margaret.

The NEA Internship Program sent specific instructions to precisely follow for shipping items to DC ahead of the training. From the first letter, I could tell they were strict. I shipped a suitcase according to the directions and flew to DC with only a small carry-on bag. I could rest easy because I was ready for the program. My daily outfits were carefully curated. I wanted everyone so impressed with my outside that they wouldn't see the damage inside. I didn't want them to notice my insecurities, low self-esteem, or fear of exposure.

My burst of enthusiasm deflated on the evening of arrival when everyone but me received the suitcase they shipped. When the host said my suitcase hadn't arrived, I thought I would die. I wanted to ask them to send me home or allow me to go to the mall and buy some clothes. They acted like it was nothing that my suitcase hadn't arrived, but I was devastated. They didn't understand how dependent I was on the image I projected. I couldn't eat, sleep, or learn. Without my clothing, I was unable to present myself positively. My self-image reflected how terrible I felt I looked wearing the same clothes every day. My fellow interns, as well as the judges, no doubt soon grew tired of my daily cry, "I don't have any clothes." Nobody seemed to understand what my missing clothes had to do with my ability to participate in the program. They didn't know I built my confidence on how I looked and not on what I knew. Without clothes, my degrees, recognitions, and national certification were meaningless.

We stayed in a dilapidated building that looked like a well-used dormitory. We were provided linens and soap, shampoo, and conditioner. The walls were covered with large, faded murals. The bathrooms were even less desirable as they were small with tiny sinks and no vanity or countertop space. The beds were uncomfortable and offered little support. It was clear the rooms were spartan to deter distractions. NEA tried to ensure we had no stress about anything outside the program, so our laundry was taken care of, but we were expected to tip the maid daily. All we had to do was be present and learn; I felt I could do neither without my wardrobe. After a week, my clothes still hadn't arrived. Anyone who came near me heard the pitiful story of how somebody somewhere lost my clothes. I hardly made it through each day without wondering what the others thought of me.

We spent most of our time in a classroom under intense judgment and scrutiny by the five NEA leaders we called judges. They were in the room every day. They didn't smile, joke, or laugh. They monitored our every move. It was like surgery without anesthesia. We worked in class from 8:00 a.m. until 10:00 p.m., seven days a week. We worked every weekend except the final one. We had major projects due each day. After only two days, I was beyond stressed, exhausted and sleep-deprived. It was only by the grace of God that I completed the program.

The program required us to create scenarios, role-play responses to the media, learn to solve a myriad of personnel problems, and maintain a good relationship with our constituents. We did not work with an actual union group while in DC. That was reserved for the hands-on experience we would get in the states where we did the internship following the training. Since I hadn't done previous advocacy for educators, I didn't know the language and expectations that most of my colleagues knew. Everyone except me seemed experienced and ready to accept a UniServ Director's position.

The cost of the training and the significant salary of a UniServ Director was a factor when things got tough and participants considered dropping out. As challenging as it was, I knew quitting was not an option. I thought the judges might have played a psychological trick by keeping my suitcase to see how its loss affected me. After a month, however, I thought, "OK, the joke's over, I need my clothes." I am grateful to God that I made it, but not without daily mental anguish and torment.

Not having my clothes stirred up childhood memories of wearing the same dirty clothes day after day, and the times Briana and I switched clothes so we didn't have to wear the same clothes to school on consecutive days. In DC, I washed my few clothing items in the room's tiny sink with hand soap. I couldn't believe I had to ask for powder to wash my clothes like I did in childhood. Not having my chosen clothes to wear, not being able to feel fresh in a daily outfit, and lacking some necessities triggered anxiety. I drowned in low self-esteem, negative thoughts, and feelings of helplessness because no one would take me to buy what I considered necessities. I blamed the judges and called this circumstance cruel and unusual punishment. Although they told me repeatedly they had nothing to do with the loss of my suitcase, I didn't believe them.

My suitcase arrived exactly one week before graduation from the program. Now I believe it was a setup by God to strip me of false confidence. The repetitive negative thoughts of Childhood Trauma did not allow me to think of anything except my perception that they (the judges) did this to me because they wanted to teach me a lesson. Years later, after I healed, I recognized my distrust of the judges, and I knew they were innocent.

The NEA Internship training program was one of the most challenging and rewarding life-changing events I ever experienced until the creation of Tower of Hope Ministries. I thought I knew what it took to get through such a demanding program: be in control and well-dressed every day and say things that made people laugh so they wouldn't see the real me. With the first plan eliminated, I still had one card left to play: to make people laugh. I repeatedly said, *OMG*. That was the hip vernacular that summer, and I thought I would fit in by using it. I wanted and needed to be memorable so NEA would think I was hirable. I did not want to go back to the Little Rock School District. Going back to the district after being accepted into such a prestigious program felt like one thing: failure. Failure was not an option for me. I had to make the

NEA trainers see me and like me even though I felt nothing was likable about me without the image my clothing projected.

Chapter 46
A VOLCANIC ERUPTION

Before attending the program, I decided not to share anything deeply personal because I knew I wouldn't be able to control the kind of emotional outbursts I feared would erupt if I shared. I could feel I had a volcano inside, but I thought I could keep it under wraps for a few more months. My livelihood was at stake. My family and the school district were watching. The participants were advised that we would return to our school districts if we failed. After graduating from the program, the stamp of success was a job with NEA. I needed the NEA Internship's stamp of success.

I had no intention of sharing anything about my childhood with the NEA trainer-judges or my classmate-colleagues. I didn't know the danger of waking my dragon—Childhood Trauma—but I knew talking about trauma intensified the pain, like pouring salt into an open wound. First, I didn't know I had open wounds, so it was always a surprise when I uncovered one. After all, the trauma happened when I was a child. What's in the past, stays in the past, right? Second, I thought because I was professionally successful I escaped the trauma because I learned how to protect myself with coping mechanisms, much like a functioning alcoholic. Third, I thought if I didn't talk about things that made me uncomfortable, whatever emotional turmoil I felt would eventually go away. Often, CT survivors think they can outrun their Childhood Trauma in multiple degrees, businesses, serial relationships, parenting, and work success. For many, like me, coping works until a new traumatic event happens; then the secret is exposed. Only years later did I learn things in the psyche don't disappear because I don't talk about them. On the contrary, not talking about them forces them to bury deeper into my psyche. I didn't get relief from the psychological pain until I talked about it, wrote about it, and prayed about it.

The final reason I wouldn't share my past with anyone at the NEA training was because I was afraid of being labeled mentally ill. I knew mental illness could mean losing a potential job as an NEA UniServ Director. I thought sharing anything personal would make me an outcast, and I would be perceived as weak. God had ordered my steps to the classroom in 1993, but in 2008, He ordered them to DC, so I had to succeed. Unfortunately, I left

God out, meaning I felt I could do it on my own once I was accepted into the intern program. Of course, I didn't say that to God, but that's what my behavior said. Doing it my way was the reason I bought the clothes and jewelry so I could be seen and accepted. With God, life is about showing up. He causes people to notice me. He had already stamped me with success and His favor, yet I stressed and worried about how to impress the judges. When I forgot to pray first, I should have expected everything else to be out of order. I felt like I needed more than God. What more does one need when they have the One who has it all?

For the first thirty days of the training, I did well. I didn't overshare and managed to protect my reputation. I thought I had successfully convinced everyone that the real me was the jovial person I presented. I didn't know the trainers were experts at recognizing people with mental illness. They gave us a battery of evaluations and measures of skills. We took the Myers-Briggs personality inventory, and I identified as INFJ (Introverted, Intuitive, Feeling, Judging), which was not a surprise. I'm caring, kind, affirming, and tend to have good insight into people. I also require significant time alone to recharge to help others effectively.

Near the end of the eight-week program, the trainers paired us for an activity requiring us to introduce ourselves to the group by sharing something about the other's background. We received specific instructions: *Name someone who made a profound difference in your early life. Tell us how they changed the course of your life.* It sounded simple enough. There were a few people who made a positive difference in my life, but the positive differences sprinkled throughout my childhood were so few that they didn't rise to the level of changing the course of my life. The negative influences in my life were stronger and more frequent. Sadly, nearly every one of the adults I encountered in childhood caused extensive emotional, mental, physical, and spiritual pain. The pain engulfed me daily.

The first classmate to speak talked about her mother. Another spoke about how her grandmother inspired her. Still another participant talked about his stepfather who taught him about life and the value of hard work. One said her godmother instilled character in her and another shared how her aunt helped her personally and financially. They talked about how they would not have made it without the individuals who played significant roles in their lives.

As they spoke, I prayed silently about who influenced my life the most. I still didn't know who I could talk about who profoundly affected my life or changed its trajectory. I felt anxious because I knew my turn was coming. I thought about saying Barney, the big purple dinosaur, who said he was everybody's friend and loved me because I knew it would get a laugh. I also knew the judges would shut it down, ask for a different answer, and tell me everything didn't have to be funny. The interns often joked that the judges were like God because their eyes were always on us and they heard our private discussions no matter how softly we whispered. The judges set the tone daily: no laughing, playing, or teasing. They were sober and serious. That environmental expectation made it more difficult for the false self to operate. Sometimes we talked and laughed until the judges arrived, but the smiles and laughter quickly turned somber.

During the internship program, I first heard the term *fake* relating to human authenticity. The judges told us they would know by our answers if we were *fake*. The fake me could laugh about anything as I had most of my life, but the real me could not lie or say what she felt. This activity was not the time for the authentic me to show up, so I went over why I had to be fake.

When it was my turn, I was comfortable because I shared with my fellow interns that I had no one who was significant to me or made a profound difference in my life. I thought that would be it. I knew we had to introduce one another and I gave my partner the exact words to introduce me. What happened next, though, was a big surprise. One of the judges, a wise older lady named Della, who had streaks of gold in long dreadlocks, interrupted my activity partner as she was about to introduce me and said, "Dora, we would like for you to introduce yourself."

What!?! Why would you want that?

My first reaction was to refuse Della's request, but that wasn't a realistic option. No one refused the judges unless they wanted to be sent home and labeled uncooperative or oppositional. Although this occurred near the program's end, we still knew we could be sent home. We also had the pressure of being blackballed from future programs and our reputations harmed. All of us wanted to be highly recommended by the judges. Their approval was gold.

I pretended to clear my throat as I stalled for something to say. I told Della I needed more time to write things down.

"Tell us. You don't need time to write anything down," Della said.

I stood up, which meant the authentic me stood up and began to speak. I had a speaking technique, so I looked directly at the interns and judges with every word I spoke, maintaining eye contact with them.

Like many of you, I wish I could say that someone from my family made a significant difference in my life. I tried to find a story like yours and sound like you all, but I have nothing positive to say about someone in my family who made a significant difference in my life. I have to tell my story, my way. Pretty or ugly, it's my story.

The truth is, the people who had the most significant impact on my life were not positive actors. When my mother passed away suddenly, I had no place to live at the age of thirteen. My great-aunt and uncle took me in. My great-uncle was the pastor of two churches and a high-ranking leader in a worldwide denomination. He was widely respected and sought out for his wise counsel. He changed my life. He was also my abuser. He sexually abused me from age fourteen until I was eighteen. My life has not been the same since.

You see, the person who made a significant difference in my life was my great-uncle. What he did damaged me so badly that I don't know who I am or who God is. His abuse ruined me. More than taking my autonomy and sense of self, my uncle took God away from me. He was a well-known and highly respected church leader who represented God. After years of abuse, I struggled to trust God, believe He loved me, and have a relationship with Him.

I paused to regain composure.

Before my great-uncle's abuse, the adults who raised me, mainly my mother and step-father, abused me. After removal from their home, other men in my family and foster home fathers sexually abused me. Despite the abuse, I had a deep faith in God and truly believed He helped me through the suffering. I felt, regardless of what happened, that I got through it all with God. When my "Christian" great-uncle abused me, however, I felt that I had no God anymore, and my life's path became long and tough. I love God, but my understanding became clouded and confused when someone who represented Him hurt me. God was all I had to rely on. I love Him, but I am no longer sure He loves me since He allowed the abuse to take place.

The room was silent. I looked from one side to the other and at each of the judges' faces. Most of the people looked shocked or sad. I could tell by their expressions they were not prepared for what I shared. Tears streamed down my face. I don't know when they started falling. The faster I wiped them away, the faster they came. My tears were unstoppable and uncontrollable—like I feared. Most of the group wiped their eyes. A few breathed heavily, clearly in discomfort. I suspect some experienced sexual abuse but refused to acknowledge it. I was the unintentionally courageous one, standing alone in a group of professional peers and judges who had the power to dismiss me or call me unstable and unfit to work as an advocate.

The volcano had erupted; let the lava fall where it may. The job didn't matter anymore. I sat down. Tissues were passed to me. I didn't look around anymore. I no longer wanted to see their faces. I was embarrassed and so hurt because I shared my story with people I barely knew and didn't trust. Stunned, I sat silently. No one said a word. I felt my life as I knew it was over. After my speech, I could have walked out the door and gone home. I was no longer concerned about what anyone thought of me, how they reacted to what I said, or my life after this program. I figured the internship was over for me. I looked around and saw tears still in almost everyone's eyes. Silence hung heavy over the room.

After a few minutes, I recovered. For the rest of the class period, I was subdued, and the judges had compassion and didn't ask any more questions. It was as if they discovered the feelings and emotions which we declared they didn't have.

After class, I walked to my room feeling ambivalent. One thought was that I had done the right thing. Another thought was it was the right thing but in the wrong place at the wrong time. After all, they were not therapists. Previously, we walked and talked as a group when we left class sessions, but this time I walked alone. I didn't mean to say what I said, but obviously it needed to be said. I felt shame, but greater than the shame was the feeling of freedom. I was mentally and emotionally free from something I had bottled up for a long time. Bringing up those memories and telling near strangers what happened was emotionally draining. I believed none of my classmates walked with me because they did not know what to say. None of them came to console or hug me, and I thought they didn't want to be associated with me. I was too overwhelmed to talk to them.

I went to the room and prepared to fall asleep, but a classmate called and said I shouldn't have shared my story with the judges because he didn't see how the judges could recommend hiring me to any of the state NEA organizations. The classmate also said that the judges probably thought I was weak. I told him I was prepared to accept whatever happened with my life, and if being authentic caused me to be disqualified, perhaps this wasn't the program for me. I was sad, but I had spoken the truth and let go of the fear of what anyone thought. I hung up and promptly fell asleep.

I woke up after a short nap and met my group to work on a project. They ignored the elephant in the room—my story—and I did, too. I didn't say much during the work session except to provide input on the topic. After the session ended, I returned to my room for the night. One of the judges drove by as I left the building and asked if I wanted a ride. I got into her car. She asked how I felt, and I said fine. Then she said, "Thank you for speaking from your heart today. You were the only person who spoke from the heart. You had so much courage, and we saw that. We know it was hard, but you should know you did the right thing."

I felt a burden drop. I knew—for once in my life—it was OK to be me and for my story to not be like everyone else's story. That's the point about my story —good or bad, it was my story. I didn't know it then, but that moment was the beginning of my healing. The secret was out, and I no longer felt the need to hide.

I said, "But what about being blackballed from the hiring process?"

She said, "You won't be blackballed. Character and authenticity are important in advocacy; you have shown you have both. You won't have a problem getting a job."

Could this be happening? The thing I feared the most—them seeing the real me—was the thing they wanted. When she said that, hope returned.

For the rest of the internship training, I held my head high and performed exceptionally and authentically in every scenario and project. After the training program, we created a project summary of the intern experience. I wrote a short story, *Dora's Magical Kingdom,* about a little girl who experienced a lifetime in her new kingdom. The story was about her experiences and lessons learned while in her kingdom as a UniServ Intern. I shared how Dora's most impactful intern experience was standing her ground as an advocate despite discourteous district personnel and the courage it took to repeatedly leave her comfort zone.

I had an exit interview with the judges about the training program. They provided feedback on my growth, areas of weakness, and how to be successful in the next phase: the field training internship. Some commented on my observable growth following the loss of my suitcase. The judges shared that they noticed my intelligence and wanted me to know I had something to offer besides appearance. They said they chose those they believed were capable and caring. After feeling like I didn't belong, hearing that I was smart increased my confidence. I looked at the clothes, but they looked at me.

After completing the training program, I landed a job in the first round of notifications. I was assigned to the state of Missouri for a semester-length internship. My primary responsibility as a UniServ Director was advocacy for NEA members. The trainer-judge said character and authenticity were important, and she meant it because there were many times when superintendents tried to get me to agree to unfair terms for their staff. I fought for fairness for everyone I represented.

I was surprised that Missouri NEA chose me for the field training portion of the internship. Both my mentors told me I would make a great advocate because the things I had been through gave me compassion for people. Instead of feeling encouraged that Missouri chose me, I felt insecure because I didn't know how much the trainers shared with the staff in Missouri. Whatever they shared, it prepared them to work with me. I worked well in Missouri and we had no setbacks or meltdowns.

Chapter 47

MOVING TO MISSOURI

I moved to St. Louis for the internship, and my son and husband planned to drive to see me on the weekends. The St. Louis office welcomed me when I arrived, and I hit the ground running. The field experience would only last a few months, after which I could be assigned to any region in the state. Missouri and its educators were a completely different culture from what I was used to in Arkansas. I had so much to learn about people—and myself.

Our mentors demonstrated the reality of working as an advocate and knew every crack and pitfall of advocacy. At first glance, Missouri was not the ideal place to begin an internship because the state law had recently changed and several districts scrambled to learn how to write and negotiate a contract. UniServ Directors were a key part of the process. I had to learn the spoken and unspoken rules of negotiation etiquette and the nuances of advocacy and bargaining—especially in the Midwest. My previous Arkansas teachers' union experience was influenced by a Southern sensibility, which differs from the Midwest culture. My internship was filled with learning opportunities and a plethora of training. By the time I accepted a position as a UniServ Director (UD), I would be thoroughly prepared.

Although I had great field experience, I wasn't ready to work in a metropolitan area, so my mentor suggested I apply for a UD position in Southwest Missouri. I was excited but quite naive about proving I could do this work. The districts in that region were mainly small, rural, and without collective-bargaining contracts. I could make mistakes, learn, and grow without the pressure of contracts, although the Joplin Education Support Professionals (JESP) had a contract, so I got some experience with bargaining. Working as a UD with supervision was great training before taking on a metropolitan area like St. Louis. I was thankful I applied to begin as a UD in the rural Southwest Missouri region.

I was asked to interview for the Southwest Missouri position as NEA Uniserv Director right before I was notified of the passing of my oldest sister, Denise. Because she was not sick, her death was unexpected. She went to her doctor for a cough and the doctor unknowingly prescribed medicine to which she was allergic, causing death due to kidney failure. I was afraid they would hire someone else if I wasn't available for the interview, so I interviewed while pushing aside thoughts and memories of my sister. Denise was my first significant loss after receiving counseling. I had no support group, and I cried excessively in those months. Grieving Denise's sudden death added to my emotional burden of moving to a new place in a new state without Drake and Michael. Looking back I see how I did what trauma survivors do: I kept going, unable to think or feel. Everything was a blur and happening so quickly.

The funeral was a de facto family reunion. Elsie's twin sister's children came from out of state. We told stories about Denise and made one another laugh until early the next morning. I laughed on the outside while concealing how overcome I was with fearful thoughts of death and dying—thoughts that plagued me for the next several months.

A week after Denise's funeral, Missouri NEA offered me a job in the Southwest Missouri region. I was grateful to God to land a job as a UniServ Director a month after I finished the field training and graduated from the NEA Internship Program. In less than a year, I moved three times. I left Arkansas for training in Washington, DC, moved to St. Louis for the internship field training, and went on to a position as a full-time UniServ Director based in Springfield, Missouri. While this was all good news, it all required transitions. It seemed all I was doing was transitioning, and nothing felt stable. Oftentimes change arouses the same emotions and fight or flight feelings in CT survivors regardless of whether the change is good or bad.

I went back to the Little Rock high school that I left nine months earlier to tell my students I was officially leaving for a new job. Everything seemed to hit at once —the death of my sister, separating from my husband and son for the new job, and leaving my students and everything I knew to go into the unknown. I could hardly walk into my classroom because I was emotionally overwhelmed. Seeing the faces of the students who looked forward to my return following the semester away was more emotional than I anticipated. I missed their first semester of the school year while participating in the field training in St. Louis. I had not taught these students, but they heard about me from their older siblings and friends and were looking forward to my return. I had to tell them I was leaving for good. It hurt to disappoint them, but I was sure the NEA job was my next step. I felt it was time to make a difference in another area. I took the same commitment and advocacy I had for students and used it for educators. On my last day at the school, I stood at the classroom door and waved goodbye. I knew I would likely never return to the classroom. I prayed for God to send someone who would love the students, protect, and teach them. I barely reached my car before the tears poured down my face. I knew the road ahead would be formidable, but God was with me.

Drake had expressed an interest in teaching and went through the same Alternative Certification program I did. He began teaching the same year I left the classroom. When Michael graduated from college, he became a teacher as well. Both of them heard my stories and how to handle difficult students. I would like to think both of them learned something from me about teaching. They are both successful, caring, classroom teachers, and I believe God answered my prayers for caring teachers like me.

My position as a UniServ Director began in January 2009. I was responsible for representing, advocating, supporting, and advising educators on job performance and working conditions in several school districts across Southwestern Missouri. I represented educators in multiple positions in schools, colleges, and universities. The territory was roughly a 100-mile radius from Springfield. It stretched from Rolla in the east to Joplin in the west to Ridgedale on the Missouri-Arkansas state line up to tiny Warsaw north of Springfield. I averaged 250 miles a day, traveling to one or two districts before returning to my apartment which was centrally located in Springfield.

In big cities, education employees have options for competitive salaries and advancement. They can transfer to other schools or districts to get relief from unscrupulous principals or superintendents. This is not true for rural areas. Some rural superintendents viewed their districts as their kingdoms. They ruled as dictators rather than as managers or Chief Executive Officers. Often, my job was to remind them of human resource practices, communication, and common courtesy. While the job description was the same as the work I did in St. Louis as an intern, the approach was radically different in the rural southwest zone of the state. There were many times I told myself I didn't sign up for the rural backwoods of Missouri when I applied for training in Washington, DC, but I knew rural Missouri was exactly where God wanted me to be—and where I needed to be. Arkansas was backwoods, too, but my eyes weren't opened yet, so the Missouri experience was new.

When I arrived in Southwest Missouri, the superintendent-as-dictator was a common situation, and many teachers were intimidated. Some had accumulated paid time off or various types of leave but called to ask for help to take time off for a doctor's appointment. Some needed representation for something as universal as maternity leave. Fear permeated their work culture. Educators hesitated to make the simplest of requests because they lacked the protection of a fair contract. On the other hand, Educational Support Personnel, such as bus drivers, food service workers, and janitors, had contracts under labor unions. Ironically, the non-professional employees had binding contracts while the professional, degreed, and certified teachers did not. The professional employees were at-will employees, meaning an employer could terminate employment for any reason as long as the reason was legal. That left room for superintendents and elected boards of education to abuse their power.

My husband and son were excited for me and my opportunity in Missouri. The job included a salary raise of nearly $10,000. We had lived in our newly-built home for five years and decided to keep it even though I moved to another state. We agreed to alternate weekends driving to see and visit one another. That worked for almost a year, even though I thought I would die during the first week away from them. The panic attacks that I thought I'd left behind returned with a vengeance. I had trouble eating and sleeping. When Drake and Michael came to visit, I ate with them, but I couldn't eat after they left. It's probably no surprise that this coincided with the expiration of my prescription of Ativan, which I took for panic attacks. I was depressed and afraid and cried excessively for reasons I could not identify.

For the first time, at the age of forty-three, I was on my own, and adjusting to living alone challenged me. Living in a different state, working a new job, and getting to know my professional community were positive changes, but all of them at once proved to be too much. I went from Harold's house to college life and from college life to marriage and Drake. I had no independent experience as a woman on my own.

I learned later that the move and the job changes were necessary for me to find healing. It wasn't until I lived alone that I realized how unprepared I was for life. I spent so much time in childhood and adolescence learning survival skills that I missed learning what was necessary to manage ordinary daily living. Drake managed our finances, our home construction and its myriad decisions, and a great deal of Michael's life and logistics. Drake kept the family calendar and arranged most of our social commitments. When I was with Drake and Michael, I could easily allow busyness to distract me when things were uncomfortable, but when I was alone, I had nothing but quiet, so my repetitive, negative thoughts were louder. I believe it was the stress of living alone that set off the second significant round of panic attacks, irrational fears, insomnia, and depression. The kinds of nightmares I had in December 2000 resumed with increased tremors and bouts of extreme agitation. I can see now that what I suppressed with medication was waiting to be revealed once the Ativan left my system.

The nightmares were suppressed memories demanding my attention. I buried the memories of my violent childhood and multiple incidents of sexual abuse because I thought that would keep them in the past where they belonged. Instead, those memories—and the emotions attached to them—attacked my body and mind like a virus. For years, I received monthly injections for allergies and sinus infections. Multiple stress-related chronic syndromes required medication. I was the definition of unhealthy, but I had no idea that my medical profile was in any way unusual. The Ativan for anxiety issues was only the tip of the iceberg. The nightmares and the illnesses were like screams from my mind and body, telling me to *Look! Look what happened to you!* I needed to understand those memories instead of running from them.

The year of living apart from my husband contributed to the demise of my marriage, but worse than separate houses was what God revealed during the time alone in Springfield. The panic attacks, nightmares, and insomnia were the warning signs of much more to come and a much deeper pain to acknowledge. Without my husband living with me, I was forced to go through the valley of revelation and grief as my mind simultaneously worked with and against me. Memories of events that I thought were long forgotten returned. I became aware of much of the abuse I suffered and began to realize how much of it was at the hands of people who professed to love God and His children.

My needs were so vast that Drake represented perfection. I never questioned anything he said or did because I knew I lacked adult skills and the ability to make sound decisions. Drake was older and had more life experience. I admired him and thought he had a healthy grip on life and its demands. It was too late when I realized he was only human and didn't have life under control. I see he was alone in our marriage in the ways that mattered. He thought he married an adult, but the reality was that I was emotionally still a child. Each incident of trauma stunted my maturity to the point my emotional development was years behind my physical age. Drake used to say, "Dora, you are not growing up. You are simply getting older." Of course, those words didn't mean much to me when he said them, but after we divorced, I began to mature and could see the truth and wisdom in his assessment. Throughout our marriage, I made childish mistakes. Drake never said it, but he would not be wrong if he thought being married to me was like raising a second child. Sadly, because I only had the understanding of a child,

I couldn't keep from hurting him. Knowing he was better without me was one thing that helped me through the divorce. I loved him enough to stop hurting him.

While living in Springfield, I began a period of maturation. I had adult thoughts (or at least that's what I called them) because they were thoughts about responsibility and what Drake and I needed to do as a married couple. I could feel the strain on our marriage as early as the first thirty days of living in Missouri, but I chalked it up to the stress of adjustment. I began to bring up previously undiscussed topics, like finances, marriage, and parenting, which sometimes confused Drake. I'm certain he wondered *why now,* since I had not mentioned those topics during our twenty-two years of marriage. I didn't know how to explain to him what was happening in my thoughts, emotions, and decisions because I didn't know. He was the one who usually said, *We need to talk,* and when he said *We need to talk,* I dreaded it like a child who disobeyed her parents. I didn't want to disappoint Drake. I knew he was good to me and took care of me. After moving to Springfield, though, I was the one who initiated the conversations. The more we talked, the more questions I had. These sessions must have been an emotional and mental strain for Drake. He carried the family for twenty-two years, and then I demanded answers dating back to year one. Surely he thought, *Where were you during the past twenty-two years?* I wish I could say I checked out, but I couldn't. That would mean that I was once there. The truth is, I never checked into our marriage. Drake carried the load until the end was in sight.

My questions turned into nights and days of heated discussions. One of them was about a piece of property Harold had bequeathed to me when he died. Although my relationship with Harold changed after I confronted him, I still kept in loose contact with him. A few days before he died, I felt led to go to the hospital and see him. He was in a coma, but I leaned over and whispered in his ear, "I forgive you. You can go now." He passed away a few days later. When we found out about the piece of property I inherited, Drake was excited about it, but I was emotionally distraught because I didn't want anything that linked me to Harold. Drake was adamant about keeping the property, and I was equally adamant that I didn't want it. There was too much emotional pain associated with it that Drake didn't understand. I didn't change my position, and the dissension continued. On another occasion, I asked Drake if we could get counseling, but he refused. I didn't know much about life, but I knew couples needed counseling when they had difficulty agreeing.

I realize now I wanted to stop being a child in the marriage; I wanted a voice, but I didn't know how to say that. I asked Drake for marriage counseling several times, and each time he rebuffed the suggestion without an explanation. Catastrophizing with all-or-nothing thinking convinced me that life would always be this way. It was as if I was locked in a building that was about to blow up, and I was the only one who knew the building would explode. That's symbolic of how I felt if we didn't get help. I saw counseling as the only escape route for us. At that time, I still had no understanding of how Childhood Trauma affected me. Perhaps with counseling, the extreme adversities I suffered as a child would have been exposed. When Drake refused, however, I went into survival mode. I felt Drake would never take me seriously because I didn't make my own decisions and didn't know how to manage money. I needed Drake to know I wanted to grow, but there was no room.

It was at that point I decided I could not stay married. After twenty-two years, the few months of living separately revealed the fragility of our foundation—the foundation initially formed in deception and distrust. Of course, what was revealed was my fragility and inability to fully participate in a loving, adult relationship. Once I faced my husband as an adult and demanded answers for his choices, he didn't like the heat of accountability, and I had no strength to continue the fight. I had no internal fortitude to establish the necessary foundation for the type of marriage we needed to make it for the long haul. I could fight for my marriage, or I could fight for my mental health, but I could not fight for both—at least, not at the same time. I felt I needed to get out of the marriage to have the space to fight for my mental health. I thought a divorce or full legal separation was the best step to take. With the emotional, physical, and mental challenges I faced, I needed space, and I wanted to spare Drake and Michael. At that point, I didn't know how my story would evolve, so I thought I'd save Drake from more heartache. Since I couldn't endure the pressure of marital conflict in addition to the mental stress I attempted to conceal, I suggested we divorce. Drake must have been at the end of his rope because he didn't oppose the suggestion.

When Drake voiced no opposition to divorce, my heart dropped. What I heard was *He doesn't want me* and *He's tired of me*. At the same time, I was ashamed of my childish behavior during the marriage. I bought a new outfit instead of paying a utility bill, or I would say I would be home by a certain time and then not call when I knew I would be late. I didn't want to feel like I had to answer to him or anyone else—the same type of thinking I had when I was a senior in high school. I was ashamed of putting him through unforgivable financial strain and emotional pain. Neither of us suggested a trial separation to consider our options. I suppose the months I lived in Missouri were enough of a separation to clarify our situation. It almost seemed like we were together one day and divorced the next. Of course, it didn't happen that way, but I knew that there was no turning back once Drake saw me as the petitioner.

I wasn't sure I could help Drake absorb and learn to live with my reality. After all, he knew many of my abusers. I was fearful how he would react, first to me and then to them. I thought the solution to my situation was divorce. I thought divorce would protect Drake and Michael from having to deal with my history. I had no idea the divorce would catapult me into a destiny molded from my history.

Many times after filing the divorce application, I wanted to talk to Drake, but he refused. I don't blame him. Even though I thought he was selfish at the time, I solely focused on myself. Now I know he gave me the best twenty-two years of his life, and he didn't want to waste another second. I get it now. But at that point, it felt unfair. I tried to buy his friendship by offering as much in the settlement as possible. I decided he could have anything he wanted except my intellectual property and writing. My writing was a record of the hell I lived through. Although I knew it might have financial value at some future point, it represented much more than income. It was my precarious tether to sanity. Drake's attorney determined I should pay most of the bills because I made more money. A year before the divorce, Drake found a job that paid less than mine, so I didn't fight the attorney's request. I blamed myself for the divorce and wanted to do whatever I could to make it less painful for him. I felt I had done the right thing in giving Drake everything. It eased my conscience, and no amount of money could do that.

Although I still had to learn about Childhood Trauma and PTSD, I knew something terrible happened to my mind and body, and I needed to understand how it continued to affect me. I can't help but wonder how many couples head for a divorce when they need time to understand what happened because one of them experienced things they can't explain. There is a very promising field of counseling called the family systems approach, in which the family members participate to understand the shared impact of issues in the family. Even if it appears that only one person has a problem, in most families, everyone is affected by the consequences. The family systems approach can be very helpful to families when a parent has unresolved Childhood Trauma.

Before the divorce, I experienced so many thoughts that I didn't know what to do with. I had no counselor and wasn't able to find one in Southwest Missouri. I knew my mind and behavior had changed, but I didn't understand why. I was like a teenager who matured from childish thinking to adult thinking. I didn't know what growing up looked like, but I knew I needed some space to do it. Sadly, I was so out of touch with adult married life that I thought if we divorced, we could remarry within a few months or after I went through whatever I needed to go through. I couldn't shake the thoughts about the significance of Harold, my abuser, officiating our wedding. I didn't want a divorce, but I wanted to be free of those convoluted thoughts, and I didn't know the best way to do that.

Before the divorce, I could not predict how life would change for Drake, Michael, and me. I couldn't conceptualize situations or analyze possible outcomes. I could not understand the emotional, physical, mental, and spiritual effects divorce would have on Michael, Drake, Drake's family, or mine. My experience with divorce was mostly limited to my sisters' situations, which I believed were improved by divorce since their divorces served to remove abusive men from their homes. At one point early in our marriage, Drake commented that if our marriage ever ended, it would be without bitterness or rancor because we were the best of friends. Neither of us had an inkling of the depth of a wound inflicted when a spouse formally rejects the other in a legal process. I saw what little bit of love we had extinguished by the rage Drake felt when he understood that I no longer wanted to stay married or to be his wife. There was nothing friendly about how we tried to come to a settlement and divide our assets.

I apologized to Drake several times at every opportunity that presented itself, but my apologies fell on deaf ears. He wasn't moved. I wanted us to be friends and protect Michael. I thought if I gave Drake everything, he would be more amicable toward me, but that was not his response. I didn't fight him for anything in the divorce settlement. My attorney repeatedly discouraged me from giving away so much, but I felt it was the right thing to do. I gave Drake nearly everything he wanted since I felt he lost everything because of me. I asked only for my journals and archive of writing materials. I gave him half of my 401K and made no spousal claim on his. I wanted to do everything possible to let him know I felt responsible for the divorce. I felt it was my fault that I couldn't think critically, so why should he and Michael suffer? I felt they had suffered enough with me in their lives, and I decided to help them however I could.

Chapter 48

MICHAEL AND ME

Before the divorce, my relationship with my son was affectionate and close. It was Drake, Michael, and me for nearly twenty-three years. We regularly walked on the local high school track, rode bikes on Sunday, danced in the Spirit as we listened to gospel songs, spent time together watching movies on family nights, and supported one another as we each celebrated our accomplishments. I admit, I did not see a divorce or an estranged relationship in my future. I thought we could conquer anything that came against us. I looked externally, ready to attack challenges that came against our family. I never once looked for an internal attack. I thought if any family—any mother-son would make it—we would. It's hard to prepare for or win invisible fights. Childhood Trauma often leads survivors into fights for which they are unprepared. This was the case with my relationship with Michael. Michael and I were extremely close, and I couldn't imagine we would ever be estranged. We talked about anything that concerned him, so I was devastated when we stopped talking. I thought because he was nineteen at the time of our initial separation, he would understand that adults have differences and aren't always able to resolve those differences. I understand now he was more shocked by the divorce than I was. Neither he nor I knew how to fix the brokenness of our relationship, so for more than ten years we didn't. Despite the depression and PTSD that continually threatened my sanity, those years held the deepest, heart-wrenching pain I ever experienced when I thought my son was lost to me.

Michael and his cousin came to visit about a year after the separation when I was still living in Southwest Missouri and working for Missouri NEA. In the previous year, I had only talked to him once or twice. Neither one of us knew how to act. I tried to buy his relationship, but I couldn't afford it. He wasn't the kind of child who could be bought. I felt I needed to do something for the pain I caused him, and the only thing I could do at that time was buy things. When he left, I knew the time we spent together that weekend was inauthentic. We were both in shock and didn't know what to think or how to respond to each other. I had lots of activities planned for Michael and his cousin, and I was glad he brought someone with him because it meant less time for him and me to sit in silence. We went on a boat ride with friends, to dinner, and laughed as much as possible. All I wanted to do was hide. I was beyond sorrowful for the pain I caused Michael and his father, but I knew a simple apology wouldn't suffice. I was learning about sexual abuse, but it would be three more years before I learned about how Childhood Trauma causes cognitive and emotional impairment.

For twelve years Michael and I had little communication. I thought about Michael daily and asked God to restore our relationship. I asked God to help him understand my pain and brokenness. I asked God for another miracle because I knew I could not bridge the gulf between Michael and me. I was the one who filed for divorce, and for a long time, I felt I had no right to ask Michael to accept me after breaking his trust. I say *trust* because he trusted us to be a family forever as I said we would, but I broke that trust. I knew it would take forgiveness and understanding to restore our relationship. Although I broke a vow to God by ending my marriage, I learned His character was forgiving, and I believed when I repented He would forgive and restore me. I believed that to my core. I believed restoration was not a long, drawn-out process with God because He waited for me to repent so He could bless me. His nature is to bless His children. God created me and loves me, but like any parent, He disciplines His children.

Every holiday, birthday, and New Year I sent a text of encouragement and spoke blessings over Michael. Most years he didn't respond, but I kept texting. I sent cards, called, and wrote letters to no avail. The part of me that did not want to feel rejection died each time I reached out to him because he didn't respond. Thoughts of restoring our relationship became stronger than the feelings of rejection. During the earlier time I reached out to Michael, I was healing, so the rejection pains were excruciating. Yet, I knew I had to fight for our relationship. Sometimes several months passed before I attempted to contact him again.

After twelve years of praying for Michael and the relationship to be restored, the Holy Spirit spoke to me one morning. He said, *Now you must speak to these mountains and command them to move.* I wrote down a list of mountains. One of them was the separation between Michael and me. The Holy Spirit guided me to write down a specific prayer to remove the separation mountain using Mark 11:24 as my guarantee: *Therefore I tell you, whatever you ask for in prayer, believe that you have received it, and it will be yours.* I prayed for sixty days and made declarations with the prayers.

After two months of speaking to the mountains, I reached out to Michael. At the beginning of 2023, I wanted to declare a blessing over him for the new year. This was the text I sent:

> *Happy New Year, my dearest son Michael!!!!*
> *I am praying and declaring that 2023 will be a year of unprecedented favor of God and man for you, blessings on the work of your hands, the beginning of the restoration of our relationship, and a harvest of healing, love, peace, and your heart's desire for all the seeds you have sown and continue to sow emotionally, mentally, physically, and spiritually into the lives of your students.*
> *God's blessing be upon you and your seed!*
> *All my love, Mom*

Michael responded with a heart emoji and reached out several times after that text to thank me. He told me he wanted to see me. He had said that before, but I knew this time it would happen. I could feel in my spirit that it was time. My faithful God allowed Michael to visit in March 2023, for the first time since the visit in 2011 with his cousin. When he got out of his truck, we hugged for five minutes.

He said, "I miss you, Mom."

I said, "I've missed you, too, and am so thankful to see you."

Our reunion began with faith in God's covenant promises, trusting God to make it happen, and aided by strength from the Holy Spirit who never let me give up the unwavering desire to see my son. My obedience led to the reunion. Michael and I continue to visit, text, and talk more frequently, but not as if we were never estranged. I understand that although we desired to see each other, our pain paralyzed us for twelve years and it takes time to mend broken hearts. I acknowledge my part in causing him pain and trust God to heal his heart like He heals the hearts of those He sends to me.

Chapter 49
GOD'S DETOX

S hortly after moving to Missouri and before the divorce, I went to a Missouri doctor so I could get a refill on my Ativan prescription. She told me that out of the ten most stressful life events, I experienced nine of them: marital strain, relocation, separation from my husband and son, a new job with increased responsibilities, my sister's death, an immune system disorder diagnosis, and culture shock from being a minority in a non-diverse geographical area. On top of that, I enrolled in a university doctoral program to get an advanced degree. Despite what I thought, the Ativan prescription adversely affected me and was extremely addictive. My anxiety level increased tenfold whenever I ran out of pills.

The doctor said, "We need to wean you off this medicine." I told her I didn't think it was a good idea to wean at that time, especially since she told me my situation was grim. She said, "Continuing this prescription is against what I believe. I don't want to prescribe medicine that I know will harm you." I wasn't concerned about being harmed. I had already been harmed. I needed safety, and the medicine made me feel safe. I had no physical feeling from the medicine; I was convinced that its mere presence made me better. I was unmoved by her argument that Ativan was not helping me or even that it was bad for me. My childhood was filled with incident after incident of people not caring about what was in my best interest—now I had a doctor trying to do the right thing and I was furious with her for not giving me what I wanted.

I urged her and tried to beg without sounding desperate. I tried to convince her I needed the medicine, but she said, "I refuse to prescribe any more of this for you." The more demanding I became, the more she saw my addiction. It took everything I had to control my urge to hit the doctor and say awful things to her. That was my first understanding of how long-term medication can create addictions and co-dependencies. I thought I needed the medication and couldn't live without it. What I didn't realize was the medicine I was fighting for was the very thing that fought against my body and worsened my situation. I refused to accept the doctor's professional and medical advice because my trauma brain and distrusting heart could not believe someone I didn't know could care for me. After all, why should I trust her? A doctor I trusted in Arkansas put me on the medication and prescribed it without any warnings of possible addictions.

"I will prescribe a medicine that won't be as harmful, but it will take a few weeks for your body to adjust to it," she said. I angrily stomped out of her office while promising to call the American Medical Association. Not once did I see her refusal to give me a drug that would harm me as taking care of me. In my mind, she refused to help me. She, of all people, knew how much I needed the medicine. I was going through some of life's most difficult times, and she wanted to change my medicine. I knew that had to be grounds for an American Medical Association complaint. Never mind that my physician said the medicine was harming my body. It couldn't harm it any more than the stress I was experiencing!

I didn't realize how long I had been on Ativan until the doctor revealed I had taken it for nine years. I didn't feel I was strong enough to wean off the medication, and I was separated from my support system. I thought I had more medical insight than the doctor. I left her office and went straight to a pharmacy before the doctor could call. I needed a refill and planned to tell them it was a transfer from my Arkansas prescription. The problem was I needed a Missouri doctor to renew the Arkansas prescription.

The pharmacist looked at me and flatly said, "That is hard to get, but I'll try." I couldn't understand why it was so hard to get in the state I had recently moved to when it wasn't hard to get in the state I came from.

I assumed the doctor called the pharmacist and told him to refuse to dispense the medicine. Looking back, I can see the impact of my lack of critical thinking. I went to several pharmacies in the small town, but none of them had it. They said they couldn't get it. That was the most absurd thing I had ever heard, and by then I saw a conspiracy.

When my husband and son came that weekend, I stayed in bed, curled into a ball. I remained in bed for the weekend with excuses about not feeling well. I tried as best I could not to let my son know what happened, but I could not force myself to get out of bed, eat, or even move. I couldn't think and couldn't sleep. I was nervous and irritable and didn't want to reveal this to my family. When they left on Sunday afternoon, I felt like I would die, and they would find my lifeless body when they came for their next visit.

Somehow I survived to tell my story. For more than a month, the doctor denied the prescription refill, and I shook during many sleepless nights. I drove only to work and to places nearby because I was afraid I might have a nervous breakdown and lose touch with reality. I was extremely anxious and unable to focus on anything other than work. I poured my energy into work and the situations I had to handle. I couldn't control my personal life, but I was able to stay in control of my work life. As I look back on those days, it's a miracle I was able to act sane during the workday. Not once during those days did I ever scream or act unprofessionally toward a member or superintendent due to my problems. It's as if God rebuked Satan from my mind long enough to do my job and drive home, but then He said *OK, Satan, you can have her again*.

Night after night, I was tormented with dreams and visions of my deceased parents beating and burning my siblings and me, chasing us with a huge stick, and coming back from the dead to torment me. Adults with parents who abuse drugs and alcohol have a higher and faster rate of abusing drugs themselves. Several of my siblings have problems with alcohol. Both of my parents drank heavily and partied on the weekends, but Elsie also drank during the workweek. She drank anytime someone gave her a drink, even early in the morning.

After nearly two months of withdrawal, endless sleepless nights, and days with no appetite, the anxiety symptoms of withdrawal from the Ativan began to subside, but I still had to fight the nightmares and panic attacks. The lack of medicine caused agitation, sleep issues, and acute emotional pain. My mind on the medicine was better in the sense that I had no thoughts or dreams about my childhood. Without the medicine, my past was the only thing on my mind, and I did not want to recall any of it. I didn't understand why this seemingly sudden change happened because I did not connect the dependence on Ativan with the suppression of anxiety or the withdrawal of it with the increase in anxiety, but that's what happened. For the first time in my life, I understood I was addicted.

In 2009, I still didn't know anything about Post Traumatic Stress Disorder (PTSD) or Childhood Trauma, but they were both heading toward me like a bullet train on a cross-country express route. PTSD is a mental disorder that usually appears within a few months after exposure to a traumatic event, such as sexual assault, combat, a natural disaster, a car accident, child abuse, or threats on a person's life. As it did for me, PTSD can lie dormant in the body for years. I suspect I may have had PTSD during childhood but lived for years without noticeable symptoms. Symptoms include negative thoughts and feelings or dreams related to the traumatic event. People with PTSD may experience insomnia, feelings of helplessness and hopelessness, bouts of crying, isolation from family and friends, emotional numbness, emotional and mental instability, hyper-vigilance, feelings of guilt and shame, angry outbursts, difficulty learning and maintaining close relationships, reduced quality of life, fear of crossing bridges, and fear of death. Thirteen million people annually are reported to have PTSD. When it became noticeable, my only option was to let it run its course.

The increasing anxiety and lack of control in my personal life brought me back to the doctor who refused to refill the Ativan prescription. She was the only physician in my area covered by my health insurance, so I was unable to seek in-network treatment from someone else. This is another example of God keeping His hand on me: by limiting my access to a single physician, I was unable to game the system to feed my junkie habit.

Culture shock was a new term for me, but she explained it. "You are in a new place and don't see many people who look like you, and you may never have lived in a place like this before. First, let me say it is normal for you to feel and think this way. You are not adjusting well to this culture change. Psychologically it's difficult, and your mind will have to adjust to your new normal. I suggest you go to church, and perhaps you will find people there you can more readily identify with and create a community."

I interpreted her suggestion to mean that I should *go find some people who look like me.* Although I had lived in the area for a few months already, I still had not seen one other person who looked like me, but I couldn't go to church because I knew for sure that would cause more problems with flashbacks and panic attacks from my previous spiritual abuse. I had no plans to return to the same place that started the pain. I knew the doctor meant well, but I couldn't go to church because I felt I couldn't trust the people in the church, especially after the so-called men of God had taken advantage of me as a child.

I also thought *Who could adjust well to this racist city?* Springfield, Missouri, is the same place where three Black men were pulled from jail in 1906 and hanged in Park Central Square at the Gottfried Tower near the replica of the Statue of Liberty. Over 1000 citizens witnessed the lynching and started a fire to burn the bodies. No one was indicted for the crimes. Not long afterward, Black residents left the region in huge numbers. Seemingly overnight, the Black population reduced from 15% to 2%.[14] Yet, Springfield was where God chose to continue my healing journey, and I am so thankful He did. It was in this racist city that I learned most about God's omnipotence,

[14]*Ozarks Afro-American History Museum Online*, 1906; *Harper*, 2012.

omnipresence, and omniscience. I witnessed first-hand His supernatural protection. He taught me He was with me wherever I went. Springfield is my *valley* experience where I learned to trust and depend on Him.

I had no idea what I would encounter when I accepted the job in Southwest Missouri, but I wasn't conditioned to look for racism, nor did I have the energy. Until I moved to Missouri, my life was primarily spent around people who shared the same cultural beliefs and background. My hometown was 60% minority, but my college experience was in an environment that was 70% Caucasian, so I was aware of occasional racial tensions. In 2000, Little Rock, Arkansas, was 55% White and I taught in a city school district that was majority Black. This meant that I had little opportunity to encounter racism head-on. I heard about it and experienced it occasionally, but not on the level that I found in Southwest Missouri.

One of my areas of responsibility was Joplin, Missouri. I had my share of racial experiences and rejection while in the southwest area, but I also met some of the nicest people there who I still count as friends. The people in Joplin knew I had no family around, so they invited me to go camping, fishing, racing, or to join whatever activities they were doing. I believed they liked me, not only as a UD, but as a person. That helped, especially since I was so far away from Arkansas family and friends.

One evening I got home a little later than usual and wanted some fresh air, so I took a walk. When I returned, I saw blood smeared on my car's passenger door and around the wheel on the front end. I hadn't hit an animal or a person, so I knew the blood was intentionally smeared. Appalled, I called the police. The responding officer apologized, "It's a shame some people want to hate people simply because of their appearance. We don't get many calls like this, but it does happen."

I wondered, *What happened? Lynchings? Beatings? Vandalized vehicles? What?* He never said what he meant by "it does happen." The more he talked, the more agitated I became. He was kind and sympathetic and assured me he would keep an eye on the apartment complex while I lived there. I decided not to move. I refused to believe we were still that far in the past. I was one of those who did not want to accept my current reality that there were some people who, no matter how much things changed, remained the same. They refused to grow and accept everyone is created by God and that no one person, gender, or group is better than another.

On another occasion, I went to a Springfield restaurant and a Caucasian man stared at me so hard that I felt anxious and decided to get my food to go.

The waitress apologized when she realized I felt as if I had to leave, but she knew she couldn't change how that man felt about this dark stranger. She saw him staring intently at me and she understood my discomfort. I went back to my apartment and broke down in disbelief that my skin color still stirred others to hate me.

After a year in Springfield, I wanted to leave. I prayed and asked God why He directed my steps to come to such an unwelcoming place. When I shared my concerns, the NEA field supervisor and state president expressed support for whatever decision I felt was necessary. I won't say I wasn't afraid every night—because I was. Most nights I tried to get home before dark. I went inside, closed my door, and did not come out until the next morning.

Springfield was not the first place I felt unwanted, but it was the first time I lived in an area where people let me know I was not welcome. Based on the time I spent in the metro St. Louis area during the internship, I anticipated more racial rejection the further I went from Interstate 44 and St. Louis. I heard about the racism in Southwest Missouri before I moved there, but I underestimated the sting of it. I naively thought people weren't like that now. Others were naive, too. When I told my Caucasian friends and co-workers about the incident, they were surprised because they also thought racism was in the past. Through this experience, I learned only God—not time—can change the hearts of the people.

Chapter 50
WHEN CHURCH HURTS

In Springfield, I got to know a young woman who frequently invited me to visit her church. She told me how accepting they were and said I should go with her. The week of Christmas 2011, I agreed to go, thinking people's hearts are softer during the holiday time of year. I remember praying to God and thinking, "I can't take another rejection. Please let me go to Your House and not be rejected." The greatest hurts in my life came from people I trusted to have my best interests at heart—people in the church who professed a commitment to God and His people. Jesus identifies specific groups of people to especially take care of: the poor in spirit, the meek, those who mourn, those who hunger and thirst for justice, the merciful, the pure in heart, the peacemakers, and those who suffer persecution—I was definitely one of those people, and the people I counted on to help further persecuted me instead of leading me to freedom.

I heard my friend's church presented an annual Christmas performance, and I thought I could give them a pre-published copy of my book *Twas the Night Before Jesus was Born* which was officially released in September 2012. The lady who invited me loved the book and assured me her church would love it, too. I wrote a poem for Michael to recite at Drake's family Christmas program when he was three years old. After the divorce, I turned the poem into a children's book, and an artist friend, Sondra Strong, beautifully illustrated each page with colorful paintings. I could picture the children in my friend's church sitting in a circle, and instead of reading Clement Clark Moore's *'Twas the Night Before Christmas*—since that version had nothing to do with Jesus—they might enjoy my Christmas story, *'Twas the Night Before Jesus Was Born*.

My friend suggested I meet with the pastor. Both of us were excited about the possibility of the book being selected for the children's program. Since it was a church, I thought it would be great if they read the book and understood another way to share the Christmas story. They could still read *'Twas the Night Before Christmas,* but perhaps they could read my book in a different part of the program. The thought that someone could benefit from my book gave me hope during my greatest time of hopelessness.

During the meeting with the pastor, I was even more excited. She told me what a wonderful book it was, how talented a writer I am, and how children would love to read this book. She was especially fond of how the book had the cadence of *'Twas the Night Before Christmas*, yet had the Biblical setting to teach children about Christ in an enjoyable and colorful way. Then her smile dropped to a semi-frown as she said, "I wish the church would allow us to use it, but I know they won't accept it. They are not ready." She acted like I offered them a million-dollar contract, and she couldn't make a high-stakes decision before going to the church leaders.

It took all the self-control I had not to burst out crying. The same God they said they worshiped had given me the story to write, but because I—a Black woman—wrote it, they wouldn't allow the children to read it. It was a long walk from her office to the car. If the pastor said I wrote something they disagreed with, I could have accepted her rejection of my book, but she simply said, "They won't accept it. I know them." My excitement and hope melted as quickly as ice in the summer sun.

When I got to the car I sobbed to God, "Why did You give me this gift if Your people would reject it? I kept asking repeatedly, "Why, God? Aren't I good enough?" I wept as I turned the car toward home.

I could barely see the road through my tears. My heart experienced something that night that no child of God should ever have to. Surely, Jesus' heart wept, too. I was overwhelmed because the pastor's words took me to the place of my ancestors, the place I thought I would never have to know, the place I thought God's people were free of—the place of being *other*. Jesus died for us, but even His death did not bring us together. The pastor's words reverberated in my mind. *They won't accept it. I know them.* Reality sank in that if I stayed in Southwest Missouri, I might be denied other aspirations. I dreamed of being another Laura Ingalls Wilder, but if they couldn't accept a little poem, they would never accept a novel. If the church wouldn't accept me, I felt there was no place for me. While I was rejected because of my skin color, Jesus was rejected because of His stand for truth and justice. As it often did, all-or-nothing thinking crept in, but this time it was more than just catastrophizing because I had too many negative experiences in Springfield related to my skin color.

When I left that pastor's office, I vowed, *One day my Christmas book will be read to the children in the church that represents Heaven. It will be accepted and read, and it will bless little children.* It was difficult for me to understand how a church could reject a story written about what Jesus taught because they weren't ready to accept how God made someone. Thank God He helped me to understand there is nothing new under the sun. People have been and always will be people, and attending church doesn't change the hearts of people. Only God's Holy Spirit can change their hearts.

Intellectually, I knew that not everyone felt like some of the people in my friend's Springfield church, but my heart knew what it experienced. Some Caucasians, on the other hand, went out of their way to welcome me and be kind. Kind people like them gave me hope that I wasn't disliked simply because of my skin color.

Chapter 51
THE EYES OF GOD

In a small-town diner in Southwest Missouri, one experience proved not everyone thought or behaved like religious people. As I waited to receive an order of eggs and hash browns, I looked around, wondering if someone would give the cue that I didn't belong. I noticed an elderly man who looked about seventy-five years old. He was dressed in pin-striped overalls, work boots, and a faded shirt. Sitting next to him was a beautifully dressed older woman wearing a summer dress and open-toed shoes with painted toenails. I glanced at her but quickly looked away because I didn't want her to give the cue. I wanted to sit and eat the plate of food that was placed in front of me.

When I looked up again, I saw a big smile on the woman's face. It was as if she knew how I was feeling. I glanced down at my phone to be sure not to look at anyone too long. Out of the corner of my eye, I saw someone coming toward me. The older man stepped close to my table.

"May I sit down?" he asked.

I was sure I didn't hear him correctly, so I didn't answer. He spoke again, "My wife and I see you sitting alone, and we don't want you to eat alone."

Before I could respond, he reached down and picked up my plate. I saw his thumb press into the hash browns at the side of the plate. I knew he didn't mean to do it because I could feel the love coming from him, but I almost forgot how kind he was when I saw his thumb in my food.

His thumb touching the hash browns almost provoked an outburst because I had an obsessive-compulsive disorder with hygiene and sanitation. I was extremely sanitary before, but hyper-sensitivity accelerated my concern into a disorder. I couldn't go to a restaurant without requesting hot water to clean the silverware. I couldn't touch the rails on escalators or the buttons on elevators. I wouldn't go near people who sniffled, sneezed, or coughed for fear I would catch their germs. I even had difficulty sharing food with my husband. I didn't think anything about my phobia until Michael at age ten told me, "Mom, you need some germs in your body."

The moment the older gentleman touched my hash browns, I recalled Michael's statement, but I didn't want to die from another person's germs. In my distorted thinking, the man's thumb in my hash browns could cause sudden death. I glanced at his thumb and imagined dirt and bacteria under his fingernail. He had calloused hands with thick fingernails, and I could see traces of dirt on them. I went into a silent emotional hysteria. I didn't feel safe enough in that restaurant to speak openly in front of the restaurant customers because I didn't know what they might do, so I took a deep breath and thought, *Calm down. This won't kill me. The people here might, but the germs from his thumb won't kill me. Relax.*

I had to think quickly. I didn't want to offend the nice couple by refusing their gesture. I was sure they saw the look on my face when he picked up the plate. *Lord, please help me. It will take a miracle for me to eat this food.* I couldn't even try to eat the food that he touched. God didn't answer my prayer fast enough, so I decided I wasn't hungry. I pushed the eggs and hash browns around on my plate and pretended to eat. I hoped they didn't notice I wasn't eating.

Bob and his wife Rebecca talked and laughed with me until breakfast was over. They talked about how God loves us and how we are to love one another. Whoa. Could this Caucasian man have said what I thought I heard him say? That we need to love one another? He wasn't simply saying it. In my heart, I knew Bob meant what he said. I loved them, but I certainly didn't love Bob's dirty thumb in my food! I understood their point and certainly appreciated it after the inhospitable ways I was treated in other restaurants.

As we talked, tears rolled down my face because I wished everyone felt the way Bob did. I wouldn't have been rejected at my friend's church, experienced the staring man at the other restaurant, or the vandalism of my car in the apartment parking lot. Rebecca passed me a tissue as she, too, fought back tears. Bob talked his way through the awkwardness, but they both let me know in their own way that they understood and disagreed with how I was treated. I was so thankful to meet Bob and Rebecca, who accepted me for who I was—not a Black person or a Black woman—but a person, another human being on the same planet who was in desperate need of love.

After we finished our conversation, Bob and Rebecca invited me to their home. I thought they must have been kidding, so I smiled and told them that I might go to their house someday. Our breakfast turned into the beginning of a great friendship. They were proud grandparents and told me about their children who lived in Minnesota and visited a few times each year. I prayed with them and asked God for a special blessing for the kindness they showed me.

Months later, when I told Bob and Rebecca I planned to leave Springfield, Rebecca gave me a handmade quilt with beguiling patterns of butterflies and bumblebees resting on a large oak tree. She took some of my favorite things—oak trees, butterflies and bumblebees—and configured them into a delightful quilt. She said the quilt represented me. She heard me talk about how butterflies and bumblebees inspired me. I didn't know who I was yet, but I was inspired by the transformation of caterpillars into butterflies and the way bumblebees defy the laws of aerodynamics, and I shared my awe during our conversation. The quilt was extra special because Rebecca made it by hand. God uses His special people regardless of their race, ethnicity, culture, economic status, or education. Bob and Rebecca not only accepted me, but they cared enough about me to get to know me and make a beautiful gift. To this day, that quilt holds treasured memories of our time together.

Another good thing about my time in Springfield was that I was recognized by the Missouri NEA for having the highest rate of educator recruitment to NEA membership. Appealing to teachers who worked without contracts was especially difficult, but word got around that I was able to advocate for teachers and influence superintendents to make improvements in school district working conditions. My recruitment rate indicated Southwest Missouri teachers not only accepted me, but they trusted me—and the organization I represented—to advocate for them. The Missouri NEA recognition was meaningful because it confirmed Bob and Rebecca's message that not everyone is concerned about race. Bob and Rebecca were convinced some people love people as God loved them and truly believe all humans are equal in God's eyes.

Jesse and Catherine are another wonderful married couple I grew to love in Southwest Missouri, and we became lifelong friends. Catherine needed advocacy, so I scheduled several meetings, and we explored her options. During our meetings, she often asked about my family, and I told her I was going through a divorce. She must have seen and heard the sadness in my voice as I talked about how much I missed my family, especially simple things like a cookout with hotdogs, reading on the porch, and Sunday dinners. After Catherine's issue was resolved, she invited me to her house for dinner.

While I thought Catherine was nice, I felt I wasn't yet healed enough to go to anyone's house. My obsessive-compulsive disorders limited the people I visited and the restaurants I patronized. Houses couldn't have pets and restaurants had to be sanitary. The restaurant had to be willing to provide hot water to soak my silverware to sanitize. I dreaded going to homes or restaurants because I didn't want to hurt anyone's feelings. In my mind, pets meant a house was dirty. To my astonishment, however, as soon as Jesse opened the door, I could see their house was immaculate. Every surface was spotless. After a few minutes, a small chihuahua came in and sniffed my feet, but I didn't panic or throw up. The dog was tiny, and the house was clean. My brain sent the message to my response system that everything was fine, and I remained calm. The first time I went to Catherine's house, Jesse grilled hotdogs because they knew how much I missed them. The second time, they served Sunday dinner with roast beef, macaroni and cheese, green beans, and dinner rolls. We developed a tradition of gathering monthly for Sunday dinner. In November, they included me at their family's Thanksgiving dinner.

Catherine and Jesse shared with me about their only son's death. He was sixteen years old and said his chest hurt, so his parents scheduled a doctor's appointment. On the morning of the appointment, they found their son dead from a heart attack. In a flash, their lives changed from parenting an active teenager and enjoying his passions and friends to the stillness of a childless home. I visited his gravesite with them and prayed silently as they grieved. Hearing such heart-wrenching stories reminded me to be grateful for what I had. I could not feel pity for myself after hearing of their great loss and emotional struggles. Undoubtedly, remembering their loss helped to put into perspective the grief I felt for the estrangement from Michael I experienced during those years.

I made other friends like Linda and Vicki in Joplin. It was because of them that I met my second husband. They made sure I wasn't alone on holidays and drove to visit me when I needed someone to talk to. They called to check on me and prayed for me as well. They drove from Joplin to Springfield to help me pack for the move to St. Louis, and they did not leave until the last item was on the truck. I am so thankful for their friendship. Linda and Vicki insisted I attend the Joplin High School graduation ceremony in 2012, a year after the historic catastrophic tornado, even though I was sick that day. I didn't want to disappoint them. I had been away from Joplin for two months, but I felt I had to return for the graduation because Linda and Vicki wanted to see me.

I was in my office one day when a member stopped by. She said, "You were so kind on the phone that I wanted to meet you." I now know her visit was a divine appointment that led to my destiny. As we talked, she revealed she was completing her doctoral degree. I wanted to return to graduate school to get mine, but I didn't know how. She told me about an evening program designed for educators. I thought and prayed about it. I had once applied for a doctoral program, but the university canceled the program, so now seemed like the time to try again. I had the support of my husband and son when I applied the first time, but without them cheering me on, I wasn't sure I could handle more stress and the demands of a doctoral program, so I didn't call. I felt God leading me to act, however, and thoughts of graduate school continued to nudge me until I decided to do what God guided me to do. I called the university representative a few weeks later.

Ronald, the recruiter, seemed excited without even meeting me, so I became excited. "It's a great program!" he said. "We take into consideration that you have a job and a family, and we want you to have time for you. Any one of those lacking will not do us any good." I thought *that's the kindest, most thoughtful thing he could have said.* I felt like this might be the place. Ronald scheduled the required writing test.

One of the questions on the test was *What are you interested in learning more about? What are you interested in changing in the world?* I wrote I was interested in learning more about sexual abuse. I knew I wanted to know more about it because that was one of the things that I had suffered. I also knew I had lost everything, and I was in a lot of emotional pain. I thought it would help to know why I was dreaming and reliving the physical abuse, neglect, and sexual abuse from childhood. I did not know the thing that hurt the most, that I most wanted to forget—the unimaginable, indescribable pain sent to destroy me—would be the very thing God used to catapult me into my destiny.

I was excited to learn more about sexual abuse, but I didn't know where to begin. Ronald warned me to choose a subject that interested me because I would study it for the next three to five years and read the research from the field. He said this area of study needed to be something that would sustain my interest. After his warning, I didn't have to think twice. I had already informally researched the subject for over a year in hopes of discovering how sexual abuse affects a child emotionally, mentally, physically, and psychologically, as well as its long-term physical and mental health effects.

My first class was on a satellite campus in a town known for its lack of diversity. I knew I would be the only minority student, but I pulled my shoulders back, steeled my spine, and prayed. I also knew if God guided my steps to my purpose, nothing and no one could harm me. That sounded good in theory, but I was a little unsettled. Still, I refused to allow fear to stop me.

A professor later told me sexual abuse was probably not the best topic to study at that university. His reasons: first, Southwest Missouri is part of the nation's Bible Belt, and there was a lot of Bible-thumping in the area. Second, the topic was taboo and still wasn't openly discussed in cities, and even less in rural areas. Lastly, the attitudes of the predominantly White, male educators who were the administrators and leaders in the university community would make it difficult. During presentations, I saw classmates squirming as if they thought *Not her again. Please let her sit down,* and *Why didn't she choose another subject?* At that time, I didn't know the research on Childhood Trauma, nor did I realize that statistically many in my classes were either survivors of abuse or perpetrators. Many of the documented issues in that region were methamphetamine use, incest, poverty, child abuse, and other rural challenges. Either way, my professors and classmates obviously preferred that I avoid such a difficult topic. During presentations, some took the opportunity to scroll their phone messages, read emails, or simply stare at me. Their *No Comment* responses validated my impressions of their disinterest and lack of support.

I maintained perfect class attendance. The university staff and students approached me with courtesy, but their lack of overt discrimination did not diminish my fear. I paid attention in class, but the concerns about what could happen outside meant I was habitually hyper-vigilant. I wanted to be prepared. I rarely felt safe or fully engaged, regardless of the kindness shown. Kindness from a few wasn't enough to cancel out the others' hate.

I rarely felt support during class. Southwest Missouri was anti-union, and assistant superintendents and superintendents I dealt with in the area school districts were sometimes my classmates. They did not want advocacy for educators because they liked running their school districts as their kingdoms and treating the educators as their servants. A crucial part of a doctoral program is the establishment of professional friendships and support networks. I could not establish trust with people who gave long stares, insincere smiles, and unwelcoming attitudes. There were many times I contemplated changing topics, if only to gain acceptance, but I persevered to learn more about sexual abuse and its impact on children.

My courage and steadfastness were gratifying. Several of my classmates spoke with me after classes and told me they, too, were sexually abused. It would have encouraged me if they had shown support during class for my topic, but they didn't, so I continued to appear to be the only one who was sexually abused and expressed interest in the topic. This kind of silence still occurs today when I speak. Survivors ask for my phone number and later call to tell me they've never told anyone they were sexually abused. While I am thankful they finally acknowledged their vile secret, it saddens me that so many survivors of sexual abuse and Childhood Trauma choose to remain quiet. The stress of keeping the secret a secret is as damaging as the secretive abuse. I'm certain many like me were sexually abused but didn't want to admit it in front of their peers. In my doctoral program, I thought of those beyond the classroom walls who were sexually abused, and I wanted to provide them a voice. As a child, I had no voice, but I was determined to speak as an adult. Others cannot shame me into silence because it causes them discomfort. I believed that if I could live through the reality of sexual abuse, they could sit through an academic presentation on the research.

Chapter 52

JOPLIN

I think of the southwest region of Missouri as the place God sent me to heal, grow, and love His people, even though a lot of them did not love me. For those who loved and accepted me, however, I choose to call Southwest Missouri a place of amazing love and acceptance. The folks who accepted me didn't simply *talk* about God. They lived Godly lives through loving and caring for His people.

My job as an educational advocate in the southwest of Missouri vastly differed from my days as an intern in St. Louis. I thought it would be similar, so I was stupefied when superintendents threatened their employees for asking for a lunch break. I informed the superintendents about Missouri laws regarding teachers' breaks, and they often acted like it was the first time they'd heard such a thing. Egregious behaviors demanded action, such as verbally abusing teachers, threatening teachers for questioning a superintendent's decision, or firing teachers for calling in sick. It was obvious that I upset the superintendents' kingdoms. The Southwest teachers were without contracts and were considered *At-Will* employees, meaning they could be fired at the will of the superintendent. Many superintendents decided that meant they could do whatever they wanted to the teachers. It was challenging to get unethical administrators to act with integrity.

The good old boy system was alive and well. Many of the superintendents treated teachers like children. Teachers feared losing their jobs, and after they told me their concern, they often said, "But I don't want you to say anything because that will make it more difficult." I could only tell God about the problem and pray for wisdom to help the teacher. God unfailingly worked it out. I took the credit for the work done in Southwest Missouri, but it was God since He answered my prayers.

I developed a unique working relationship with the superintendent and teachers of Joplin. I couldn't do as much for teachers without a contract or the ones who asked me not to say anything, which meant I often felt trapped. Joplin's superintendent, Dr. C.J. Huff, was an exception. He and I were both new to the district and knew God. In our first meeting, I told Dr. Huff that God put him in charge of His people and that Dr. Huff would answer to God for his treatment of them. He agreed. That agreement on our mutual accountability was beneficial to have in our tool kit when working on solutions. We both wanted to do the ethical and moral thing. As a result of our close working relationship, the Joplin teachers were less intimidated and better able to participate in their advocacy. I heard I should keep work and personal life separate or it would come back to bite me, but I adopted Joplin members as my family and went to their family events. This was good for me, especially after I filed for divorce and lost the close family relationship I previously enjoyed.

Two years into my position in Southwest Missouri, I experienced, along with the citizens of Joplin, another trauma—a devastating tornado. It made national headlines and changed my life forever. It exacerbated the PTSD, night sweats, nightmares, and fears that I consistently experienced.

Sunday, May 22, 2011, is etched in my memory. It started as a brisk, sunny morning, but by mid-afternoon, the sun hid its face behind ominous clouds. I still couldn't listen to any kind of media because I couldn't tolerate the negativity. Negative news made me anxious, and dramatic or violent TV programming interfered with my sleep. I had no idea of any intense weather warnings, but I knew dark clouds meant serious weather. As I drove toward Springfield from a family visit in Arkansas, I could tell a storm was brewing. Dime-sized hail hit the windshield, and strong winds buffeted the car. I grasped the steering wheel with both hands to keep the car in the lane. The closer I got to Springfield, the louder the winds howled. I hoped I'd make it to my apartment before the storm peaked. I accelerated and felt the wind lifting, pushing, and pulling the car as I struggled to steer. The sky was dark, and I could see it was much darker to the west.

I called the Joplin union's president to inform her that something ominous was approaching. She said the news reported a tornado touched down, but she was fine. Then she added, "Glen went to town near Range Line Road, but I think he's OK. I pray he saw it coming and knew to get to safety." She sounded a little concerned about her husband, but not hysterical.

Then the call dropped. I called back several times, and she didn't answer. I felt my heartbeat quicken and my palms grew sweaty. I started to panic because I didn't know what to do. I was helpless and knew the Joplin president must have felt helpless, too. I could feel my body going into fight or flight mode. *Has something happened to her? To her husband? What do I do now?* I thought about the Joplin educators I represented. They weren't only my job. They were a chosen family.

I was afraid to get out of the car and run to the front door of my apartment. My soon-to-be-ex-husband was in Arkansas and unable to help me. I used to rely on him in moments of distress, but he wasn't with me to tell me what to do or how to handle things. I waited in the car for nearly an hour hoping to hear from the Joplin president. When she finally called, she didn't sound upbeat at all. The words poured out of her in a torrent of reporting.

"Glen said he saw everything. There was a huge tornado. He went into our house and got in the bathtub until it passed. He said he could hear the winds churning and knew it was not good, but he survived. He doesn't yet know the extent of the damage to the city, but he said it hit hard and it's not good."

I felt relief for her and her husband, but also a heaviness as I anticipated the tornado's damage. My anticipation did not begin to match the reality of the catastrophic damage to the city of Joplin. The damage was calculated at $2.8 billion, making the Joplin tornado the costliest single tornado to date in US history. The insurance payout was the highest in Missouri's history. One hundred fifty-eight people died, and over eleven hundred were injured, making the Joplin tornado one of the deadliest US tornadoes.

Early the next morning, with my heart racing, my mind bombarded with fear of driving, and my body trembling, I headed to Joplin to see the damage and to support the local leaders of NEA groups in the Joplin area. The EF-5 tornado had 200+ mph winds. The ravaging winds smashed everything in the storm's path, leaving the area in rubble and looking as if a fire had torn through it, burning homes and buildings to the ground. I didn't even get twenty miles from home before I had to return because Interstate 44 was closed due to the damage in the areas between Springfield and Joplin. Not only was my personal life in shambles from the divorce, isolation, and mental and emotional anguish, but the one area that looked great all the time—my professional life—was disintegrated.

The Missouri National Education Association (MNEA)—the organization I worked for that represented the educators in Joplin—made sure every Uniserv Director had an emergency plan to help educators and was ready to execute the plan in an emergency. This was an emergency. I located the plan. People need plans because when an emergency strikes, there is little or no time to put one together, and even if there were time to put one together, it would be hard to think under such duress. Our emergency plan gave directions for what to do. Our first step was marking names on a roster of employees verified as survivors. The president of the Missouri Association and I prayed and waited until we heard from every educator on our list. Neither she nor I knew what to say as we dialed each member's number, praying and hoping they were safe.

It would be nearly two weeks before anyone except President Obama and the media could enter the Joplin area affected by the tornado. The President came in with Federal Emergency Management Agency (FEMA) personnel for a status update and a quick review of the damage. My first in-person visit to Joplin wasn't until about three weeks after the tornado hit. The city still looked as if the tornado had happened the day before. My state supervisor, another state representative, and I were emotional as we quietly walked around. Most people were in shock. Help from around the world poured in to help Joplin. I smelled smoke in the air from fires burning across the area. A large spray-painted X marked the condemned houses. Vehicles had caved-in rooftops, and their back seats were smashed against the front seats. I hoped no one was in those cars. I wasn't mentally or emotionally prepared for the things I witnessed. People had begun cleaning up, but I couldn't see any progress, because as far as I could see, the houses were reduced to slabs and crushed like soda cans. The scene looked like an apocalyptic movie where stunned residents roamed the streets searching for lost family members, photographs, or keepsakes among the debris.

In the days and weeks after the tornado, I heard many stories of near-misses and miraculous survivals, as well as stories of children who now panicked at the slightest wind and rain. I couldn't tell them I was already traumatized, and hearing their stories increased my panic and anxiety. I listened to every story of anyone who wanted to talk. Often, I didn't know what to say or what not to say. The tornado changed Joplin, but it also changed me. Panic and anxiety increased during the year of tornado recovery. I needed to find relief.

One of Joplin's stories was about the high school graduation, which ended only minutes before the tornado hit. Joplin Superintendent Dr. C. J. Huff decided a few days earlier to move the graduation ceremony from the high school to a nearby college campus. When parents complained, Dr. Huff didn't budge. When I heard about his decision, I knew the Holy Spirit directed him to change venues. The tornado demolished the high school at the same time the students and their families left the university arena to return to Joplin, a distance of about ten miles. Standing in the middle of the worst devastation, I couldn't help thinking, *This is not good, but thank You, God. It could have been so much worse. If You had not directed Dr. Huff to move the graduation to the university, those families would have been in the high school, and all of them might have died because the high school was destroyed. Thank You for saving the children, parents, and educators from destruction by placing them out of harm's way as they celebrated the children's academic milestone.*

Dr. Huff guided the district through its rebuilding process and preparations for the next academic year. Joplin got through the physical tornado and the emotional hurricane and rebounded stronger. Dr. C.J. Huff was nationally recognized for his courage and resilience. Four months later, he lightened the mood with a little humor when he spoke at a convocation for the Joplin School District at the beginning of the 2011-2012 school year. I'll never forget his words. He said, "As I prayed and thought about what I needed to do next, I googled, 'What to do after a tornado for dummies.'" That broke the somber mood, allowing everyone to laugh and smile again.

A few weeks after the tornado, I began to have outbreaks of weeping, periods of deep sadness, recurring nightmares, anxiety, panic attacks, and insomnia. Being in the presence of those who survived and spending time with those who had lost loved ones caused my previous PTSD symptoms to intensify. Storms and high winds contributed to my anxiety and panic attacks. Dark clouds or heavy storms set my body to fight or flight. During severe thunderstorms, I hid in the bathtub. Fear engulfed me. I thought I had left behind what happened in my childhood only to have Joplin churn those memories up. It rendered me helpless because of the constant re-experiencing of emotional upheaval from the traumatic childhood events. I naturally began circumventing situations that triggered traumatic memories.

I later discovered it wasn't only the tornado that intensified the PTSD attacks. It was the life stressors that came with living in Springfield. I went to graduate school, dealt with a divorce, managed a high-pressure job, and then the stress of recovering from an E-5 tornado increased the emotional overload. Environmental hazards and exposure to contaminated air and debris piled onto the other concerns in my life. Days consisted of crying upon waking, crying on the way to meetings, crying on the way from meetings, and waking throughout the night in terrible sweats and drenched clothing, only to cry again. This went on for months.

I knew I was going through a lot, but I couldn't see how it fit together in the puzzle that was my life. I sought counseling only to have the counselor, at our first session, tell me her problems. I decided I didn't need to pay her to hear her problems, so I did not return to her office.

I didn't know what was happening, but I knew these symptoms weren't ordinary or common. The tornado set me back spiritually because I was unsure of my relationship with God. Once again I couldn't understand why God allowed this to happen. Hadn't I been through enough? I wasn't sure I could bear the pain of the educators because of the pain I was already carrying. In my quest for help, I thought about what the Joplin Superintendent did following the devastating tornado when he needed help in the crisis. He turned to God and Google. I turned to God because I used to talk and pray to Him as a little girl. But when I needed God most, I realized I had no relationship with Him. Although I had been in church most of my life, I didn't know Him. I began to learn about Him, but I was hurt by the church and unable to read the Bible to find guidance or comfort. I reflected on my earlier memories of God when I dreamed of being a teacher, and He answered me. He made it possible for me to be a successful teacher for fifteen years. Although I didn't know if God loved me, I knew I loved Him. I would find out later I could only love Him because He first loved me.

Because of my spiritual wounds, I could not pray aloud, so I wrote letters to God. I told Him what I could remember of my childhood and asked for His help to overcome what happened. I told God the memories of childhood abuse surfaced, and I didn't know what I did to cause them to appear. I didn't know anything about PTSD. I told God I thought my childhood was over and I asked Him why I was reliving the abuse, the beatings, the torture by my parents, the shame, and the insecurities. I searched Google for *bouts of crying and extreme sadness,* and *PTSD.* I read about sexual abuse and its impact on a child. I learned the after-effects of sexual abuse caused the bouts of crying and sadness. I didn't yet know that the physical and emotional abuse contributed to it as well.

I believe God led me to search engines and browsers, as if He guided me to the exact articles I needed. I had terrible anxiety attacks, so I found an article that explained anxiety and compared it to the waves of an ocean. The writer said I shouldn't panic during the highest tide of the wave because it would only last a few seconds. That helped tremendously because the attacks came from nowhere, and I didn't know what to expect or when to expect them. I learned how to ride the waves of anxiety. At times, they became so strong that the seconds felt like hours as I waited for the waves to pass over me.

I believed God could speak. I wasn't sure He would speak to me and I didn't know anyone who said He spoke to them. Given the fact I was spiritually scarred, I felt I might not be the one He would speak to if He were going to speak. I wrote in my journal daily. I wrote letters to God and recorded daily conversations with educators and conflicts with superintendents. I wrote about my internal conflicts, environmental and cultural challenges, as well as the sleepless nights and nightmares I endured. If something aroused an emotion in me, I gave it space in my journal.

I read that exercise was helpful when overcoming negativity and stress and that exercise benefits the mind as well as the body, so I began a rigorous exercise program. I ran every morning, and I worked with a trainer at a gym three evenings a week. He focused on strength training movements. It helped keep my mind off my problems as I focused on taking care of my body. As I became more fit, my confidence increased and some of the anxiety lessened.

Many mornings I found it difficult to run because I wanted to sit in the house and cry. There was no one to make me get out of bed, walk, cook, eat, or go to work. I knew I had a choice to do those things—*or not*. With those *or nots* came consequences. I had to choose to help, push, and encourage myself. Every day I reminded myself that I recovered from the breakdown in 2000, and I will recover from this one. I repeated aloud, **You are going to come out of this storm. You are an overcomer. You survived a horrific childhood. You will overcome this.** I had done a lot of motivational speaking throughout my career and recalled several things I told others to do. It was time to take my own advice. I recalled some of the speeches I wrote for my son Michael and how they inspired others, with phrases such as, *I will make a difference, I will not give up,* and *listen to the still, small voice inside.*

I lacked family support while going through the divorce because my family members were struggling with their own issues. I was close to my sister, Briana, but she was in an abusive relationship and couldn't be emotionally present for me. I had a few nieces who were close to my age. One was in treatment for breast cancer, and I felt I couldn't burden her since she was fighting for her life. She changed how our family saw cancer because she was strong, beautiful, courageous, and faith-filled. All I can say is she never had a doubt God would bring her through, and He did. She has been cancer-free ever since. At the time, however, I felt my situation might be too much for her to take on.

I was crawling spiritually, but at least I was moving. I felt a little stronger because I went from writing letters to whispering small prayers. I still couldn't pray out loud, but I could say a few words to God. When I finally prayed my first prayer aloud, it sounded like this:

God, You know what I've been through. You see me and know me. I am messed up. I don't know everything that happened in my childhood, but I know it affected me and is still affecting my mind, my emotions, and my life. If You had anything to do with those people who abused and misused me, I don't want anything to do with You, but if You are the One True God I read about when I was young who helps Your people, I ask You to help me. I heard You can do anything. I read You can do anything. Will You heal me? I am a prime candidate. Will You heal me emotionally, mentally, physically, and spiritually? I will tell everyone what You did for me, and I will not be ashamed.

Interestingly, this was the beginning of my prayers to God. I was afraid of being deceived again, but I was desperate and needed help. I felt like I made it clear to any evil forces that I wanted no part of the deception. I proceeded with caution. My need for help was greater than my fear of receiving the help. I didn't think help could be worse than PTSD. I shall always remember that when I needed help, God helped me.

Chapter 53

JOURNAL BENEFITS

I began writing at the age of thirteen, shortly after finding my mother near death. I didn't call it journaling. *My writing* was what I called the poems, essays, and speeches I wrote during my adolescence and marriage years, as well as the letters to God I wrote while in Springfield. I had no counselor during the divorce process, so writing became my preferred way to process my thoughts. Later I read about the benefits of journaling and realized journaling is what I'd been doing. I bought stacks of blank journals and set aside time to write. Each morning and evening I wrote details of my daily experiences. Journaling became a time to think about how things or people made me feel, process my emotions, and put those events into perspective. It helped me tackle fears, brought suppressed memories to the surface, and increased self-awareness. Journaling helped relieve stress and introduced me to positive self-talk. In short, journaling gave me a voice. Much later, I found research that supported my experience: expressing myself relieved pain and my critical thinking skills improved as stress was identified and processed. Journaling was therapeutic.

It is good to know that no matter where we are spiritually or emotionally, God hears us. As part of my healing process, I first questioned if He had anything to do with the abuse, probably because the people who abused me said they knew Him. Second, I told Him what the abusers did to me. Third, I told Him who I thought He was and what I heard he could do. Finally, I promised God that if He healed me, I would share it.

I did not come to God because I had such great faith. I came to Him because I had great pain that I hoped He could heal. It was my mustard seed faith.

I am thankful He didn't require much. God let me know I was not *like* the woman with the issue of blood in Mark 5 who needed healing so much, she risked everything to touch the hem of Jesus' garment. I *was* the woman with the issue of blood. The people who came to Jesus came because they were in desperate need of help and heard He would help them. His only requirement was for them to (1) have faith, and (2) tell others what He did for them. I shared my prayer in this book because I want people to know it's okay to ask God for help. He wants to help His children.

I often get asked how long I've been healing. I wish I could say I was healed instantly, but that's not how it happened. If I were to pinpoint the beginning of my healing journey, I believe it began at the 2008 internship training program in Washington, DC, when I revealed Uncle Harold's sexual abuse publicly for the first time. The emotional breakdowns in 1999-2000 were certainly warnings or pleas for attention from my mind and body. I took off work for a semester, but I didn't *do* anything to improve my situation apart from getting medication. In both situations, I felt something unusual happening in my mind and emotions that I couldn't explain. In the NEA Internship Program, when I answered the question, *Who was the most influential person in your life and how did they change your life?* I tried to create a false narrative, but I couldn't. I could think of one or two teachers who influenced my life, but their influence wasn't imprinted in my hippocampus like the negative experiences of Harold and the others who abused me. The abuse was stuck there because, during the traumatic event, adrenaline rushed through my body and the memory was embedded into my amygdala. My amygdala recorded the event as something extremely emotional based on my response. Because the event was embedded in my amygdala, I continued to live as if trauma recurred daily.

The next significant phase in my healing journey was when I left my sheltered home and family in Arkansas—Drake and Michael—and moved to Springfield, Missouri. I was under the perpetual pressure of my job in a new environment with cultural, social, and spiritual stress while recovering from traumatic memories. However, the most challenging issue was the spiritual stress. The perceived lost relationship with God caused extreme stress because I treasured my former relationship with God. I use the term *perceived lost relationship* because it was how I perceived God to be and not how the Bible speaks of God's character. I know now my feelings and perceptions were based on the negative ideas, confusion, and religiosity I was taught in Harold's church and the one I attended in Little Rock.

That church *training* is why I thought God would love me only if I did everything right. I couldn't do everything right, so I questioned His love for me. After the breakdowns in 2000, I couldn't pray, read the Bible, or do many of the things I once did. I felt disconnected from God and thought He was mad at me. As bad as it was, the sexual abuse didn't affect me like the disconnection I felt from God. I felt God had betrayed me, He couldn't be trusted, and He didn't love me. I did not understand how God could allow something so detestable to happen to me.

As I began reading the Bible, I understood more of what He requires to walk closely with Him. He requires me to love mercy and justice and walk humbly before Him and my fellow man (Micah 6:8). As I obeyed that instruction, I felt closer to Him each day, so naturally I was drawn to conversations with Him. The conversations with Him led me to read His Word, and reading His Word renewed my mind, and renewing my mind transformed my life. After He transformed my life, He used me to transform others' lives. My perceived relationship with God hindered my true relationship with Him. Anytime I experienced adversities, I regretted the loss of the perceived closeness to God. I worshiped God with my mouth, but my heart was far from Him.

Along with the milestone markers of separating from my family and taking on a high-stress job was the stress of living in Southwest Missouri, ineffective therapeutic counseling, a previously unidentified addiction and its unexpected withdrawal, PTSD, an estranged relationship with my son, and racial tensions in the community. Instead of the problems decreasing, they continued to multiply. Each day was simply a checklist to get through. I wasn't living. I merely existed. I didn't understand why God allowed me to exist since I couldn't see the point of my life. I certainly had no purpose. It's a miracle how God kept my mind from ever contemplating harming myself or others. I knew God was Sovereign and believed He approved everything in my life. Knowing this helped me to understand God's power and my frailty, but it also contributed to thinking God was punishing me. I felt helpless as I suffered relentless nightmares, unyielding panic attacks, and unforgiving traumatic memories.

Moving from Springfield to St. Louis was the next step in the healing process. I dealt with ongoing PTSD, but I also experienced Social Anxiety Disorder, depression, added tensions due to racial bias at the university where I continued to pursue my doctorate, and the extended estrangement from my son. Work demands intensified the emotional conflict between what I wanted to do and what I had to do.

Chapter 54

SPRINGFIELD TO ST. LOUIS

Near the end of 2011, I was afforded the opportunity to transfer to the St. Louis NEA office. I had prayed for months that God would allow me to leave Southwest Missouri. Springfield was a difficult episode, and I longed to get away, even though Southwest Missouri was also the place where I met God. It holds a special place in my heart. It was bittersweet when I left, but more sweet than bitter, because I needed a respite from the rejection and lack of diversity.

Moving to St. Louis was not as simple a decision as I thought it would be when the opportunity presented itself. Southwest Missouri was the place where I met God and began healing, so leaving was not easy. In fact, by the time the offer was extended, I felt perfectly fine and confident that God led me there and that I was in my purpose. I understood and saw the importance of asking God to direct my steps. If I asked Him to direct my steps when things got hard, I knew I could overcome obstacles by following His leadership.

I searched for the Proverbs 3:6 scripture of God's promise to *direct my ways if I acknowledged Him*. I had a lot of head knowledge about God but very little heart knowledge. In Springfield, I learned how to have a real relationship with Him and began to have heart knowledge. So I prayed.

The NEA Human Resources director frequently asked for my decision, but I put her off by saying that I wasn't sure yet but would let her know shortly. *Shortly* turned into weeks and then months. It was the first time I waited and trusted God to make a decision. Other times I asked, but either didn't wait or did not know how to wait. This time I waited and expected clarity.

Unlike the bad experience of believing God would keep me safe when I went to Texas under deception, this time I waited until He gave me neon lights and flashing signs. I refused to allow the bad experiences with church people to make me distrustful. If God were willing to give me a chance to try trusting Him, I would give Him a chance. After all, the first time I trusted the church people—not God—because I had no *relationship* with Him. I had *religion* with him. It was challenging to learn how to listen to a still, small voice, especially after listening to *a voice* in 1999 that contributed to my emotional breakdown. I did not want to trust any voice again. I needed concrete confirmation. I vacillated between praying out loud and writing prayers, but I wanted to talk to God in conversation.

One evening after work I read the Bible, which I liked to do in the morning before work and at night before going to bed. I usually read a chapter in the Old Testament and a chapter in the New Testament because I was thankful to be able to read the Bible again. For years, it hurt too much to read the Bible because I feared God as the uncaring judge who struck people down without warning. In Springfield, my faith grew stronger, and I began to trust Him to guide me.

That evening while reading the Old Testament, I ran across the scripture: "The reason the dream was given to Pharaoh in two forms is that the matter has been firmly decided by God, and God will do it soon" (Genesis 41:32). Instantly, I knew I would be moving soon because this was my next step. No earthquake or fire was falling from heaven, nor did an angel come to tell me. I knew that verse in Genesis was my answer and that I would soon move to St. Louis. I felt relieved from having to listen for a voice to speak. Earlier, I told God I couldn't trust His voice anymore, and I wanted confirmation when He spoke because I wanted to obey Him.

For the first time, I understood God speaks to us in many ways: through His Word, His Holy Spirit, and through other believers. God speaks to our souls through our dreams while we sleep and by visions when we're awake. We can know God communicates with us by the peace accompanying His revelations. Hallucinations or voices from mental disease are accompanied by fear and anxiety. This *knowing* through His Holy Spirit came through my spirit softly and gently while I studied the Bible. For the first time, I felt safe and confident in trusting God to lead and guide me. As I learned and listened without acting on a decision, I could recognize when something was from the Holy Spirit. Also, when I read the scriptures, I recognized certain words jumped out without thinking about them or meditating on them. Knowing is not a feeling. It is something I acknowledge in my spirit. It is where I have peace. The peace leaves me knowing the next step to take. It is not an impulsive decision. Although the Human Resources Director wanted an answer immediately, I didn't give her a decision right away because I knew I had to pray and ask God for direction. The morning after reading this scripture, I called my HR Director and accepted the job in St. Louis.

I thought I would be happy about the move because I would no longer be in an area with a culture as foreign as the one in Southwest Missouri. I could go to almost any restaurant or business and see people who looked like me. I thought that was what I needed. It turned out those were only some of the things I needed, but they didn't help as I anticipated. I thought relocation to an urban, metro area would alleviate most of my problems, but the root of my problems was not from external forces. How some people in Southwest Missouri treated me made me uncomfortable, however, changing my environment without changing what was happening internally only provided temporary and sporadic relief. I needed treatment for the cause of my discomfort, not just treatment for the symptoms.

The certainty of God's revelation that I should move brought peace, but the uncertainty of the process of moving raised a new set of concerns. I began to feel and think things I hadn't felt or thought before. I was sure I could do the job, but I had doubts after speaking with people from St. Louis who warned me that St. Louis had a different breed of educators than Joplin and its surrounding areas. In Joplin, educators appreciated my efforts and understood if I had to cancel a meeting. I was told that St. Louis educators weren't as understanding. I felt insecure and thought, *What if I can't or don't understand something?* St. Louis area school districts had legally collectively bargained contracts, and each school district had a unique contract. I was newly healing from PTSD. My memory and comprehension were not yet fully recovered. I handled more than forty school districts in the rural area of Southwest Missouri, but Joplin was the only district where the employees had a union agreement. I learned it and knew it exceptionally well, but I began to doubt I could learn everything I needed for the districts I'd be required to serve in St. Louis.

Insecurities escalated as I questioned my ability to work effectively in St. Louis. I gave my word, and I believed that God gave me His Word to move, so I moved. My insecurities intensified when I had to work with larger districts and serve more people. The same is true spiritually. Attacks, doubts, and insecurities gain strength when we attempt to do greater things. Big changes such as a promotion, marriage, or childbirth bring more stress. We want to teach God's ways, spread the gospel, and make a positive difference in the world, but the enemy comes for us when we work for God's Kingdom and walk in our God-given purpose. The doubts multiplied. Satan used nervousness, insecurities, lack of confidence, fear, and *what-ifs* to keep me from obeying God.

I turned the *what-if* around on the enemy. I told him, *What if I grow, am stretched, and accomplish more than I ever imagined? What if I learn things I never knew I could do?* and *What if I fail at trying to grow?* Duh. That's why it's called growth. Babies don't walk without ever falling. It is impossible. Falling and failing are part of growing and learning. When I permitted myself to fail—and to leave St. Louis if it didn't work for me—I had peace.

Now that I was free to move, I realized Drake and Michael were no longer available to help with the move. Not only that, they were no longer speaking to me. I figured they, too, were in emotional pain. Had I known the divorce would hurt them so much, I am certain I would have stayed married and continued to suffer silently until my death—which undoubtedly, would have come sooner rather than later. I mistakenly thought because our family was so close, they would understand that I went through something intolerable. It was unimaginable to have neither of them in my life after twenty-three years together. I was ill-prepared for the reality of divorce. I even thought that after we got through it—and I was better—that we would reunite. Boy, was I living in a false reality!

What I see now is that I needed a skilled counselor to help us navigate the uncharted waters because it was a life-or-death situation. I believe marriage is for life and that vows are meant to be kept. In my case, even though I had several reasons, I broke my vow. I forgave myself because I saw only hurt and pain through the lens of Childhood Trauma as long as Harold's name was on the marriage certificate. Viscerally, I needed the divorce because Uncle Harold, who sexually abused me, was the same man who performed the marriage ceremony. His sanctimonious deception was a parasite eating me from the inside. When I pointed this out to Drake, he didn't understand how damaging Harold's role was. After I recovered the memories of Harold's abuse, I could only feel that my marriage to Drake was cursed. I felt like Drake and I weren't married because a fake preacher performed the wedding, and I thought divorce was the only way to get the stain of Harold's deceit and treacherous hypocrisy off of us. My health and well-being declined because I tried to keep the secrets, protect the people involved, and be strong for Michael. The stress of keeping secrets meant that I tried to control not only my life but also Drake's and Michael's.

With the newfound freedom of my single life came many fears because I was deluged with countless ideas and opportunities to make decisions. On one hand, it was exciting to make my own decisions, but I often hesitated between the exhilaration of independence and grief for the loss of my marriage. For the first time, I felt *human thoughts and emotions* that were new and foreign. Most mornings, I wanted to go back to sleep immediately after waking. I was depressed because I lost my best friend, Drake. He helped me grow beyond who I was when we met. Even though I often wanted to hibernate in bed, some people at my job needed help. They became my reason to get up and keep going.

Like other trauma survivors, I didn't take time to grieve the loss of the relationships with Drake, Michael, or my in-laws, nor did I know I needed to grieve them. Moving away from family and friends, losing my five-year-old home, and realizing the enormity of the childhood I lost through the abuse— none of those things were acknowledged as losses that needed to be given time and attention. I wept many nights, but I didn't grieve. I believe grief is good and is meant by God to provide an emotional catharsis. We should feel better after recognizing a loss and its value to us. Instead, each day, I felt increasingly sadder.

In the intervening years since the divorce, I've had many insights into how difficult it was for Drake to be my husband. He never said how challenging it was to be married to an adult with a child's mind when it came to decision-making, though he never left or threatened to leave, not even once. He had tremendous patience, and regardless of what happened in the end, I believe he did his best to help me. It was unfortunate that he was unable to insist that I address my mental health, but I would not wish the struggles he went through with me on anyone else. Few are prepared to handle loved ones with mental challenges because society doesn't prepare people to deal with those with unresolved traumas and mental disorders.

I know Drake wasn't prepared for his wife and the mother of his child to have a mental disorder. Many times he treated me like a child and explained why I should pay the gas or electric bill instead of buying a new dress, why I couldn't spend money before I got it, and why we shouldn't paddle our toddler. There were times he taught Michael about life, and I recall thinking *I must remember that* because I didn't know it. I still remember when Drake told Michael the biggest areas in life to control are what the mouth speaks, what the ears are allowed to hear, and what the heart chooses to feel. He advised Michael to carefully select friends because they can change life for better or worse. Drake said if friends do good things, they can enrich life, but if friends get into mischief, they can adversely change life. Most adults take this for granted because this type of knowledge and basic life skills come from the instructions of loving parents. My childhood was too occupied by surviving abuse to pick up any valuable parental advice. I did not know these fundamental principles—and while I knew I didn't understand what others seemed to—I didn't understand why.

During the final three months before moving to St. Louis, I managed to pack only one box. Not only did I pack one box in three months, but I made no other movements to facilitate the move across the state. I didn't even reserve a moving truck. A few days before I was to move out of the Springfield apartment, Jesse, Catherine, Linda, and Vicki came to help me. I forgot I had even asked them to come. I quickly got on the phone and called around to rent a self-hauling truck. I didn't know what size to get, so I reserved a small truck to move an apartment filled with furniture. I later discovered that spatial intelligence—the ability to understand space and how items take up space—is often a trauma casualty. Estimating the size of my goods, difficulty calculating how much time it takes to go from one place to another, and figuring out how to make things fit into a cabinet, suitcase, or trunk are challenges that had an impact on how I managed time and planned projects.

Thank goodness, Jesse immediately realized I needed a larger truck and went and got one. In retrospect, my brain shut down because it couldn't process the stress of moving. The peace I felt when I decided to move deserted me as fears flooded my mind. I didn't know what to do. I hoped my friends didn't notice my emotional numbness, but I'm sure they knew something was off. They each took a room, packed the boxes, dismantled the furniture, and loaded everything onto the big truck. That day I was in a daze, physically drained and mentally in shock. I went through the motions but was not engaged in the process. My friends loved me, and I knew they loved me. Our friendship survived the upheaval of moving without preparation.

My friends spent the day packing and loading the truck from 9:00 a.m. to 4:30 p.m. After packing, I told them I couldn't drive because I was dizzy. That was only partially true. I couldn't drive because my mind was unstable, and I had panic attacks. The move was a reality check. Even though I had been divorced for a full two years, it hit me like a ton of bricks that my son and husband were not going with me. I was on my own. I faced the world as a single woman.

Jesse and Catherine agreed to drive to St. Louis, and I agreed to pay them for helping me move. He drove the rental truck and towed my car on a trailer. I rode in the car with Catherine. I was thankful God gave me good friends. We arrived in St. Louis around 8:00 p.m. and unloaded the truck immediately. I assumed they would spend the night, but as soon as they unpacked and assembled my bed, they hugged me and left. I was exhausted and emotionally and mentally frozen, but I knew I had work to do. I sat in the middle of the beautiful, new apartment and cried like a baby. I felt like the kid in the

Christmas movie when he realized his parents accidentally left him home alone to go on a vacation trip. I couldn't call anyone and ask them to get me. I faced the fact that I was truly alone—until I was aware that I wasn't alone.

Moving to St. Louis was what I believed God led me to do, so I knew He was with me. After a few minutes of sitting and staring at the walls, I got up and tried to walk around the condo, be grateful, and pull my emotions together, but I couldn't. Each time I stood up, I fell to my knees and wailed. This had to have been how King David felt when he wrote, "Oh, that I had the wings of a dove! I would fly away and be at rest" (Psalm 55:6). I would have flown away to rest like David. The more I suffered and struggled, the more I remembered how those in the Bible struggled and suffered, too. Heroic Biblical characters came to life, but I realized they weren't heroes. They were ordinary people, like me, who trusted God through the tough times. *They came through and so will I* is what I believed, because as long as we see Biblical people on pedestals, we will think they had superpowers or were somehow different from us. They weren't. God used people like Joseph, Naomi, and Job who suffered great losses. God used David, who wanted to conceal his sin and made a grave error when he had his soldier, Uriah, killed after David committed adultery with Uriah's wife. God also used Jacob after he deceived his brother Esau and stole his inheritance. These humans made fundamentally human mistakes, but God used them to show us He uses broken, weak, and imperfect people to accomplish His purpose. Knowing this made a difference in my belief that God could use me, and I would overcome this difficulty.

I spent the first night in my beautiful condo in the same fog where I spent three months without packing to move. I woke early and looked around to see if the move was a dream. Although few looked like me in my new complex, I knew I could see those who looked like me nearby or go to any number of St. Louis neighborhoods and experience my culture in restaurants and churches. The search for people who looked like me would be a short one. My housing search was limited to fairly new places because I knew they wouldn't have mold or mildew, which are issues in flood-prone St. Louis. I wanted my space to be gorgeous, and I was willing to pay the cost because I had a well-paid job. I thought I needed a place to help erase my losses and past, so I was willing to pay whatever it took to get it. What I didn't know was that *no such place existed.* I kept misjudging the root of my problems and sought *external* things that I thought would bring *internal* peace. The superficial decisions I made to escape inner turmoil only exacerbated the pain and imprisoned me in a jail of self-deception.

I walked around the new condo complex discovering its two large swimming pools, a cinema room, and a huge party room available by reservation for events of up to 200 people. I soon learned the complex lit up like Las Vegas nearly every night. People hung out at the pools and frequently had impromptu get-togethers by grilling meat and setting out bowls of chips and dip. It was a mecca for the lonely and those looking to meet others. I smiled until I realized I had no family or friends from my old life to celebrate my new life, which made me sad. Part of the difficulty of moving is that we want people from our former life to go with us into the new life and share the blessings. It had been four years since I left Arkansas, and I was still too ashamed to talk with those from my old life. I hoped the new surroundings and job promotion would bring relief to my anxiety and peace to my mind, but I learned money can't buy happiness. It can purchase a beautiful home, buy the best mattress, or fund beautiful vacations, but it can't change the ugly images embedded in the memory.

Each day following the move, I realized how difficult it was to think critically, analyze issues, and solve problems. The inability to reason explains why I usually asked Drake for help when making decisions. He alone made most of the decisions because he had a wife who could not discuss the pros and cons of difficult situations. I credit him for what he did during those twenty-three years of marriage. I have nothing but gratitude for him. Of course, he wasn't a perfect person or a perfect husband, but with the damage to my brain, he was what I needed. He had no idea of how damaged I was and how what I sought when I looked for a husband was a father—someone I had never had. My heart had a father-sized hole in it, looking for love. My first father, Buck, was an abusive monster. A quick string of foster fathers and brothers-in-law followed who sexually assaulted me. Then, my great-uncle Harold made me his surrogate wife. How could Drake know and understand this insanity when I was unaware?

In St. Louis I worked long hours each day without complaining because the long workdays and nights occupied my mind and emotions. I now know it was avoidance, a coping mechanism after trauma. My job left little time to feel or think about personal things. I hadn't yet learned that past traumas can stay stuck in the amygdala and prefrontal cortex until they are acknowledged, processed, and released. Dr. Felitti, a world renowned researcher and expert on Childhood Trauma, shed light on the subject through his world-changing

Adverse Childhood Experiences Study. At this time, however, the topic wasn't widely discussed and certainly wasn't part of the public discourse. It was at least another five years before the words Childhood Trauma drew worldwide attention and another few years before they drew my attention.

Chapter 55
THE GOD WHO SPEAKS

President Obama gave the commencement keynote speech at the 2012 Joplin High School graduation, exactly one year after the deadly tornado. During the mind-numbing emergency days following the 2011 tornado, the President promised Joplin students he would speak at their commencement if they finished the school year. He encouraged them and told them it would be challenging, but if they stayed in school, held on in the tough times, and graduated, he would return to speak at their commencement ceremony.

The Superintendent of Schools, Dr. C.J. Huff, and the NEA president invited me to the graduation. Their invitation was special because of the working relationship the Superintendent and I had established. We could set aside our differences through Christ and do what was best for the educators. Dr. Huff and I agreed our faith made the difference. When it was officially announced that President Obama would speak, I wanted to return for that momentous day. The Superintendent said people worldwide called requesting tickets, but I did not request a ticket for several reasons. One, I would have to cross several bridges, and although the panic attacks had diminished, I still had them. Two, I knew people worldwide wanted to go, and I no longer worked in that region. Lastly, I knew how stressed and pressured the Superintendent was, so I didn't want to add to his burden by asking for a ticket. I was pleasantly surprised when he called and said the White House would contact me about the security requirements.

It happened exactly as the Superintendent said. The White House sent emails with instructions to obtain a security clearance. I was excited to attend the event with President Obama because he meant so much to me and many other Americans. Obama's presidency was historic in many ways, and Joplin was a rural area where I would not have expected a president to visit. Seeing a president after the endless turmoil in my life was an honor.

The week before the commencement, I excitedly anticipated the event, but shortly before the graduation, I became quite ill and decided I couldn't attend. I emailed the White House, and they said I could not give my ticket to anyone because that person did not have security clearance. I desperately wanted to go, but I felt sicker the closer it got to the graduation. I prayed, but still felt too sick to drive. Upon reflection, I see this was a prayer of desperation, not faith, as I prayed in the past. The morning of graduation, I received an email saying I was invited to the VIP reception, but I still didn't feel well enough to attend.

I lay in bed, full of regret and feeling sick. Joplin was at least a four-and-a-half-hour drive from my apartment in a community west of St. Louis. At 5:00 a.m. I tried to get up, but my head fell back on the pillow. My eyes were swollen, my ears ached, and I was dizzy. I was in no shape to drive to Joplin. I kept thinking, *This is a once-in-a-lifetime opportunity. I can do this!* only to fall back on the bed. I wanted to get up, but everything around me continued to spin. I fell back to sleep. There was no use in trying. I was beyond sad that I would miss seeing President Obama in person.

At 9:00 a.m. I woke up and heard a voice say, *Get up and go to Joplin.*

I was familiar with voices, but this was different. This was a still, small voice that I would have missed if I wasn't very quiet. During my healing journey, I avoided adhering to voices because hearing voices contributed to my earlier mental breakdown. This was the same voice that told me what to write for Michael's speeches, to take Michael to speak to a conference, and ultimately, to become a teacher. The voice was clear and recognizable.

I responded with my sick voice, "I don't feel like it."

Then the voice said again, *Get up and go to Joplin.*

I lay back down. As I was dozing off again, I heard the voice louder, *Go to Joplin! I know you're sick, so if I told you to go, I must plan on healing you. Now go!*

That time, the voice got my full attention. I did not answer back.

I staggered nervously to my feet, tottered to the closet, and grabbed the first dress I saw. It was a black and white polka dot, ankle-length, fitted dress. I grabbed red high-heeled shoes and a red purse and sprinted out the door. No shower, no brushed teeth, no washed face. No obvious effort to groom or try to look professional. I was afraid to look back lest I transform into a pillar of salt like Lot's wife (Genesis 19).

It was almost 10:00 a.m. when I left the parking lot. My hands shook, but I knew I didn't want to hear that voice again. I headed west on Interstate 44 to Joplin. I no longer felt sick. I drove to Springfield without an issue: not one dizzy spell or moment of nausea.

I stopped at a Springfield hotel to freshen up because I knew the hotel rooms in Joplin were already booked. I drove to Joplin for the VIP reception, where I recognized people I had worked with during the previous three years. The caterer provided beautiful treats and snacks. I mingled and shook hands with the dignitaries. I felt I didn't belong there because no one in the room looked like me. I glanced around at the people lining up to speak to the various local, state, and national dignitaries. I stood back and watched. I had no desire to be noticed or seen. I needed that kind of attention before I began my healing journey, but I didn't need it now.

Social Anxiety Disorder (SAD) made me feel like people scrutinized and judged me. I feared those around me could recognize my fear. I felt anxious, and I mentally rehearsed what I would say to people, so I stood in a back corner and hoped no one would approach me. I didn't like answering questions in unfamiliar situations or talking with people I didn't know. I know it is typical for introverts to feel uncomfortable in social settings, but this anxiety was not normal because of the extreme fear, insecurities, and panic attacks. The PTSD exacerbated my situation, and the lack of support and diversity was dreadful because I feared rejection. Ironically, before the manifestation of PTSD and SAD, I was comfortable in most social settings.

I soon exited the VIP reception room and headed to the arena. Because I worked with the district, I was given a preferred seat near the stage with the local NEA president. Our seats were a few yards from President Obama, but I could hardly enjoy the momentous occasion because of plaguing thoughts of the return drive to St. Louis. I looked around the packed stadium and thought to myself, *I am here. I am here. Don't worry about the next moment. Enjoy this one.* I was thankful for the opportunity but was in such a terrible place emotionally I couldn't fully enjoy the moment and absorb its meaning to me and the people of Joplin. A limited number of people were invited to Joplin's graduation, and I was one of the 4,600 people packed into the gym. I smiled the biggest smile and told myself if I never had another opportunity to see a president speak in person, I will have seen this special one. Obama's speech was inspirational and interrupted many times by applause. I knew God granted me a favor by having the Superintendent invite me, healing my morning illness, and protecting me from anxieties on the highway and across the bridges from St. Louis to Joplin. I was thankful.

I learned an important lesson from the experience of opposition in the form of that morning's illness. Whenever we struggle or face mountain after mountain of adversity, we should fight harder and fly higher—like the eagle does in a storm—because there is something greater above the clouds. In this case, I saw the first African-American president and experienced his love for

Joplin's resilient parents and children. It was an experience I couldn't fully comprehend until after it was over. Giving up before we get to the top of the mountain or climb out of the valley deprives us of the strength that comes from doing both of those challenges.

After the graduation ceremony, my Joplin NEA friends and I headed to the parking lot, but as we exited the arena doors, my aching feet reminded me I'd been wearing high heels for most of the day. I spotted a golf cart parked near the exit door and figured it was for those who needed physical assistance. Judging from my foot pain, I certainly qualified. I noticed a Missouri National Guard soldier standing near the cart and asked if he could drive my friends and me to our cars since we were parked almost a mile away. The soldier politely explained the carts were for those who needed them—for those who can't walk, he said. I thought about the high heels, my aching feet, and back pain. I decided I was unable to walk and needed the golf cart.

I tilted my head, smiled and asked again sweetly, "Are you sure you can't take me to my car?"

A tall, athletically built, light brown man with Major Washington on his uniform walked over and said, "Yes, ma'am, what can I do for you?"

I didn't know where he came from, but I was instantly offended because I thought *they saw a Black woman who had questions* and *because they didn't know how to deal with her, they got another Black person to help her.* I was insulted that they needed to go get him, so I didn't want to talk to him because I knew I might show anger. Everything the racist people in Southwest Missouri said and did while I lived there rose in me; I could feel their mistreatment, discrimination, bias, and racism.

Bewilderingly, this thought came: *Be kind to strangers because you entertain angels unaware.*

So I answered his questions.

"Are you handicapped?"

"No."

"Part of the President's entourage?"

"No."

"And you don't look elderly," he said.

"I know, but my feet ache."

I sighed and tried to help him feel my fatigue and aching feet.

"I understand, but I can't bend the rules, even for you."

I gave a half-smile like I understood him not bending the rules for me, but I wanted him not only to bend them but to break them and throw them away. I knew this commander could bend the rules for me, so I looked at him. My friends stood near me but were not listening to our conversation as they chatted with others leaving the arena.

The answer to my request was, no, they couldn't take me to my car. I thought the commander would turn and go back to his post after he informed me he could not break the rules for me, but he didn't. We talked briefly about the opportunity to see and hear President Obama, but I barely engaged in the conversation. I didn't even look too closely at him or see his attractiveness.

I had been married for twenty-three years, single for nearly three years, and newly learning to date again, but I wasn't doing it well. I couldn't pick the right man for me. I repeatedly had bad dates. I went out with men who were desperate—desperate to go to the movies, desperate to have sex, desperate for any sort of human contact, it seemed. I even talked on the phone to a man for three months before I found out he was married! By that point, I didn't want to look at a man, nor did I want him to look at me. After the previous married man, I slipped back into catastrophizing, thinking men are liars and that I should avoid them altogether. I knew I needed more healing and spiritual discernment before I resumed dating. I wrote in my journal the night before the commencement, *I am in such a wonderful place, and I don't need a man in my life, and it feels so good!*

Major Washington asked if I was married. I told him I had recently gone through a divorce, and he said he wasn't married, either. I was so distrustful of men that I doubted his answer and felt I needed to remind myself that I was not interested in meeting anyone. Our small talk continued. I told him I lived in St. Louis, thinking that information might deter his interest in me. I tried to be polite in case he was an angel, but I also thought *this angel should know when someone doesn't want to be bothered and fly away.*

"So what do you do?" he asked.

"I work for NEA. What do you do?"

He said he had been in the military for twenty-six years. I still wasn't interested. I DID NOT want to hold this conversation and grew annoyed. Unfairly, I made him pay for the men who treated me poorly, even though I didn't realize that's what I did. The only thing I liked about him was the uniform. I admire and respect those who serve our country, and he served for a long time. My respect and honor for his service, not my interest, is what engaged me in our conversation.

"I am also in grad school," I said. I thought that might derail his interest in me, not that there was much reason to think he was interested, but I wanted to squelch it if he was. I didn't want him to complicate my life. I wanted to push him away with indifference. I was trying to cross bridges without panic attacks, and I didn't need one more thing on my scale because it was already tilted.

I thought, *Lord, please don't let this man ask for my phone number. Also, please forgive me in advance for what I am about to say to him—if he is an angel.*

I knew I was about to be rude because I didn't want anything to do with him and I interpreted his gaze as if he thought *She was single and delivered to my doorstep.* Talk about projecting my expectations!

Major Washington said he was from St. Louis, but while securing the area for the President he stayed in Joplin and slept on a cot. I was briefly in the Army ROTC in my early college years, so I knew what sleeping in the woods and on cots was like. It was not restful. I figured he had to be tired, and I sympathized with him.

He was respectful, but I remained suspicious and kept guard rails and security bars around my heart because of bad experiences with dishonest men. I was not interested in another lying, married man. Thank God, the other lying, married man was solely a phone relationship.

"So, what is your…?" As he began his question, I was ready to give him a piece of my mind, but I heard the still, small voice say, *"You should be nice to strangers,"* so I closed my lips. I thought quickly, "Lord, please help me be kind to this man."

"So, what is your field of study?" he finished the question. What a fool I would have been to snap at him for asking for my phone number when he didn't! *Only a fool answers a man before hearing* (Proverbs 18:13). I certainly didn't want to be a fool.

I loosened up a little after my near-fool experience and talked about my studies. Major Washington spoke of his military leadership training courses and his challenges with some of them. I told him I might need tutoring in statistics because it was so challenging. He smiled and told me statistics wasn't his favorite class, either.

My friends indicated they were leaving, so I told Major Washington that meeting him was nice.

"How do I…?" he started.

I knew not to assume, so I let him finish.

"How do I get in touch with you if I need help with statistics?" He smiled because he knew that wasn't my favorite subject.

Then I smiled and said, "You can look me up at nea.org. Go to mnea.org and click on my name. Keep it short if you send a message because it's my work email." I walked away and hoped he would forget.

He didn't forget. By the end of the week, he emailed, "Coffee?" I knew immediately this man paid attention to details.

I learned his name was Mitchell. We went for coffee and had such a good time getting to know one another that it led to dinner. I didn't know it then, but I began dating the man I would eventually marry—although it would take almost five years for that to happen.

Chapter 56

NO ESCAPE

My St. Louis job was extremely tough. Once again, I was tasked to work with a non-diverse district with few teachers who looked like me. My mentor was kind and taught me so much, but he had the advantage of doing the job for nearly thirty years and was retiring with a great record of success. I took over his territory and faced scrutiny because I wasn't him and did things differently. Advocating was not difficult for me. Advocacy is part of my core nature. Helping teachers resolve disputes with administrators was gratifying. Helping groups negotiate contracts offered the opportunity to improve teaching and learning conditions. The difficult part was representing those who did not want me to represent them because of my skin color or because my values didn't accommodate their wrongdoing.

I wanted the teachers in metro St. Louis to trust me as the teachers did in Southwest Missouri, but the St. Louis population was not the same kind of people. Because I wasn't who they were used to, they second-guessed most things I did, which caused more insecurity. They protested when I encouraged someone who harmed a student to leave the profession. My caseload was heavy, especially on top of dealing with PTSD and anxiety. However, working 12-14 hours a day Monday-Sunday, is not good for anyone, even if not dealing with personal struggles and PTSD. It didn't help that the PTSD was repeatedly triggered because the job requirements were in direct conflict with my values and beliefs.

The violations I was dealing with were serious and often involved financial misdealings, ethics violations, professional misconduct, and sexual crimes— especially child sexual abuse. Representing employees accused of violating the state statutes, and sometimes the penal code, required a mind fully functioning on all cylinders. I needed to know human resource policies, criminal law, and the education statutes to work out resolutions in children's best interests. What I didn't see initially eventually hit me full force: I was often required to represent and defend people who abused children. I was forced to *Defend, not Judge*. I didn't anticipate how triggering it was to hear a teacher admit they sexually violated a student. After defending the person, I felt horrible. My childhood abuse fully intersected with my professional duties. It would take a while, but I eventually learned that I could not work in conflict with my values. The words of Dr. Martin Luther King ultimately rang loud and clear: "If a man hasn't found something worth dying for, he's not fit to live." I would face a reckoning that threatened my life. Unbeknownst to me, as I waited to find that thing I was willing to die for, it found me.

My job could be considered a dream job, except for too many work hours. The job came with special perks, privileges, and prestige, and introduced new and interesting people daily. I had the opportunity to hone my speaking skills when I was selected to be one of NEA's Trainer of Trainers. I made nearly $100,000 in salary. On top of that, I had an MNEA credit card with a $3000-a-month allowance. My palate may have been limited because of the lack of food in my childhood, but I more than made up for it as I regularly took clients and distinguished guests out to eat. My manager trusted me, and I never took advantage of that trust. I had great support from the entire St. Louis NEA office staff, secretaries, and field representatives. I should have had the time of my life. Instead, it was the life of my time, meaning, God set that time aside for me to go through emotional pain and continue healing.

I thought I had finished healing when I left Southwest Missouri. I didn't understand that I had only gone through preliminary healing and that healing was a journey that would continue for the rest of my life. I didn't yet understand that a child couldn't experience extreme adversities and be free overnight or after a year, or even, in my case, several years. The childhood and adolescent abuse occurred over the course of eighteen years, yet I expected the healing to be complete in a few months or a few years. I didn't understand that it would take time, commitment, healing, and Jesus to undo the damage done to my mind, body, heart, soul, and spirit.

I continued journaling and praying, but the intensity of my workload increased my anxiety. I was finally able to recognize triggers and residuals—things that activated negative memories or launched PTSD attacks—and work through them, but there wasn't much time to breathe. I was headed straight for another massive breakdown. My mind lost some of its effective function. Researchers Hayes, Vanelzakker, and Shin report that hallmark symptoms of PTSD are difficulty with focus, planning, and problem-solving.[15] The PTSD impaired my ability to think, listen, and come up with strategies for those I represented. I began to feel anxious and nervous after confrontations with

[15]Hayes, Jasmeet P., Michael B. VanElzakker, and Lisa M. Shin. 2012. "Emotion and Cognition Interactions in PTSD: A Review of Neurocognitive and Neuroimaging Studies." *Frontiers in Integrative Neuroscience* 6, no. 89 (October) 1-14. Doi: 10.3389/fnint.2012.00089.

superintendents. On top of that, I couldn't keep up with the workload because my emotions were out of control and robbed me of the time I needed to think, create solutions, and document action steps.

Several times during meetings and conferences I sneaked away from my colleagues to cry in solitude. I reapplied my make-up and rejoined them to be the life of the party. I wanted to show my mentors how much I appreciated their support, so I hid my pain and became the person I thought everyone wanted. The more I hid my pain from others, however, the more my pain exposed itself to me. I was in constant emotional turmoil because my life became performative instead of authentic. I had no one I trusted to unburden myself and hear them say, *You've been through a lot. It's okay to cry.* It took several episodes for me to find a pattern and to understand what the loss of control signaled.

I refused to break down, although my mind and body sensed an approaching problem. I fought through the anxiety until I couldn't fight anymore. The unyielding schedule and overwhelming workload continued unabated for nearly two years. The St. Louis job was too much for me while I was in the early phases of healing from trauma. I cried when I was alone in the car, between appointments, and in the evenings when I got home from work. Sometimes I had to reapply makeup and wear sunglasses, even on cloudy days, to hide the bags under my eyes caused by crying and lack of sleep. I knew something had to change because I couldn't continue under that stress.

I loved advocating and fighting for teachers, but my job didn't leave time for me. It often conflicted with my beliefs and values and left me feeling as if I betrayed myself. I didn't know how to set healthy limits. Even while sleeping, my mind didn't rest. I dreamed about resolving conflicts between union members and school districts. I didn't take vacations because I knew the backlogged workload would be unmanageable. Besides, when I put work aside, I still had to deal with ongoing residuals and reminders of my horrific childhood, the aftermath of the divorce, and the loss of authenticity, my personality, values, and beliefs. Everything that made me unique was lost. I chose work hands down over examining my personal life and the healing I needed. I thought that if I stayed busy with work, eventually the emotional pain would go away. It never did, regardless of how busy I stayed or how successful I was in my job. I still had repetitive, nagging thoughts about my childhood abuse, past mistakes, the divorce, the loss of my relationship with my son, the pressure of the job, the distasteful aspects of human behavior, and the fear of what people would think if I left my dream job. Day and night, I fought for my mind and tried to determine my next steps.

One cold January day in 2014 as I sat in my office, something unexpected happened that forced me to make the decision I felt I could not make. I tried to speak, but couldn't. No words came. I could hear others talking in the next room but could not produce a sound. My secretary called me. She knew I was sitting in the office, so she came to the door when I didn't answer. She looked in, saw me, and ran to call 9-1-1. I could hear everyone speaking around me, but I could not reply. I couldn't say or write anything. I thought I might be having a stroke. The reports of recent NEA employees across the nation who had stress-related strokes flashed through my memory. Many of them were in their early 50s. I was in my late 40s, but I knew I was under a lot of stress.

I was rushed to a hospital and kept overnight. This was the first time I had stayed overnight in a hospital since giving birth to my son twenty-three years earlier. I felt the loneliness of not having family near me. Although my ex-husband and son were notified of my hospital stay, I didn't expect them to drive hours to be with me. I hoped Drake or Michael would call to ask how I was, but they didn't. I knew they were both fighting their own dragons and private battles during this time.

Pam and her boyfriend, Sam, whom I met in St. Louis, were at the hospital with me. She and I worked together on a project. Pam and Sam, who later became her husband, refused to leave the hospital. He slept in a chair next to my bed, and she slept on a sofa in the room. Love from friends who gave up their beds to be with me was a new experience. I was stunned that someone who barely knew me could love me. I tried to figure out why she would do such an unimaginable thing. Of course, I would do it for her, even though I didn't know her well, but I couldn't fathom anyone doing such a caring thing for me. From what I learned and heard about Pam, she had a loving heart.

I recorded Pam and Sam's decision to stay at the hospital as a *Jehovah Jireh* experience. God provided someone to be there like He provided the ram in the bush for Abraham when he needed one (Genesis 22:13-19). Several other people I barely knew were present. One of them was a lady named Judith. She lost her adult son a few years before I met her, and we connected immediately. Judith, Pam, and Sam offered to stay through the night so I wouldn't be alone at the hospital. This confirmed that we don't have to worry about tomorrow when we obey God, because He's already there and knows what we need. He places everything we need where we need it when we need it. All we have to do is show up each day. The hospital stay helped to grow my faith in God.

Many others called the ER when they heard I was rushed to the hospital. I thought I was a worker, an advocate, and an employee, but I learned I was so much more. I realized the power of love, which is real, and I had nothing to do to merit it. Love is something people have in their hearts, and I didn't have to understand it. It comes from God, the Father of Love, and flows from their heart to others. I was overwhelmed with their love and friendship. Judith and others called the hospital so often that the nurse remarked, "You have lots of family." She didn't know why they were calling; they knew I didn't have family in St. Louis. Now I realize the nurse was correct. I did have lots of family with me. The love expressed during a time when I felt I had no one helped me understand family is more than the blood you inherit from natural birth. It is also the Blood you inherit from Spiritual birth. I was surrounded with love.

Throughout the night, I slept on and off, fitfully at best. My mind raced with thoughts. I was skeptical of love from others. I continued to glance at Pam and Sam as they slept wondering how I could repay them for their kindness. Several times, I wished that they hadn't stayed with me because I felt indebted to them. Kindness, in my experience, usually had a price tag attached, and I didn't know how much I'd have to pay for what they gave me. I knew they made a sacrifice that I might not be able to reciprocate. I wondered when I would get the chance to show them I have the same heart and would do the same for them. Since healing, I have learned love is not transactional. When kindness is given with expectancy, it loses its authenticity. Real love is given, not planned, measured, or monetized. It sees a need and moves to satisfy it through compassion. People who give love remind me of Jesus. The Bible states that Jesus was moved with compassion for people and healed them on many occasions. I have learned we don't give love to get, we get to give love. The hospital experience taught me to enjoy generosity and kindness from those who know the true value of getting to give.

Although Mitchell and I began seeing each other after the Joplin commencement, we decided to keep our relationship strictly a friendship at that point. We were both recovering from difficult divorces that had drained us emotionally and financially, and Mitchell was also in the National Guard and was sometimes deployed. Despite our non-dating status, I unrealistically expected him to be at the hospital for me. It is common for Childhood Trauma survivors to place their feelings and expectations on others and be disappointed when others don't do what they expect. It is distorted thinking, implicit expectations, and attentional biases from cognitive and behavioral difficulties. Mitchell's absence hurt because I thought he understood the unspoken rules of friendship. Since learning about Childhood Trauma, I know it robbed me of the tools I needed to have healthy relationships and interactions with others. I could only see that Mitchell wasn't there for me and felt rejected.

It seemed with most decisions, I thought people intentionally did things *to* me. I couldn't see that most people did what was best for them—and didn't factor me into their decisions at all. I took things personally and decided that people were actively doing things to hurt me. I am sure I thought this way because Buck and Elsie, my primary caregivers, did so many hurtful things directly to us. Being in a relationship with me was difficult because I was persistently up and down and in and out of my feelings. One minute we were lifelong friends and the next I wasn't sure if I could ever trust again. I had a good deal of *all-or-nothing* cognitive distortion. My negative thinking patterns tried to ruin meaningful relationships and damage learning opportunities. I think it was a protective mechanism to avoid hurt feelings.

I learned from the hospital experience that feelings are not facts. CT survivors often get stuck trying to separate real feelings from real facts. My feelings of rejection were real, but it wasn't a fact that Mitchell rejected me— as I would later find out. I also learned that I developed unrealistic expectations of others and placed demands based on what *I would do for them*. Until I learned that others come with their own set of triggers and residuals that have nothing to do with me, I was frequently disappointed by people. As God healed my mind, He gave me revelations and understanding of my thoughts and unrealistic expectations of others. He showed me how my thinking was skewed, and that it wasn't that people didn't care enough for me when they didn't do the things I thought they should do. When I looked through the lens of healing, I saw and better understood others' actions. The more I healed, the more I understood others instead of believing others should try to understand me.

At the hospital, I ran on a treadmill the next day for heart, lung, and brain evaluations. After the tests, the doctor concluded I was under severe stress and recommended time off. Without the expensive tests and subsequent medical bills, I could have told him that. I wanted to call my ex-husband and ask him what to do. I thought about calling my son to tell him something happened to his mom that she couldn't explain. I thought it might help to talk to my siblings and tell them I needed some of the advice I had once given them to get me through it. I wanted to call my friends and tell them I was at my worst and find some solace and comfort in their words of sympathy. Nevertheless, I did not call anyone. If only I had someone to tell me what to do! This would be the second time since beginning my healing journey that I had to make a life-altering decision on my own. The first was when I decided to leave Springfield and move to St. Louis. Although I had made life-altering decisions from the time I ran away from foster homes, this was different because I had begun to heal and could *feel*. I didn't understand my new feelings, and they affected my decision-making process.

Drake no longer spoke to me. My son, Michael, was still processing the fallout from the divorce so I couldn't call him. My family members were busy slaying their giants, and most of my friends lived in other states and didn't understand the full extent of my situation. No one I trusted could help me. Mitchell couldn't help because he had only recently returned from a deployment and was processing the loss of several elderly family members, including his mother and father. I needed to decide whether or not to keep my highly-stressful job. I saw my situation as saving *me* or the job. Although Mitchell did try to convince me to keep my job, I felt he didn't understand that I had no choice because of my physical and mental health. I felt no one understood or could help me through the pain, so I woke up alone and went to sleep alone and prayed about what to do.

An email I received about a month earlier requested prayer for a lady named Marion who worked for NEA. I didn't know her, but she was doing the same work as I was. She had no time for herself. She was about my age and had a bright future ahead of her, but one day in the blink of an eye, everything changed. She had a stroke and was unable to speak and walk, and it was suggested that her workload had become too much. With that in mind, for the rest of the day at the hospital, I went back and forth with the decision *to quit or not to quit*. I wondered if Marion had exercised, taken personal time, or worked a schedule like mine. Email updates about Marion popped up in the weeks following her stroke. I didn't know her, or why I got the emails and updates on her situation, but whenever I got one, I took a moment to pray for her. I felt a connection to her. One email said she didn't get any warning that she was having a stroke and that she was fighting to regain strength in her body and mind. The thought *this could have been me* was haunting, but not enough to give up my job, my status, and what I defined as deserving of respect. I prayed for Marion, but I heard something deep inside say, *I need to let this job go before the same thing happens to me. It's too much for me with the personal stress I have.* I quickly dismissed the thought by determining I could handle everything. It was the first time I had made such a big salary, and I lived in an expensive, gorgeous condo. I could fly wherever I wanted and whenever I felt like it, with only one problem: I never had the time to do it.

I tried to ignore what I knew to be true, but the more I tried, the worse I felt. I hadn't told anyone that I was considering giving up my job because I knew they would try to convince me otherwise. They might not understand what I experienced and how dangerous the job was for me. However, my priorities were so messed up that I was willing to lose my mind before losing my job until the thought came that *I didn't have a choice in this matter. I must leave my job. I have PTSD.* I mentally composed a resignation as I prepared to leave the hospital, but I didn't believe I would actually do it. I knew once I resigned, the money would stop, and I would have no one to help me.

I was released from the hospital with the recommendation that I take off work for a while. I thought what the doctor asked was impossible and unreasonable. The sheer work of the job required seven days a week to stay on top of things. How could he suggest I take off work for a while? It didn't help that my attitude was: *I will work harder.* I felt I had to prove to the Missouri NEA that I could do the job. Failure was not an option. I did not want to disappoint anyone. How could I justify walking away from making almost $100K a year? I calculated the advantages of staying vs. leaving. The calculation revealed *If I leave, I will survive and heal, but if I stay, I may die.*

From childhood, I felt I had to prove that I was a hard worker, that I could achieve the same as others, that I was dependable, loyal, and had value. This came from the seeds of low self-esteem and unworthiness that were sown in childhood, took root, and manifested in a lack of self-value. My image said I was successful and nothing could keep me down. It said I was strong. But inwardly I felt unsuccessful and weak. I struggled to keep from failing. I had not yet made the connection between the healing I needed, the friction of my work and values, and the unendurable expectations I imposed on myself. My mind and body could not tolerate the disharmony and signaled through episodes of crying and PTSD flashbacks that I needed help, and I needed help immediately.

Chapter 57

THE LONG JOURNEY TO FREEDOM

I knew what I had to do. It took about a month, but I eventually turned in my resignation letter. I prayed, fasted, screamed, hollered, and moaned, but I already knew I had to let go of the job even though it validated me. That job said, *You have arrived! You are somebody. You are valuable. You are smart. You are not who your mother said you were.* I thought I needed that job SO badly. Everyone I knew, from the backwoods towns of Arkansas to the big city of Washington, D.C., had heard about me and my work. I played in the big leagues in the arena of education unions. Who could let that go? Leaving that job was equivalent to returning to Arkansas and letting everyone know that life beyond the small town was too much for me to handle. In my mind, resignation announced that I had failed. Failure was yet another big disappointment. Inexplicably, leaving the job made me feel like I would never bounce back from the divorce. Leaving the job meant that I had no mental capacity to solve my issues. Leaving the job meant that I had no value to give to the world.

Although research findings and theories consistently emphasize an association between Childhood Trauma—specifically physical and sexual abuse—and the development of suicidality, I did not have any thoughts of suicide. Interestingly enough, despite the great pain and turmoil we experienced, neither did any of my siblings. I credit it to faith in God. When asked where we got such faith, I say faith is what we had when we had nothing else—and we had nothing else. We knew we had to believe and trust God because we couldn't trust Elsie and Buck.

I knew prioritizing my health was the next step. I knew I could no longer work at all, not just for the NEA. I couldn't mentally perform work tasks anywhere. The near-constant crying was uncontainable. I had to leave meetings and conversations to run to the bathroom to break down in private. The external conflict became too much, and I knew that I needed a break from the internal conflict to get back on the track to healing.

I chose my health. The hours and workload, the conflict with my values, and the lack of any personal time were too much for me while juggling a divorce, PTSD, and grad school. Shortly after I sent the resignation email to

HR, I received the call I expected. The HR Director was caring and understood my plight, however, she encouraged me not to quit but to take a little more time off. She told me they were willing to hire a temporary director in my place until I could regroup. I couldn't tell her the problem was that I didn't know how long it might take me to regroup. I couldn't tell her it might take months or years because I didn't know. It hurt that I couldn't tell her *yes, please give me a few weeks or months, and I will return stronger than ever.* All I knew was I needed some time. Each time she asked me to reconsider, I told her no. I knew I needed to follow this decision to its conclusion.

Once I told my friends what happened to me, they asked why I didn't contact them. Each time I struggled to sort through the details, I broke down. For the first time, I was intensely aware that I lacked critical thinking skills. I saw unmistakably that decision-making was difficult because of my inability to fully analyze a situation, hypothesize the possible outcomes, and devise a solution. I grieved for the abuse that destroyed the critical thinking part of my brain. For years, I had leaned on Drake's sound advice for big decisions. As long as I had Drake to think for me, I was unaware of my critical thinking deficit, but without him, it became obvious I could not sort through the options and ramifications of a decision, and I was afraid to make a decision for fear it would be the wrong decision. At that point in my life, I made decisions based on how I felt, not by weighing facts, opinions, or research. Instead of creating a plan to choose the optimal solution for a problem, I went with what felt right. Occasionally, by chance and with God's help, I made a good one.

PTSD made it impossible to hold a job that required working with people. With every decision came increased stress. The increased stress caused massive depression, and I was aware of my depressive state because it was difficult to get out of bed or make decisions. I cried and worried excessively, isolated myself from people, and felt overwhelming guilt. Even so, I didn't know how seriously depressed I was.

Before moving to St. Louis, I learned to pray and wait for God. My life was difficult, and it was challenging to make decisions, but after I moved to St. Louis and developed full-blown PTSD, things got worse. It came in like a whirlwind to buffet my mind and set me off-kilter, making it impossible to make a well-thought-out selection. University studies have linked young adults' unhealthy risks and impaired decision-making to extreme stress and Childhood Trauma. Knowing this helped ease the guilt and shame I had for making poor decisions. It was impossible to make a good decision when I had no faculties to do so. Making decisions with a damaged brain is like dancing with one foot because function is impaired.

I knew quitting NEA was the correct choice for my mental and emotional health, but it was not the right choice for my financial health. Some decisions I felt secure about and was confident that God confirmed them. Others I felt were more like the flip of a coin. I learned a lot about God from this experience. I questioned if financial security was more important than my mental and emotional health. To live within my means, I made an effort to adjust my steak-and-potatoes dauphinoise appetite to one that was content with beans and rice. I went from crème brûlée to off-brand pudding. For someone who spent so many years truly hungry, the years I ate in great restaurants on my expense account were a time of learning how delicious good food can be. My palate had developed a desire for food. It was yet another loss to grieve when I realized those days were over.

I finally got past the *what-ifs* and came to grips with the resignation. When people asked what I would do after leaving MNEA, I couldn't answer because I hadn't thought beyond the resignation. I could only think about taking the doctor's suggestion to protect my health. I had no plan for anything else. Part of why I didn't know was because I trusted God to guide me even though He didn't lay out his entire plan. He told me to obey Him, and the more steps I took in obedience, the more His plan unfolded. I didn't know what I could and couldn't do.

After I turned in the resignation letter, the walls of my life collapsed. For days, I stayed in my beautiful condo in shock. The job I thought I couldn't live without was gone, my marriage was over, the relationship with my son was estranged, my health had failed, my mind was broken, my emotions were unstable, and I feared my financial situation was precarious. The worst of these was the loss of my relationship with my son. We had always been close. I read books to him, dropped him off at school, watched movies with him, threw him parties that made his friends wish I was their mom, traveled with him to his engagements, taught him about God and the importance of prayer —and at this crucial point in my life, we weren't speaking to one another. I couldn't wrap my head around him being alive and us not communicating. I had never imagined that hurt and pain could lead to such a separation.

I thought I resigned from work to regain my sanity. However, soon after resigning, my mind was consumed with my son and my estranged relationship. While my job was overwhelming and had great demands, I discovered the job wasn't the actual problem that caused much of the mental and emotional anguish. It was my estranged relationship with my son. I thought about him day and night. I wanted to tell him how sorry I was for hurting him and that I did my best, but when I did get up enough nerves to call him, he didn't answer. The other times I didn't call him because I knew it would only hurt him more if I called. I also knew there were no words to justify the emotional pain from the divorce I passed on to him. It seemed I would never overcome this intense pain.

When I wasn't working I only wanted to lie in bed and cry. No one knew about my pain because I was too embarrassed to share. I nursed my private fire of loneliness, mental anguish, and financial distress. Who *could extinguish these fires?*

Each time I thought about my emotional and mental state, I knew resigning was the right thing to do. I continued to have nagging thoughts: *I made a mistake. Call and get your job back. It was the first time I've made that much money, and it may never happen again. I shouldn't have resigned. I finally arrived, and then I let it go. Now, I'll return to the little one-room trailer I came from. I lost everything, and now I'm losing my mind. Who quits a well-paying job they enjoy without knowing what they will do next?*

I gradually learned to think things through and ignore impulses and feelings so I could make decisions based on facts instead of treating choices like lottery numbers. I learned God has a method when He speaks and guides believers. I learned to trust Him and the process. There was no one to tell me what to do. It was challenging, but I learned to place my trust and confidence in God instead of people. I paid a high price for my earlier spiritual laziness. I was misled, deceived, and manipulated because I trusted and believed what someone else told me about God instead of seeking Him independently and developing a relationship with Him. My excuse was that I was afraid of Him and wounded by His people. The difference at this point was that I had to trust Him. I was still afraid but felt there was no choice but to go to Him again.

For several months following the resignation, I often sat on the floor and sobbed. I left the condo only to go to the on-site gym where I walked on the treadmill and lifted weights. I knew I needed exercise to help with stress, so I did sit-ups, calisthenics, pushups, and planks. I couldn't control my mind, but I could keep my body in shape. After working out, thinking the sunshine would brighten my day, I sat by the pool, but I was in such despair that only the SON shining within could help. Whenever someone came near me, I left the pool and returned inside. I couldn't hold a conversation with anyone without breaking down, and I never knew when I would burst into tears. After three months, I thought about getting a menial job, but I knew I couldn't. Whatever this was, I had to allow it to play out. Every day I woke up with a thick cloud over me, holding me down, monopolizing my thoughts and emotions. My feelings were a rollercoaster, but my feet felt leaden. Each night I went to bed hoping and praying the next day would be different. For a long time, the days melted into each other without differentiation. I often prayed for Drake and Michael to have as much peace as they could while they adjusted to the loss of our family. I prayed for them day and night because I saw and felt the consequences of my actions. Next to a slow, painful death, it couldn't have been more difficult.

By 2014, my relationship with God was steadily growing. I studied His character and recognized His voice, and when He guided me to do something, I did it. Although I didn't know God's plans for me, I knew He was with me and would use me to help people one day. I thought it involved public speaking because that was my passion. While I didn't yet know what His plan looked like, I knew as I obeyed Him, every step I took brought me closer to realizing the fullness of my purpose.

Miraculously, I could still read and focus on research in between bouts of tears. That is another confirmation that God sent me to graduate school because, even after the breakdown, I could return to university classes to complete the doctoral degree. Transferring to the main campus in St. Louis was more expensive, and I had to make 401K withdrawals to pay for it, but I thought it would be worth it when I got a job. I knew God instructed me to get the doctorate, and He would reveal in His time why I needed it. He continued to teach me that where He guides, He will provide. Some semesters I worked as a graduate assistant where I managed a copy machine and made copies. I had very little contact with anyone except to drop copies off to the professors. Other ways God provided was to have people who borrowed money from me repay me, and I used the money to enroll in class. If it had not been for these seeming coincidences, I would not have been able to continue in the doctoral program because I didn't have any more money to withdraw.

I experienced some supernatural manifestations of God's power and favor in my life. One of those manifestations led me to Church on the Rock in St. Peters, Missouri. Another manifestation was finding my St. Louis counselor, Arella. I wasn't trusting of counselors because the Southwest Missouri counselor burdened me with her problems and made counseling unappealing. However, I was at the point where I knew I needed guidance. I prayed and asked God where to look. The Holy Spirit said to call the church I attended, but the church secretary said they couldn't make recommendations or give preferential treatment to members. I told her, "God told me to call and ask, so I'm being obedient." There was silence on the other end. Optimistically, I thought if anyone understands that God still speaks to people, surely the church should know.

One of my biggest mistakes was thinking God speaks to everyone like He speaks to me, and thinking people hear God like I hear Him when He speaks to me. I don't mean that in a prideful way. I mean it most humbly, but I know it is true. Don't get me wrong; God doesn't speak to me every time in an audible voice. That's only happened a few times, and it was frightening. He speaks in different ways. I believe people don't take the time to listen to Him speak and establish a relationship with Him so they can recognize His voice, because I didn't either. After recognizing my great need for direction and understanding, I had to trust that He was speaking to me. I knew He would never allow me to be deceived again like I was about the Texas visit to Deion Sanders' house.

I held the phone because I knew God had me call the church, so I waited for the secretary to think or do whatever she needed to do to provide the information I requested. I expected direction since I did what He told me to do. Then she said, "Ma'am, this is not a recommendation, but a counselor was in my office a few days ago, and her card is still on my desk." Before she finished talking, the Holy Spirit said to me, *That's the one. Get the contact information.*

I called the counselor and scheduled an appointment as soon as possible. In our first meeting, Arella said that she prayed about giving up private counseling. Despite that, she counseled me for almost two years before leaving private practice to work in a corporate healthcare setting. I am sure God kept her business open for me. Arella was a licensed Christian counselor who lived her beliefs. She believed in the scripture and believed God—along with therapy—would heal me.

It seems popular among Christians to say they see a Christian counselor. When I ask if their counselor teaches scriptural healing, they often ask what I'm talking about. I've learned many Christian counselors leave *Christ* out of their sessions, which leaves their clients feeling hopeless. How sad that they confess the God of all hope, yet they don't share that hope with their clients. In my mind, Christian counseling should be based on the belief that Jesus desires for people to be healed of their physical, emotional, mental, and spiritual infirmities based on the covenant promises of God.

Through Arella's Christian counseling and support, I grew exponentially. I loved her counseling techniques of listening, caring, praying, believing, and trusting God so much that I use them today to help those God sends to me. I wasn't employed when I met her, so she counseled me for two years without charge. She made such an impression, I will never forget the help and support she gave when I needed it most. God used her to transform my life. Now, I endeavor to transform the lives of those God sends to me.

The best thing about moving to St. Louis was meeting with Arella. She explained the trauma I endured in my childhood and how it affected my thoughts, beliefs, values, and self-esteem. She further clarified the work I needed to do in conjunction with the work God had already begun doing. She gave assignments to complete between sessions and told me what to expect emotionally, mentally, and spiritually as I moved through the process.

Arella's therapy worked to improve communication, behavior, and coping skills. She used guided activities to strengthen my self-concept. The most important thing she did, however, was to pray for me at the end of each session. I felt her faith in God and that she knew she was in her purpose. While she didn't teach the Bible, she did let me know her help, and mine, came from God, because she could only do so much. I am grateful that she wasn't afraid to tell me to read scriptures and pray them over myself. I followed her counsel, and with each visit I grew stronger.

From the first time I went to Arella, I felt stronger spiritually because she taught me how to fight spiritual battles. Arella began sessions by asking how I had been the previous week, and she didn't think I was crazy when I shared the spiritual battles I experienced. I told her more about the spiritual battles than the physical and emotional ones. Surprisingly, each time I told her what happened, she told me how to combat it and what God said to do about it. The increased spiritual strength made me emotionally, physically, and mentally stronger, as well. I received revelation after revelation in each session with her. By the end of our sessions, I knew I was transformed and would never be who I once was. I am so thankful for such a Spirit-filled counselor who recognized the mental, physical, emotional, and spiritual battles Childhood Trauma survivors face.

Arella didn't take long to diagnose me with PTSD and clinical depression. Miraculously, with her support, I began to emerge from the depression. She told me to continue the routine I developed and the activities she assigned. I looked forward to our weekly sessions. Each time I met with her, I felt increasingly free. I learned the power of not only Christian counseling, but anointed counseling from her. I've had counseling sessions with a therapist, psychologist, and psychiatrist. With Arella, I experienced freedom in a way I did not experience in former therapeutic sessions. My life has never been the same. I needed someone who had a relationship with God and could help me believe Divine healing was possible. In my situation at that time, I was not a candidate for mental health medication. My wounds were spiritual, and my healing had to address them from a spiritual standpoint.

Chapter 58

CRACKS IN THE SYSTEM

I accepted the reality of living off the funds from my 401K until I got better. Even without young children, I was ineligible for government assistance like the Supplemental Nutrition Assistance Program (SNAP) and Medicaid, and I didn't qualify for unemployment because I voluntarily resigned and terminated my employment contract. It didn't matter to the government agencies that I had an emotional and mental breakdown. Since I was emotionally unable to function and mentally unstable, I couldn't imagine getting even a menial job. It hurt to think I had lived in the United States and paid payroll taxes since my first job at age fourteen, but when I needed help from the same system I paid into, I was denied. Added to my suffering and feelings of rejection was the rejection from the programs that were supposedly created for those who fell on hard times. Not only had I fallen, I was incapable of getting up by myself.

Thinking of applying for other types of assistance caused feelings of inadequacy, so I did my best to eliminate those thoughts. I didn't apply for welfare because I previously worked for DHS and knew the qualifications. I was unemployed, but because I had savings I would have been denied. Also, I didn't want welfare to be my source of income. I'm sure some of my reluctance to the idea of receiving welfare was due to my previous family experience with it. I had enough of the state's assistance when I was a child, and I wanted nothing to do with it in adulthood.

My financial situation exacerbated my problems. I went from having excellent healthcare to no healthcare—another disappointment. Each day I lived gave me an excuse to cry. I continued withdrawing money from my 401K to pay bills and living expenses. The 10% penalty for early withdrawal plus the income tax on the withdrawal was news to me. My traumatized brain did not critically analyze the next steps following the resignation. Now I know the wisest thing to have done before resigning was to secure less expensive housing, but I didn't think I could endure another transition, so I believed I had no choice. Undoubtedly, this belief that I didn't have a choice limited me from thinking beyond what I believed could happen. The Bible says, "According to your faith be it done unto you" (Matthew 9:29) and, "All things are possible if we believe" (Mark 9:23). I lived in an expensive condo and paid exorbitant rent because I felt I couldn't endure losing one more thing. The condo was a shelter against reminders of my childhood and being tossed from pillar to post, changing addresses every few months, with the next place a step down from the previous one. Foster homes were serial exposures to abuse and sexual assault. I lost the one beautiful home I could call mine in the divorce, so when I could finally afford a little bit of luxury, the condo was a proclamation of worthiness, something I deserved to have and appreciate. Each time I thought about moving, I despaired. I recognized no option but to stay in a beautiful environment that drained my savings.

At a point of desperation, I decided to reconsider government assistance. Perhaps I could receive a supplement, even if only for a short time. I was convinced I needed income, food, and help. The quicker my savings account drained, the more acceptable assistance looked. Another thought stuck in my head: I had worked since age fourteen, so I might qualify for Social Security Disability (SSD). The website said it was for people who couldn't function or were disabled. At first, I thought I could never apply because that would admit how terribly bad my situation was. The more I read, though, the more I thought about applying. The site indicated a long wait for the application process, but I decided not to give up. I wrote down the advantages and disadvantages of the program. The advantages outweighed the shame or guilt I thought I would feel. My emotions were less of a concern than the fact I needed help and had little choice where it came from.

Two weeks after applying, I was notified to complete the paperwork and wait for an interview appointment. I never doubted that I qualified. I figured that when I told them about my childhood, they would approve my application. I was mentally and emotionally ready to do whatever was needed to get temporary assistance. I thought the hardest part was acknowledging I needed help.

My first appointment was with a tall, Caucasian man. Although I was confident I couldn't be denied, his expression and demeanor seemed calloused. As a government gatekeeper, he was someone experienced in denying applications. As soon as I encountered him, I thought I already saw a NO in his eyes and a DENIED stamp in his hand. I knew his demeanor wasn't a false front. He had the power to either help or push me further into despair. I hoped that he would help because I didn't think anyone in such a position ever had.

The government functionary asked me to rate my mental processes on a scale from 1 to 10. I rated mine a 2 or 3. He asked me questions: *Can you dress yourself in the morning? What day is it? How's the weather?* He delved into my childhood, and I answered his questions, not realizing the danger of waking the giants. I felt I had to be candid to get help. He cut me off mid-sentence and was short with his explanations. He sternly warned me, "Some people die waiting for approval because the approval process takes anywhere from one to two years. Most people are denied and have to file an appeal." I couldn't help but think about unemployed people like me who had little resources—no food, no dignity left, and no support—who worked hard and put money into the system and needed the system's help.

I had a mental picture of people who suffered child abuse and lost their minds and couldn't work anymore, only to be denied. These were people like me. I burst out crying. "Sir, are you telling me I could be denied? I told you everything, and it's the truth," I sobbed. "I only need about a year to get back on my feet. I will work again." I tried to assure him I was not *one of them.* I told him I didn't even want to be in the system, but I couldn't work. "I want to work, but I can't work right now," I sobbed.

Like many impersonal government functionaries, he said bluntly, "Thank you. You will be notified of our decision." He didn't offer an *I'm sorry you had to endure so much, that's so sad,* or, *You will come through this.* Nothing. He escorted me to the door and said, "Have a nice day."

Defeated, I walked out of his office. I cried several times over the next few days when I thought of how impersonally he treated me, but I also thought his harsh words and attitude were worth enduring if I got approved for assistance. I knew people abused the system, but the system needs to show compassion to those who suffer. I believed I was in desperate need of help. I wanted a little mercy and understanding as I struggled mentally and emotionally, but he didn't extend it. Still, I stayed optimistic and waited for the call. I struggled to fill out the paperwork and cried my way through each page. Part of the process was to submit past medical history records along with the application for approval. I had to pay for my medical records to be sent to his office, but I did it because I felt like the system was for people like me who needed a hand-up, not a handout. Instead, I felt I got kicked and stomped down. I was overwhelmed by the experience.

Even though the application cost time and money, I tried to stay hopeful. I called to inquire about the status of the application and was told, "It's only been two months. You should be prepared to wait at least twelve months." I feared I would be on the streets in twelve months and began to panic. It didn't matter that I had college degrees. I was certain that I couldn't function in society. I wasn't emotionally or mentally stable. I felt the inertia from the SSD office was their decision. I couldn't depend on the system as a child, and I couldn't depend on it now. I was disappointed because I wanted time to process my mental and emotional states and not worry about how I would eat or pay bills. I continued to use the dwindling 401K while waiting. At the time, it felt like more of what I experienced as a child, and it aroused triggers and residuals. Once again, I could not think critically and see anything beyond my feelings and situation.

Thankfully, it didn't take twelve months to hear from the SSD office. I received a letter of denial four months after my interview. I appealed and went to appear before the Administrative Law Judge (ALJ) two months later. The ALJ office informed me he was retiring soon and if I missed my appointment with him, I would have to start over. I knew I wouldn't miss it.

After seven months of waiting for the application decision, my nightmares, terrors and tremors were less frequent, but I wasn't ready to go back to work. I was better than I was, but I still had emotional outbursts. Almost two years had passed since I resigned and lost my source of income and sense of self-worth. I was desperate and not too proud to beg by that time.

Kindly, the Administrative Law Judge asked specific questions. He said, "Ms. Wallace, I read your application file, and I am so sorry you had to endure so much." His statement validated my feelings, and after he apologized for what I endured as a child, I started weeping. Tears flowed as I answered his questions. I was grateful he acknowledged my pain.

"I see you haven't worked anywhere in almost two years. Why not?"

I told him, "I am unable to control my emotions and need a little time to get better." Previously, I sent him an email summarizing the events of my childhood, the divorce, and loss of employment. I hoped it would help convey the emotional and psychological upheaval. "My memories of what happened hit me at once, your Honor."

He said, "Yes, I can understand that, but there are many jobs I think you can still do," and he read a list of jobs. I bowed my head in embarrassment because he had already announced I had two degrees. Then he asked, "Would you be willing to work one of these jobs?"

I responded. "I want to work, but I am not able to work right now. I know I will be back working again soon." The jobs he recommended were positions like Walmart greeter, security guard, waitress, and janitor. *What did he not understand?* I did not need any kind of contact with people. I didn't trust myself, and I didn't know what I might do or how I might respond. I needed time and space to get through my recovery. I kept thinking *If only I can get approved for a year, that's all I need. I will show them. I will keep my word.*

The judge pulled out a binder and spent the next several minutes flipping through it as if he were looking for something. Occasionally, he mumbled to himself about something not being enough. I waited, my mind a whirlwind of thoughts. I wanted to beg him to read my journals. I had brought dozens of them to court with me, but he didn't ask for them. I kept thinking that recalling the abuse and reliving so much of it in dreams and nightmares would only be worth it if the judge could understand the connection between Childhood Trauma and the inability to function as an adult. I must've begun crying again because the clerk passed a box of tissues to me.

Finally, he looked up and said, "I want to help you, but there isn't any way I can, based on the rule book. You don't meet the criteria for income assistance." He listed a few other jobs that I should be able to work, including home health, cleaning jobs, and data entry jobs—all of which involved facing the public, communication, and documentation. I knew I couldn't do those jobs because I couldn't focus or keep my emotions in check. The sad part was I couldn't help him understand my emotional state, and based on what the interviewer wrote, he believed I could work.

I thought I would go into full-blown panic mode, but I didn't. I was surprised the judge denied me help because he didn't see the current-day results of my childhood beatings, starvation, neglect, and the burnings and hangings of my siblings as *enough*. I steadied my nerves when I wanted to fall on the floor and scream at him, *Please help me! I've been let down so many times. I need help.* Instead, I listened to him say, "Thank you, Ms. Wallace. I can see you've been through a lot. I hope things get better for you."

He hoped things would get better for me. People say that when they don't have the power to change your situation. He had the power to help me, but he didn't. He told me I didn't meet any criteria for assistance. I understand he followed policy, but I also understood how policies worked because I had worked for a government agency with policies. I knew there was always someone to review policies and procedures when a case manager deemed it necessary. Ultimately, I concluded I didn't know what to say so he could circle a policy and grant me assistance. The Administrative Law Judge's decision triggered my distrust in the state to help me when needed. I questioned how others with less Childhood Trauma in their lives received assistance. I also questioned why society had nothing in place for those who had major distressing transitions back to back. I felt like he heard my story and wished me well. Was there no program available to help me get free counseling or food? How could he, in good conscience, live with himself after I shared my story and he saw my degrees and saw how deranged I was? What person with two degrees would settle for a $20,000-a-year job? He knew I wasn't lying because he had my tax returns. He saw how much money I made in previous years. I listed several names of people who could verify my story was true. Even if he didn't believe anything I said about my childhood, he could surmise something happened for me to leave my high-paying job. He didn't even offer a referral for mental assistance. None of that mattered to him, because he decided to deny my claim. I had done everything I could. Still, I was denied.

I wanted to scream, "You *hope* things will get better for me? Your *hope* is the reason suffering people who have complex trauma die without getting help."

Your *hope* has caused some people to become homeless.

Your *hope* makes people stop believing the system is for them and can help them.

Your *hope* steps on the weak and crushes them.

Your *hope* causes people to be hopeless.

Your *hope* denies those who need help the most.

Keep your hope. May the Righteous Judge help me and others like me!

I felt rejected, dejected, and hopeless as I left the building. I suffered emotional pain from recalling the memories to tell the judge my story because I hoped it would be worth it in the end. I opened Pandora's box and dreamed about Buck and Elsie and the beatings, burnings, and hanging. I dreamed of the nights Briana and I spent at the hospital with Buck. I even dreamed that I was going to be burned on the stove. These nightmares woke me in a panic with a pounding heart and wet clothing from fear sweat. I had to relive the abuse memories only to have the ALJ tell me that I didn't meet the criteria for help. If I had been approved, the pain would have been worth it. Without the approval, I only saw more difficulty ahead. I had a mind full of terrible memories, no job, little money left in the 401K, and a whole lot of shame.

My healing journey did not seem like healing. Instead, it seemed to be a long journey filled with unrelenting pain and no sign of future release. I was stressed about the possibility of homelessness. I was thankful I still had a car to sleep in if it got to that point.

Chapter 59
HEALING MATTERS

When deciding whether or not to initiate a healing process, I think many feel they should let sleeping giants lie. I once thought that as well. The only problem with that logic is it ignores the fact that sleeping giants turn over, move, sneeze, get hungry, and wake up. People may think if they leave the giant alone, it will sleep forever, but that is not true. By *giant*, of course, I'm talking about PTSD and the other *trolls* that accompany it. For others, their giant might be fear, shame, low confidence, passivity, personality disorders caused by earlier trauma, or whatever holds them in bondage. I awakened my giant, and soon the trolls of PTSD were present, as well: nightmares, night sweats, middle-of-the-night panic attacks, intrusive memories, phobia of bridges, avoidance of people who triggered painful memories, extreme sadness, grief, anxiety, crying spells, and frequent overwrought reactions to various types of stimuli.

I survived repeated psychic assaults for nearly three years after moving to St. Louis. Because I wasn't working, I had few distractions and could seek answers and concentrate on healing. I acknowledge that even though I didn't feel like it at the time, I was privileged to be afforded a type of two-year sabbatical so that I could focus on mental health. I understand that my situation was unique and that most people couldn't understand why someone with a college degree couldn't work and needed time to heal. Depending on the severity of the trauma, some survivors can fight through their healing journey while also maintaining a marriage, parenthood, education, and financially supporting themselves and/or a family, while others give up on life or, like me, are so emotionally and mentally unstable that everything is shut down.

In the Tower of Hope programs I founded, I've seen participants dedicate daily time to follow the healing assignments while maintaining their employment and accountability to others. With a support group, proper guidance, and direction, survivors can do many things I couldn't do because I had none of those. I also resigned from the Missouri NEA position and concealed my situation from my family and most of my friends. My wounds from people were so deep that I could conceive of no other approach. I would not recommend my solo approach because the only thing that got me through was faith in God and standing on His covenant promises that no matter what I went through, because I loved Him, He would rescue me. And He did rescue me.

What I see now is that God customized my rehab experience. My prayers were often deep moments of silence, and I wrote many poems and reflective journal entries that I could see were therapeutic as I wandered through my mind making connections and trying to find solutions. I was isolated from distractions and disruptions, I was productive in spurts, and I kept physically active, which was great for my body and mind and helped the thought processes mend and create.

My days had a routine: wake up, pray, and write in my journal; sit on the balcony, and pray some more, which generally triggered weeping. I shed tears until I was exhausted, fell asleep, and woke up on the balcony with wet clothing from the tears and the heat of the spring and summer months. I ate a few bites of food, but only for survival. In the afternoon, I watched a TV western and went to the condo gym. I compulsively cleaned my apartment and followed cleaning with a small meal. I took long walks, listened to inspirational recordings, and recited declarations. Often, I cried some more. I listened to Gospel music while walking and cleaning. I watched more TV westerns in the late evenings until I fell asleep. I avoided the news and any sort of programming that stirred emotional reactions. I didn't go to movies or talk to anyone who provoked strong emotions. Self-awareness is important, and I found it essential during healing. Knowing which stimuli provoked emotions helped me find self-control.

Grief caused most of my tears. I grieved the loss of childhood, innocence, my authentic self, and marriage. I grieved the loss of the little girl I thought Dora could have been had she not been so abused and misused. I grieved for never having loving parents and for the losses of my siblings—both their deaths and their losses of sanity—as well as the loss of some of their children. I even grieved the damage to the relationship with my abusive great-uncle Harold, whom I called Dad. I grieved the lack of understanding I had about what happened. I grieved the loss of the loving God of my childhood innocence.

I learned about the God of fire, brimstone, and punishment while staying with Harold and Agnes. After the breakdown following the recovery of the memories of Harold's abuse, I couldn't understand why the God of fire and brimstone didn't punish Harold for his evil acts. I was terrified of God because church people described Him as a punisher and not as a loving, forgiving, compassionate, and merciful God. In the aftermath of the breakdown, I sought to understand things: How could God look away from the suffering I went through at the hands of my parents? How could He allow the men of the church to sexually abuse me and go unpunished? How could He watch me suffer breakdowns, divorce, and the loss of my family and home? How could God let me suffer from PTSD, personality disorders, and crippling phobias? How could this happen to me, and why? How was this the work of a loving God? How could He work this out for my good? What was the purpose of my suffering? Inexplicably, I still loved and had deep reverence for Him.

During one of my bouts of extended crying, I heard that still, small voice say, *Write down everything I give you because one day, you are going to use this to help others heal.* I grabbed a pen and wrote down the steps He gave me to facilitate my healing. He said they would be paramount to helping others to heal.

I did these activities intentionally and expected something observable and measurable. It also helped to know that there are scriptures in the Bible where God promised to heal Believers. After thirty days of intentionally using the guided steps to healing, I began feeling and thinking differently. I had already come a long way since I first spoke declarations, wrote in my journal, exercised, read God's Word, paused, and reflected, but this time was different from the healing that started in Springfield because this time was focused. This healing came with mental clarity, revelations, joy, and a closer relationship with God. I still cried frequently, but the crying spells didn't last as long, and after a few months of consistently doing the healing steps, the crying spells subsided. I learned not to look for a quick deliverance but rather a progressive deliverance. It wasn't my favored tempo, but I accepted it. I had to learn to appreciate God's timeline instead of my wish for instant, microwave healing.

In Springfield, they were my survival skills, but in St. Louis, they became my living skills. The more I incorporated them, the more enjoyable life became. Prescribed by the Springfield doctor who took me off Ativan, I took a low dose of Buspirone to treat my anxiety, but the healing activities allowed me to thrive. God revealed that using them was paramount to continue healing, and I needed to do them daily. Each day, I healed more, laughed more, and cried less.

A huge learning experience was linking God's healing to how I valued myself, how I thought God valued me, and how my parents treated me. I believed I was low on God's priority list and didn't mean much to Him. I never doubted God's healing power, but I doubted He would heal *me*. When my healing didn't come overnight, instead of thinking that healing takes time, I concluded God didn't hear my prayers or that He didn't think I was worth healing. John 9:1-41 is the foundational scripture of Tower of Hope. God helped me understand that when Jesus comes to me, I must be willing to do something to get something, exactly as the blind man was willing to do whatever Jesus told him to receive his sight. I was willing to do the healing assignments to get my mental, physical, emotional, and spiritual healing.

God taught me I had a role to play in my healing. The thought that Jesus wanted me to *do something* to heal was a new idea. It didn't seem right. God had the power. Also, scripture talks about how you can do nothing to inherit or bring about your salvation. I thought the same about God and healing. I couldn't imagine why He wouldn't heal me in an instant like He did the woman with the issue of blood (Luke 8:48), the man with leprosy (Luke 5:12), the man with a withered hand (Mark 3:5), and the centurion's servant (Luke 6:13). After all, Jesus healed those people suddenly and immediately.

In my human effort to try and understand why God did not heal me instantly, I concluded that the brain and heart are not like a broken body part. Drake used to tell me the brain needs time to come back up like a rebooted computer, and his analogy helped me handle my mental breakdown. In the Bible, Jesus never told anyone *Your heart is healed*. He told them what to do to heal their heart, such as the cases with Nicodemus, His disciples, and the Scribes and Pharisees. Because everything flows from the heart (Proverbs 4:23, Matthew 19:21-24, John 3:1-21), I can see why it requires more internal work.

My expectations set me up for disappointment. I wanted my healing to be God's rescue of me. He wanted me to accept responsibility for my healing, believe He had already healed me through His work on the cross, and begin walking in it. I was one of the people God healed where the healing depended on obedience and working to ensure healing was complete, such as when He told a man to go wash in the pool of Siloam (John 9), told another to take up his bed and walk (John 5:8-16), and the ten lepers who were cleansed to show themselves to the priest (Luke 17:14). All of them were healed when they obeyed. God wasn't going to simply touch me, and poof! I would be healed. It took a while for me to grasp that I was already mentally and emotionally healed. I had to accept His covenant promise of healing, commit to my healing by doing what I knew to do, and wait patiently for my healing to manifest. The key was waiting for the healing to manifest naturally (Isaiah

53:5). By His stripes, I wasn't healed. By His stripes, I am healed. This means Jesus already did it, and it only needs to be manifested. So if I am healed but don't feel healed, it may be because I am no longer walking by faith, but rather I am walking by sight. That was the other hard work of doing what I could while God did what only He could do.

Transformational healing began the moment I started the actions. Although the change was slow, it was still change. Each day, I grew stronger, but I still wanted my change to be like when Jesus cursed the fig tree, and from that moment, it withered from its roots (Matthew 11:12-25). I wanted to see immediate signs of healing, and I was often discouraged. There wasn't anyone I knew who had gone through Childhood Trauma and could tell me how the healing transformation took place. The more I learned about God, the more patience I had with myself and for my healing. I didn't know what a healed person looked like, but I knew how unhealed revealed itself. Emotional outbursts, uncontrolled anger, jealousy, and insecurity do not identify a healed person. Healed individuals were not manipulative and controlling. They did not have chronic physical illness, signs of personality disorders, schizophrenia, panic attacks, and tormenting dreams. Healed people did not cry frequently. As I met new people in public and shared my story, they often told me they were healed. Yet, I could see they were dealing with the same physiological, psychological, behavioral, and spiritual problems I did. I was not looking for more of the same. I expected and prayed for true healing and deliverance. I believed there was more and expected more.

As I matured and grew in the attributes of God, I noticed there was often a significant time delay between Biblical characters praying and the manifest answering of their prayers. For example, Abraham waited twenty-five years for the promised son (Genesis 12 and 21), and Joseph waited more than thirteen years for the promised dream (Genesis 37-45). David waited about fifteen years to become King of Israel (1 Samuel 16, 24 and 2 Samuel 5). Hannah was barren for many years (1 Samuel 1-2), and Ruth remained patiently with her mother-in-law, Naomi, after the famine (Ruth 1-2). God used waiting as a time of testing for His servants and to encourage their faith to grow in Him. As revealed by their behaviors, I doubt Biblical characters appreciated waiting on God any more than we do. Doesn't God know modern Christians live with the expectation of *now* and are known as the microwave generation who wants everything fast and if it's not fast, we lose interest?

On the contrary, many of my deliverances were miraculous and immediate, like when God broke spiritual strongholds, such as religious thinking. Religion and tradition keep believers in bondage. God enlightened my understanding through scripture, thus breaking my spiritual strongholds. He also delivered me from the demonic strongholds of negative thinking that kept me from having hope that things would change, or that convinced me I was too broken to fix.

From 2010-2013, I took copious Holy Spirit-led notes about healing as He revealed them to me. As I heard the still, small voice dictate, I wrote. My first manuscript was nearly 400 pages of reflection. I wrote many times throughout the night about my early life abuse, hunger pangs, and foster homes, the near-death experiences of my stepfather Buck, the nights in the hospital with Briana, Elsie's abandonment episodes, her death, the depression, and my journey to sanity.

The writing was beyond difficult, not only to recall but also to relive. Recalling the events caused excruciating emotional and physical pain. I didn't have to struggle to recall some of the traumatic episodes since they were in my memory. However, I suppressed others that took weeks and months to recall and place in the correct history of my life story. For example, I suppressed the memory of the time Elsie drove drunk and backed off a bridge. In the flashback, I was six years old, riding in the back of a pick-up truck and unable to find something stable to hold on to. I was petrified of drowning as she laughed and threatened to go completely off the bridge into the water as I slid around in the bed of the truck. I remember shaking and crying, but there was no one to rescue me. After witnessing the brutal beatings, burnings, and hanging of my siblings, there was no reason to think she wouldn't follow through with destroying us. No doubt this experience was the genesis of my bridge phobia. I processed the images from the flashbacks as they came to me and wrote about how those things felt as a child at that moment.

I suppressed the memories of my great-uncle Harold's sexual abuse until a friend told me, as I drove across a bridge, that her uncle sexually abused her. As my friend shared, somehow my brain recovered both the memory of my mother's erratic threat and Harold's abuse, although it would be another year or so before I had the dream that forced me to acknowledge our relationship as abuse. The bridge phobia that developed from my mother's drunk driving and threatening to drive us off a bridge made me feel as if I would drown when crossing bridges, so I developed a phobia of bridges. What began as a caring conversation with a friend turned into more than a decade of ongoing panic and anxiety attacks, tormenting memories, and nightmares. For twelve years, I balked at bridges. Extreme anxiety and panic attacks flooded my body when I approached them. In time, my faith in God, belief in the power of healing, and belief in the Scriptures helped me address the phobia and regain the ability to drive across bridges.

I began writing prayers to help process the disturbing thoughts and affirmations to provide hope. I went through the process of the healing assignments morning and evening for a full year, and then continued for a second and even a third year as I experienced the early stages of healing. During these years, although I knew there was growth and improvement in my relationship with God, I still wasn't fully trusting Him—not with the kind of faith that I would later develop.

Chapter 60
EMERGING FROM THE TRAUMATOSE COMA

O ne of the best things about my struggle during this time was that I knew God and trusted Him. Before the divorce settlement, I had worked for twenty years for financial independence and was debt-free. The divorce left me with debt, which compounded when I left my job and had to liquidate the savings upon which that former independence was built. It was a bitter pill. I felt hopeless until I reminded myself that I would never have to go through deception and manipulation again because God opened my eyes to understand what happened, how it impacted me, and that healing is a process that takes time.

With opened eyes, God also gave me the grace to forgive myself for the things I didn't know and the people I hurt—especially my innocent son, Michael. I learned while there were consequences for my blindness, there was grace to help me through it. I may have felt as if I traveled more than once down the road of deception, but I didn't. I was on the road to recovery and had been traveling for a few years. Each day, I reminded myself that I would never have to go through this again. Each day, I increasingly understood how the world worked and told myself it wouldn't always be this way. It was as if I had been in a *traumatose* coma for years and miraculously came out of it.

Traumatose isn't in the dictionary because I made it up. However, to trauma survivors and overcomers, it is a real word that expresses what it feels like when one experiences PTSD and frequent panic/anxiety attacks and lives in a constant state of survival with waves of overwhelming fear. *Traumatose* is how survivors live, move, think, and act based on their trauma-affected brain. They make decisions and do things unconsciously, unable to analyze problems, find solutions, or think about how decisions impact others. *Traumatose* might be similar to brain paralyzation, with the exception that one can make choices but not think critically. There is brain activity, but survivors are emotionally and mentally unresponsive to their environments. That's why I call it *traumatose*. Whatever the term used, it was a long, hard journey back to life. I am thankful to God I survived the *traumatose* coma.

Miraculously, after the period of the *traumatose* coma, I was mentally competent and healthy. I began to understand the depth of my wounds, and I felt a freedom that accompanies understanding. Based on the research and knowing what I now know about PTSD's effect on the brain, it is a miracle I had any quality of life. Although I did the healing steps and healing occurred, I was unprepared for PTSD and its challenges. Lack of social and family support and not fully understanding the symptoms and behavioral manifestations of PTSD made healing more difficult. Although I did not have support from others, I had internal support through the Holy Spirit and the assignments He gave me, and I stayed committed to doing whatever it took to heal. Despite the increased emotional upheaval, I am certain that continuing to exercise, write, reflect, listen to inspirational recordings, and read the Bible were instrumental to staying mentally competent and healthy.

Providentially, I was better spiritually after the *traumatose* coma—and that's a miracle, too! Hope returned. I learned about God little by little in Springfield, but my relationship with God catapulted into high gear when I moved to St. Louis. It may have been because He wanted me to feel His presence 24/7 to know He was with me in the heat of the battle or because He was about to give me a huge assignment. Nonetheless, I went from struggling to trust God's leading to understanding it and hearing His voice. I also understood the other ways He speaks, such as through the Bible, His Holy Spirit, and confirming His word through others. He trained my ear to hear His voice. He said, "My sheep hear my voice and a stranger they will not follow" (John 10:4-5). Previously, I didn't know His character or attributes or have a relationship with Him. Although I knew scripture and was in church most of my life, I didn't know God. Like a new Christian, I had to learn and trust God to teach me everything He wanted me to know.

My past gave me an experience of religion with God. My present gave me the experience of a relationship with God. The difference was significant.

As I grew spiritually, I learned to listen, trust, and wait for God when I needed direction. I learned deception could come if I looked for another person to tell me what to do. Looking for a sign or answer from others only set me up for more deception. I learned instead to pray, consider the pros and cons, and seek counseling from Spirit-filled people. This was huge growth! My confidence was now in God and not humans. For the first time, I had a strategy when making decisions: pray for direction, ask for wisdom, expect

God to answer, get wise, Godly counsel, and act on the decision. Those were miracle steps for me! When I followed those steps and things didn't go as I thought they would, I considered it part of God's plan. I had no shame or guilt when things appeared to go awry because I knew I had acknowledged God, and He promised to direct my path (Proverbs 3:5-6, Psalm 37:23). I also believed God was with me (Romans 8:31, Psalm 56:9), and He would work things out to bless me in the end (Romans 8:28).

I had to take a year off from coursework and studying because it was too much for my exhausted brain and nerves. Graduate school in St. Louis challenged me on another level. When I doubted my cognitive abilities, I reminded myself of previous rigorous programs I had done, like the application process for the National Board Certification in 2007, which involved a lot of research and learning following the completion of my first Master's degree in 2006. I often had to revisit my accomplishments to affirm that I could study and learn.

I studied the importance of self-awareness, so I was careful about where I went, what I did, and who I talked to during my years out of the workforce. I was attentive to my thoughts, feelings, and emotions when talking to people throughout the day. For one year, I mainly processed more elements of my loss, worked out, wrote in my journal, wrote prayers and declarations, studied scriptures on healing and covenant promises, and began to receive counseling. The words of Norman Vincent Peale and Earl Nightingale came back to me.

During my first breakdown, I found audio recordings of Earl Nightingale that I had listened to for several years. I read *Think and Grow Rich* by Norman V. Peale and *How to Stop Worrying and Start Living* by Dale Carnegie. As my mind returned, these were the only books and audio recordings I could listen to. I thought they were to help me through that breakdown, but I now realize they were to help me through my continued difficulties. They taught me to think positively and to persist without giving up. I contribute faith in God and positive thinking for the strength to overcome obstacles. I recalled the words until they replayed in my mind even while I slept. I reprogrammed my mind to think positively. Little did I know that positive thinking would help me through several breakdowns. I am thankful God, in His infinite wisdom, prepared me years earlier for what I needed when I needed it.

It wasn't until I left Southwest Missouri and began counseling with Arella that the observable healing outcomes were revealed. One of the first things the counselor said was, "You have done a lot of healing on your own." She and I both knew it wasn't me. It was God's guidance in the healing process. I shared what I did, and she assured me the worst was over because I had done a lot of hard work. However, mentally, I was still in a horrible place, and I couldn't imagine the worst being over. It was time for effective spiritual and psychological counseling.

I shared with my counselor some of the Holy Spirit's healing work, such as writing unmailed letters apologizing for choices and decisions that didn't represent my authenticity, apologizing to Drake for ending our marriage, and attempting to make amends with my son for hurting our family. I asked for forgiveness for doing things that didn't align with my values. Negative behaviors that contributed to ending my marriage included financial irresponsibility and social immaturity. Damaging behaviors to others were things that didn't align with my values and made me regretful after I did or said them.

One of the things people lose after sexual abuse is their authentic self. It takes persistence, hard work, and time to recover authenticity. I wrote several poems as I searched for my authentic self. Often, I didn't know if what I did was the real me or part of who I was conditioned to think I was. I found myself at the same time others met the real me. Despite recognizing my authentic self, I was afraid of who I might become when I let go of who I thought I was, even though I knew I had to find the real me. I wasn't sure she was worth finding, but God had a purpose for her, and no faded or broken copy was acceptable. I did several things to help the authentic me emerge. I wrote poems and prayers, spoke God's promises over her, fasted, and prayed for God to allow her to emerge. I envisioned what she might look like and who she might become. I knew she was there, buried deep in pain. Next to divorce, continuing to believe my authentic self would emerge one day was one of the most difficult things I have ever done.

Little by little, the real me emerged, and she was beautiful. I liked things about her I had never before liked. I liked her genuine compassion to help people, her sense of humor, her kinky hair, brown skin, and perky lips. I came up the rough side of the mountain, but not without purpose. I studied the Bible and read how God intentionally took the children of Israel, His chosen people, around the difficult way instead of giving them the shortcut (Exodus 13). He said they weren't ready to fight yet, so I knew He had a reason to take me up the rough side of the mountain, allow me to endure heartache, and let me struggle for years with no help in sight. He took me from pain to purpose.

I made a few decisions without asking anyone because I knew God was in it. One was the decision to resume attending church. After the spiritual abuse I experienced in the Arkansas churches, it took Jesus to get me to return. Except for a few funerals, I refused to attend church for fifteen years. Following my breakdowns, I went from attending church several times a week to only going once a year. Don't get me wrong. I longed to attend church and be with people who loved and served God. My problem was after being treated so poorly by those who claimed to love and serve God, I didn't know who the genuine Christians were. I understood more clearly that Jesus was persecuted by those who claimed to be sent by God, especially the Pharisees and Sadducees, who repeatedly challenged His authority and repeatedly tried to catch Him contradicting or violating the law.

For me, spiritual abuse was worse than sexual abuse because it took away my hope, faith, and trust in God. Spiritual abuse is the ultimate betrayal and hurt. I didn't go to church in Springfield except for Christmas with my secretary, and I didn't plan on going when I moved to St. Louis. I was fine with God, but I had challenges with His people.

During my first month in St. Louis, a stranger approached me in a restaurant and invited me to his church, Church on the Rock. He said it was Family and Friends Day. Perhaps he was being kind by calling me family. I tried to return the kindness because he fulfilled the Great Commission issued by Jesus in Mark 16. It was a kind thing to do, but I couldn't be led to church simply because of a stranger's kindness. His kindness could have been pharisaic. A week later, my secretary asked if I had a church home and mentioned a wonderful church in St. Peters, Missouri. I stopped her mid-sentence because God was teaching me how He speaks in various ways to confirm what I was thinking and feeling in my spirit, so I asked her if it was Church on the Rock, which she confirmed. Although I felt led by the Spirit to go, I thanked her and told myself that I loved God, but I would not be going to Church on the Rock. I couldn't fathom going to any church. The church hurt was too painful.

I rebuked every thought of people suggesting I return to church. I was certain it could NOT be God leading me to the place that caused so much pain. I had a long talk with God and thought He understood it was too painful for me ever to go back. Although I didn't get a response from God personally, I felt secure that He was fine with my decision until He reminded me these were His people and that I couldn't ignore, hate, despise, or reject them while loving Him. I reasoned what was impossible with man was possible with God.

Several times, I asked God's forgiveness for my rejection of His people, but I wanted nothing to do with them.

One Saturday, I woke in the middle of the night and heard a voice saying, *In the morning, you need to go to Church on the Rock.* I wanted to pretend I was confused, but I knew God was omniscient and knew everything. He knew I didn't want to go because I was afraid to be hurt again. I always wanted to obey God, so I searched online for Church on the Rock in St. Peters, Missouri, the following day. I was interrupted by several panic attacks as I dressed and had to let them run their course. I wasn't spiritually healed enough to understand the power and authority I possessed to rebuke the attacks. I cried as I drove to the church. I felt like God betrayed me, but I knew He guided me even when I didn't know why. The father wound from Harold made me feel betrayed by God. A father wound affects a survivor of Childhood Trauma, especially sexual abuse by a father or father figure, by creating an inability to feel or express emotions, be intimate, or interact freely with love. In adulthood, a father wound may be transferred to the Heavenly Father with the same dysfunctional relationship dynamics. I could not trust God—even though I understood I needed to trust Him—until I recognized and processed the effects of my father wounds from Harold serving as my surrogate father.

As I drove into the parking lot, people waved and smiled. I was angry after what I had suffered, but they waved and smiled. The people at this church hadn't done anything to me. Seeing them reminded me of the other churches I attended and of the other church people who inflicted abuse. It was an emotional overload.

People at the doors to the church smiled and welcomed me. I didn't appreciate their effort because I didn't want to feel welcomed. I wanted to go home where no one would hurt me. I trusted God, not them, but I could not understand why He led me to them. In the sanctuary, I saw a diverse congregation of several ethnicities and cultures in the sanctuary. *Surely, heaven must be something like this!* Even so, I wasn't ready to go to heaven yet. Throughout the service, I was anxious and trembled. The pastor's wife spoke and prayed over the congregation. *Wait, I liked that.* I liked her prayer. She prayed for me without knowing me. She prayed for those with depression. *That was me.* She prayed for those who had mental problems. *That was me.* She prayed for those laden with fear. *That was me.* She rebuked the enemy. After she spoke, the pastor prayed for me, too. He said, "God, heal those who have *church hurt.* I stand in the gap for them now. I speak healing over them."

Who are these people? How did they know me? Their prayers deeply touched me, but not enough to want to return.

Although I didn't want to return, I knew I had to continue to go until God said I could stop going. Each time I attended services, the pastor and his wife prayed over the congregation and spoke of healing. I kept waiting for God to tell me, "OK, that's enough. You proved you love me. Now you don't have to go anymore," like He did with Abraham (Genesis: 22:12-14), but He never did. After I had attended a few months, God spoke to me and said, "You can't love Me and not love My people." That was hurtful because I couldn't trust church people. How could I love them when I didn't trust them? I had misapplied the scripture about what was impossible with man but was possible with God (Luke 18:27) to fit my agenda of protecting myself from church people. God told me that I couldn't dislike His people whom I could see while loving Him whom I couldn't see. I knew then this LOVE thing would require more work, growth, and maturity.

When I understood, I learned how to accept people and take them at their word until they showed me differently. I also learned I couldn't judge a person solely by one thing they said or did because people are human and make mistakes. God gives grace to the humble. Dr. Maya Angelou said, "When people show you who they are, believe them." I concluded that whatever a person consistently does is who they are, and I became able to give grace to people when they hurt me. As my eyes opened and I watched their behaviors, I gave them grace but learned I didn't have to give hurtful people space in my life. Spiritual maturity assigns a character to a person based on what they do consistently or over time. Spiritual maturity is transformational. I have been at Church on the Rock since I resumed attending church because I continue learning and growing from the leaders' teaching. My life has been immensely enriched under their leadership. I matured when I accepted the fact that there are no perfect people, so there can't be a perfect church.

Chapter 61
THE STRANGER

By January 2016, it had been nearly two years since I left my prestigious and well-paying job. My emotions were stable, and my behavior was more predictable. I was definitely on the road to recovery because I felt the urge to return to graduate school and look for work. With a nearly depleted bank account, I prayed, *God, please help me. I need an income. Please let me get a job. I will work anywhere.* Although I said those words, I didn't mean them per se. By anywhere, I meant somewhere using my Master's Degree in Secondary Education. Since He is all-knowing, I assumed He knew that and would consider it when providing a job for me. Again, I thought God was clear on my desires even though I was less than clear in my communication and intention.

I wonder how long we suffer needlessly because we want our will to be done instead of God's Will? And then when we pray *His Will Be Done,* Heaven opens up. I didn't feel stable, but I needed a job that didn't require too much thinking. It had to be a simple job where if I forgot something, the consequences weren't dire. Any job would do, and if I got fired for an emotional outburst, it would be fine. I would find another job.

Deciding that I would work didn't eradicate my fear of what I might do if someone said something triggering, but I had to eat and pay bills, so I prayed about where to apply. At this point in my life, I prayed about everything because I learned and accepted that God had nothing to do with the sexual abuse and deception I experienced in church. I prayed for God to give me a job I could handle in a place where He wanted me to be. I had no choice but to trust God to keep my mind and emotions in check because I had to do something. The fear of not getting a job and running out of my savings became greater than the fear of working with people again.

Although I had two degrees, I was emotionally and mentally limited in what I could manage. At that time I still wasn't sure of my actions or reactions in a public place, so I felt it was best that I not hold a public job. I put in a few applications and waited to be called for an interview. I thought I might have sounded too educated for some of the positions, so I turned in a few resumes without listing my degrees. I had a few bites, but no catches. I had gone to several employment agencies and businesses looking for a job, but none of them found a placement. I asked about hospital jobs where I could do data entry, but no one hired me. It was extremely discouraging to be overqualified for a menial job while I felt I was too emotionally and mentally unstable for a professional job.

Each time I thought about the denial of the SSI Disability, I broke down. I saw people who could work but chose to get assistance instead. I wasn't trying to beat the system, I only wanted the system not to beat me. On top of the stress, nightmares, terrors, and PTSD, I had to figure out how I would continue to pay the tuition and fees to complete the doctoral program. Michael, Drake, and my family thought I still had a nice job and that I was doing extremely well because I was too embarrassed to tell them I resigned, nor did I tell any family or friends I had an emotional and mental breakdown. I was ashamed to tell them I hit rock bottom and that I wasn't doing well. After all, I was the one in the family who made money, had a beautiful family, and was successful. How could I deny them that proud family moment? I could not tell them I was now looking for *any* job that could help cover my bills.

I didn't go without food when I was unemployed because lessons from my childhood kicked in. I knew how to cook black-eyed peas, which I least prefer, but I figured they kept me alive as a child and would keep me alive in my time of need. There was a period in my childhood when I ate them seemingly every day. No cornbread, only black-eyed peas. In a way, I regressed to childhood because I didn't keep many groceries in the pantry. It was one thing to endure poverty as a child when I didn't expect much or know better, but another thing entirely to be poor as an adult after experiencing a comfortable life with some luxury—or at least, I felt poor. Of course, I was measuring where I was by where I had been not too long before. In my calculation, from employed to unemployed, I was poor. I can see now that it was a matter of perspective. I still had a luxury apartment, a college education, and assets that poor people rarely have.

I walked into a small Chinese takeout restaurant on a Wednesday and looked at the posted menu on the wall. I knew I could buy egg rolls since they came in an order of two for $1.00. They were filling and lasted a long time in my stomach. I had eaten enough black-eyed peas. This Wednesday, I would not eat black-eyed peas. There was too much suffering associated with them.

I noticed a tall man of medium build standing beside the counter. At a glance, it appeared he was waiting for his order because he wasn't standing at the front of the line. In case it had changed, I asked the cashier the price of the egg rolls to confirm how little I could afford and then ordered them. I pretended I had money and asked the stranger about the chicken broccoli. Right away, I felt an overwhelming presence and could hardly talk to him. The sensation was a new experience. At the same time, I sensed he would buy me some food. I simply *felt* it.

The man responded, "I haven't had the chicken broccoli, but order what you want." I knew enough scripture by then to know how God works. I perceived this was a man from God, and I knew if he were, he would know I was hungry and would feed me.

I had to ignore my previous experiences with men and their motives, otherwise I might have missed this God encounter. I focused on the unexplainable presence of God I felt. My mind went back and forth with competing thoughts. I felt like the Tin Man in the *Wizard of Oz* who needed a brain. Now that I had gotten one, I wanted to use it. I analyzed everything. I thought perhaps the man offered to purchase the food and get something from me, but I wasn't attracted to this man, nor did I feel he was interested in me. I carefully analyzed the situation and realized I felt a supernatural presence surrounding him. I was nervous and slightly overwhelmed, but I didn't let that get in the way of my appetite. I was ravenous.

Again, he said, "Order what you want," so I asked for chicken and broccoli with egg rolls and walked to the back of the restaurant to wait for the kitchen staff to prepare the meal. I felt a little sad that I had gotten to the point of prompting a stranger to purchase food for me. I thought I had been at my lowest, but this moment seemed even lower. I sat near a window to allow my tears to flow freely and be away from the kind man.

I felt the stranger approaching me, knowing he would sit near me. I *felt* his presence. I wanted to tell him not to, that I was contagious and some of my low self-esteem, depression, and emotional and spiritual pain might jump on him, but I couldn't. Of course, I knew it wouldn't work. I felt I was too broken, damaged, hurt, ashamed, and depressed to have such a sublime presence near me. The closer He came, the more I wanted to run out of the restaurant without the food, but I was hungry. I felt trapped.

He sat down beside me. I pretended to look out the window. I didn't want him to see my emotions or uncontrollable tears. I stared at the parking lot as we sat in silence. Then he said, "God doesn't want this for you."

First, because of the strong presence of this man, I was afraid. I was afraid that he might say that I had disappointed God. I was ashamed to appear so needy that a stranger bought me food. I didn't ask him what he meant because

I thought I already knew. I listened as he explained, "God has great things in store for you. You don't know who you are in God's eyes."

The tears came faster. *God was the one allowing me to go through this? Didn't He know I had nothing and was nearing homelessness?* I wanted to tell the stranger that if God had anything great, now would be a good time to give it to me. I couldn't control my tears. The more I wiped them away, the faster they fell. Finally, I sobbed, "I don't have any money because God won't give me a job." Who can fight with God?

"You are going to get a job," he responded promptly. *Whoa.* He sounded convinced God was getting me a job. I felt encouraged. I had the thought: *Any job will do.* I thought I meant it.

"You are going to get a job at Walmart."

I stopped him mid-sentence, "Wallllllllmart?!?!? Sir, do you mean THE Walmart? I have several degrees," I said, as if that would explain something to him.

He didn't respond. He seemed unimpressed. I thought maybe he didn't hear me, so I repeated it, hoping that God would tell him the other places I could work since he knew so much about God. I should have been happy my mind was strong enough to work again no matter where, but I had not yet learned how God honors a thankful heart. Proudly, I smiled at him and repeated, "I have several degrees and can do almost anything. I made a résumé without my degrees listed, so I wouldn't be overqualified for jobs that don't require advanced education."

He said, "I know. You will get a job at Walmart." He repeated the same thing he had said earlier. I realized his mind was unchanged, but I sure wished it would. I knew I had to do what this man said. I can't explain it, but I knew he was right.

I asked childishly but seriously, "Sir, is it OK if I get a job at Target?" I tried not to shop at Walmart, much less consider working there. My previous NEA colleagues would think I was a traitor if they found out I worked at Walmart since we were discouraged from shopping there and encouraged our members to boycott in protest of Walmart's employment practices and anti-union policies. Although I no longer worked with NEA, I still felt a loyalty to it and to oppressed workers. I shopped at Walmart occasionally, but after working for NEA, it wasn't my store of choice. The idea of working there did not appeal to me.

This man, whoever he was, meant what he said. All I could think about was Walmart. What would I do there? I couldn't imagine. I was horrified that he said Walmart.

While I thought about Walmart, the man continued, "God is going to use you, but there are things you must learn first. You will get a job at Walmart before Friday. You have many gifts and talents that you don't know you have."

At that time, the only talent I counted on was public speaking. I wasn't sure about writing. I loved to write poetry, so if that counted, that was two talents. My employment history indicated I could teach and train teachers in best practices for reaching students. I had a proven record of advocacy and problem resolution for Missouri NEA. Not to mention, I am one of those people who rarely hesitate to speak to a stranger, as evidenced by this conversation. Since the breakdowns and leaving MNEA, however, my self-confidence had taken a big hit, and I didn't consider working with teachers something that I could or might do again.

The kind stranger started telling me about himself. "Twenty years ago, I felt called into the ministry but wasn't ready. I preached for a few years and then decided God never told me to *go*. I merely went after He called me." Hmmm, that sounded familiar to me. Perhaps the man was deceived by his lack of waiting on God for the *go* sign. The man continued, "I stepped down, and many were disappointed in me when I did, but I knew God hadn't said *go*. Ten years later, He said *go,* and I went. I was ready. You don't want to go until He tells you to *go.*"

I felt this encounter was supernatural because the stranger confirmed first that there was a call, but then there was a waiting period before going. There is also a period required to train and develop to serve effectively. The waiting period is for equipping. Most people are not fully equipped and ready during the call. I wrote a poem while in Springfield titled, "Why Not Me?" I was inspired to write the poem when God taught me about His character and the waiting period. The poem speaks of people God called but did not tell them to *go*. They erroneously *went* because they thought *the call* was enough. In the poem, those who were called differed from those who were called and *released* to go. I knew from the poem if God ever called me, I needed to wait until He said the word, *go. Go* would signal that he had equipped me with everything I needed for the assignment.

God helped me to understand that calling is the first step. He called Moses, Joseph, King David, and the disciples, but they were released only at a specific time. The stranger taught me that God will let me know when it's time to go after He calls. Sure enough, God called me years before He sent me. I am thankful for the teaching from this stranger because when I felt called by God, I did not move until I heard the word, *go*. When I get an idea now, I still wait for God to release me or tell me when to go. It helps me to avoid moving in the flesh and acting because I have an idea or feel I can do the work. The truth is we may be able to do the work in the beginning stages, but the ones who didn't wait for Him to send them seem to wane, whereas those whom He sends get stronger over time. God does exactly what He promised to do for them: *Renew their strength like an eagle* (Isaiah 40:31).

I thought I'd try again to ask the stranger if Walmart was the only place I could work. I asked him the third time, desperately trying to escape it.

"What if Walmart doesn't hire me?" I wanted him to say something about the other jobs I had applied for since he knew so much. He never mentioned any of them. I finally accepted that I was to be obedient to this stranger. I had been taken in by deception many times, but I had been healing and learning to discern situations and spirits for nearly five years at this point, so I knew this wasn't deception. I resolved to drink from the bitter cup of shame and humiliation yet again, or at least, that was my perception during the healing years because I still had too much pride to see this as an opportunity rather than a punishment. I did not feel grateful to God because I couldn't visualize the heaven-sent golden time of equipping He provided me.

I thanked the kind stranger for the meal and told him the idea of working at Walmart was difficult to accept, but I would do it. We walked out of the restaurant together, but because I was so distraught over the idea of Walmart, I didn't look back at him as I got into my car and drove away. Upon leaving, I thought it was kind of the man to buy dinner, counsel me, and give directions. I thought critically about everything that happened and asked myself: *Did he try to get anything from me? Did he try to seduce me? Did he try to get personal information? How did I feel while talking with him? Why was he so kind to me?* I concluded each answer was *no* because he never asked my name or where I lived. He only offered advice and help as he met me in a time of need and provided answers to my prayers. I knew this was not of the flesh. I knew God alone sent him.

While I accepted that meeting the kind stranger in the Chinese restaurant was a supernatural experience, I couldn't fathom God sending me to work at Walmart because Walmart didn't fit my perception of how God did things. Experiences like this helped me to be less critical of the children of Israel and their disobedience.

The day after I met the stranger, I didn't do anything he told me to do because I felt I could get a better job and knew I was overqualified to work at Walmart. Instead, I went to a hiring agency, which is an example of how easy it was for me to do the wrong thing, even when I was 100% sure what to do. It's called rebellion. I don't like this word, but that was what I did: I rebelled against authority, which is quite common for CT survivors. It's not wise to do it with God.

At the hiring agency, a middle-aged Caucasian man behind a desk asked a few questions:

Will you be on time?
Will you come back after your first check?
Will you miss work if you don't have a babysitter?
Will you use the bus ticket?

Mentally, I rolled my eyes as he went through his questions. He had an application indicating that I was once a licensed, certified teacher and I worked for Missouri NEA. Why did he ask these ridiculous questions?

Then he looked up and said, "Oh my! I see how much money you made at your last job and your education credentials...." His voice trailed off as he flipped my résumé over and read more.

"You should be interviewing me. I don't have the education, training, or skills you have." He didn't smirk or sound sarcastic. He merely stated the truth of what he read. "You are overqualified for this temporary job."

I held my tears, knowing he told the truth. I wondered if he thought that overqualified people didn't need jobs. I'd heard human resource screeners automatically assume overqualified people won't stay. However, with high turnover rates at some companies, why not get six good months from a responsible professional rather than a bad year with an irresponsible unprofessional? I didn't factor in the costs of hiring, training, and developing, or the possibility that other professionals weren't as responsible as I thought I was. Maybe HR is more of a numbers game than I know. He said he wished he could help, but because of my education, he couldn't. I wished I hadn't shared that I had degrees, but it was too late. He couldn't unknow.

I left feeling defeated, dejected, and desperate. I had a pity party in the car for a few minutes before the stranger's words popped into my head. *Go to Walmart. You will get the job before Friday.* It was Thursday. I spoke to the stranger on Wednesday and half-completed the Walmart application. I thought

Walmart wouldn't call because I couldn't get a job anywhere. If Walmart didn't call, I wouldn't be disappointed. I submitted online résumés daily, and every answer was a variation on the theme of over-qualification: *We couldn't do that to you. It wouldn't be fair to give you a job making less than you deserve,* or *You wouldn't be happy at this job.*

Instead of going home to finish the Walmart application, I went to another temporary agency where they advertised they hired on the spot. Everyone sitting in the place looked beaten down by life. I greeted the employee at the counter, handed over a résumé, and told her I could do most any office, education, or training work. I added that I would learn if I didn't know something.

The woman took my résumé and read it as I stood waiting. Then she said, "I'm so sorry, but we don't have anything you can do."

I wasn't past begging, but I knew it wouldn't work, so I turned around and walked out. When I got outside, I heard an inner voice say, *Go to Walmart. You will get a job by Friday.* With each rejection, I heard the still small voice say, *Do what the stranger told you to do.* He told me *that door would open other doors.* I try to obey God quickly when He gives instructions, but in this situation, I found it difficult to humble myself and complete a Walmart application.

The more desperate I became, the more appealing Walmart seemed. I shook my head no, but my heart said *Yes, I must be obedient.* It was nearly 5:00 p.m., and I was tired, desperate, and hungry. I went home and had another pity party. As I began to cry, I heard the voice again: *Go to Walmart. You will get a job by Friday.* I contemplated applying for jobs until 8:00 p.m. On my computer, I pulled up the half-finished Walmart application that I began with no intention of completing. I couldn't believe I was applying for a job at Walmart! Although I cried, I knew I did the right thing because I felt at peace. I also knew I would get a job because of the stranger's words. His words were as if God spoke.

As I hit submit on the Walmart Careers webpage, I felt a weight fall from me. All I could think was *I can't believe I applied to work at Walmart!* It was surreal, like an out-of-body experience. I fell asleep in disbelief, but I quickly became a believer the next morning.

Walmart HR called Friday morning. "Hello, Ms. Wallace. You applied for a job, and we want to know if you can come in for an interview at 10:00 this morning."

I arrived professionally dressed because that was the only way I knew how to dress for an interview. I wore blue and white—the standard interview blue suit with a white blouse, stockings, and heels.

The interviewer didn't ask about my previous job, although my work history was on the application. Turnovers were high, and she was probably glad to see someone dressed professionally for a job interview. She didn't ask about my goals or plans to move up in the company. She discussed Walmart's expectations, policies, and procedures. I could tell Walmart needed a worker as badly as I needed a job, and she wasn't concerned about how long I planned to stay. It was a tonal shift from the other companies that wouldn't hire and often predicted I wouldn't stay long because I was overqualified. I was overqualified for Walmart, yet they offered me a job. The interview lasted about fifteen minutes.

Then she said, "You applied to push carts?" She asked as if she thought there was a mistake on the application. I was surprised, too. I clenched my teeth and lips together, so I didn't seem ungrateful or too snobby. At that point, I needed a job. Pushing carts was not my dream job, but it would work for now.

I didn't recall applying to be a cart pusher. St. Louis has torrid temperatures in the summer, so I knew not to do that. I couldn't explain what happened. Perhaps the stranger had something to do with it. I didn't know, but I knew I could not be a cart pusher in real life. At that point, I prayed *Lord, please excuse me from pushing carts. It is enough to work at Walmart.* When I completed the application the night before, I remembered that the online system kept freezing. I had to exit the system several times and sign back in to finish the application. Perhaps that's what happened, but I did not request a position as a cart pusher. I was desperate, but not that desperate.

"No, the computer froze up several times while I was in the application system," I said.

"Okay, well, we thought you wanted to push carts. There's an opening for that right now. What other job would you like to do?" She asked.

"I applied, I mean, I thought I applied, for cashier or something clerical," I stumbled.

She consulted her computer and said, "I see several cart pusher positions but not much else." Disappointedly, she looked up at me, "It doesn't look like we have anything else right now." I wanted to say *Praise the Lord! God is going to give me another job at some other place.* I strongly felt that God didn't call me to be a cart pusher.

Yessssss! I thought. *I don't have to work at Walmart, and perhaps the stranger was not a messenger from God.* I felt like I had caught God in something He couldn't escape. The interviewer searched again for a position on her listings. She found nothing but tried encouraging me as she said, "Positions come open every second."

I waited for a few minutes as she scrolled through the list. I didn't want to be rude, but I was about to thank her for her time and leave. Somehow, I avoided getting a job at Walmart. Then her eyes widened, and she smiled like she was doing me a favor as she announced, "Looks like a position came open a second ago for a Customer Service Representative."

I was stunned. I prayed for a job—but not this one nor this place, but I can't tell God how to answer my prayer when I pray. The CSR position opened because it was for me. I did not want to work at Walmart, and especially not in customer service, but I knew I had no choice. I was stuck on the words *customer service at Walmart.* I guess it was payback time. I recalled how rudely I treated Walmart customer service representatives before I healed. I had a nasty attitude and was disrespectful. Now, it would be my turn.

The interviewer asked me, "Do you think you can work in customer service?" Her question was not if I *could*. Rather, she asked whether I *wanted* to work as a Walmart CSR. I was still lost in thought. "Are you okay with that?" she asked again, looking directly at me. I needed time to talk to God. I wanted to talk to Him about how I felt regarding Walmart, but He wouldn't hear me like He wouldn't hear Moses when Moses told Him he was too inarticulate to represent God to His people. I was like a little kid waiting for permission from an adult when I already knew the answer—I simply didn't like the answer.

"Great, I accept it." I felt my mouth say those words, but my heart said, *No, thank you.* I knew Walmart was exactly where I was supposed to be, so I said, "Thank you for hiring me and giving me a chance to work." Up and down was the battle between my head and my heart. *Yes. No. Of course not. What if someone sees me? There are other places to work. I am crazy for listening to that stranger. I have degrees!* Despite those thoughts, I knew this job offer was God's work. I had to ignore the dissenting non-God thoughts.

"Ok, we'll see you Sunday." The interviewer's voice interrupted my indecisiveness.

It didn't take a second for me to respond in a high-pitched tone that I'm sure she noticed and heard, "Sunday? I'm sorry, ma'am. I don't work on Sundays. I work at my church on Sundays, so I can't work here." I was serious. I was a greeter at church and took my church work seriously because I was thankful I could attend church. I viewed it as work for God, and I couldn't stop working for God to take this job God provided. I knew Hebrews 10:25 said Believers should not neglect to get together to encourage each other. God gave me grace when I couldn't go to church due to church wounds, but at that point, I was healing, and I didn't want to miss church.

A hidden smile came into my heart as if to say to God, *It looks like Walmart won this one.* Of course, God knew my smugness, but I felt He had hit a hard obstacle because this was Walmart! For once, I rooted for Walmart. I admit I wanted to tell God *I'm so sorry that the repulsive job you had for me at Walmart didn't work out.* Truthfully, I was glad for this obstacle. I never wanted to work there anyway. Surely, God tested me to see if I would accept such a low position. Any minute now, God would do me like he did Abraham, telling me I passed the test and that I don't have to work at Walmart. I was sure He knew I had too many college degrees to work there. I had silently hoped Walmart would say no, yet I knew in my heart that God, in His omnipotence, could overthrow Walmart's power if He wanted me to work there.

I thanked the recruiter for the interview and began to leave because I knew God would not have me work on the Sabbath. It was a personal conviction that I would not compromise. I felt great because I chose to stand for something I valued. Roy E. Disney was right when he said, "When your values are clear to you, making decisions becomes easier." It was easy for me to say no to working on Sunday because that was a no-compromise zone.

Then, something jolted me out of my self-congratulatory reverie. The interviewer looked up from her schedule and said, "Well, if you don't tell anyone, we will let you skip Sundays. But don't tell anyone because everyone who works for Walmart must work on Sunday." She repeated as if I didn't understand the first time that every employee worked on Sunday. She said, "Even managers work on Sundays." I thought *Yes, ma'am, managers would be a part of everyone.*

I understood. I looked at her, and she reiterated, "It's mandatory."

You already explained that, I thought. *Why are you continuing to tell me? I understand, and I am okay with your decision.* I never commented after she said it was mandatory because I was clear I wasn't working on Sunday. That was my value, and I didn't need to explain it further, so I walked toward the door. As I reached for the doorknob to exit the interview room, she said, "But since you don't work on Sundays, we can change the schedule—but seriously, you can't tell anyone." I thought, *Woman, if you hire me, I will tell everyone because I don't want to work here anyway. You don't have to do this. Please don't change your mind on my account. Stick to your rules and policies.* Instead, I meekly said, "Thank you so much." I knew God had opened the job position for me and made that woman hire me. She walked me to the front entrance and told me I was to report to work the following week.

Chapter 62

WALMART CSR

As I watched a Walmart training video, I thought, *I can do this. I should be a trainer. Maybe I can work in customer service for a few months and transfer to training.* I was not content with a job as a Customer Service Representative. I wanted to do anything except customer service. I hadn't begun working but was already trying to help God find another placement that wasn't so detrimental to what I called "my character" or would more closely match my education and experience. I reminded myself that God sent me to this job for a reason and that I needed to be obedient. I convinced myself that I wouldn't be a CSR for more than thirty days, so I adjusted my attitude, telling myself I could endure almost anything for thirty days. God never mentioned the number thirty to me, but I had to think of something positive to help me endure the enforced humility. Surely, He wouldn't make me stay any longer than that, especially with the multiple skills and talents I had! I guess I needed something to help me get through the early days at Walmart, and I thought knowing it was only for a short time would help. Thankfully, I was stronger emotionally and mentally, but I was still financially insecure. I needed money to pay my mounting bills, but more important was my obedience to God because obedience gave me an unexplainable peace. I knew a job without obedience to God would have only helped in the short run. I had to obey God if I wanted to continue to heal.

I worked at a large Walmart Supercenter in a suburban area. Once I decided I wouldn't be there longer than thirty days, I was the best employee I could be. I smiled daily, and the store manager shared weekly reports of what the customers had said about me. They said I was consistently pleasant and helpful, which increased my confidence.

One of my requests to God was to let me make more than minimum wage, and HR told me I started at three dollars above minimum wage. I thought that was good, but after only a few months, I received a notice of a raise. I was so excited. God heard my prayers. As hard as I worked, I assumed I would get at least a five-dollar raise. I went the extra mile and a half.

Customer satisfaction and pleasing God were the two most important things to me.

The manager praised me and relayed how the customers talked and that some had even said they went home when I wasn't at work and returned when I was there. I smiled because it proved I was making a positive difference. I wanted God to get the glory because I worked for Him. The manager continued to rave about how I went above and beyond for the customers and that some had even called the home office to sing my praises. The more she talked about how great an employee I was, the wider my smile grew. Then the great news came. I was on the edge of my seat.

"You're doing such a great job. You are getting a five cents-an-hour raise," she said.

My balloon burst. I used to get $5,000 raises on my NEA job, and Walmart came with five cents an hour more? What had I fallen to? From the prefrontal cortex to my brain stem, I silently yelled, *What is five cents? You can keep that. Don't ask me to come into this office again for five cents. Five cents is an insult and does not encourage me. It makes me want to quit!* God was still working with me about the Fruit of the Spirit (Galatians 5:22-2). I was especially lacking in self-control.

Instead, I held my peace. "Thank you for the raise."

I'm sure my lack of gratitude spoke louder than my acknowledgment. I was infuriated because I felt insulted by this minimal raise. I walked out of the office smiling, but I felt anything but joyous.

Thank God, it was the end of the day. I had no smiles left in me, not even for Jesus. God was healing me and blessed me with a job. Why did I feel so unloved and ungrateful? I walked back to the service desk in unbelief. *How could they offer me, as educated as I am, only five cents more an hour? How could they not know this was unfair? How could they think someone with my skills and talents would even want to work at a service desk for one minute— much less every day? How could they?*

The angry thoughts and ingratitude haunted me for days. I had taught workshops and conducted training on positive thinking for over fifteen years, but I struggled when I needed to apply that training. I am thankful for the training because it allowed me to fight through the negative thoughts, or I know it would have been worse. I was in a low place with no confidence. Mitchell was my friend, and we hung out together and sometimes went to social events together, but I didn't want to unload my problems on him since we weren't technically dating. I didn't want to weigh him down with my struggles, so I soldiered on alone.

God taught me the power of words and affirmations, so I had to think about everything I said before I spoke. The scripture, *You shall be satisfied with what comes from your mouth* (Proverbs 18:21-22 and Mark 11: 23) often came to mind. I knew that God would give me what I said because speech attracts action; however, I found very little I could say to protect my pride since pride is not something God intends for us to protect.

After only four months at the beautiful suburban Walmart, I had a dream that made me aware I would transfer to another Walmart: the Walmart in Ferguson, Missouri. Ferguson is the St. Louis municipality where a Caucasian policeman shot Michael Brown on August 9, 2014. More than two thousand National Guard troops patrolled the streets for eight days because of public uproar from riots protesting injustice after the district attorney refused to indict the police officer. Two years later, Ferguson still wasn't an area where I wanted to work. After the horror of past dreams, I knew not to trust any dreams without God's confirmation. If I were to transfer, He would have to make it clear to me. Ferguson was the demographic opposite of the suburban community where I began with Walmart. I thought I was tested and tried by fire on every hand, but I was not afraid to go to Ferguson because I knew God's character enough to know that if He sent me, nothing and no one could touch me. I requested a transfer and spoke with the managers. I felt their trepidation because of Ferguson's reputation, as they strongly advised me not to transfer. I was comfortable at the suburban Walmart; I enjoyed the customers' praise and dreaded working somewhere less appealing. Ironically, the community of Ferguson eventually hosted the first year of meetings for Tower of Hope Ministries, so moving to the Ferguson Walmart was part of God's plan.

I dismissed many dreams, especially after I had the dream to drive to Texas in an ice storm and thought God told me to do it. Now, I know not to act on a dream without confirmation. I had the transfer dream again, but God showed me that a co-worker would transfer to Ferguson first, and I would follow later. Again, I rebuked that dream and asked God for more confirmation, not because I had no clarity but because I didn't want to transfer. I was blessed that He didn't discipline me for that disobedience! God knew I wanted one more confirmation because moving was a huge transition, and past deceptions haunted me.

Four months after the second dream, my co-worker transferred to the Ferguson Walmart. I heard that still, small voice say *Be ready to transfer in a few months.* That was the final confirmation. At that time, I couldn't transfer to Ferguson even if I wanted to because there was no opening, but God opens positions when He's ready, as I had already experienced. For the time being, I waited.

I continued to strain my brain to discover how working at the Ferguson Walmart would benefit me. I felt a deep rejection by God as I waited for a month. Rejection is familiar to survivors of Complex PTSD (C-PTSD) due to chronic traumatization over long periods. I felt triggers and residuals from multiple perceived rejections. Another trait I noticed about myself and survivors of trauma is how easily discouraged we are. I believe it is because of low self-esteem. It doesn't take much to believe that we can't do something or are not worth it after being raised to believe we aren't worth anything and treated like we have no value.

Finally, Mitchell weighed in, "You have to take your own medicine. You give everyone else such great advice about being strong, and now it's time to take your own sip. Why can't you do it?"

His words hit me like someone with amnesia whose memory returns in a flash. Clarity flooded in. I realized I was fighting against God when I needed to submit to Him. I didn't think I could submit to God because I couldn't imagine Him leading me to work at another Walmart. I thought I would only be at the first Walmart for thirty days, yet it had been five months. I knew I had to transfer and continue my God-given path, so I applied again to transfer. I also felt the transfer was necessary and would prepare me for whatever He called me to do. The stranger's words returned to me and confirmed that first I was called, but I would have to wait to go. A few weeks later, a position opened, and I began working at the Ferguson Walmart. The transition was challenging because I worked for ungrateful twenty-year-old supervisors who were distasteful and disrespectful. With each move, God provided me with an opportunity for growth, and I did not appreciate it, but I learned more about myself and the healing I needed with each transition.

A few weeks after working in the Ferguson position, my friend Debra and I met for lunch. I hadn't yet told her I worked for Walmart. I kept it a secret from almost everyone and told the few who knew not to tell anyone. I decided it was time to tell her. I had met Debra seven years earlier when I worked for Missouri NEA in Springfield. Although she lived in St. Louis, we had met at one of the Missouri NEA conferences. She was the vice-president of her local at a St. Louis school district where she was first a teacher, then an administrator. In 2014, she was still an NEA member. She boycotted Walmart her entire adult life because she didn't like the ways she experienced maltreatment of employees, its anti-union position, and because of the massive income differential between the Walton family members who directed the Walmart empire and the front line workers.

Debra and her union leadership staff wrote the first collectively-bargained contract for her district. Her district adopted and knew the value of union representation. She still has a strong sense of social justice and equity. Knowing her values and commitment to her belief in boycotting Walmart discouraged me from sharing about my job. Although we were close, I had kept most of the details of the previous two years from her. She only knew about my divorce but did not know any details about my breakdown, resignation, and subsequent healing journey. She never challenged my charade when we were together. She let me know that she loved me as I was and never asked probing questions that might have uncovered what happened.

I looked away so as not to look her in the eye. "I have something to tell you. I haven't told you because I was too ashamed. I am sorry. You've never judged me, but I couldn't discuss it. I simply couldn't tell you about it."

"What is it? You know I don't care what it is. I'll still feel the same about you," she assured me. She didn't have to. I knew she was an excellent friend and accepted me as I was. She thought highly of me, encouraged me, and believed I could do anything I set my mind to. She supported me through the Springfield years and during my time in St. Louis without knowing the details, and I felt bad for not telling her about Walmart because keeping it a secret had nothing to do with her. It had to do with me and my insecurities.

"It's not you. It's me. I couldn't tell you," I assured her.

After everything I had been through, she was still my cheerleader. She and I often talked about how one day she would work with me and my organization, Tower of Hope Ministries. I had so much hope and wanted her to have hope for me. None of the stuff I went through supported that hope, but she was optimistic nonetheless.

"I have been working," I said to test the waters. She continued to smile and encourage me as was her way. I was looking for her demeanor to change, but it didn't. As far as she knew, I wasn't working. She remained calm as I saw her processing underneath her beautiful, purple-framed glasses.

"Where?"

"Well, that's what's so hard to tell you. I feel like I betrayed my values and those who believed in me. I am so sorry. I don't know why it's so hard to tell you." I stumbled over my words. She's kind, loving and generous, but she's growing in the fruit of patience. She cut me off.

"Where is this place that you're so ashamed of? It's not a nightclub, is it? I mean, you're not pole dancing or anything, so why would you be ashamed?" she said, smiling. Pole dancing was about as high on my list of preferred jobs as the one I had at the Ferguson Walmart.

"I'm working at Walmart. I already know how you feel about it, but God told me to get a job there. I don't know why. I prayed and prayed, but I couldn't get a job anywhere else, and Walmart was the only place that would hire me. I know exactly what you want to say." I rambled on, trying to think of everything she could and would say or think before she said it. Maybe it would soften the blow of her words. I continued as she listened. I didn't need quietness or stillness, so I rambled on. I needed words. "I feel so bad, and I don't understand why God sent me there. Out of all the places to work, He sent me to Walmart, and I am struggling." I felt the tears fall. "This can't be what God has for me. Maybe I made a mistake. I don't think I'll be there long —at least, I hope I won't. I am so disappointed, so I know God is disappointed in me." I had already been at Walmart for almost a year. I don't know why I said I won't be there long. The truth is, I had already been there longer than I expected. I must have gone on too long, and she looked at me with excitement and a huge smile.

"What a great place for you!" she exclaimed.

I had to ensure she heard where I said I worked because that wasn't the expected response, so I repeated, "I work at Walmart."

"Yeah, I know. I said that's a great place for you for the type of work you do."

What does she mean for the type of work I do? I thought. *I help heal broken people.*

She said simply, "Dora, that's *The Well*." The expression on her face and voice told me that she expected that I would know what she meant, as if what she had said would've been clear to anyone listening.

I was perplexed. I had no idea what she meant by *The Well*. Debra is not one to preach or teach Jesus openly, so when she spoke, I knew God was speaking through her.

"Remember, *The Well* was where a lot of people met Jesus. All kinds of people came to Him at the well to be taught, healed, and set free. It was where the poorest of the poor came and met Jesus. *The Well* is where everyone eventually had to go to get their water for the day. It was a common meeting place in His day. If Jesus were here today, He would heal people at Walmart."

Wait, what just happened? Did she teach me a lesson about Jesus? Wow!

My eyes opened. My heart felt like it would explode. I understood her explanation as if a spiritual bolt of lightning had shot through my brain and illuminated everything I needed to know. If it were a movie, the clouds would've parted, the sun would've come streaming through, and a chorus of angels would have sung hallelujah! I wanted to sing the Hallelujah Chorus!

"So I represent Jesus," I said, needing confirmation of my understanding. I was a Bible scholar at sixteen years old, yet here I was needing to be taught that Jesus was with the poor and hurting people of His time. "God sent me to Walmart because He wanted me to help *those* hurting people!" That was enlightening. Wow!

It's odd how many Christians think that if they can only leave their current job and go *someplace* to work for God, they can serve Him. We don't think He's where we don't want to be or where our flesh cringes, but He is. We are closest to God in the humblest state of humility.

"How did you end up at *The Well*?" she asked.

Suddenly, my perception of Walmart changed. I felt accepted and proud to work there, and I could tell the story. I explained about my fruitless job search that ended with the stranger in the Chinese restaurant who told me I would have a job at Walmart by Friday.

"So, which one?" she interrupted. She never liked to be led on. She needed details and needed them fast. "Is it the one near your neighborhood?"

"I was in St. Peters. They loved me there. I know it sounds weird, but I enjoyed working there. I enjoyed the work, helping people, doing things no one else wanted to do. For me, it was more than a job. It was customer service."

She smiled, "I am not shocked you like it. You are committed to whatever you do. I am glad you like it." I wished everyone had a friend like Debra.

I stopped her.

"But that's not the end of it. I don't work at that store anymore. I had a dream that I was supposed to transfer to another Walmart, and I did, but that's not it either," I exclaimed, feeling relaxed.

"So, which store did He send you to?"

Debra was already half smiling like she knew how God worked. Again, Debra prefers details over unnecessary talking. I needed her not to yank the rug from under me. The transition to Ferguson had already done that.

"Ferguson."

Debra laughed, and so did I. I didn't need to say anything. She was 100% sure God led me there. To go from a store where I never had a customer complaint to a store where everyone had problems upon problems had to be God's direction. The betrayal I felt by God when He sent me to Walmart turned out to be part of His Faithfulness. He wanted to use me at *The Well*.

Debra was laughing so hard she could hardly ask any more questions. I was laughing, too. "Wow, you went from St. Peters to Ferguson," she chuckled.

Debra lived near Ferguson and was very familiar with the community.

"So how is it really, working at Ferguson?"

I told her I had learned a lot from the people at *The Well*. I also told her I learned to accept what I could not change.

I am eternally grateful for the clarity I got about my purpose at Walmart. Perspective can indeed change everything. After the conversation with Debra, my perception of Walmart changed. I went from dreading work to going in early, volunteering to stock the shelves, volunteering to work with the toughest customers, and being exceptionally kind to them. Please note: it took the Fruit of the Spirit every day, and the days I lacked Fruit were when I ended up in my supervisor's office explaining what happened. My assignment at Walmart lasted eighteen months, much longer than I would have anticipated.

Instead of looking for problems with the customers, I looked for answers to help solve the customers' problems—and there were many daily. Sometimes, they couldn't find the ladies' T-shirts, sour cream, or the WD40. Whatever they couldn't find, I gladly volunteered to help locate. While helping them, they would talk about how they suffered emotionally, physically, mentally, or spiritually. I listened to them. Often, they needed encouragement. Some asked me to pray with them. I was surprised that they would ask a stranger to pray with them. Interestingly, I was never afraid of being fired for praying with customers. I considered it to be part of my job. It wasn't on my job description for Walmart, but it was for Jesus. Since Jesus hired me, I thought doing His work at *The Well* was fine. The store managers and customers noted my friendly attitude and excellent customer service. What a difference it made to find my purpose! There were days my co-workers and customers challenged me in my purpose, but at *The Well,* I learned self-control and to practice the Fruit of the Spirit and the strength of humility.

The Walmart experience helped me to understand what I meant when I told God, *If You need somebody, send me.* What most of us mean is *If You need somebody going where I'm already going and traveling the road I'm already on, and in my comfort zone, You can send me.* Once I told God I would go, He could use me. I surrendered, and it was too late to say that I didn't know what I was saying—which is what I assuredly felt. I permitted God to inconvenience me anytime, use me anytime, and transfer me anytime if he needed me. What was I thinking?

I learned many things at *The Well,* but the biggest lessons were humility and trust. The meaning of true humility is to be a willing servant. Saying that I trust God and trusting Him are two different things. I learned humility required that I not care about my reputation and credentials. It is unashamedly choosing, like Moses, to be with *the least of them*—the oppressed and broken. Humility is serving people who have nothing to give beyond *thank you.* Humility is putting others' needs first. Humility is helping someone who may never say thank you. It serves everyone as if they might be Jesus or an angel in disguise.

While working for Walmart, I continued to work on my doctorate. I swept Walmart's floors, learned the cash register system, and was yelled at by angry customers, all while experiencing PTSD. It was extremely stressful to recall which buttons to push for returns. I asked God to help my brain learn the process. There were times I wanted to run to the back of the store and cry, and I did, but I knew God sent me there to heal my mind. Through this experience, I learned God gives me clarity and help to do whatever He tells me to do.

From then on, I never worried again about doing something God told me to do. I would tell Him, *OK, You told me to do this, so here I am trying to do it. I need You to teach me how to do it.* Every time, no matter the situation, He taught me. That was my process: first, I confirmed God told me to do it. Once that was settled, whatever I needed for the job was His responsibility to provide, whether financial support, healing, protection, or courage. He provided whatever I needed wherever He sent me. Sticking with that sequence takes the onus off me. Working at Walmart was stressful, but I see how God used it to humble me while healing my mind at the same time. Since I previously had a mental and emotional breakdown, I couldn't handle much pressure, and it took God's healing hand to restore my brain.

I learned the reality of being a willing servant and the truth that I wasn't. Working at *The Well* illuminated the heart problem I had. Servants are willing because they know they work for the master, not vice versa. The willing servant is agreeable when the master's plan changes without prior notice. The willing servant's only agenda is to serve the king. I was previously a servant, but not a willing servant, because I would only work if I approved the work He had me to do. Before I learned that Walmart was *The Well,* I was an unwilling servant, and I found it difficult to work there because it seemed anyone could. I thought it was a waste of my time since it required no special skill set, which was ironically the very reason I took the job in the first place. After the lesson on *The Well,* I was a willing servant. How long I stayed at Walmart didn't matter because I knew it was God's purpose and someone needed me. Willing servants love God's people. Every day I went to work, I prayed God would lead me to the person who needed me and that He would show me how to help them.

An example is the man who came into the store shortly after his release from prison and stood before my register. "Good morning. How may I help you?" I said with a genuine smile.

He said, "I just got out of prison and don't want to go back. I don't know what to do."

He looked at me as if he knew I had the answer he needed. I looked at him like I had the help he needed—because I did. Several people waited in line behind him, but I knew I could not let him leave without helping. He was desperate.

"Sir, you don't have to go back to prison. You can live a better life," I said, right there in front of co-workers and customers. This man's desperation was the reason I was there. I didn't care about losing my job. I only had the job because of God. "Would you like me to tell you how? If you say no, that's fine, but I hate to let you leave thinking you have to go back to prison." I talked while continuing to process an item return for him. No one could say I was talking too much. I had learned how to work and talk. Customer Service Representatives are keenly aware of the cameras aimed at us.

"I just need help. If I do what I did before, I will go back to prison," he answered.

"You have to change your mindset." I wanted to keep it simple, so even a fool couldn't misunderstand. "Have you heard of Jesus? He can help you with your mindset."

"Yes, but I don't know much about Him."

"All you need to do is believe in Him and believe that He wants more for you. When you begin reading and applying His Word, He will help you stay out of prison. You can begin with one chapter or one verse a day and focus on that," I said.

Looking confused, he asked, "How do I do that?"

I tried to think of ways to stall him so I could answer his questions. I wondered if whoever watched the camera feed thought I was standing and talking to the customer without carrying out a Walmart task.

"You must accept Jesus into your heart, and your ways will change as you grow in Him," I said. "You were taught wrong, and how you live is wrong. You can't hurt people, take things that aren't yours, or expect someone to take care of you. I know life is hard, but you must be a man and do everything you can to teach your children the right things so they won't go to prison."

He looked at me as if to ask *How do you know why I went to prison?* I hit a button for his signature.

"Got it?"

"Yes," he said.

With the camera pointed at me and customers waiting, I couldn't figure out how to pray for him, so I shook his hand and said, "May God watch over you, protect you, and keep your feet on straight paths. Repeat after me, *I repent of my sins and accept Jesus as my Lord and Savior.*" He repeated my words as I shook his hand. We smiled, and he turned to leave as the next customer approached the register.

"Good morning. It's my pleasure to help you at your local Ferguson Walmart," I joyfully exclaimed.

Someone reading this may think *That woman needs Jesus because she stole time at work. She should only do Walmart's business and not talk to the customers about God.* I thought those same things until I repeatedly helped people who asked for prayer or help to make a life-altering decision. Many wanted to understand something that happened, like the man who didn't want to rob or kill again. He wanted to know what to do to get out of the criminal life because he felt helpless to control his behaviors and choices. Taking a minute to pray for and guide him in the right direction was more important than taking any amount of money I made. Several people told me they tried to commit suicide, and while searching for an item, I was able to tell them how to process their anger, bitterness, or hatred so they could live life. The more I thought about it, the more I remembered the religious people in Jesus' day who talked about Him for violating the law on the Sabbath when he healed someone. They didn't celebrate the man's healing. They looked for ways to discredit Jesus.

I worked while talking to people seeking help. So, I say to the religious person, I could not in good conscience ignore pleas for help and assistance. I could help them, so I shared a few words of wisdom and a few minutes of Walmart's time and showed them how God saw their sorrow to give them hope. It was a win-win. Walmart made money, and the customers got help at *The Well*. My work at *The Well* initiated my understanding of how to help God's people. I am eternally grateful for it.

Chapter 63

ROMANTIC RESTORATION

Mitchell and I had known each other nearly four years. We met in 2011, and 2012 was the beginning of our recovery, emerging from a dark place full of suffering and loss. Mitchell and I prayed separately for God's direction on how to proceed with our relationship. I prayed several times for the Lord to take him out of my life if we weren't supposed to be together, but He never did, so we continued to grow in our friendship. Mitchell's family suffered several deaths, which splintered their closeness, and at that time I wasn't close to my family, either. We had difficult divorces that took a toll on our finances, friendships, and families. We were both starting over after losing everything. The only thing the both of us still had was the heart to find love again, still trust God, and start all over. We grew closer as we came out of our dark places.

I believe love helps us find our way out of the darkness.

I was ready for that next step, but I was still convinced that Mitchell didn't think of me that way. It was clear he liked me, but did he love me? I still struggled with doubts. *You work at Walmart. What educated person works at Walmart unless they are the manager?* I felt I had nothing to offer him. Since God didn't remove him, I thought I would help God out by removing him myself because being in a relationship with him forced me to face things about myself, such as how I didn't like conflict, which is the case with most CT survivors. I also didn't like having to trust him with my heart. I was fine as long as we agreed on things. When I ran away from him emotionally, I expected the Holy Spirit to show me things about Mitchell and how he wasn't right for me. Instead, He revealed things about me. He showed me that I had never experienced an adult relationship. Agreeing with someone on everything or allowing someone to make decisions for you all the time is not a relationship.

When Mitchell and I had difficulties, I always sought for a way out and began thinking about leaving him because I didn't know how to handle conflict. After my mind was healed, I couldn't agree with him on things that didn't give me peace. I was living in my authentic self, and unless you are a passive person, living in your false self, or emotionally immature, you will have conflict. That conflict made me uncomfortable because I didn't know I needed to learn relationship skills. I had been married for over twenty years, and I thought if anyone knew how to have a relationship, I did. I thought I was qualified to teach a class on relationships and marriage. The Holy Spirit revealed to me after several conflicts with Mitchell that I needed to learn how to compromise and that years of marriage don't make you a marriage expert. Understanding the dynamics of marriage, compromising, forgiving, unconditional love, and support in the marriage make you a marriage expert.

When Mitchell and I had differences, I would think he would never call again. That was just a wound from past relationships, childhood abuse, and insecurities. I would become so emotionally upset that I would hang up the phone, leave his house, or just shut down. When he would call to say goodnight, I wouldn't answer. In the beginning I was shocked he called after I wouldn't talk to him or answer his call, but he would explain to me conflict is part of relationship. Each time we disagreed and he came back, I grew to understand that conflict was an inevitable part of a mature relationship and that it didn't mean he would leave because of it.

One of the stresses that came with the relationship with Mitchell was dogs. While I enjoyed being with him, I didn't like being with dogs, and he had dogs. Not small dogs. Big dogs. Not only was I afraid of dogs, their presence caused me anxiety because of my issues with cleanliness. I realized that none of the life changes I encountered could evolve smoothly, not even our relationship! I had to deal with dogs and the stress of *what if we ended up together*. I also didn't like living with the prospect of Mitchell having irregularly scheduled short and long deployments in his career. Both dogs and deployments were equally disruptive to my healing journey.

With Drake I didn't have a big wedding because I was hurrying to get married and change my name. I thought I needed a name change for people to see me as worthy. I wanted to marry Drake to show Harold I could get somebody and prove to the community that I was worthwhile. I didn't know that even if I had married a prince from a royal family, I would still have felt inadequate because changing my outward situation couldn't help my inward problem.

This time around, I wanted a man to ask me to marry him. In my hasty youth, I didn't think about the emotional impact of asking Drake to marry me until I began to heal mentally and feel things emotionally. I wondered whether he felt emasculated or if my haste conflicted with his romantic dream. Very few women in my generation asked their boyfriends to marry them. We were the leading edge of feminism, it's true, but my rural Arkansas culture was not ready to drop some of the traditional expectations of romantic behavior. The more I matured and healed emotionally, the more I regretted asking Drake to marry. I should not have married at all because I did not have the faintest idea of love or how to have a healthy relationship. I married out of fear, afraid that no one would find me worthy to marry. I did not merely deal with low self-worth; I had no self-worth. How could I? Daily, my parents made sure to let us know that we were nothing and would never be anyone of significance. Harold reinforced their lack of respect and regard by sexually abusing me for years. How could I grow up healthy after chronic verbal, emotional, mental, physical, and psychological abuse as well as physical neglect from my parents and caregivers? I had no self-esteem, massive insecurities, and crippling fears. For most of my adulthood, I lived in constant fight or flight. I expected rejection and abandonment because that was the recurring pattern of my childhood, hardly a recommendation for a romantic involvement.

I had no voice in my marriage because I couldn't think or make critical decisions. I was there physically but absent emotionally and mentally. Drake asked for my input, but I was like Imani in the movie *Coming to America,* who responded, "Whatever you like, Prince Akeem," to every question asking her preference. That's how I communicated with Drake. He made the major decisions. When we bought our new house, he asked about lighting, fixtures, and paint color preferences, and I told him, *Whatever you like is fine.* He did an amazing job building and decorating the house, but the pressure of making so many decisions alone must have been overwhelming. As I healed, I appreciated the sacrifices he made.

I didn't share with Drake my symptoms of PTSD, nor did I want to. How could we talk about it when I was too emotionally immature to approach the subject? Also, I hardly knew what was going on in my mind. I thought I should keep quiet lest everyone think I was crazy. Proverbs 17:8 says, "Even a fool is thought wise if he keeps silent, and discerning if he holds his tongue." I interpreted it as *Keep your mouth closed, and people may think you're crazy, but if you speak, they will have no doubt.* I didn't want to illuminate my mental state and eliminate the doubt for those who suspected something wasn't right with me. Drake may have hoped everything would be fine, as some men do in a relationship with an emotionally immature woman. I say men because women, by nature, usually notice when something is off in a relationship, whereas men are frequently not as intuitive and are sometimes caught off guard. Most men are satisfied that things are fine if the house is standing, bills are paid, and vehicles are in good shape. Men are wired to provide and protect. Most women want to change or improve things.

After years of studying and researching Childhood Trauma and its impact, I realize that while I was physically a twenty-two-year-old woman when we married, emotionally, I was operating like a much younger girl. I am sure I sounded mature and like I had it together, as many trauma survivors do at first glance. I was socially adapted, dressed well, and was intelligent, but I didn't have my life together. Unbelievably, I didn't know how much I didn't have it together. Many survivors use *masking* as a way to conceal their true thoughts and behaviors for fear of being rejected or criticized or to create or maintain normalcy. Whether it's the rose-colored glasses in speaking of the future or academic masking in educational settings, it is an unhealthy coping mechanism. I spent a lot of time and energy masking.

Drake was my everything. It was one thing to love him, but it was another to make him responsible for my every physical, mental, and emotional need. Now I cringe when I hear a person say that someone or something is their everything. When I had a problem, I went to Drake for the solution. I never had to think to solve a problem. I thought he was so wise, and I knew I was unwise. I thought I knew nothing, and he knew everything. I can see now that Drake was the father I never had. He was gentle and respectful and explained life to me. It would be inaccurate to describe our marriage as one of equals. Even though I had a college degree, I had no real-life experience navigating adulthood, especially parenting, financial management, and planning for the future. For the first twenty years of our marriage, I was fine going through life with Drake as my voice. He took care of me and our son. He handled our finances and planned our futures and vacations. It was only after I began to understand some of the trauma and started to *feel* that I also emerged to gain a voice for myself.

When Drake and I divorced, I was not only devastated, I felt lost. My brain was unused to functioning on most of the non-academic levels. My brain had little experience in solving life's problems or planning future events—the role of the brain known as *executive function*. My brain knew how to survive, but it didn't know how to live and make the most of the life I had. For many trauma survivors, thinking is all or nothing, with nothing in between. When survivors have to make life-altering decisions, they must have Godly counselors to help them understand the impact of their decisions. After studying the impact of Childhood Trauma, I decided if I ever married again, I would first discuss important things such as faith, childhood adversities, and finances because those issues have long-term consequences. Marriage means I would be part of my spouse's long-term consequences, and he would be a part of mine. Ignoring the importance of discussing big issues is like intentionally keeping the other person in the dark about things that will impact the relationship over time. It starts the relationship with lies and deception; nothing good comes from a foundation of lies and deception. I know, because I intentionally kept my past from Drake because I thought if he knew the truth about me, he wouldn't marry me. I understand now that no one has the right to take away someone else's choice. The good news is that when God is a part of the marriage covenant, and couples resolve issues with Godly counseling and love, all things are possible.

Mitchell's and my adversities leveled our playing field and gave us a connection that others couldn't comprehend. Unless you have been raised in a wherever-you-lay-your-hat-was-your-home environment, or a small home with six siblings as he was, or in a family of constant lack as I was, you wouldn't understand what it is like to lose your home. For both of us, we lost more than just a physical home. For us it was a loss of identity and all we had worked for. We didn't just decide to be together, stick together, and remain friends. We both knew what it was like to have people around you who were not loyal to you, didn't support you, didn't believe in you, and took advantage of you, so we made a commitment to treat one another the way we wanted to be treated and see where it led. It led to four years of friendship. We told each other that, whatever happened, we would be there for each other until someone else came along, if that was the Lord's will. Mitchell understood my story more than he understood my dedication and desire to help people who shared my story. He didn't always understand my purpose, but he was willing to stick it out.

During childhood and adolescence, I rarely spoke of what happened to me with anyone other than my siblings—and even they were uncomfortable with the subject because it exposed their hidden dragons. I felt I had no one to talk to or confide in. I didn't learn how to talk about things or work things out like most teenagers and college students do. The downside to my social and emotional isolation is that I didn't get the message that what happened to me was abnormal and unacceptable. Without someone to listen to me and express their shock and horror at my experiences, I unwittingly normalized the abuse.

It wasn't until I independently faced stressful life events that many of my Childhood Traumas revealed themselves. The stress of leaving Drake and our son to take a new job in a different state exposed suppressed memories. Leaving my husband and son and moving to an isolated area provided the impetus to *feel*. I often panicked because I didn't know what to do with my feelings or how to address them. In the past, I ignored whatever few feelings I had, but ignoring them didn't work without the distractions of my husband, son, and nearby family members. These feelings arose because circumstances in Springfield and Southwest Missouri triggered memories that revealed the extent of my childhood abuse.

I was well into my forties before I realized that my parents did not treat me humanely. Their level of torture and abuse was unimaginable and indescribable, although I have tried to describe it in this memoir. Because my parents brutalized me so badly, I didn't see the sexual abuse by my uncle, church leaders, relatives, and foster fathers as criminal offenses. Even though I was barely in my teens, I thought I loved my great-uncle Harold and respected him as a man of God. In my twisted mind, I thought I helped his ministry with my compliance. I was never informed that no one should be allowed to force me to have sex. I had not learned that I had the right to withhold consent. I had never heard the term *statutory rape*. To a great degree, I escaped most of the social exposure most children have. I was rarely included in conversations in other people's homes, and talk of sexual abuse was not the kind of conversation held at school, so I believed most people experienced what I did but didn't talk about it.

By the time Mitchell and I seemed to be headed toward the altar, I knew our marriage would require me to think, count the costs, analyze, and be ready to accept the challenges of married life. I couldn't compare marriage to Mitchell to my previous marriage because this time I could and would speak and think. I read books on marriage, received marriage counseling, talked with long-married couples, and attended marriage seminars. I prayed often and asked God to teach me what I missed or didn't know that I needed to know, and He did. He often told me how to think about something after a discussion with Mitchell.

By 2016, I was emotionally mature and understood the meaning of marriage. I knew it would mean *until death do us part*. At the same time, however, I still had doubts about Mitchell's feelings for me regardless of how many times he told me he loved me.

It was a few days before Christmas, and Mitchell and I were sitting on the couch talking. I was feeling emotional because I felt like he should have already asked me to marry him if he was going to. After four years, I felt that our relationship needed to take a turn. Either we should be heading toward marriage or we should go our separate ways. There was a lot I wanted to say that night, but nothing came out. Going through my head was Uncle Harold's proclamation from long ago, "Why buy the cow when you can get the milk for free?" At least this time I knew I could dismiss that negative saying because Mitchell wasn't getting any free milk! We had determined to wait on God and marriage before having sex. I know that is an unpopular route to take, but it was what we felt was the right one for us, especially considering my past.

Without warning, I blurted out, "What are your plans for us in the future?"

"You mean with the relationship?" he asked.

"Yeah, I just wondered what you were thinking, that's all." I didn't want to put any ideas in his head.

"It's funny you should say that," he said, looking down. "I had prayed to God and told him I would ask you to marry me if you went one year without quitting me."

Remember, I didn't like conflict, so every time we had a disagreement, I would walk out, tense up, and leave. I sat there trying to remember the last time I'd done that. It happened a lot in the first few years, at least once a month. But now, I couldn't remember the last time I quit him.

He looked up at me, smiling as if he knew something I didn't know.

"It's been exactly one year today."

I surely didn't know it had been one year.

"Are you serious?" I asked.

"Yes. In fact, when I woke up this morning, it came to me that today was one year. So I'm shocked you asked me that today."

I sat there waiting for him to tell me *what now*. But just like that, the conversation ended. I took that to mean he wasn't interested in moving forward. From that point on, I was waiting for the moment he would let me down, or looking for the way I could let him down first. This time, though, I wasn't worried about what I would do or what would happen to me. This time I thought *It's been really wonderful having a nice, respectable man like Mitchell, but God will send me someone else if he no longer wants to be with me.*

I felt I had to begin planning my life without him in case this was the end. Mitchell hadn't told me it was the end, but he didn't tell me it was in the middle either. So, I immediately went into overdrive self-preservation with default plans—do what I needed to do to be sure I was fine, put up my emotional defense walls, think the worst, and hope for the best. This is one thing trauma survivors are known to do. We lessen the pain by not only preparing ourselves for the worst but also being the first to end a relationship. Otherwise we will feel rejected, and that is much too painful.

For the first time, I was making a decision by myself with God, and it felt scary but good. I knew if I made the wrong decision, God would guide me through it and reroute me back to His plan and purpose. This time I understood the scripture, *"All things work together for good for those who love the Lord and are called according to his purpose"* (Romans 8:28). I understood that no matter what happened, I wouldn't just barely make it. I would triumph gloriously over and through every obstacle and setback.

Mitchell had been called on duty and would be gone for a few weeks or a month because of social upheaval in Ferguson. It was a great time to make my big emotional escape. There was just one problem. I had given him my word I would take care of his two dogs, which were like his children. One was a German Shepherd and the other was a Brittany Spaniel. I didn't like dogs, had never liked dogs, and didn't want dogs. Yet, he had two dogs, and I was willing to care for them while he was serving our city and our country.

Every morning, I would get up and drive thirty minutes to his house and drive thirty minutes back over in the evening to care for them. The military had given him a possible release date, so I knew he would be home the following Saturday. I did not want to see him because I felt this was the end of us, and I didn't like long goodbyes. I had had enough tears and heartaches already to last me a lifetime. I thought if I left for my planned trip to see my goddaughter Alicia a day early, I would avoid the long goodbyes and heartache. I booked my flight for the day before he would return. He would be on the way home, and I would be on the way to the airport. Sounds cruel, but I was in self-preservation mode. I spoke with him and avoided any conversation about "getting married or future plans." For the first time I knew my value and my worth. I knew I was a daughter of the Most High God, and I had great purpose. Of course, my love for him didn't change, but if someone does not share their plans with you, you have to make a decision—though painful—to move on, unless you want to be in a ten or twenty year relationship as a friend.

I had been with Alicia nearly a week when Mitchell called and told me he was planning a trip for us. I thought to myself *I don't want to go on a trip with him now. Why didn't he plan this trip when we were together?* In my mind we were already broken up. I just agreed to the trip, hoping he would forget. We had gone on trips together before. Mitchell and I had boundaries while dating. He would sleep in one bed, and I would be in the other. This was an agreement we had made to honor God and our relationship. We believed if we honored God, He would honor us. At the end of my stay in Philly, I concluded God sent me there to help me gather my thoughts and help redirect my attention from a man to HIM, to understand who I was in Him, and to let me know I was not the same woman I was when I got the divorce. Survivors of Childhood Trauma and PTSD often get "stuck" in a thought or a belief, and they reject the truth of what is. For example, if they believe a man or woman is their husband or wife, or a job is theirs, regardless of the evidence or what anyone tells them, they will continue to believe that. This is especially true for Believers, who can be deceived into thinking their desire is the same as, "God told me to ask and I would receive." I had experienced deception before, so I was concerned my feeling that Mitchell was my husband was deception again.

I took the latest flight back to St. Louis, and Mitchell was there waiting for me at the airport. He was always patient. He drove around and around until I picked up my luggage. Every few minutes I would catch myself thinking *he's such a nice and patient man.* Then I would quickly tell myself *You have to be ready to move on. So what if he's nice, kind, a great conversationalist, you have fun with him, you love him, and you can't imagine your life without him?* I had finally learned it's not enough for me to "feel" good about someone. I had to know that God chose this person for me and that I could spend the rest of my life, for better or for worse, with that person. I had to get a picture of for better or for worse. There was a time I could barely talk about today much less for better or for worse. For it to last, he had to feel the same way about me, and I never knew how he felt. He wasn't a garrulous, praise-filled, I-am-so-glad-you-came-into-my-life kind of man. As I was discovering my authentic self, God was sending me someone who would help me to become who He created me to be.

The trip Mitchell planned was for the two of us to visit his niece in Florida. As far as I knew, we were just two friends going on a trip. He told I me I would need a white dress because we were going to an all-white party. I still wasn't excited. I thought this would be a nice trip, but nothing special. It was now the first week of February, and we would be leaving for the trip around the 9th and wouldn't return until the 16th. It did register in my mind for a split second that we would be together on Valentine's Day.

After my divorce, I learned the importance of communication. I learned I needed to mature emotionally, express myself, have a voice, and be more confident. I wasn't going to try to hide my flaws. The first marriage I thought the more he knew about me the less he would want me, so I didn't want him to meet people from my hometown. This time around I wanted him to know my childhood was horrendous and it had damaged me emotionally, mentally, physically, and spiritually. He never flinched. He never made me feel bad for the things that happened to me. I could tell it was hard for him, so I would only tell him things a little at a time. In my current state of doubt, I began to think Mitchell no longer wanted me because of all of those things I shared with him.

But if he was rejecting me, I thought, why would he take me on this trip? Then I remembered we were very good friends, and he really cares for me, but maybe not enough to marry me. Then the twins came to visit me: low self-esteem and doubt. I knew not to let them stay too long.

The day came for us to leave. He was so excited. We were ready for friendship and fun in the sun. We got to the airport, and he walked in front of me and told me to stay back while he took my driver's license and gave it to the clerk. The lady looked at me and smiled. Then she waved for me to come on though. The flight schedule said we were flying to Denver. I did wonder why we had to go to Denver first, and he calmly told me because our best friends were going with us (Pam and Sam), the same couple who had stayed with me in the hospital overnight. We could have ended the trip there, I was so excited. We loved being around them. We always had so much fun together. Like us, they had previously gone through terrible divorces, and God had brought them together, but not yet to the point of marriage. Mitchell told me we were all going to fly to Florida together, and we had to fly to Denver because of friends and family mileage. It all made sense to me.

When we arrived in Denver, they were already there waiting. Pam was just as in the dark about the trip as I was, and I couldn't wait to discuss it with her. She was usually great at knowing everything. This time she knew nothing. I told her I had to bring something white, and she told me she was told to bring boots. We did conclude they had pulled one over on us. In fact, we only found out where we were going when they announced it was time to board the plane—to Cancun! We were all excited. I did think it was very nice of

Mitchell to pay so much money for us to go on a trip together just to relax. It was even more special knowing I couldn't buy a pack of bubble gum on my Walmart salary. This meant he really cared for me, at least in my mind. I began to relax a little.

We arrived at the luxurious hotel in Cancun. It was breathtaking. We had dinner dates that he and Sam had scheduled; all we had to do was show up. We could eat whenever and whatever we wanted. I had never been on a vacation like this. I didn't know what to think or feel except to enjoy this vacation time with him and our best friends.

On Valentine's Day, Pam and I were told to wear white to dinner. I knew Pam hadn't brought anything white, so I was surprised when she came downstairs dressed in white! Sam had packed her a white outfit. Both men also dressed in white. Immediately, people began taking pictures and making comments. "How cute! They look darling, don't they, honey?" All kinds of butterflies filled my stomach thinking about how sweet it was of Sam to have surprised Pam and bought her something to wear. I thought to myself that I wished a man would surprise me one day and do something like that for me. As we sat in the lobby waiting for our reservation, a song came on: "There's a Ribbon in the Sky for our Love." I still didn't think anything about it. It would not be unusual for that song to be playing on Valentine's Day.

Five minutes after we were seated, a man came to us with four wine glasses. As Pam and I sat talking about how nice that was, Mitchell burst in on our conversation and began talking.

"I remember when we first met, the kindness you showed me, and all the things we have gone through together. You accepted me for who I was, and I asked myself if I were dying, who would I want by my bedside, and I said Dora. I love you, and I'm so glad I met you."

I felt myself get nervous: palms sweaty, mouth dry, and heart beat increased like I was about to go on stage unprepared. I could hardly focus on what he was saying, I was so nervous. I didn't understand why I was nervous, when he was the one speaking.

He went on, "I want you in my life and I can't imagine my life without you." I was already feeling overwhelmed that he was so kind to share these words about me with friends. We had read the *Love Languages* book and taken the quiz as part of getting to know one another, so he knew my highest score was in affirmation. It still didn't cross my mind what he was about to do or say. After all, I had made up my mind that I was moving on, and he and I would be the best of friends. No hard feelings. Then he dropped down beside the booth on my side.

"Will you marry me?"

What! Did this man just ask me to marry him? Immediately I became emotionally numb. I couldn't think at all. I just sat there—numb.

He took out a beautiful Halo ring. Then thoughts raced through my mind. *What are you doing? He loves me. He loves me not. Wait, but that's not for real life.* My thoughts slowed down. *What does love mean? What do I do now? I have been wanting and waiting for four years to marry him, and now it's time. Here he is asking me. Am I ready? He's asking me to marry him. Somebody please help me. Is he asking me to marry him because he feels sorry for me?*

Lord, help me to answer him.

Then I dismissed the negative thoughts with the Truth. No, he asked because he wants me, loves me, and he genuinely wants to be with me.

As fast as the insecurities, lies, and negative thoughts came, they left. Mitchell finished his proposal to me. Then Sam dropped down on his knees and proposed to Pam. I was still emotional from my proposal. Now this. It was too much. It's not that I wasn't excited. In fact, I was overly excited and didn't know how to express it. I didn't know what to do, but thankfully Pam knew what to do. She started hollering and screaming, so I started hollering and screaming, too.

We sat there until our dinner came, talking about the superb job they did of hiding the proposal from us. Mitchell and Sam told us they planned it all back in January, but actually talked about doing something in December. That made Pam and me feel even more special because they loved us so much, they thought ahead. It also didn't escape my notice that Mitchell was already planning the proposal when I asked him about our future.

I shall always remember the amazing love I felt in that restaurant that day as we all shared that special moment. We knew God had brought us all together, and He would keep us together. We all knew these were divine marriages, not made in heaven, but sanctioned by heaven to be lived out on earth. I am so grateful to God for healing my heart and changing it so that I was able to feel love, express love, and enjoy it. That's the abundant life only Jesus can give.

Chapter 64
THE WEDDING

Now that we were engaged, I had a new problem: how to pay for the wedding. I had plans of what I wanted, but zero money and a job at Walmart. I had achieved one of my biggest dreams: to get engaged without asking a man to marry me. Waiting for Mitchell to ask me was a big step against my own insecurities because I still felt that impulsive thought that if I didn't do the asking, we would never get married. I felt it was too much to ask to have the kind of wedding I'd always dreamed of. I should be happy just to go to the Justice of the Peace.

Our first conversation about the wedding, I just sat in tears because I knew I had a lot to offer in love, support, and faith but nothing to offer financially. I just told him we can do whatever he felt comfortable with. Mitchell knew what I had wanted because I had told him about my first wedding, how I'd asked Drake to marry me, borrowed my wedding dress, and felt I didn't have a choice because my uncle had told me no one would want me. He knew I didn't know what love was the first time, and I married quickly to change my name. He knew I didn't have a real wedding and always wanted one. He also knew I would be settling if we were married at the JOP.

Like the Israelites, I had selective faith. I had faith to get me there but not keep me there. I think this happens when we want something so badly (the dream job, car, child, whatever), but when times get extremely difficult, we lose faith. That's exactly what the Children of Israel did. They had faith that God would send them a deliverer to rescue them from Egypt, but lacked faith for Him to take them into the Promised Land.

I knew God as the One who healed me from physical and mental illnesses so I could work again, but I hadn't yet experienced God on a financial level. I had heard *Where He guides, He provides,* and *Where He leads, He feeds.* Catchy clichés, but were they true? It took a while for me to willingly allow friends to do special things for me because I wanted to be financially stable and independent. God was spiritually feeding me. I thought I should always be giving because the scripture says, "It's more blessed to give than to receive" (Acts 20:35). Jesus simply said the one who gives more has more joy because he can bless many. Without vigilance, I learned giving can turn into pride. It's prideful when it's my time to receive, and I feel shame, or if I feel stressed about what I don't have and how people may feel about me or my reputation. There is no shame in receiving.

My new reality was learning to act and trust God's provision as I obeyed Him. In the past, like so many Christians, I prayed and waited, hoping and expecting God to do it all Himself. After I had been on my healing journey a while, I learned God will do a little and expect you to do a little. He will also send people to do things for you, so you have to be willing to receive other people's kindness as gifts from the Lord.

Mitchell told me the Justice of the Peace was out of the question. Even though we both had little money left after our divorces, he was a financial planner, so he created a budget, and we made our dream a reality. We both wanted an elegant wedding surrounded by people who loved us and who would be genuinely happy for us. Everything else would be icing on the cake. I didn't know then that Mitchell used his savings for a new truck to give me a wedding because he said I deserved a wedding. Even years later, writing this brings tears to my eyes when I think someone loved me so much that he asked me to marry him and wanted me to have a proper wedding. It meant he listened to me and he valued me.

All of the pieces fell into place just as God ordained. We had a beautiful, outdoor, October wedding in a lovely park that just so happened to be available on the very day we needed it. The man who walked me down the aisle was Fred, a man God sent me as a father figure when I moved to St. Louis. He had never had a child, and I had never had a father, and he chose me to be his daughter. He was the one to give me away. Jessie was a mother figure to me. She had lost her son a year before I moved to St. Louis. She treated me like her daughter, and I had her sit in the seat of honor as Mother of the Bride. The four of us still spend a lot of time together.

About a month before the wedding, a good friend named Beverly told me God told her to come and care for any needs I had for the wedding. She also told me God told her to buy me a wedding dress. I thought that was nice, but how could she buy me a dress that I'd not tried on? I went ahead and bought my own dress even though God had told me I wouldn't have to buy a wedding dress because He would provide it. I wanted the experience of shopping for one, but I also wasn't trusting God wholeheartedly; so, with the little money I had, I bought a discounted dress. It wasn't my dream dress, but it would do. It always costs us when we don't wait on God!

When Beverly came down the week of the wedding, she took me shopping and made sure I had everything I needed. I remember thinking, *This is what it feels like when you have a mom who supports you and pays your wedding costs.* She also brought two beautiful dresses with her, one for the wedding and one to change into afterward if I wanted. I thanked her but thought there was no way it would fit, but when I tried on the wedding dress, I was in shock. It fit in every area. It was perfect! It was a long, flowing, white dress with a sheer flap that moved with each step I took. It was breathtaking. All I could think about was how beautiful I would be in this dress that God had bought for me. I knew it was my wedding dress after I tried it on. It looked like it had been made especially for me. I was overwhelmed with love.

Finally, the day of the wedding came. Pam and Sam had gotten me a room at a very exquisite hotel in St. Louis for me to enjoy the evening before. They made sure the room was beautifully decorated with rose petals on the bed and throughout the room. I sat on the bed with the Bible open, thanking God for allowing me to have a wedding and loving friends and family to celebrate with. I felt this was something God did not have to do, especially since I had been married before. He knew my hopes and dreams this time around for a wedding and gave me the desires of my heart. I was overwhelmed with his lovingkindness. Perhaps this is what King David felt when God chose him to be king of Israel. He told God, "Who am I, Sovereign Lord, and what is my family that you have brought me this far" (2 Samuel 7:18)? I sat and wept.

I remembered my first wedding which really wasn't a wedding. We didn't invite but seven people, and they all came. This time my family and friends were coming from near and far to celebrate with me. I knew I was blessed. I mostly lay before God that night and asked him to bless our wedding, our marriage, and our visitors who were attending the wedding. Mitchell and I had already fasted and prayed together that God would bless the people attending our marriage and that He would get the glory. We wanted Him in every aspect of this marriage. That night as I sat in the beautiful hotel room surrounded with rose petals and chocolate, I reflected on God's blessings, on His miracles, on how I had met Mitchell, and on how our relationship progressed in spite of our inadequacies.

Here I was again, starting over. This time I was a mature woman in mind and spirit. I had chosen my husband out of love and not out of fear that I wouldn't find a man or that a man wouldn't find me. This time I felt equipped and ready for marriage, its ups and downs, its setbacks, whatever it came with. I didn't know what the future held for us, but I knew who held our future. We had gotten marriage counseling, taken love language courses, marriage courses, seminars with Jimmy Evans and his wife, been in difficult situations, had difficult conversations, shared our expectations, handled conflicts, and agreed this time we would fight our way through any difficulty. Us + God = Success. We had done all we could do to set ourselves up for success. We felt ready enough. Now I realize ready was a bit of an overstatement. Thank God for our foundation in Him!

The day of the wedding, I was saturated with more love in one day than I had experienced in my entire life. I wanted to scream, shout, and cry all at the same time. I wanted to yell, "God, is this really happening? You really did smile on me after all I've been through." Pam was there to be sure I had everything I needed. Another wonderful sister from the church did my makeup. While dressing, there were times I felt I didn't deserve this. I pushed those feelings aside and focused on God's grace and love for me. As I walked down the paved little entryway to meet Mitchell, the sheer flap swayed with each step I took. Yes, I said paved. The park had a long walkway for me to walk down which was for me like walking down the aisle at a church. My diamond shoes were glistening in the sunlight. It was seventy-three degrees, and there was no rain. The sun was shining bright, but it wasn't hot. It was the most beautiful day anyone could ask for. God had answered our simplest prayers and was smiling on us. Everyone who attended said they could feel His presence.

The wedding ceremony was performed by my sister Jolene's husband, so it was extra special for me. The reception was held at the park immediately following the wedding. After the ceremony, we danced. Jolene and her husband of eighteen years were the first ones on the dance floor. It brought me great joy to see her happy for me because she knew firsthand the intense pain I had endured. I had never felt so loved.

Unconventional Love

I searched for your love high and low
I searched in familiar places hoping it would show
I searched the past for a clue
I searched everywhere but couldn't find you

I searched for it in extravagance
but it could not be found
I searched for it in elegance
where true love can never abound

I searched for it in a dozen roses
I searched for it in the fantasies of my mind
I searched for it on a cruise around the world
I searched for this love I thought I would never find

I searched for it in shopping malls
I searched for it in the stillness of the night
I searched for it in the darkness
I searched for it in dry places where no fire could ignite

I searched for it on top of the hill
I searched for it like others do
I searched for it in the recesses of my mind
I searched for it until I said "I give up. I'm through."

I searched until my feet were tired and ached
Finally I prayed and asked to the Lord, "Lord how much more can I take?
So I decided to stop searching and let HIM find my man
And now here I stand with you, my Dearest Mitchell, my unconventional man

No you didn't come as a knight in shining armor
or with the dozen roses in your hand
or with a $1,000 shopping spree
smooth words telling me how much you wanted to be my man

You came to me with your love and friendship
You came to me with Eagle eyes
You came from God above
I know He sent you because
You came to me with an unconventional love

Chapter 65
A GUARDIAN OF FREEDOM

Mitchell and I agreed to wait to go on our honeymoon because I needed the money for graduate school and had deadlines to meet. I was writing my dissertation proposal for my research study. Upon approval of the dissertation proposal, I only had one year to complete the study. It was approved a month after we married. Everything was working out. I couldn't have been happier. Now that the wedding was over, I could turn my attention once again to graduating.

Then we got the news that Mitchell was being deployed to Kuwait. Immediately I felt myself kick into the survival brain. My first thought was *How will I make it with these dogs?* I know you were probably expecting me to say *How will I make it without Mitchell?* But I knew God would help me make it without him. I just wanted to know how He would help me with the dogs! We had only been married nine months, and he was about to leave for about a year. We sat there and hugged, and I assured him I would be fine and the dogs would be, too.

His dogs were his children. My mind kept wondering how I would concentrate on my dissertation and also make it work with the dogs while he was gone. It seemed impossible for a while, but the closer we came to the date, the more God gave me peace. Here was another situation where I had to pray and trust God, so I asked Him to help me be strong and if Mitchell would return home safe. He answered me that He would protect Mitchell and bring him back safely. Now whenever I felt anxious or nervous, I would meditate on what He told me, and then I was fine.

The Army may be the earliest to rise, but it can't beat God, because God never sleeps. Three weeks after Mitchell received his papers to deploy to Kuwait, I was awakened in the middle of the night with an urgent sense to pray for him. I prayed for him to not go to Kuwait. I didn't know why he didn't need to go to Kuwait, I just felt led to pray that. When I woke up the next day, I told Mitchell about the prayer. He told me the Army doesn't usually change its orders once they have been sent. I told him they will this time because you are not supposed to go to Kuwait. You're supposed to go to Jordan. A month later, Mitchell received new orders that he was to report to Jordan instead of

Kuwait. Mitchell told me he was so glad he was rerouted to Jordan. God is amazing!

The day he left, Mitchell hugged his two dogs as if he was afraid he wouldn't ever see them again. They were both older, outside dogs. Caesar, his German Shepherd, was almost thirteen and ailing, and Macy, the Brittany Spaniel, was fifteen. As I watched him hug them out the kitchen window, it looked like they knew he would be gone for awhile. Animals know a lot more than humans sometimes. I couldn't help but pray *Lord, do I really have to be here with the dogs? I am not a dog person.* He knew when he married me I was not a dog person just as I knew when I married him he was a soldier. He was probably praying the same prayer for his dogs that I was praying, "Lord do my dogs really have to be here with her? She is not a dog person." The dogs barked goodbye, and I am sure they were crying because I wanted to cry, too. I wanted to cry twice. One cry for Mitchell leaving and the other cry for leaving me with the dogs.

I remember the first time I met Mitchell's dogs. I had known him at least a year before meeting his furry babies. Looking back, I can see the wisdom. I was still dealing with OCD, and dogs were something I saw as unclean. I had witnessed and experienced God doing all kinds of miracles, but I wasn't yet ready for the Promised Land with the giants. And Caesar was a giant to me! He was huge. When I talked about him to people, I described him as a pony. When I met him for the first time, Caesar came in from the outside and licked my face. He tried to jump in my lap, but he was larger than me and weighed more. I immediately went into freeze mode because I couldn't escape. I thought I was going to die from sudden shock. I loved Mitchell, but I didn't know how to express my love for him without expressing my disgust for his babies. I just sat there shaking, hoping the pony wouldn't sense my fear.

I thought for a few minutes I might have misheard God when He told me Mitchell was my husband. In my mind, there was no way God could give me such an impossible task. Mitchell told me the dog was wagging his tail, which he explained meant the dog was happy. I wanted to tell him, *"Well I am not, so can he please go someplace else and be happy?"* Instead, I sat there in shock for a few minutes. Macy didn't come near me, and I didn't go near her. Now we would all be forced to be together. This didn't sound like something a loving God would do.

It wasn't long after Mitchell's deployment that I was outside giving the dogs water and I heard a voice say, "I'm using these dogs to teach you how to care for my people." I had never heard of God using dogs. I thought to myself

How can you teach me to care for your people using dogs? Then he gave me examples of Moses and David caring for physical sheep and they were great leaders. I pondered on what He had said to me. Instead of, "Feed my sheep," like He told Peter, God was telling me, "Feed my dogs."

I began to pay close attention to the dogs' behavior, personalities, likes, and dislikes. I even read books about them so I would know what to expect. Although I had been around them now for four years, this was different because I had received a "Divine assignment" to learn how to care for them. It was like I had just brought the dogs home. I felt like someone was standing over me, or I was in a dog trainer's class. I had to be careful to remember to feed them, walk them, observe them, play with them, talk to them, and let them know I loved them. For me, this would be a nearly impossible task since I didn't like dogs, but I knew I couldn't do like Moses and ask God to find someone else. There wasn't anyone else.

When Caesar became ill, I remember praying for him and anointing him with oil and asking God to heal him because I didn't want him to die while Mitchell was away serving his country. I took him to the vet, and as we sat in the room waiting, I noticed Caesar was anxiously walking around, prancing back and forth. I was nervous, too. When the doctor walked in, Caesar got so nervous that he pooped. My mouth dropped, but the vet continued his conversation with me as if nothing was happening. I couldn't half hear anything he was saying because of my nervousness and the poop. Caesar pranced and pooped until he had made a circle in the room. Meanwhile, the vet scolded me about how I was taking care of Caesar. I told him how afraid I was and that it was more than I felt I could handle. He cut me off in mid-sentence.

"This is your dog and he is your responsibility," he said, "so when anything happens, you have to do something."

I wanted to walk out, but I wouldn't know what to tell Mitchell, so I stood there and let the vet vent on me. Caesar must have felt anxious for the doctor's harsh words to me because he pooped as he came closer to me. By this time I was about to pass out from being in the enclosed room with poop everywhere, the vet's harsh chastisement for not knowing what to do for Caesar, and for Caesar's pain. Just when I thought I experienced the worst, Caesar tried to come between my legs, but he was too tall. I stood there, legs shaking and about to join him in pooping. I was standing in poop, lips shivering, hands shaking, and tears welling in my eyes. But something transformational happened when Caesar tried to go between my legs this time.

I realized he needed me and wanted me to be close to him because I represented safety and security. To him I was his mommy. I cried more because I realized I couldn't give him the safety and protection he needed.

I'm sure the vet admitted Caesar to the hospital to help me. When I picked him up a few days later, he told me he saw a little blood in his stool but nothing to be concerned about. I felt there was more he wasn't telling me, but I couldn't ask. I would have to continue to pray and ask God to heal him.

God answered my prayer and let Caesar live to see Mitchell again, but he died a few months after Mitchell's return. I took his death hard, which was shocking to me. God sent the dogs to me to help me overcome fear and Obsessive Compulsive Disorder, to learn how to lead and care for His people, and to triumph over difficulties. I am grateful for my experiences with those dogs, even the vet experience, because I can laugh about it now.

Chapter 66
BEAUTY FOR ASHES

I never asked God *why me* when it came to my difficulties, but I did ask Him why there was so much pain in my life. I told Him I had nothing, experienced nothing but pain, and knew nothing except suffering. One day, He answered with a poem called, "Why Me?"

Why Me?

Today I asked God, "Why me?" and this was his response.
"When mankind, whom I created, lost his way, and I had to send a redeemer,
How many times do you think I asked, "Why Me?" I will tell you---not once.
I'm glad you asked these questions. They are asked by everyone I call.
Who told you to call me? Why don't get someone else? Am I going to have to
*   suffer?*
It makes me think they never knew me at all.
Why me? Why me? is their constant cry.
I am too young, too old, too sick, too tired—one after one they offer an alibi.
I will never leave you nor forsake you. I wait for a response, but they never reply."
Then God said, "They beat my son for your sins and whipped him time and time
*   again.*
For this I had no response.
How many times do you think I asked, "Why me?" I will tell you—not once.
I understand your hurt, pain, and even frustration when you suffer day after day
*   and relief never comes.*
You look for my presence and don't see a body
but in my physical absence, you got to understand, that's when your faith
*   blossoms.*
I understand your million and one questions, and you want answers right now.
Why was I created? When will all this be over? and How much more do I have to
*   take?*
My answer to you, my child, is this: Trust me. I have not made a mistake.
I understand your journey. It is a trip that you must take alone.
That's why I separated you from the world, not me. I hear your every groan.

You must not be anxious on your journey
Because each day there will be something new to learn.

Lean on me when you can no longer walk. I will carry you.
I am your best friend. I see your fears—I am concerned.
You must take it one day at a time.
In your haste, you overlook my smallest creations and the lessons each one can
    teach.
Smelling the flowers reminds you of me, and the setting of the sun does, too,
But you choose to focus on things that have no meaning, things that stress you.
You must not focus on which season you're in. Focus on who sends the seasons.
You must not focus on what you're going through and try to figure out all the
    reasons.
I don't work like the man I created. I am God, I am ELOHIM, I am JEHOVAH.
I don't always make sense to man. Remember the Ark, the animals of their kind,
    and Noah.
I am Alpha and Omega. I am EL ELYON and Yahweh.
Finite knowledge cannot figure out infinite wisdom.
I am a God of unity and strength, not of all the dissension and schism.
The church where I built my foundation is being turned into a place of deception
    and degradation.
The place where my people who are hurt should go is being turned into a place of
    shame—I know.
The place--I named it the The House of Prayer,
A place of serenity, a place where you know I will be there.
It shall be called a place of shelter to protect you from the storm.
My House of Prayer is now being transformed.
Transformed into something that does not resemble me yet carries my name.
False prophets and preachers are leading my people astray,
Taking from the poor and giving to the rich
They are doing it all in my name

So you ask me the question, "Why me?" Your heart has been tested and tried.
You know how it feels to be misled, mistreated, and denied.
You have borne shame, frustration, and sorrow.
You know what it's like to have to beg, steal, and borrow.
You have been abused by those I supposedly sent.
You waited for my voice, others just went.

You have been broken into little pieces. You wonder, why you?
Look around at my world—how many are truly serving me?
Only a small percent.
I am searching for those who are true.
I am searching for those I can use.
I am searching for the wounded, the downtrodden, and yes, the abused.

My child, I am searching for you."
So the next time you are tempted to ask, "Why me?"
This should be your response,
"Why not me?" Can you respond like this—just once?

Dora J Wallace, February 2, 2010

It wasn't quite the response I expected from God, but I finally understood. I was His servant, and His servants suffered for His name's sake. I didn't understand why He allowed me to suffer like I did as a child. In this fallen world, no one is exempt from suffering. I didn't understand why children were not exempt from suffering, and I had more questions, but I didn't ask God. I pondered them. I meditated on them and wondered why I had to suffer chronic Childhood Trauma and sexual abuse and never feel loved. There were many questions, but I did not want God to answer them immediately. I was probably afraid of the answer. After He answered the *why* question, I kept my questions quiet. How silly of me to act as if God didn't know what I was thinking.

I continued to study the impact of trauma on the brain and experienced a greater understanding of why I wasn't able to comprehend, love, and enjoy life. The more questions I answered, the more questions I posed. I wondered how I made it as far as I did in life and made as many friends as I did, and the questions that never seemed to find a satisfactory answer, such as *How was I able to get married? How did I survive having a child? How did I stay married for such a long time?* My big question was: *Why did I experience so much pain?*

God's thoughts are larger than our thoughts. It wasn't until He revealed answers that I saw how narrow and minuscule my thoughts were. My thoughts focused only on me, while His thoughts focused on others. My thoughts were inward while His expanded outward. My thoughts focused on my pain, while His focused on others' pain. Every question I was asking God was about me. I never would have thought His answer would set me on a path to change the trajectory of my life and catapult me to my destiny. While I was in His presence and wrapped up in me and my pain and suffering, He led me to the book of John, the ninth chapter. I read it several times. As I read it, I saw I was the blind man. Let me elucidate.

The scriptures that resonated in my spirit were verses 1-7 in the New International Version:

¹As he went along, He saw a man blind from birth. ²His disciples asked him, "Rabbi, who sinned, this man or his parents, that he was born blind?" ³"Neither this man nor his parents sinned," said Jesus, "but this happened so that the works of God might be displayed in him. ⁴As long as it is day, we must do the works of Him who sent me. Night is coming when no one can work. ⁵While I am in the world, I am the light of the world." ⁶After saying this, he spit on the ground, made some mud with the saliva, and put it on the man's eyes. ⁷"Go," he told him, "Wash in the Pool of Siloam" (this word means "Sent"). So the man went and washed and came home seeing.

What I learned was this:

Verse 1: *As He went along, He saw a man blind from birth.* Jesus saw a man with a condition from birth. **That was me**.

Verse 2: *His disciples asked him, "Rabbi, who sinned, this man or his parents, that he was born blind?* My mouth dropped when I read this verse. It was like the disciples asked Jesus the same questions I asked God. I wanted to know: *Why so much pain? Was God punishing me as a result of my parents' wickedness? Was I cursed? Was God angry with me? Why the loss of my childhood? Would God ever be able to use someone as broken as me?* And the big one—*Why did God allow it to happen?* **That was me.** I'm certain this wasn't the first time I had read John 9:2, but I now had new clarity and revelations.

Verse 3: *Neither this man nor his parents sinned, said Jesus, But this happened so that the works of God might be displayed in him.* I heard that I wasn't born this way and didn't go through the abuse because of my parents. **That was me.** I went through this because the world is evil, and people do evil things. Then I heard the still, small voice: ***I had an appointed time for your healing and to display it.*** God knew what happened, but He also knew in His infinite wisdom that He had a set time to heal me from what happened.

Verses 4-5: *As long as it is day, we must do the works of Him who sent me. Night is coming, when no one can work. While I am in the world, I am the light of the world.*

Verse 6: *After saying this, He spat on the ground, made mud with the saliva, and put it on the man's eyes.* Jesus challenged the religious believers' thoughts about God and how He works. Jews believed there was some power in the spittle, so if Jesus left it at His spittle, they might have been more willing to accept the man's healing, but Jesus made clay, which had nothing to do with the spittle, and anointed the man's eyes. He might have been teaching them God's healing is not limited to only what men think He can do.

Verse 7: *Go, he told him. Wash in the Pool of Siloam. So the man went and washed and came home seeing.* Interestingly, the pool in which Jesus told the blind man to go and wash is named Siloam, which means *sent*. Jesus told the blind man to **do something.** Jesus could have healed the blind man on the spot. Instead, He sent him to do something. The man's healing would not have been complete had he not done what Jesus told him. Doing something is required of the Tower of Hope Ministries' participants. Jesus died for us and rose from the dead. That's His part of the healing process. He requires us to **do something** to participate in our healing.

After reading those verses, my thoughts were positive but didn't make me feel any better. I wish I could say I had immediate joy, but I can't. I was still in deep emotional and spiritual pain because I wasn't fully convinced that God had no hand in my suffering. I kept telling God, *It hurts so much,* and I tried to grasp what He was saying, so I repeated it aloud: *You chose me to display Your supernatural healing power. You did this so I could show Your healing power. You hurt me so others could see You.* I had been seeking and getting to know God for several years, but I didn't yet understand His character. I didn't have enough growth to understand this level of sacrifice. Not only was I not happy, I also sobbed uncontrollably. I cried until I had no tears left. Then I hugged my pain because there was no one to hug my grief. I stopped my conversation with God because I was in too much emotional pain.

I kept thinking. God did this *to me* for His glory to manifest later. Understanding that made it hurt even more deeply because He is God and could have stopped it. Then I heard a voice: *No, that's not how God's character works.* The still, small voice spoke up and said, **God didn't do this to me, nor did He want this to happen to me.** *My suffering happened because of the sinful world, and God, in His infinite wisdom, knew this would happen and set an appointed time to heal me of it.*

For a moment, I felt betrayed by God, forsaken and rejected. This was my Gethsemane. The emotional pain was too great for me to see the big picture. Finally, I understood.

In John 9, Jesus revealed to the disciples that the man's condition was in God's plan because God's mighty works would be revealed through the man's healing.

Once I finished sobbing, I dried my eyes and realized I had a new sense of purpose not yet revealed. I knew God wanted to use me one day to do great work. He wanted me to help others like me.

God didn't wait until I was married again or finished with a degree program to begin using me to help others. I had worked at Walmart for eighteen months until I married Mitchell and was able to leave it to finish my doctorate, which I did in May of 2018. But while I was making wedding plans, still working at Walmart, and studying for my doctoral degree—when I thought I couldn't add another thing to my plate—God did. He had called me, and I waited to be sent, but now was the time to *GO*.

At the beginning of my healing journey, the Holy Spirit led me to write down everything, but it wasn't until six years later that the Holy Spirit revealed why I needed to keep a written record. I am thankful God doesn't reveal every step of His plan for us at once because it would overwhelm us. I wouldn't have been able to handle it if He had told me during my healing journey that I would create a program that helps others like me heal. I certainly would have run like Jonah (Jonah 1:3). I love how God introduces those He calls to an idea, which seems like a small thing at the moment. After all, who doesn't want to make a difference in somebody's life? I liked the idea of helping a few people along the way. That didn't seem like much.

Once I knew my purpose, I began looking for others who had endured Childhood Trauma. I began by telling people my testimony. The natural outcome was that when I shared about how God was healing me of my Childhood Trauma, others would tell me about theirs. Early on, finding others willing to admit the impact CT had on them was daunting. Many I spoke with said their trauma didn't impact their adult life at all. I thought maybe they didn't understand what I meant, so I used simple terms to describe it. I read the research and lived the experience of the consequences. Yet, others with similar traumas in their childhoods said they were happy and had no long-term effects. It made me wonder if it was only me—and those in Dr. Felitti's study—who suffered from the debilitating effects of Childhood Trauma.[16]

Later, I learned that people were unwilling to acknowledge their discomfort. Many of them did not connect their Childhood Trauma to their adult dysfunctions, chronic physical illnesses, emotional outbursts, controlling behaviors, impulsivity, and mental challenges, so in their perspective, they didn't experience Childhood Traumas. Some denied their reality, and some even felt hopeless because they had lived with the disruption for so long that they could not conceive of another way of life. I hadn't made the connection myself for over thirty years, so I understood.

Making the connection between trauma and adult dysfunctions was freedom. Jesus said, "You shall know the truth and the truth shall make you free" (John 8:32). The truth was I wasn't crazy, but something crazy happened to me, and it caused me to do some crazy things. Still, I know how the trauma changed my brain, affected my behavior, changed my identity, and wired me to fear. The freedom of truth changed my perception of pain, suffering, and life. I went from *Woe is me* to *Strong is me*. When I received the revelation that childhood pain connected to my adult purpose, my happiness was indescribable. I went from extreme weakness, grief, self-pity, shame, guilt, unforgiveness, and feelings of rejection to supernatural strength, joy, guilt-free shamelessness, comprehension, forgiveness, and God's acceptance.

I began using the writings and recordings God provided for my healing to help other people heal as well. This led to establishing the program Tower of Hope, later called Tower of Hope Ministries (TOHM), to help people who have difficulty adjusting to life from the staggering effects of trauma. Although my focus was on those who were dealing with the long-term effects of Childhood Trauma, it didn't matter whether they suffered the trauma in childhood or adulthood. As long as they admitted they needed help, I didn't turn them away. I wanted them to know there was hope even though their trauma had left them emotionally, mentally, spiritually, or physically damaged and feeling hopeless. I wanted to offer them tools to heal their hearts, help them succeed, and make informed decisions.

The tools and strategies began with one goal in mind: to help people process the trauma that happened and heal from it so they could enjoy life. I understood their struggle and pain. My research certified me as

---

[16]Felitti, Vincent J. 2002. "The Relation Between Adverse Childhood Experiences and Adult Health: Turning Gold into Lead." *The Permanente Journal* 6, no. 1: 44-47. Doi: 10.7812/TPP/02.994.

knowledgeable, but my adverse childhood experiences (ACEs) qualified me as an expert. I knew its devastating effects and impact on the body, soul, and spirit. Trauma was one area of life about which I knew much.

When I started Tower of Hope in August of 2017, I still struggled to feel valuable because I didn't think I had much to offer, even though I was a National Board Certified Teacher with fifteen years of teaching experience. The extent to which we assign value to ourselves by the *things* we can afford and allow them to define our identity is intriguing. When I lost those *things*, I lost my sense of value, self-confidence, and self-esteem. It was difficult for me to understand Moses' story of how he was trained in the best schools and raised in the royal court, but when God called him to speak, he told God he stuttered and wasn't good at speaking. I'm certain he was once self-assured and confident that he could do anything.

After healing, I questioned my speaking ability and whether I wanted to be a motivational speaker. I lost the desire, courage, and confidence to speak before a group of listeners. I was bewildered. How did God expect me to speak and train people when I felt ill-equipped? I had to learn that God's calling me had little to do with my abilities and more to do with His capabilities. He was capable of doing beyond what I could imagine. God takes the natural and makes it supernatural. My passion for helping people and my faith in God overrode fear and lack of self-confidence. I came to survivors with experience, a caring heart, and a God-sized purpose. Somehow God was able to take everything that happened to me—all the abuse and suffering—and use it to help me understand those who come to Tower of Hope Ministries.

TOHM participants pour their hearts out. I am not surprised by anything they tell me they have said or done because I have seen and experienced so much. Sometimes, when they share something they've never shared with anyone, they expect me to judge them, scold them, look in awe, or tell them about unpardonable sins. Neither God nor my counselor, Arella, did that to me, and I won't do it to them. Nothing about Childhood Trauma shocks me because I know whatever horrible thing they did or experienced wasn't their fault. I also know it wreaked havoc on their life, and they need healing and deliverance, not criticism and judgment.

I wanted Tower of Hope to be a place where people aren't judged on their past but are freed from it. I knew the students came with distrusting anticipation, heart-wrenching regrets, painful decisions, and a desire to be authentic and to find a hopeful future. I knew because they were me, and I was once them. I wanted TOH to be a safe place for people to come and heal. They would agree to go through a rigorous process of deep soul-searching, attend monthly meetings, participate in class activities, and do assigned homework, just as I had to do in my one-on-one rehab with God, counselor Arella, and Dr. Phil's book *Self Matters*. I still consider Dr. Phil one of my counselors; that's how influential his book was in helping me.

Although I knew my work to help CT survivors was immeasurable, I also knew it wouldn't come with a handsome salary. I calculated the distrust, skepticism, and fear of trauma survivors and prepared to do my work without charging a fee. It's a good thing I did because that's what it took. The year 2024 was the seventh year of the program, and the seventh year I have not received a salary. I didn't create and provide the program to earn income. I did it to fill a gaping need in the fabric of the community. I want people set free to live the abundant life Jesus promised. Like Elijah, God sends the ravens to feed me through timely donations and gifts from like-minded people.

Some fifteen years on, God continues to heal my mind, body, heart, and soul from the brokenness, dysfunction, and pain of Childhood Trauma and the drama it causes. The best way to describe the healing process is to think of an onion. There is an outer layer that protects the flesh of the onion. Inside, there are layers upon layers of onion flesh. Closer to the core of the onion is the strongest scent of the onion. Healing is the same process. At Tower of Hope, we often say we have to get to the root of the problem and not just the fruit from the problem. The root of the problem emerges when we refuse to only keep addressing superficial symptoms.

For those who have had complex trauma, it can take years of removing outer layers to get to the core of their pain. The more I healed and studied Childhood Trauma, the more God revealed about the healing process. I found support for healing for the struggles, and I did the hard work of *doing;* God did the *undoing* of the damaging affects on my mind, body, heart, and spirit.

Chapter 67
God's Global Positioning System

With each test I overcame, God prepared me for the next thing. The abuse prepared me to teach, teaching prepared me for the National Board Certification process, and the rigorous process of the NBCT prepared me for Tower of Hope Ministries. The state teacher certification process took three years. The patience I acquired through the NBCT was transferable because I would need it to work with the participants who come to TOHM to be healed. If I had laser focus through the NBCT process, I knew God would help me achieve a passing score. I apply the same approach when helping students who come to TOHM. God sends them to TOHM, and if they do the work, they will be healed and delivered. Most importantly, NBCT taught me to trust God, which is what I have to do in my work with TOHM. The entire program is based solely on my assurance that God sent me and is with me to help His people heal.

It took nearly eight years of the Lord's training, beginning in Springfield and continuing in St. Louis, before I was ready to step into leadership with Tower of Hope Ministries. I saw God orchestrate my steps as He did for King David, from herding sheep to leading his people or from the pasture to a pastor. Although I am not a church pastor, I see why I needed to learn how to care for, pray for, and lead God's people whom He would send to TOHM. They came like I was: abused, broken, deceived, rejected, and misguided. I learned how to extend the grace, mercy, patience, and compassion God extended to me. God's GPS led me directly to the place and people He wanted me to be with.

I found God's Global Positioning System (GPS) and training excruciatingly painful because I was required to take positions and go places that humbled me, but that ultimately led to creating a program to help His people heal. I did many things I previously considered unfathomable: I left teaching to advocate for educators, went to work in a geographical area where I went three months without seeing another person of color, experienced first-person racism and discrimination, lived alone for the first time in my life at the age of forty-three, left my prestigious and highly paid job, and finally, worked at Walmart.

In hindsight, I see it was His method to make me a bold, humble, courageous, and unrelenting warrior who fights for the captives and the oppressed, but during that time I only saw and felt the pain. I didn't understand that God has a purpose for each of us, and all we need to do is yield to Him and He will lead us to that purpose. It makes sense now because we often spend too much time trying to find our purpose instead of getting to know the God who gave us the purpose. Only He can lead us to it. When we yield to Him, He leads us to it. The pain is so great that perhaps this is why many Christians opt out of the training and tell the GPS to take them directly to their purpose. The problem is that the training makes one able to endure the pain, suffering, rejection, lies, misunderstandings, setbacks, and disappointments. The training equips us with the mercy, grace, compassion, humility, and love we need for our purpose. If we arrive at our place of destination before the training, we will undoubtedly accomplish some things, but it will be a struggle and extremely stressful. When we have the proper training, we know God's GPS directed us, and when we arrive, we know the pressure is on Him and not us.

God called me, but I didn't know what that *calling* looked like. I could count on one hand the leaders I knew who lived the life she or he preached, so God would have to teach me what He meant by *calling* me. Whatever He did in and through me, I wanted to be real. I wanted God to anoint me, and I wanted Him to transform the lives of those He sent to me, so I asked Him to do those things. I couldn't ask anyone else because I didn't trust anyone to teach me. From my history of spiritual abuse, God knew trusting spiritual leaders was not an option for me.

Thankfully, God meets us where we are. The spiritual abuse would forever be a reminder to pray always, value God's people, remember leaders are judged harshly, and wait until God sends. I followed the examples of Biblical leaders called by God who completely submitted to him, such as Samuel, King David (except for committing adultery), Jeremiah, Ezekiel, Daniel, and Paul, to name a few. The problem was I found flaws in many of them. I wanted a perfect person, but couldn't find one, so I concluded Jesus would be the one to teach me leadership. The first lesson Jesus taught was that none of the Biblical characters are perfect. He wanted me to know I was not, either. I had many flaws. God chooses to use fallible people to show forth His power.

The second lesson I had to learn was humility. Working at Walmart was the first test, and I failed many tests on humility. It seemed almost impossible to achieve. Jesus was humble and displayed great humility, but I couldn't. I couldn't let people walk on me or turn the other cheek when they were disrespectful. I tried. I finally gave up and told God the truth. I couldn't do it. That's when He showed me it wouldn't be by my might, nor power, but by His Might and Power (Zechariah 4:6). That's when He gave me the OJT (On the Job Training) at Walmart, and I prayed daily for humility until He answered my prayer. I was excited until He revealed that humility would take some work. I wanted desperately to take a humility pill and wake up humble. I thought I was already humbled. I don't know why, since I had been independent since age eleven. I didn't understand until God demonstrated that I was prideful by default. It was a part of the extreme independence I developed because there was no one to love, protect, or provide for me. I was unaware that childhood self-sufficiency can breed pride as an adult. I also noticed pride, next to deception, is one of the biggest challenges of the TOHM participants who need help to heal. I understand their difficulty. God taught me humility at Walmart in my work as a Customer Service Representative. I thought I would die, and in reality, the prideful part of me had to die.

I told God I would do what He wanted me to and tell everyone what He did for me if He healed my mind, body, heart, and soul. I made my brave declaration before He told me what He wanted me to do, who He wanted me to help, and how He wanted me to do it.

He said, "I am sending you to people like you."

I was so shocked I could not respond when God initially revealed His assignment.

There was no feeling like it when I finally understood and accepted why I was created. It was the same feeling when I found out for whom I was created to serve. Frankly, at that point, I wanted nothing to do with His plan for me. I almost had another breakdown. I would be helping those like me? That should have been a happy time, but I knew the challenges I would face. Thanks be unto God, He told me it wouldn't be up to me to heal them. It was God who would heal them. I would merely be the vessel/instructor to lead them to their healing.

I cried for days thinking of the minds and hearts of the people who experienced trauma, and even more thinking of them coming to me for help. I forgot the promise He made: "No man shall be able to stand before you all the days of your life. I will be with you as I was with Moses. I will never leave you nor forsake you" (Joshua 1:5). The assignment seemed bigger than the promise, and I knew I had another impossible task ahead.

When I stopped crying enough to think about what God said, I knew it wasn't left up to me to do anything alone, so for that reason, I wasn't overwhelmed. I knew I wasn't the Healer, but I knew the Healer, and He would be with me to teach, guide, strengthen, anoint and answer my prayers to heal others. I also knew His directions and instructions would not always align with what people think should be done or how they think their healing should occur. In the same way the religious people of Jesus' day had difficulty understanding the works of Jesus, today's religious people have difficulty understanding the works of His twenty-first-century disciples. In the end, I knew if they followed the instructions God led me to tell them, they would heal exactly as the blind man was healed.

I would become a surrogate mother for those He sent by helping those who had given up on their dreams and purposes. Like me before healing, they would come with a loss of identity, broken and lost dreams, few or no skills, low self-esteem, little or no strength to fight, and nothing left to fight for or with. I am the one to carry their dreams until they are strong enough to carry them again. The surrogate mother knows, regardless of the people for whom she is a surrogate, that each process begins with a pregnancy and ends with a baby. I wrote a poem that included the word surrogate while living in Springfield after hearing Dr. Tererai Trent speak. She sparked an interest in me to become a surrogate mother for those who had lost their hopes and dreams after their abuse. Not yet knowing my purpose, I had an insatiable desire to help survivors of Childhood Trauma.

Experiencing and overcoming Childhood Trauma didn't mean I would automatically have compassion for others. Recognizing that only God's grace brought me through it and healed me gave me humility and compassion for others. Compassion is not only feeling sorry for someone. It is truly desiring and yearning to help someone and see them healed. It's never giving up on someone. I wanted it, studied it, and fasted and prayed for it until He gave it to me. Compassion keeps me praying, believing, and trusting God for someone else's miracle. Tower of Hope Ministries was born out of this Divine compassion to help others suffering from Childhood Trauma and to help them find freedom from trauma's bondage.

The Holy Spirit is the Teacher, Trainer, Guide, Wisdom, and Strategist for TOHM's Triumph Over Trauma program. I consult Him every day for every decision and for every student. I invite Him into every session as I tell Him I don't know anything and cannot help these people without Him. Their needs are too great. Only He knows what each person needs and how to rescue them. Only God through His omniscience, omnipresence and omnipotence can help emotionally, mentally, physically, and spiritually deprived individuals. Regardless of their problem, I believe God can help them because He helped me. My testimony is so miraculous that when I meet people with similar stories, I tell them, *If He did it for me, He will do it for you* and He always does. TOHM's total dependence on the Holy Spirit is one thing that separates us from other programs. We ask God what to do, how to do it, and wait for Him to tell us. Then we tell the students, and when they do it, they are healed and delivered. Learning our God is the same God Abraham, Moses, King David, the Prophets, Paul and the Apostles prayed to makes a difference for us. We know when we pray, He hears us, and if He hears us, He will answer us.

In working with trauma survivors, I discovered there are several kinds of survivors:

- those who believe revisiting the trauma is too much
- those who feel like as long as they are not dead, they are doing great
- those who feel that acknowledging their trauma betrays their families
- those who checked out mentally and emotionally because what happened to them was too painful, and they want to ensure no one could ever hurt them again
- those unwilling to do the work to heal, so they get stuck in the process

Those who had already lost family and friends and material things, like me, had nothing to lose by seeking healing, doing the necessary work to heal, and, upon completion, helping others heal. That's what we do at TOHM.

Gideon was a man whose purpose was to deliver God's people from bondage and oppression. He saw himself as ill-equipped to be a deliverer, so he asked God for confirmation of his call (Judges 6:36-40). God obliged Gideon by answering his request. I often cried and wondered why God called me or if I heard him correctly, especially when times were stressful. I felt like Gideon, that I was the least of who should have been called. I believe God sends us to do the impossible so He alone can get the glory. I often think about how I, who was least likely to be chosen because I had mental and emotional problems and couldn't handle much pressure, was chosen to help those who have mental and emotional problems. What is impossible with man is possible with God.

Chapter 68

WHEN PAIN AND PURPOSE COLLIDE

Michelangelo is best known for his great artwork from Genesis on the ceiling of the Sistine Chapel and The Last Judgment on its altar wall. As a result of his work, he is known as one of the greatest Renaissance artists of all time. That is the Michelangelo that everyone reads about and remembers, but there is much more to his story. Michelangelo actually suffered significant Childhood Trauma. He was taken from his mother at birth and raised by a wet nurse, but returned to her at age three only to lose her again to an illness at age six. Afterwards he lived with a nanny and her husband where he endured physical and mental abuse. It was when he lived with the nanny and her husband, a stone cutter, that Michelangelo learned of his great love for marble and painting. Although he suffered great loss and was raised by a foster-type family, he gained his purpose by being introduced to art. In short, the thing that brought him the most pain—losing his mother at such a young age and the abuse of his foster parents—is the thing that opened the door for him to become one of the greatest Renaissance artists.

Pain and suffering are a training ground, a catalyst that God uses, not just for the purpose in our lives but for the battles, to build spiritual muscles and maturity. But we have to be careful not to get stuck "in the battles" because our pain can turn into pity INSTEAD of purpose and fury INSTEAD of faith to believe that God is using it to frame our purpose. The battles are sent to deter and derail us, but we have to keep going.

The only hope for some people like me who suffered complex Childhood Trauma is God. If I did not have that hope, I would have given up. It was this hope that kept me grounded like an anchor when everything around and within me was stripped. This hope came from faith that God was with me and one day He would turn everything around. For these reasons, I never gave up hope that my life would get better and that God would bring me through it.

During my darkest days and nights, I lay in bed and quoted Psalm 91 which I learned while living with my Uncle Harold. He made me sit at the big dining room table that seated twelve to fourteen people. He would sit at the end, and I would sit next to him every Saturday evening and sometimes during the week and read the Bible to him. He read on a second or third grade level, so I would read and cross-reference scriptures for him. Even as a young teen, it was my favorite thing to do. As I read, I researched the historical meaning and definition of words. I didn't know it, but my early exposure to these Bible studies increased my faith. Repeatedly hearing the stories of how God chose the unlikely, such as Ruth the Moabite, to serve Him, and how He called some of the Biblical characters like Joseph, Jeremiah, and Daniel at a young age planted seeds of hope in my mind that one day God could use me to help His people.

What I could never unravel is why I had to endure the Childhood Trauma, why I continued to relive the trauma and nightmares, and how God would use everything that happened to me to reveal His purpose for my life. So for years, I was captured by pain until my pain collided with my purpose. My faith provided the foundation I needed to turn my pain into purpose and avoid turning it into pity.

As an adult, when I suffered emotional and mental pain from childhood adversities, I asked myself if I was the only one going through it. At the time, I hadn't heard anyone speak openly about their childhood abuse, so I thought my family and I might be the only ones who suffered. Consequently, I kept most of my suffering to myself. I suffered in silence! However, when other brave people shared their stories with me, I realized my family and I were not the only ones who endured extreme adversities in childhood. It was then I felt a fire inside me to help others who suffered extreme adversities in their childhood. Each time I met someone who shared their story of abuse, the fire set ablaze because I didn't want others to think they were crazy as I once did when I didn't have the tools to process, skills to navigate, or words to express what I went through. It wasn't until I studied the effects of trauma on a child's brain that I fully understood the depth of trauma I endured.

I learned I wasn't crazy, but something crazy happened to me.

My overwhelming pain would have been unending if I had not chosen to heal and create a program to help others heal. Tower of Hope Ministries is for those who don't have the skills and knowledge to navigate the enduring effects of their abuse and to help them overcome the long-term challenges associated with it. Our mission is to help people triumph gloriously over trauma through research-knowledge and faith-based strategies. We help transform survivors of trauma into overcomers. I also get a bonus as I help others heal because current research reports that helping others helps us.

Regardless of what happened in your life, God can do the same for you as He did for me and many others—turn your pain into purpose. Everyone has a story, but when we allow God to write our ending, He recycles the pain. If we refuse to wallow in self-pity, regret, shame, and, "Why me," God can bring about a miracle by causing our pain to collide with our purpose and produce a win-win for everyone.

A survivor of abuse is often unwilling to expose their abuser and talk about what happened. They deny their abuse, suppress it, or think, like I did, that if they don't talk about it, it won't affect them. Abuse affects a person despite their efforts to conceal it. They can't control its effects, but they can control how long trauma affects them—the sooner they acknowledge what happened, the sooner the brain can process it and place it in a proper vault: the long-term memory. Unprocessed Childhood Trauma continues to activate the nervous system to respond as if the trauma is continually recurring. Trauma survivors can relive the traumatic event for weeks, months, and even years.[17] A proper resting place for the trauma is in the memory after it is recognized, acknowledged, and grieved. Establishing personal safety, finding emotional security, and restoring damaged relationships is ongoing.

After years of intensive healing through education, therapy, and spiritual journaling, my mind healed, and I was transformed. I was happy and delivered from the emotional prison and ready to help others find their deliverance. Little did I foresee that I would continue to recover childhood memories and to heal in unpredictable areas for another several years.

Ongoing healing is not as dramatic as the initial healing because it's more like filling in memory gaps and finding the context for memories of events. Writing this memoir was extremely important for many reasons. Writing helped me establish a timeline of everything that happened. It was an exercise in placing my memories in sequence to understand the context in which things occurred. I could precisely determine my age when certain events happened and know who was involved. It helped me to calculate my siblings' ages to better understand that my previous thoughts of them as *older* or *grown-up* were simply because, as the youngest, everyone was older than me and seemed grown-up. It helped me absorb the fact that each of my siblings

---

[17]Van der Kolk, Bessel A. 2014. *The Body Keeps the Score: Brain, Mind, and Body in the Healing of Trauma*. Viking Press.

either ran away from our parents or was removed by the child welfare agency. It helped me comprehend that my siblings were not adults simply because they left home. It allowed me to give them grace for not coming to rescue me because they were abused children who ran the first chance they got. Their survival was all-consuming.

I don't have triggers and residuals like I once did, and my nervous system is no longer on alert and ready to be activated at a moment's notice. My body and mind have thoroughly processed every traumatic event I can recall, which allows me the freedom to live and enjoy life. I don't have panic or anxiety attacks, nightmares, or any of the debilitating disorders I once had. However, healing is a process, so I suspect I will continue to heal until Jesus returns. The good news is I don't have to wait to die and go to Heaven to heal. I enjoy the fruits of healing and helping others heal—right now, right here.

I am continually amazed at the power of God and how He heals the participants in TOHM programs. I feel like Job, when he said, "I had heard reports about you, but now my eyes have seen you" (Job 42:5). I now know the power of God because I know what He did for me, and what He's been doing for TOHM the past seven years. His miraculous healing power has freed participants from personality disorders, depression, panic and anxiety, addictions, PTSD, multiple types of mental disorders, emotional and eating disorders, and physical illnesses. He heals those who come suffering from the debilitating and crippling thief called Childhood Trauma.

I realize my steps were ordered to endure the pain, be strengthened in suffering, and overcome so I can do this work. Dr. Sherblom, one of my college professors, changed my life as I sat drowning in my ocean of pain surrounded by PTSD when he said, "Some people have to be the bridge that carries others across." With those few words, I saw myself as a bridge helping others to safety. It's amazing that the very thing I feared—a bridge—is the very thing God would call me to be for others. Being a bridge gave me the strength to look outward instead of inward. It made me want to help others even more. It made me believe God would use my pain to bring others to gain. We all suffer, but it helps when we know our suffering will help others. I don't want others to lose their families, homes, identities, dreams, desires, and finances as I did.

I have learned God does not change. The God who healed Naaman, King David, King Hezekiah, and Job in the Old Testament is the same God who healed the ten lepers, the paralytic, the blind men by the roadside, the one who raised Jarius' daughter and Lazarus from the dead in the New Testament.

He is the same God—I AM WHO I AM—who is healing the physically and mentally ill, emotionally numb, and spiritually dead in TOHM. He is the same God who will heal you because He does not change. We can count on Him to do what He says He promises to do. I encourage you to trust Him today that what He is doing for TOHM, He will do for you.

I understand the Sovereign God, in His wisdom, planned for me to be in the world during the Childhood Trauma awareness period. Children have historically experienced trauma, but never before has there been such widespread knowledge and exposure of the long-term consequences of Childhood Trauma and abuse. I am grateful to be living during this time. Without a doubt, Tower of Hope Ministries was created for such a time as this.

God has been faithful and continues to be faithful to Tower of Hope Ministries. The program continues to grow without any public advertisement. I don't recruit because the Lord's healing speaks for itself. People come from several walks of life, bringing their pain and suffering, and Jesus meets and exceeds their expectations when they do the healing assignments, attend the monthly sessions, seek His face, and prioritize their healing. The greatest testimony for Jesus was, and always will be, a transformed life.

When He healed the Samaritan woman at *The Well,* He told her to, "Go and sin no more" (John 4). She told everyone about Him when she spread the good news of healing and deliverance. She revealed a transformed life. When Mary Magdalene, the woman from whom He cast the demons, became a missionary and a loyal disciple, she revealed a transformed life (Luke 8). After Peter denied Jesus, he repented, became Godly and sorrowful, accepted forgiveness, and became a preacher. He led the Pentecost crusade, winning 3,000 souls in one day (Acts 2:41).

I learned early on that healing is great for those in pain, but healing doesn't transform lives. While it can lead to a transformed life, healing itself doesn't transform lives. Only a relationship with Jesus transforms lives. At TOHM, we teach people about the Covenant Maker and His Covenant Promises so they, too, might experience His everlasting healing, and more importantly, have a relationship with Him. Everyone who desires can experience everlasting healing and wholeness with God upon accepting Him as their Savior.

As you read this book, it is my prayer that you will encounter *Jehovah Rapha, The God Who Heals* the sick, hopeless, depressed, suicidal, and mentally challenged. For those who need to experience the One, Jesus came to provide salvation. I pray that after reading my story, you will understand that regardless of what happened in your life, God can take messes and give messages and turn your tests into testimonies and your pains into purpose. As long as I focused on my loss, pain, and disappointment, I could not get a true picture of how great God is. When I stopped exalting my problems and began exalting God over my problems, He exalted me over my problems. When you trust God and exalt Him, you will always win. It has been difficult, but I have never traveled alone, and neither will you.

I believe this is your appointed time to heal. I look forward to continuing this great healing journey with God and you.

Your sister and overcomer in Christ,
Dr. Dora J. Washington

Scan to donate to
Tower of Hope Ministries

We may not be able to stop every child from being abused, but we can ensure every adult has a safe place to heal. Your tax-deductible gift helps us to do so.

TOHM is a 501c3 organization

ABOUT THE AUTHOR

Dr. Dora Washington is an author, advocate, and speaker and is an expert on Childhood Trauma and its effects on adults. She has a Doctorate of Education (Ed.D) and is an advocate to increase awareness of the long-term effects of childhood trauma. Her personal story is one of triumph over a childhood of physical, emotional, and sexual abuse, abandonment, starvation, and poverty. After discovering a path to healing through God's help, she Hope Ministries to help others like herself overcome trauma and live and founded Tower of abundant life.

Tower of Hope Ministries is dedicated to transforming trauma survivors into healed overcomers by empowering them with H.O.P.E. (Heal, Overcome, Persevere, Educate). Using research knowledge and faith-based strategies, Tower of Hope's programs are designed to help people with trauma to do more than just survive their past. They teach them how to overcome and triumph gloriously over trauma! For more information, go to www.towerofhopeministries.com.

"The thief does not come except to steal, and to kill, and to destroy.
I have come that they may have life, and that they may
have it more abundantly."
John 10:10

Want to know more?

Scan this QR code for exclusive
photos and content.

REFERENCES

Al Odhayani, Abdulaziz, William J. Watson, and Lindsay Watson. 2013. "Behavioural Consequences of Child Abuse." *Canadian Family Physician* 59, no. 8 (August): 831-836. https://www.cfp.ca/content/59/8/831/tab-article-info.

Bradley, M. M., M. Codispoti, D. Sabatinelli, and P. J. Lang. 2001. "Emotion and Motivation II: Sex Differences in Picture Processing." *Emotion* 1, no. 3 (September): 300–19. Doi: 10.1037//1528-3542.1.3.300.

Bremner, J. D. 2006. "Traumatic Stress: Effects on the Brain." *Dialogues in Clinical Neuroscience* 8, no. 4: 445–461. Doi:10.31887/DCNS.2006.8.4/jbremner.

Carver-Thomas, Desiree, and Linda Darling-Hammond. 2019. "The Trouble with Teacher Turnover: How Teacher Attrition Affects Students and Schools." Arizona State University. *Education Policy Analysis Archives* 27, (April): 36. Doi: 10.14507/epaa.27.3699.

"Child Maltreatment Statistics." 2024. American Society for the Positive Care of Children. https://americanspcc.org/child-maltreatment-statistics/.

Cikanavicius, Darius. 2019. "Trust Issues That Arise from Childhood Trauma." Psych Central. https://psychcentral.com/blog/psychology-self/2019/09/trust-issues#1.

Douglas, J. W. B. 1973. "Chapter 15: Early Disturbing Events and Later Enuresis" in *Bladder Control and Enuresis*, 109–17. Spastics International Medical Publications. William Heinemann Medical Books.

Felitti, Vincent J. 2002. "The Relation Between Adverse Childhood Experiences and Adult Health: Turning Gold into Lead." *The Permanente Journal* 6, no. 1: 44-47. Doi: 10.7812/TPP/02.994.

Feriante, Joshua, Tyler J. Torrico, and Bettina Bernstein. 2023. *Separation Anxiety Disorder*. StatPearls Publishing.

Hart, Heledd, and Katya Rubia. 2012. "Neuroimaging of Child Abuse: A

Critical Review." *Frontiers in Human Neuroscience* 6, no. 52 (March): 1-24. Doi: 10.3389/fnhum.2012.00052.

Hayes, Jasmeet P., Michael B. VanElzakker, and Lisa M. Shin. 2012. "Emotion and Cognition Interactions in PTSD: A Review of Neurocognitive and Neuroimaging Studies." *Frontiers in Integrative Neuroscience* 6, no. 89 (October) 1-14. Doi: 10.3389/fnint.2012.00089.

Järvelin, Marjo Riitta, Irma Moilanen, Leena Vikeväinen-Tervonen, and Niilo-Pekka Huttunen. 1990. "Life Changes and Protective Capacities in Enuretic and Non-Enuretic Children." *Journal of Child Psychology and Psychiatry* 31, no. 5 (July): 763-774. Doi: 10.1111/j.1469-7610.1990.tb00816.x.

Kenrick, Douglas T., Vladas Griskevicius, Steven L. Neuberg, and Mark Schaller. 2010. "Renovating the Pyramid of Needs: Contemporary Extensions Built Upon Ancient Foundations." Association for Psychological Science - APS. *Perspectives on Psychological Science* 5, no. 3 (May): 292–314. Doi: 10.1177/1745691610369469.

Khadr, Sophie, Venetia Clarke, Kaye Wellings, Laia Villalta, Andrea Goddard, Jan Welch, Susan Bewley, Tami Kramer, and Russell Viner. 2018. "Mental and Sexual Health Outcomes Following Sexual Assault in Adolescents: A Prospective Cohort Study." *The Lancet - Child & Adolescent Health* 2, no. 9 (September): 654–65. Doi: 10.1016/s2352-4642(18)30202-5.

Kimble, Matthew, Abhishek Sripad, Rachel Fowler, Sara Sobolewski, and Kevin Flemming. 2018. "Negative World Views After Trauma: Neurophysiological Evidence for Negative Expectancies." *Psychological Trauma: Theory, Research, Practice and Policy* 10, no. 5: 576–584. Doi: 10.1037/tra0000324.

Kirk, Mimi. 2017. "How Childhood Trauma Adversely Affects Decision-Making." *Pacific Standard*. https://psmag.com/social-justice/childhood-trauma-adversely-affects-decision-making.

Larsen, Emmett M., Luz H. Ospina, Armando Cuesta-Diaz, Antonio Vian-Lains, George C. Nitzburg, Sandra Mulaimovic, Asya Latifoglu, Rosarito Clari, and Katherine E. Burdick. 2019. "Effects Of Childhood Trauma On Adult Moral Decision Making: Clinical Correlates And Insights From Bipolar Disorder." *Journal Of Affective Disorders* 244, (February): 180-186. Doi: 10.1016/j.jad.2018.10.002.

Lieberman, Matthew D., Naomi I. Eisenberger, Molly J. Crockett, Sabrina M. Tom, Jennifer H. Pfeifer, and Baldwin M. Way. 2007. "Putting Feelings Into Words: Affect Labeling Disrupts Amygdala Activity in Response to Affective Stimuli." *Psychological Science* 18, no. 5 (May): 421–428. Doi: 10.1111/ j.1467-9280.2007.01916.x.

"Linking Childhood Trauma and Addiction in Adulthood." 2018. Silvermist Recovery - Addiction & Mental Health Treatment in Western Pennsylvania. https://www.silvermistrecovery.com/2019-guide-the-link-between-childhood-trauma-and/.

McLanahan, Sara, and Gary Dandefur. 1994. *Growing Up With a Single Parent: What Hurts, What Helps.* Harvard University Press. Doi: 10.2307/ j.ctv22tnmnn.

Regier, P. S., L. Sinko, K. Jagannathan, S. Aryal, A. M. Teitelman, and A. R. Childress. 2022. "In Young Women, A Link Between Childhood Abuse and Subliminal Processing of Aversive Cues is Moderated by Impulsivity." BMC Psychiatry 22, no. 1 (March): 159. Doi: 10.1186/s12888-022-03770-0.

Substance Abuse and Mental Health Services Administration Center. 2014. "Chapter 3: Understanding the Impact of Trauma" in *Trauma-Informed Care in Behavioral Health Services*, 59-89. U.S Department of Health and Human Services.

Urban.org, 2022.

Van der Kolk, Bessel A. 2014. *The Body Keeps the Score: Brain, Mind, and Body in the Healing of Trauma.* Viking Press.

Walker, Pete. 2013. *Complex PTSD: From Surviving to Thriving: A Guide and Map for Recovering from Childhood Trauma.* Azure Coyote Publishing.

Zotev, Vadim, Raquel Phillips, Masaya Misaki, Chung Ki Wong, Brent E. Wurfel, Frank Krueger, Matthew Feldner, and Jerzy Bodurka. 2018. "Real-Time fMRI Neurofeedback Training of the Amygdala Activity with Simultaneous EEG in Veterans with Combat-Related PTSD." *NeuroImage: Clinical* 19: 106-121. Doi:10.1016/j.nicl.2018.04.010.

www.ingramcontent.com/pod-product-compliance
Lightning Source LLC
Chambersburg PA
CBHW071132130626
46553CB00004B/1340